Work...ng
with Animals

The UK, Europe & Worldwide

Working with Animals

The UK, Europe & Worldwide

Victoria Pybus

Distributed in the USA by
The Globe Pequot Press, Guilford, Connecticut

Published by Vacation Work, 9 Park End Street, Oxford
www.vacationwork.co.uk

WORKING WITH ANIMALS – THE UK, EUROPE & WORLDWIDE
First Edition 1999
Second Edition 2003
by Victoria Pybus

Copyright © Vacation Work 2003

ISBN 1-85458-297-6

Cover Design by
Miller Craig & Cocking Design Partnership

Illustrations by John Taylor

Typesetting by Brendan Cole

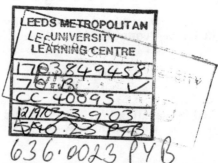
Printed and bound in Italy by Legoprint, SpA, Trento

Contents

PART I – THE UK

PROFESSIONS AND QUALIFICATIONS
Overview 15
The Veterinary Profession 16
Veterinary Surgeon 16
Veterinary Practice 17
Other Employment for Vets – *The State Veterinary Service – Animal Charities*
– Veterinary Inspector – Army Vet – Research & Teaching 19
Qualifications & Training – *University Veterinary Schools* 20
Veterinary Nurse – *Qualifications & Training for VNs – College Courses – Job*
Hunting – Pay and Conditions 22
Other Animal Practitioners
Chiropractor/Osteopath 28
Physiotherapist 28
Behaviour Counsellor 29
Animal Technician 30
Working on Farms
Farm Manager – *Training and qualifications* 32
Farm Worker – *Training and qualifications – Pay and Conditions* 33
Organic Farming 34
Other Animal Care Qualifications 35
BTECS 35
Choosing a College – *Animal Care College* 40
Work Schemes for Americans 41

ANIMAL WELFARE ORGANISATIONS
Animal Health Trust 42
Blue Cross 43
Celia Hammond Animal Welfare Trust 44
The National Animal Welfare Trust 45
The People's Dispensary for Sick Animals 46
The Royal Society for the Prevention of Cruelty to Animals – *Working for the*
RSPCA 48
The Wildlife Hospital Trust (St Tiggywinkles) 50
The Royal Society for the Protection of Birds 51
Wood Green Animal Shelters 54
The Scottish Society for the Prevention of Cruelty to Animals 54
Independent Animal Rescue Centres – *Animals in Distress – Burstow Wildlife*
Sanctuary – Friends of Animals League – Last Chance Animal Rescue –
Wildlife Aid 55

WORKING WITH DOGS & CATS

Dogs

Kennels 57
Guide Dogs Association 59
Dog Rescue Centres Employing Kennel Staff 59
Courses & Training for Canine Work 60
Microchipping 61
Dog Trainer 61
Dogs for the Disabled 62
Canine Partners for Independence 62
Guide Dog Trainer/Mobility Instructor 63
Hearing Dogs for Deaf People 65
Dog Groomer/Canine Beautician 65
Dogs in Uniform 69
Private Security Dogs 69
Dog Warden 69
Greyhound Racing Kennelhand/Trainer 70
National Canine Defence League 71
Search & Rescue dogs 73
The Kennel Club 74
Free Enterprise – *Dog Walker – Dog Day Care Centre* 74

Cats

Cat Only Veterinary Practices 76
Cats' Protection League 76

WORKING WITH HORSES

How to Find a Job 78
Types of Stables 79
Qualifications – *NVQs – BTECs – BHS – ABRS* 79
Groom/Assistant Stable Manager 82
Riding Instructor 82
Racing – *The Jockey Club – Stud Work* 83
Horsebox Driver 87
Horses in Uniform – *Mounted Police – Army* 89
Farrier 90
Physiotherapist 92
Saddler 92
Equine Rescue Centres 93
Seasonal Work with Horses 95

ZOOS, SAFARI PARKS. AQUARIA & CIRCUSES

Zoos and Safari Parks

Zoos – *Zoo Keeper* 98
Safari Parks 101

Aquaria

Marine and Freshwater Biologist – *Working in aquaria, Sea Life centres* 102

Directory of Zoos and Aquaria

Directory of Zoos and Aquaria 105

Circuses

Circuses 110
Overview 110

Employment 111

OTHER OPPORTUNITIES
Pet shops – Qualifications & Training 116
Heathrow Animal Reception Centre... 117
Animal Sitting.. 117
Waltham Pet Centre... 118
Showbiz Animal Agent 118
Rabbits... 119
Volunteering/Work Experience with Animal Projects – *Useful websites* 120

DIRECTORY OF UK ANIMAL ORGANISATIONS 124

PART II – EUROPE

EUROPE-WIDE ORGANISATIONS
Finding a Job 133
Sources of Information 134
Languages 135

WESTERN EUROPE
Mutual Recognition of Qualifications in the EU – *Certificates of Experience* ... 136
European Union Work Experience Schemes 137
Student Exchange for non-EU Nationals – *CIEE – SWAP – Student Work Abroad Program* 138

Country Guide
Austria – Belgium – Denmark – Finland – France – Germany – Greece –
Iceland – Ireland – Italy – Luxembourg – The Netherlands – Norway –
Portugal – Spain – Sweden – Switzerland.. 138

CENTRAL & EASTERN EUROPE & RUSSIA
Country Guide
Bulgaria – Croatia – Czech Republic – Estonia – Hungary – Latvia –
Lithuania – Poland – Romania – Russia – Slovakia – Slovenia – Ukraine 186

PART III – WORLDWIDE

NORTH AMERICA
The USA 209
Entry & Working Visas... 209
Exchange Visitor Programmes
Internships – *Through BUNAC – Through CIEE* 210

Organisations Offering Internships..212
Volunteer Work...223
Career Opportunities – Veterinary – Horses – Agriculture – Zoos 227
Canada 230
Entry & Working Visas..230
Exchange Visitor Programmes..230
Volunteer Work...231
Other Opportunities..232
Quebéc 233

AUSTRALIA & NEW ZEALAND

Australia 234
Entry & Working Visas – Students – Working Holiday – Special Schemes 234
Other Opportunities – Vets – Horses – Zoos – Sea World
Volunteer work 239
Welfare and Wildlife Protection..241
New Zealand 243
Entry & Work Regulations – Work Schemes – Getting a Work Visa 243
Conservation 244
Other Opportunities – Farm Work – Horses – Animal Welfare.......................245

ELSEWHERE

Africa & the Indian Ocean
Botswana – Egypt – Ghana – Kenya – Madagascar – Morocco – Namibia
– Nigeria & Cameroon – South Africa – Swaziland –
Tanzania – Uganda & Congo – Zambia 247
Asia
Borneo and Indonesia – Japan – Malaysia – Mongolia – Sri Lanka – Thailand
– Turkey – Vietnam 254
South & Central America
Argentina – Belize – Bolivia – Brazil – Chile – Costa Rica & Puerto Rico –
Ecuador – Guatemala – Mexico – Peru – Surinam – Venezuela.......................260

APPENDIX

OTHER IMPORTANT ORGANISATIONS TO CONTACT
Animal Charities Working Overseas...271
Worldwide Organisations with Animal-Related Projects..............................276

Preface

Most of us have probably thought at some time that we would like to work with animals. There is an understandable human fascination with the astonishing variety of species who share this planet with us, and through a knowledge of whose behaviour we gain insights into our own. This is not only true of the higher mammals such as primates, dolphins and elephants, and of familiar domesticated creatures like dogs cats and horses but of the whole array of other creatures from ants to zebras.

Working closely over a period of time with some individual animals can produce a bond as deep as with any human, as many pet owners, zoo-keepers and animal trainers will testify. Nonetheless, the reality of working with animals is likely to differ from any ideal, imagined version. The majority of veterinary surgeons deal mainly with domestic pets and farm livestock at all hours and in all weathers. Jobs with animals also involve dealing with humans, either the owners or in the interests of public relations. Many jobs caring for animals involve long (and smelly) hours of hard physical work, more often than not for little financial reward.

While not everyone gets to be head ranger in an African game reserve, a flying vet, a top jockey or a lion tamer, virtually anyone can join an animal conservation project helping to protect nesting sea turtles or caring for monkeys in a primate orphanage, provided that they can afford the airfare and the volunteer's financial contribution. If this is not possible, they can volunteer to assist a zookeeper at the local zoo, or animal sanctuary.

Anyone intent on a job or career with animals should note that there is a difference between working with animals in agriculture, science or entertainment, and working for animals where the object is to improve the treatment and welfare of, and respect for animals. All types of organisations and professions that deal with animals, some of them with directly opposing agendas, are included here.

Since the first edition of this book opportunities to volunteer on animal projects around the world have continued to increase, and we have included many more of them in this second edition. For those wanting to work with horses there is a new section on seasonal work at riding establishments.

To summarise: working with animals can be done on any level from helping out as a volunteer at an animal sanctuary, zoo or conservation project to following a career as a vet or aquarist and perhaps becoming a specialist in a particular field such as wildlife medicine or cetaceans (whales and dolphins). Which ever you choose, your perception of animals particularly, and the world around you generally, will be illuminated.

This book tells you what the jobs are, what they involve, how to qualify and train, and how to get all kinds of work in the UK and worldwide.

Victoria Pybus
Oxford, June 2003

Acknowledgments

The author and publishers wish to thank the following in no particular order for their invaluable help in compiling this book: Jacqueline Seguin (Canada), Don Stacey (Circus writer), David Jamieson (editor, *King Pole* magazine), Helena Cotton (British Veterinary Association), Daniela Klein de Oliveira for ad hoc interpreting in an Austrian animal refuge, Dr Hannah Buchanan-Smith (primate specialist), Daniel Bennett (biologist and sea turtle volunteer), Paul Bagshaw (conservationist and volunteer kiwi counter), Marion Fossett (former lion-tamer), Juan Romero (aquarium curator), Hugh Stanley (veterinary surgeon), Bob Westacott (former Chief Equine Welfare Officer, Redwings), Claire Tuck (animal care student), Alison Whittock (trainer of assistance dogs), Kate Corbett (amateur jockey), Simon Buscuttil (RSPB area manager).

Special thanks also to Richard Perron of quantum@t-online.de for the current zoo information which he so kindly supplied.

Part 1

The UK

**Professions,
Qualifications & Training**

**Animal Welfare Organisations
Dogs, Cats, Horses,**

Zoos, Safari Parks & Circuses

Other Opportunities

Professions and Qualifications

OVERVIEW
Animals are part of our daily lives and our relationship with them is a complicated one. For instance, we make a distinction between those with which we share our homes (and whose company and affection delight us), and those we consume as sustenance. We make money out of animals, yet rely on them to compensate for our disabilities (dolphin therapy for depressives and the disabled, guide and assistance dogs for the blind, deaf etc). We harness and harvest their natural talents and properties, and put them to labour for us. Despite all the benefits they confer on *Homo sapiens*, there are many instances when they are shamefully neglected or deliberately mistreated. It is small wonder that there is no shortage of people wanting to work with, and for the benefit of animals; it is the least we can do.

The majority of animal work is connected with animal care, husbandry and medical areas. Animals are just as accident and disease prone as people, the difference being that they cannot explain their symptoms. The following section deals with the main animal oriented professions and trades and how to train and qualify for them. Details of employment with individual organisations can be found in the other chapters of this book.

Many people are attracted by the idea of working with animals and a good many of them will have started in a volunteer capacity or have had some other experience of pets or livestock. However, before setting the wheels of ambition in motion it is advisable to give some consideration to what working with animals might entail and in particular the following points:

O If you really love animals then working with them can be very rewarding and worthwhile.
O There is some excellent training available in the UK for all kinds of work with animals.
O Some workplaces such as laboratories for animal experiments and intensive or battery farms may not be suitable for animal lovers with acute sensibilities.
O The work can often be dirty and smelly and frequently not for the squeamish.
O Some jobs can be repetitive.
O Many jobs with animals involve working outdoors in all weathers and temperatures, and can be physically strenuous.
O Veterinary, research and farming jobs are not for the sentimental.
O There are health and safety risks such as diseases transmittable from animals to humans, and the possibility of injury from being bitten, kicked etc.
O There is a lot of competition for study courses, especially veterinary science, and they can be very difficult to get on to.
O Most jobs with animals are low paid especially compared to industry, and there may be little chance of promotion.
O Most jobs with animals involve dealing with people as much as animals so good interpersonal skills are most important.

What goes for other types of job also applies to jobs with animals, i.e. the more qualifications and training you have the more interesting and responsible work you can apply for.

This section deals with the different careers with animals and gives background information as well as information on the qualifications necessary.

THE VETERINARY PROFESSION

VETERINARY SURGEON

The popular fictional image of the vet tends to be of a heroic figure battling his or her way through appalling weather conditions in the middle of the night to help a distressed animal give birth by the light of an emergency lantern while a storm rages around outside. Reality is mostly less dramatic, but vets do have to provide an out of hours emergency service.

There are about 17,700 vets registered with the UK's Royal College of Veterinary Surgeons (Belgravia House, 62-64 Horseferry Road, London SW1P 2AF; 020-7222 2001) including those who have retired and those working overseas. Approximately 11,100 of vets registered are active in the UK. About 9,200 of these work in practices of which there are 2,213 (excluding branch practices). By far the majority (1,169) are mixed practices followed by small animal practices (768). Large animal practices have declined to about 30 and there are 63 practices specialising in equines. About 1,200 vets are employed in the State Veterinary Service and universities, and 660 in private sector industry pharmaceutical companies and other organisations and about 300 work for Animal Welfare Organisations. There are also vets working for the Army, zoos, local authorities and a few other sundry organisations.

Hugh Stanley, who has dual Irish/US nationality, studied Veterinary Science at Edinburgh, qualifying in 1984. After several years in a small animals/exotics practice in Essex he took a job in Hong Kong in 1992. In 1999 he qualified for residency in New Zealand through the points system but changed his mind and decided to stay in Hong Kong.

Hugh Stanley describes his veterinary career after qualifying

The veterinary school in Edinburgh arranged for some of us to spend sixth months in Botswana after qualifying. One of the projects we helped with out there involved looking at village poultry populations. The chickens were very free range and difficult to catch, so we used to bribe the children with sweeties to catch them for us.

Back in the UK, I got a job as a veterinary adviser for a pharmaceutical company. Then I joined a small animal practice in Essex. As well as the usual family pets, we got a high proportion of rottweilers and parrots. The practice also dealt with exotics and I was on-call zoo vet for the area.

I was offered a job in Hong Kong which I took up in 1992. I got the job through a colleague who had established several clinics there. When I went to Hong Kong there were only 21 private vets; six years latter there were about 120. My clinic was located in Repulse Bay, which is the exclusive part of town. Having said that, there was no sense of class about my local clients, they were just very hospitable and very pleasant people who happened to be rather rich. When I first arrived, I was asked to make a house call and then stay for dinner. In my ignorance, I turned up in my shorts and safari shirt, only to find myself walking in to a room full of bankers in suits. I didn't go to Hong Kong for the money, but I was rather pleased when my salary trebled in three years and tax was 15%. It's all changed now of course with the Asian economy crisis.

Small animal practice is pretty much the same kind of work wherever you are in the world; it's the after hours experiences that make the difference. Having said that, in Hong Kong it was a seven days a week practice, and it was usual to see as many as 40 to 70 animals in a period of three hours. This meant that you would spend 15 minutes with one client, and maybe 60 seconds with another. I worked with an interpreter who took down the animal's history prior to the consultation and then during the consultation the interpreter would interpret and I would diagnose, prescribe etc. and then go on to the next client in the next consulting room leaving an assistant to dish out the medicine and collect the fee.

The perception of medicine is different in Hong Kong. I had to give an injection to virtually every animal, even if it was a placebo, otherwise the clients would throw the medicines away in disgust as they left.

There are also pet crazes. In recent years the Chinchilla, a South American rodent, was the designer pet. They cost about £600 ($1000) each. They are not a usual small animal for vets. I had to do a crash course from the internet. The internet is invaluable for a crash course on any strange animals.

I would say that the problem of working in Hong Kong post Chinese takeover is that most of the expats and Hong Kong residents who were there long-term and accumulated animals have now left. The people who are going there now are likely to be there for a year or two and so they are less likely to have pets.

With my US passport, I could go and work in the States, but I would have to take the State National Veterinary examination as UK qualifications are not recognised in the USA.

Further information on working in Hong Kong, and ex-Commonwealth countries, Europe, etc is available from the British Veterinary Association (020-7722 2001).

Foreign Vets in the UK

The UK employs a higher number of foreign vets than most other countries. Currently there are over 200 from EU countries and about the same number from the Commonwealth countries i.e. Australia, New Zealand, Canada etc. The high annual intake of foreign vets is of some concern to British Veterinary graduates.

VETERINARY PRACTICE

A typical veterinary practice has three or more vets working in partnership. This has advantages in that it enables a range of expertise to be provided under one roof and helps share the burden of unsociable hours that vets invariably have to work when covering emergencies and running evening surgeries. A veterinary surgery is a business with the same aims as other businesses: while clients' welfare comes first, the overheads must be covered and a living made: difficult when you think that buildings, equipment, maintenance, staff and a 24-hour service must all be paid for. Nonetheless, there are good earnings to be had; typically, a successful urban veterinary surgery could make a minimum £50,000 annually for each partner. There are of course vets that earn much more than the average particularly if they have a renowned expertise in a particular field like equines, and hold a veterinary professorship, but these are in the minority.

The typical urban general veterinary surgery treats a variety of familiar domestic pets: cats, dogs and a range of small furry and feathered creatures, and some that are not so traditional: snakes (large and small), other reptiles and exotic pets are becoming more common. Rural surgeries usually opt for mixed practice that deals with a wide range of species including farm livestock, equines, zoo inmates and domestic pets, or to specialise in one or two of these fields.

Hugh Stanley, who qualified in veterinary medicine at Edinburgh, worked in a small animal/exotic practice in Essex. His strangest patient was an 11ft, 14 stone Indian Rock Python with a gum infection, which was brought to the surgery by its owner. Hugh describes the experience:

Pythons have a tendency to get this condition. The treatment involved fiddling about in its mouth. I wouldn't say it actually liked it, but it was very tame and amiable and very well cared for. The owner was totally in love with it.

Rural vets normally have to do more travelling than urban ones as larger animals cannot normally be brought to the surgery. Covering up to 100 miles a day is not uncommon. Any vet can be called out to deal with an injured pet or one too ill to be moved.

Larger animals cannot be brought to urban surgeries

Vets who work with farm livestock are concerned not only with treating individual animals but also with general animal health and welfare. Modern farming methods mean that vets are involved in helping maximise productivity, artificial insemination and animal disease control programmes.

A rural vet may well have a 'part-time' appointment as a Ministry veterinary inspector. Part-time appointment is generally a euphemism for spending a lot of the practice's time testing bovines and other livestock for disease, inspecting livestock markets and ensuring that hygiene and welfare standards are met in abattoirs. Producing written reports and certificates is a integral part of the job.

Other establishments that are required to have regular official veterinary inspections include greyhound race tracks, equitation centres, zoos, breeding and boarding kennels and pet shops. Such inspections are carried out on behalf of the local authority.

Vets may also be consulted on the welfare of animals being used for scientific experiments in laboratories.

OTHER EMPLOYMENT FOR VETS

The State Veterinary Service

Vets employed by the SVS advise DEFRA (the successor to the Ministry of Agriculture, Fisheries and Foods) and are involved in special investigations, the control of disease and as consultants to improve the welfare of farm animals. The SVS has national headquarters in Cardiff, Edinburgh and Surrey and five regional centres each with its own Animal Health Office. Veterinary surgeons work from one of the regional centres which also have a complement of technical and support staff. One arm of the SVS is the Veterinary Field Service (VFS) whose duties include carrying out inspections of diagnostic nature. In the event of the outbreak of a notifiable disease such as foot-and-mouth or BSE, state veterinary field officers are responsible for seeing that statutory legal obligations are carried out to deal with the outbreak.

Duties of vets employed by the SVS include:

O   Disease monitoring and surveillance
O   Control and eradication of notifiable diseases
O   Special investigations and surveys
O   Meat and poultry hygiene inspections
O   Improvement of animal welfare

Charitable Animal Welfare Organisations

Animal Welfare organisations employ a few hundred vets between them. Of these the Peoples' Dispensary for Sick Animals (PDSA) is the largest national organisation and has about 200 vets on its books. Working for the PDSA. can provide a wide range of experience in small animal treatment. For detailed information see the section *Animal Welfare Organisations*.

Veterinary Inspector

Somewhat different from hospital work is the round of establishments, which handle animal slaughtering and carcass processing. These premises require veterinary inspections to ensure they meet certain standards. In the case of meat processing plants this means carrying out meat hygiene and general plant and storage inspection for import and export. In the case of abattoirs, vets check that animals are properly stunned and dispatched as humanely as possible.

The Army

Working in the Royal Army Veterinary Corps involves mainly the care of the Army's dogs and horses (plus a few regimental mascots). During their service they may work in a variety of locations around the UK or Germany or Cyprus. They may also get involved with animal rescue in trouble zones. During recent times, in Bosnia, an Army vet serving there was instrumental in the process of helping to save the 60 remaining horses at the Lippizaner stud in Prnjavor. Army vets serve on a short commission basis, although there may be a few regular commissions as well.

Further information can be obtained from:

Royal Army Veterinary Corps Division (RAVC): RHQ RAVC, Defence Animal Centre, Melton Mowbray, Leics LE13 0SL; ☎01664 411811; fax 01664-410694; e-mail DAC.HQ@dial.pipex.com

Research and Teaching Posts

The activities of vets employed by pharmaceutical companies and research institutes tend to be confined exclusively to research and development. Research institutes include the Agricultural and Food Research Council, Medical Research Council and the Animal

Health Trust. Pharmaceutical companies and other commercial work can involve biomedical research and technical guidance on the development of drugs, vaccines and food additives. Investigations into medical or veterinary problems can be done on a consultation basis.

Vets employed by university veterinary schools teach and carry out research often linked to the faculty animal hospital.

QUALIFICATIONS AND TRAINING

The entry standards for a degree in Veterinary Science are very high and in practice the six schools in the UK demand three A-levels or five Highers at grades A/B before they will even consider you (even though the minimum requirements may be lower). Chemistry is essential and other suitably scientific subjects are Biology, Physics, Zoology and Mathematics. The subject requirements vary from one university to another and it is advisable to check this even before starting 'A' Levels. Even if you achieve the maximum grades, a place is not guaranteed as there are only about 400 statutory ones (though a few more places above this minimum may be offered by individual schools) and the competition is therefore prodigious. However, anyone who is determined to be a vet will not let this deter them. It is virtually a prerequisite that candidates will be able to show some experience of working with animals, which they have done in their free time or during the school holidays.

The UK's six universities which provide courses leading to a degree in veterinary science are Bristol, Cambridge, Edinburgh, Glasgow, Liverpool and London. The course takes five years (six, in the case of Cambridge).

The requirements of the course are such that veterinary students usually have to spend the vacations gaining experience in a veterinary practice which means that it is usually impractical to supplement the cost of the long course by earning money during the holidays.

USEFUL ADDRESSES & INFORMATION

University Veterinary Schools

Bristol: Veterinary Admissions Clerk, University of Bristol, Senate House, Bristol BS8 1TH; ☎0117-9287679; www.vetschool.bris.ac.uk/courses. In addition to BVSc Degree, the school offers the following: BSc in Veterinary Nursing and Practice Administration, BSc Equine Science, BSc Animal Health and Welfare.

Cambridge: The Department Secretary, Department of Clinical Veterinary Medicine, University of Cambridge, Madingley Road, Cambridge CB2 OES; ☎01223-337600; fax 01223 337610.

Cambridge: The Cambridge Intercollegiate Applications Office: Kellet Lodge, Tennis Court Road, Cambridge CB2 1QJ; ☎01223-333308; www.vet.cam.ac.uk/ applications.

Edinburgh: Admissions Officer, Faculty of Veterinary Medicine, Royal (Dick) School of Veterinary Studies, University of Edinburgh, Summerhall, Edinburgh EH19 1QH; ☎0131-650 6178; fax 0131-650 6585; e-mail VetUG@ed.ac.uk; www.vet.ed.ac.uk.

Glasgow: Admissions Officer, University of Glasgow, Veterinary School, 464 Bearsden Road, Bearsden, Glasgow G61 1QH; ☎0141-330 5705; fax 0141-942 7215; www.gla.ac.uk/Acad/FacVet/admissions

Liverpool: The Admissions Tutor, Faculty of Veterinary Science, University of Liverpool, POB 147, Liverpool L69 3BX; ☎0151-794 4281.

London: The Registrar, The Royal Veterinary College, University of London, Royal College Street, London NW1 OTU; ☎020-7387-2898; fax 020-7388 2342; www.rvc.ac.uk; undergraduate courses: Bachelor of Veterinary Medicine (BVetMed), BSc Veterinary Science, Veterinary Nursing (jointly with Middlesex University).

Veterinary Hospitals

British Veterinary Hospitals Association: Oak Beck Veterinary Hospital, Oak Beck Way, Skipton Road, Harrogate HG1 3HU; ☎01423-561414; fax 01423-521550; e-mail admin@VetHospital.co.uk; www.VetHospital.co.uk.

Anchorage Veterinary Hospital: South Walsham Road, Acle, Norfolk NR13 3EA; ☎01493-750255; e-mail roger.clarke@breathmail.net

Cheadle Hulme Veterinary Hospital: 2/4 Queen's Road, Cheadle Hulme, Cheshire SK8 5LU; tel: 0161-485 8444; fax 0161-4866156.

De Montfort Veterinary Hospital: Merstow Green, Evesham, Worcestershire WR11 4HB; ☎01386-446095; fax 01386-765415.

Earlswood Veterinary Hospital: 193 Belmont Road, Belfast, BT4 2AE, Northern Ireland; ☎028-9047 1361.

The Veterinary Hospital: Colwill Road, Estover, Plymouth PL6 8RP; ☎01752-702646; fax 01752-773305; e-mail vets@vethospitalplymouth.co.uk.

Braid Veterinary Hospital: 171 Mayfield Road, Edinburgh EH9 3AZ; ☎0131-6672478; fax 0131-6620414; e-mail vets@braidvet.co.uk.

Veterinary Associations and Other Organisations

British Veterinary Association: 7 Mansfield Street, London W1M OAT; ☎020-7636 6541; fax 020-7436 2970; e-mail: bvhq@bva.co.uk

Association of Veterinary Students: c/o BVA, 7 Mansfield Street, London W1M OAT; ☎020-7636 6541; e-mail: avs@rvc.ac.uk

Association of State Veterinary Officers (ASVO): c/o State Veterinary Service, 1A Page Street, London SW1P 4PQ; ☎(DEFRA phone number) 0207-904 6000.

Association of Veterinarians in Industry (AVI): c/o Penny Alborough, John C Alborough Ltd, Lion Lane, Needham Market, Suffolk IPG 8NT; ☎01449-723800; e-mail penny@jcagroup.com. AVI members' activities include participating in field trials, acting as locums, sales and marketing, technical writing and working in diagnostic laboratories.

Association of Veterinary Teachers and Research Workers (AVT&RW): www.avt rw.mri.sari.ac.uk; c/o Dr. Alun Williams of the University of Glasgow; e-mail A.Williams@vet.gla.ac.uk

British Association of Homeopathic Veterinary Surgeons: Alternative Veterinary Medicine Centre, Chinham House, Stanford-in-the-Vale, Faringdon, Oxon SN7 8QN; ☎01367-718115; www.bahvs.com.

Society of Practising Veterinary Surgeons (SPVS): 2 The Old Gun Room, Blagdon Estate, Seaton Burn, Newcastle-upon-Tyne NE13 6DB; ☎01670-78 90 54; fax 01670-789359; e-mail office@spvs.org.uk; www.spvs.org.uk

British Small Animal Veterinary Association (BSAVA): Woodrow House, 1 Telford Way, Waterwells Business Park, Quedgeley, Gloucestershire GL2 2AB; ☎01452-726700; fax 01452-726701; www.bsava.com. Runs specialised courses for vets and publishes veterinary text books.

Ireland

The Veterinary Council of Ireland 53 Lansdowne Road, Ballsbridge, Dublin 4; ☎+353-1 6684402; www.vci.ie. For more information on Ireland, see *Ireland* in Europe section.

Veterinary Publications

State Veterinary Journal: www.defra.gov.uk. The official journal of the State Veterinary Service (SVS) of DEFRA (Department for Environment, Food and Rural Affairs). Covers disease control, animal welfare and public health and consumer protection. Published twice yearly.

The Veterinary Record: the journal of the British Veterinary Association, 7 Mansfield Street, London W1M OAT; ☎020-7636 6541; fax 020-7637 0620. Weekly. Subscription included in BVA membership of £185 per year.

Veterinary Practice: published by A E Morgan Publications, Stanley House, 9 West Street, Epsom, Surrey KT18 7RL; ☎01372-741411; fax 01372-744493; www.vpmag.co.uk. Monthly. Free to all practising veterinary practices, college libraries etc. or £15 per year subscription to anyone not eligible for free issue.

Journal of Small Animal Practice: published by the British Veterinary Association. Monthly.

Veterinary Times: Published by Veterinary Business Development, Olympus House, Werrington Centre, Peterborough PE4 6NA; ☎01733-325522; fax 01733-325512; e-mail: vbd@vetsonline.com. Weekly.

The Veterinary Journal: Published by Baillére Tindall, 24-28 Oval Road, London NW1 7DX. Edited by Andrew Higgins of the Animal Health Trust. Six issues a year.

UK Vet Publications: Kennet Building, Trade Street, Woolton Hill, Newbury, Berks. RG20 9UJ; ☎01635-255511; fax 01635-255445; www.ukvet.co.uk. Publishes *UK Vet Companion Animal* (8 issues a year), and *UK Vet Livestock* (7 times a year).

Journal of Animal Breeding: Editor: Richard Murray, University of Liverpool, Veterinary Teaching Hospital, Leahurst, Neston L64 7TE; ☎0151-7946029; fax 0151-794 6065. Annual.

VETERINARY NURSE

Behind every efficient vet or veterinary practice there is a hard working veterinary nurse, or nurses, managing the fort. The veterinary nurse makes the appointments, holds animals while the vet examines them and carries out treatments, prepares animals pre-op (for instance shaving the operation site) and assists with administering and monitoring anaesthesia. During the operation VNs hand the vet surgical instruments and dressings, clear up after the operation and monitor and treat the patients post-op if the practice has hospitalisation facilities. Also on the technical side the VNs help with X-rays (positioning the animal and developing the films) they order supplies and drugs, give some injections under direct veterinary supervision and collect and analyse specimens with simple laboratory tests. They also maintain equipment and sterilise instruments.

Other duties include clerical ones: maintaining and filing records and dealing with correspondence. They also advise owners on vaccinations, neutering, worming and other routine treatments. Most VNs do not accompany vets on their rounds although in a large, mixed practice they may help treat large animals outdoors.

There are about five thousand qualified veterinary nurses in the UK.

QUALIFICATIONS AND TRAINING FOR VNS

The British Veterinary Nursing Association oversees the interests of its members in training or when qualified. Applicants for the Royal College of Veterinary Surgeons' training scheme have to have at least five GCSEs or '0'levels' at grades A, B or C including English and two science subjects, or a science and mathematics. Applicants must be at least 17 years old. Upwards, there is no limit.

The first step is to secure a placement, or the promise of one, at a veterinary practice or similar, which has been approved by the Royal College of Veterinary Surgeons as a Veterinary Nursing Approved Centre or Training Practice. The approved centre or training practice is where the trainee gets practical experience and some tuition from employers and colleagues. The theoretical part of training can be done in various ways including self-study and correspondence courses, but the most usual is to attend a part-time, full-time, day release or evening college course, depending what is available in the area. Training takes a minimum of two years and includes study of anatomy, physiology, first aid, theatre practice, kennel and hospital management, quarantine procedures, laboratory work, anaesthetics, dispensing, radiography and dark room developing. Two examinations must be passed: usually Part I is taken a year after enrolment and Part II at the end of two years leading to an NVQ (National Vocational Qualification), or the Scottish equivalent, S/NVQ at levels 2 and 3.

The British Veterinary Nursing Association has a career information pack available direct from the BVNA, (Level 15, Terminus House, Terminus Street, Harlow, Essex CM20 1XA). Please enclose £5, which also covers postage.

VN College Courses in England
SOUTH EAST
Berkshire College of Agriculture: Hall Place Burchetts Green, Maidenhead, Berkshire SL6 6QR; ☎01628-824444; fax 01628-824595; e-mail enquiries@bca.rmplc.co.uk; website www.bca.ac.uk; full-time and part-time.
Brinsbury College of Agriculture & Horticulture: North Heath, Pulborough, West Sussex RH20 1DL; ☎01798-877400. Part-time day release.
Canterbury College: New Dover Road, Canterbury, Kent CT1 3AJ; ☎01227-811111; fax 01227-811101; part-time day release.
Farnborough College of Technology: Boundary Road, Farnborough, Hampshire GU14 6SB; ☎01252-405555; fax 01252-407041; www.farm-ct.ac.uk; part-time day release.
MYF Training: Hippodrome House, Birchett Road, Aldershot, Hampshire GU11 1LZ; ☎01344-773226; part-time day release.
Sparsholt College: Winchester, Hampshire SO21 2NF; ☎01962-776441; fax 01962-776587; e-mail enquiry@sparshot.ac.uk; part-time day release.
Plumpton College: Ditchling Road, Plumpton, Nr. Lewes, East Sussex BN7 3AE; ☎01273-890454; fax 01273-890071; e-mail enquiries@plumpton.ac.uk. Part-time day release.

SOUTH WEST
Bicton College of Agriculture: East Budleigh, Budleigh Salterton, Devon EX9 7BY; ☎01395-562300; fax 01395-567502; www.bicton.ac.uk
Bristol University: School of Veterinary Science, Langford House, Langford, Bristol BS18 8LJ; ☎0117-928 9517; fax 01934-852037; full-time BSc. Hons in Veterinary Nursing and Practice Administration.
Duchy College: Rosewarne, Camborne, Cornwall TR14 OAB; ☎01209-710077; fax 01209-719754; Full-time block release.
Lynwood School of Veterinary Nursing: Station Road, Wimbourne, Dorset BH21 2NY; ☎01249-466825; fax 01249-466825; e-mail jarvik@wiltscol.ac.uk. Part-time day release.
Wiltshire College-Lackham: Lacock, Chippenham, Wiltshire SN15 2NY; ☎01249-466825; fax 01249-466825; e-mail jarvis@wiltscol.ac.uk; part-time day release.
Vetlink School of Veterinary Nursing: c/o Orchard Veterinary Group, Wirral Park Road, Glastonbury, Somerset BA6 9XE; ☎01458-210818; fax 01458-210040; e-mail nursing@vetlink.co.uk; part-time day release.

MIDLANDS
Moulton College: West Street, Moulton, Northampton NN3 7RR; ☎01604-491131. Part-time day release.
Hindlip College: Hindlip, Worcestershire WR3 6SS; ☎01905-451310; fax 01905-754760; www.pershore.ac.uk; Part-time day release and block weeks.
Warwickshire College: Moreton Morrell, Warwick, CV35 9BL; ☎01926-318333; fax

01926-318000; e-mail enquiries@warkscol.ac.uk; part-time day release plus block weeks.

EAST ANGLIA
College of West Anglia: Landbeach Road, Milton, Cambridge CB4 6DB; ☎01223-860701; fax 01223-860262; part-time day release.
College of Animal Welfare: London Road, Godmanchester, Huntingdon PE18 8LJ; ☎01480-831177; fax 01480-831291; www.caw.ac.uk; full-time BSc Hons 4 years (Royal Veterinary College Potters Bar); part-time day-release (Huntingdon, Oldham, Leeds, Potters Bar Edinburgh).
Otley College of Agriculture & Horticulture: Ipswich, Suffolk IP6 9EY; ☎01473-785543; fax 01483-785353; part-time day release.
Writtle College: Chelmsford, Essex, CM1 3RR; ☎01245-424200; fax 01245-420456; e-mail postmaster@writtle.ac.uk; full-time block release and part-time day release.

NORTH
A.C. Training: Hope Enterprise Centre, Scot Lane, Wigan, Lancashire WN5 OPR; ☎01942-737424; fax 01942-202797. Part-time day release.
College of Animal Welfare: Abbey Veterinary Hospital, Leeds; www.caw.ac.uk. Part-time day release.
East Durham & Houghhall: Houghhall Centre, Durham, DH1 3SG; ☎0191-386 1351; fax 0191-386 0419. Part-time day release.
Hopwood Hall College: Middleton Campus Rochdale Road, Middleton, Manchester M24 6XH; ☎0161-643 7560; fax 0161-643 2114. Part-time day release.
Knowsley Community College: Rupert Road, Huyton, Knowsley, Merseyside L36 9TD; ☎0151-477-5701; 0151-477 5703. Part-time day release.
Life Ltd: 3a Church Street, St. Helens, Merseyside WA10 1BA; ☎01744-24062; fax 01744-617174; e-mail nvqanimal@aol.com. Part-time day release.
Myerscough College: Myerscough Hall, Blisborrow, Preston, Lancashire, PR3 ORY; ☎01995-640611; fax 01995-640842; www.myerscough.ac.uk. Part-time day release and full-time BSc (Hons) in Veterinary Nursing and Practice Management.
North Trafford College: Talbot Road, Stretford, Manchester M32 OXH; ☎0161-886 700; fax 0161-872 7921; www.northtrafford.ac.uk. Part-time day release.
Rodbaston College: Rodbaston, Penkridge, Staffordshire ST19 5PH; ☎01785-712209; fax 01785-712209. Full-time block release and part-time day release.

VN College Courses in Wales/West
Abbeydale Veterinary Training: 20 Glevum Way, Abbeydale, Glos. GL4 9BL; ☎01452-300596.
Hartbury College of Agriculture: Hartpury House, Gloucester GL19 3BE; ☎01452-830065; fax 01452-700629; e-mail 100655.732@compuserve.com. Full-time block release, full-time BSc (Hons), and part-time day release.
Holme Lacy College: Holme Lacy, Hereford HR2 6LL; ☎01432-870316; fax 01432-870566; www.pershore.ac.uk. Part-time day release.
Pencoed College: Pencoed, Nr. Bridgend, South Wales CF35 5LG; ☎01656-860202; fax 01656-864875. Part-time day release.

VN College Courses in Scotland
Barony College: Park Gate, Dumfries, DG1 3NE; ☎01387-360251; fax 01387-660395; www.barony.ac.uk. Full-time block release and part-time day release.
College of Animal Welfare: Royal (Dick) School of Veterinary Science, Edinburgh; www.caw.ac.uk. Part-time day release.
Edinburgh's Telford College: Crewe Toll, Edinburgh EH4 2NZ; ☎0131-332-2491; fax

0131-315 7510; www.ed-col.ac.uk
North Highland College: Ormilie Road, Thurso, Caithness, KW14 7EE; ☎01847-896161; fax 018847-893872; www.uhi.ac.uk/Thurso. Part-time short block release.

Veterinary Nurse Open Learning (Correspondence) Courses
Animal Care College: Ascot House, High Street, Berkshire SL5 7JG; ☎01344-628269; fax 01344-622771; e-mail animalcarecollege@cavill.org.uk; www.animalcarecollege. co.uk Two-year course designed for students employed at an ATC who are not within easy reach of a recognised Royal College of Veterinary Surgeons course. Should be registered with the BNVA before beginning the course and can go on to do the BNVA Course afterwards. Cost £280 per year plus VAT.

ABC Level 2 Certificate for Animal Nursing Assistance (ANA)
Anyone who is without the qualifications necessary to be accepted for the RCVS Veterinary Nurse training scheme need not despair. It is possible to qualify for acceptance by following the above (usually abbreviated to ANA) which is a course which is a training for those wishing to follow a career in animal care within a veterinary practice.

The ANA course covers general husbandry and care of a range of small animals normally encountered within a veterinary practice. The student also learns practice clerical and reception skills including handling finances and product retailing. In order to be eligible for this course the candidate has to be available for full-time (35 hours a week including time spent at college) work at a veterinary practice (not necessarily an ATC practice), or part-time employment (20 hours not including college time) in a veterinary practice. If a satisfactory level is achieved students are allowed to progress to the RCVS Student Veterinary Nurse course. Even if students do not gain sufficient results, their ANA training will be recognised by other animal care sectors such as veterinary reception, kennels and animal welfare organisations.

Colleges Offering Approved Pre-Veterinary Courses
A.C. Training: (01942-737424).
Barony College: (01387-860251).
Berkshire College of Agriculture (01628-824444).
Bicton College of Agriculture: (01395-562300).
Cambridgeshire College of Agriculture & Horticulture: (01945-581024).
Canterbury College: (01227-811111).
Chichester College (formerly Brinsbury College): (01798-877400).
College of Animal Welfare (Godmanchester): (01480-831177).
Derby College: (01332-836600).
Duchy College: (01209-722100).
East Durham & Houghhall (0191-386 1351).
Greenmount College: (028-944 26601).
Hadlow College: (01732-850551).
Hartpury College: (01452-700283).
Holme Lacy College: (01432-870316).
Hopwood Hall College: (0161-643 7560).
Llyfasi College: (01978-790263).
Moulton College (Northampton): (01604-491131.
*Myerscough College (Preston): (*01995-640611).
Pencoed College: (01656-302600).
*Pershore College: (*01386-552443).
Plumpton College: (01273-890454).
Rodbaston College: (01785-712209).
South Downs College: (023-9279-7979).

Sparsholt College:(01962-776441*).*
Warwickshire College: (01245-420705).
Writtle College: (01245-420705).

Further Qualifications
Diploma: qualified VNs are eligible to enrol for a Diploma, details of which are available
from the BVNA (01279-450567).
HND Veterinary Nursing and Management: a three-year, full-time programme offered
by Bicton College of Agriculture in Devon (☎01395-562300; www.bicton.ac.uk).
BSc (Hons) Veterinary Nursing: offered by the College of Animal Welfare Edinburgh,
College of Animal Welfare Potters Bar, Hartpury College of Agriculture, Myerscough
College. Bristol University offers a BSc (Hons) in Veterinary Nursing *and* Practice
Management.
Further details of veterinary nursing top-up degrees or direct entry degree course from
Barbara Cooper on 01480-831177 or e-mail bc@caw.ac.uk or from Middlesex University
website www.mdx.ac.uk or the Royal Veterinary College website www.rvc.ac.uk.

Modern Veterinary Nursing Apprenticeships
Lantra, the land-based industries organisation and veterinary employers are in the process
of developing a framework for an advanced modern apprenticeship and a Scottish
modern apprenticeship. The modern apprenticeships will make it easier for veterinary
nurses to access wider skills and learning with a basis of key and core skills. Successful
candidates will receive some funding for enrolment, tuition and examination fees.
Further details on modern apprenticeships from Lantra (c/o Royal Agricultural Centre:
National Agricultural Centre, Kenilworth, Warwickshire CV8 2LG; ☎024-7669 6996).
Lantra's remit is to deal with all land based careers included in which are: small animal
care, veterinary nursing, farriery and all equine careers, plus agriculture and livestock.

JOB HUNTING

The BNVA keeps job seekers' details on an employment register which members can use
free (Non-members pay £6) for a period of four weeks. The BNVA register is circulated
to employers who then contact prospective employees direct. If you have not obtained a
post at the end of four weeks you can have a free extension for the same length of time.
The register is for VN students as well as for qualified VNs seeking temporary (locum)
and permanent positions. It is also possible to contact ATCs direct; just send the BNVA
an SAE requesting a list of addresses in your area.
Note that as well as veterinary practices qualified and student VNs can apply to animal
centres run by the PDSA, RSPCA and Blue Cross. Further details in the Animal Welfare
Organisations chapter. The Dogs Home Battersea (020-77622 3626), one of the largest
rescue centres in the country for dogs and cats employs fourteen VNs.
Other ways of getting a job include advertising in the Veterinary Nursing Journal
and the Veterinary Record. Some VNs become practice managers which entails a lot of
administrative work and can include training and teaching other VN and support staff.
Qualified VNs can also work in other establishments for research or teaching
establishments, zoos and so on. There are also opportunities abroad (see section two).

USEFUL ADDRESSES

British Veterinary Nursing Association: Level 15,   Terminus House, Terminus
Street, Harlow, Essex CM20 1XA; ☎01279-450567; fax 01279-420866; e-mail
bvna@bvna.co.uk; www.bvna.org.uk.   Has a jobs section on its website. Also
publishes *Veterinary Nursing,* the journal of the BVNA which is available from the
above address on subscription (£35 per year for a qualified veterinary nurse), six issues
per year. Has a jobs vacant section.

Veterinary Employment Services: Cornerways House, School Lane, Ringwood, Hants. BH24 1LG; ☎01425-482888; fax 01425-482999; e-mail vets@employment.com; www.vetsemployment.com Vet nursing agency for the UK. No registration fee and locum positions from Scotland to the Channel Islands.

USEFUL WEBSITES

www.netvet.wustl.edu – US site which has links to thousands of animal-related topics.

www.rcvs.org.uk – The Royal College of Veterinary Surgeons website has an excellent section for veterinary nurses with information on training, exams, career development. Also useful for getting up-to-date list of approved veterinary nurses training centres.

www.vet.record.co.uk – online version of *The Veterinary Record*. Has useful job section for veterinary nurses containing details of the job adverts that have appeared in the magazine.

www.vetnurse.co.uk – aims to be first internet port of call for veterinary nurses in the UK. Has nearly 2000 members so far. Offers news, magazine and job sections, and a forum for the exchange of ideas and practices and experiences. Also a revision section for veterinary nursing qualification.

www.vets-in-practice.com – recruitment website for the veterinary industry throughout the UK. Offers permanent and locum positions. Also a register of qualified veterinary nurses and locums available for short and long-term cover. Can also be telephoned on 0870 160 2600.

It is not unusual for veterinary practices to take on untrained staff and train them themselves. Practices vary from one veterinary surgery to another and many vets prefer to tailor their staff rather than hire a trained VN who has been taught to do things in a different way. This is fine for the vet as the VN will learn their way of doing things to perfection, but is not advantageous for the VN who may in consequence acquire a restricted knowledge which will not help them to get a job in another practice. However, working at a veterinary practice on a voluntary basis is an excellent way to get an idea of whether you are really suited to being a VN and it will help you get a full-time place later on.

Pay and Conditions

Typically in the United Kingdom there is no standard pay for veterinary nurses and salaries vary from area to area. Student VNs are paid usually from £6,000 to £9,000 a year and qualified VNs (those who have passed the Part II exam) from about £11,000 to £15,000. Another factor influencing pay is whether or not the post is residential which some are. The job applicant should however expect to receive additional recognition from employers for academic qualifications and length and range of experience. Head VNs should expect to receive from £14,000 to over £17,000.

OTHER ANIMAL HEALTH PRACTITIONERS

CHIROPRACTOR/OSTEOPATH

It is not only humans that have back and other skeletal problems which is why there are a number of chiropractors that choose to treat animals. There are 70 professionally trained chiropractors who do this in Britain and Northern Ireland, dealing mainly with horses and dogs, although other creatures such as cattle are also treated. In theory, any vertebrate animal can be a potential patient for this kind of manipulative and holistic treatment.

Chiropractic is a hands-on discipline, which involves removing bony misalignments in the skeletal system by swift, precise adjustments.

It is a scientific and systematic discipline studied at degree level. Courses in Chiropractic for animals are harder to locate than human ones. The respected McTimoney College of Chiropractic (Kimber House, 1 Kimber Road, Abingdon, Oxon, OX14 1BZ; e-mail: chiropractic@mctimoney-college.ac.uk) runs a two year postgraduate Diploma course in Animal Manipulation designed for those who already have training in relevant therapies (human chiropractic, physiotherapy, osteopathy), and who have proven experience of working with animals. Veterinary training is not essential. There is a chiropractic and osteopathic pathway. Osteopathy involves not only manipulating bones but also massage of the soft tissues to increase circulation and speed recovery. At the time of press, this was a relatively new idea spearheaded by qualified osteopath Tony Nevin of Cheltenham who has proved its efficacy on a variety of creatures from wrens to wolves, and from bats to cheetah. He proposes setting up workshops to teach the basics to other osteopaths. As with chiropractic, it is usual to qualify for treating humans and then extend the skills to animals. Further details can be obtained by sending a stamped addressed envelope to Tony Nevin (The Vineyard, Berkeley Street, Cheltenham, Glos. GL52 2SX).

PHYSIOTHERAPIST

Physiotherapy is a growing area of animal care. Unlike the title veterinary surgeon, anyone can call themselves a physiotherapist, but not a chartered physiotherapist. Members of the Chartered Society of Physiotherapists (MCSP) have to have reached a high academic and practical level of training. Physiotherapists treat a range of musculo-skeletal injuries and conditions using their hands (joint and soft tissue mobilisation and manipulation) and electrotherapy (ultrasound, laser, muscle stimulators).

As with chiropractic, it is necessary to qualify to treat humans first. This involves three to four years at university (depending on the course) and two years of postgraduate work as a Chartered Physiotherapist with people. Animal training takes place under the tutelage of a 'Category A' member of the Association of Chartered Physiotherapists Animal Therapy (ACPAT) and chartered physiotherapists have to be ACPAT members before they can practise on animals. There is a legal requirement that animal physiotherapy is performed only with veterinary approval and in any case liaison with the referring veterinary surgeon is essential.

In the autumn of 2002, The Royal Veterinary College awarded 20 Master's degrees in veterinary physiotherapy to the College's first batch of graduates of their two-year course. At the time of press there were 38 undergraduates studying on the course, 19 in each year. The course is a collaboration between King's College London and the Association of Chartered Physiotherapists in Animal Therapy (ACPAT). The course is very popular and has an annual intake.

The two main areas of animal physiotherapy are: large animals (horses, cattle etc.) and small animals (dogs, cats, birds, goats etc.).

Further details of ACPAT training can be obtained by sending an s.a.e. to ACPAT, Morlands House, Salters Lane, Winchester, Hampshire S022 5SP; www.acpat.org or telephone Kate Hulse (07879 814683; e-mail katehulse@hotmail.com).

BEHAVIOUR COUNSELLOR

Animals, like people can develop bad habits and exhibit delinquent behaviour. In the USA the proliferation of 'pet psychiatrists' in recent years was regarded with some derison by the average British pet owner. However, where the USA leads Britain often follows, and the UK version, called Companion Animal Behaviour Counselling, is now a recognised profession. There are about 60 registered with the Association of Pet Behaviour Counsellors (01386-751151) and other organisations such as the Federation of Canine Behaviourists and Professional Dog Trainers, and the UK Registry of Canine Behaviourists.

As a glance at any Yellow Pages under Pet Services will show, there is no shortage of self-advertising pet counsellors. It is probable that the majority of these practitioners do not have formal pet counselling qualifications as there is no regulating body or career structure for this profession, though the Association of Pet Behaviour Counsellors is trying to encourage those with a proper training to sign up to a standard code of practice. One of the best known animal behaviour therapists in the country, is Roger Mugford who runs The Animal Behaviour Centre in Chertsey, Surrey (01932-566696). He employs about a dozen staff and also does a nice sideline in intellect stimulating pet toys.

Academic qualifications

A background in behavioural studies, veterinary medicine, psychology or biological sciences are all useful. There are universities offering behavioural science courses including Bristol, Edinburgh and Reading universities. In recognition of the fact that animal behaviour is now an expanding area of animal health care the University of Southampton (023-8059 5000) has a Diploma/MSc in Companion Animal Behaviour Counselling as a postgraduate qualification. Entrants are normally graduates in veterinary science, psychology or biological sciences, but can be from other professions. The course comprises 18 modules and is part-time up to five years duration if needed. It covers various aspects of ethology (natural animal behaviour), the effects of domestication, animal biology, veterinary science and human psychology. The last because many animal behavioural problems derive from human causes. Owing to the fact that many humans no longer have a close relationship with nature, they tend to anthropomorphise their pets and then find that the animal is taking advantage and dominating them. The Southampton course is academic rather than vocational and includes a legal component as behaviourists are increasingly called as paid expert witnesses, especially in dangerous dogs cases.

There is also an undergraduate version of Southampton's qualification, a Certificate in Applied Animal Behaviour which can be done part-time over 4 years. The typical candidate for this course would be a veterinary nurse whose practice wants to expand the services its offers. Non-academic, short courses include Talking Dogs, offered by Broomfield college in Derby (0800 028 0289), which is for one day a week for five weeks.

Another possibility is a Foundation Degree in Animal Management and Behaviour offered by Bishop Burton College in Humberside (01964-553000; www.bishopburton.ac.uk).

Non-academic Courses

The Natural Animal Centre in East Sussex, whose goal is 'to create an Animal Behaviour University' offers courses on Positive Horse Magic, Equine, Canine and Feline Behaviour, Complimentary Therapies and others. Positive Horse Magic is also offered as a self-study programme. In addition, The Natural Animal Centre takes on animal carers and trainers who work in exchange for formal and informal education in the behaviour of animals and instruction on how to train them using positive reinforcement. Applicants should be over 18 and preference is given to those who can stay a year.

Employment

It is important to note that most pet behaviour counsellors are self-employed. If they are very successful they may run their own practices and do consultancy type work for which there is a growing demand. However, the overwhelming majority of pet counsellors also rely on other sources of income including writing and lecturing. The Blue Cross animal welfare organisation which deals with traumatised rescue animals employs a few behaviour counsellors, and veterinary surgeries are increasingly offering behaviour counselling as part of their services; other organisations may follow suit. Other demand is from individual members of the public who are increasingly referred to pet counsellors by vets.

Useful Addresses

Association of Pet Behaviour Counsellors (Administration Only): P.O. Box 46, Worcester, WR8 9YS; ☎01386-751151; fax 01386-750743; e-mail apbc@petbcent.demon.co.uk; www.apbc.org.uk Can supply a list of behaviour counsellors. For careers information send £3.50 to the above address for an information pack, or consult the website.

Association of Pet Behaviourists (see Association of Pet Behaviour Counsellors).

The Centre of Applied Pet Ethology (COAPE): P.O. Box 6, Fortrose, IV10 8WB; ☎0800 783 0817; www.coape.co.uk Offers seminars and courses on pet behaviour open to those wishing to study animal behaviour therapy. Send an A5 envelope for a brochure.

ANIMAL TECHNICIAN

Animal technicians generally work with laboratory animals and this is an ambiguous calling for an animal lover as it depends on the belief that what you are doing is essential to help cure deadly human diseases and advance science for the benefit of all. It is however a tricky area ethically. In 1997 2.5 million experiments were carried out on primates, dogs, cats, guinea pigs, rabbits, hamsters, rats and livestock in laboratories throughout Britain. Amphibians, fish and insects may also be used. Every laboratory has to have a licence granted by a Home Office Inspector. Under conditions published by the Home Office in 1998 the pursuit of profit is no longer a justification for experiments on animals, so pharmaceutical companies developing drugs duplicating those already on the market under a rival marque, are not be permitted to carry out animal testing. Furthermore, the suffering inflicted on animals has to be justified on a utilitarian basis i.e. it has to be outweighed by the benefit experiments can bring to people by advancing health, science and education. So while animal experiments are allowed to continue, their use is likely to be increasingly restricted. About 20% of animal experiments are related to 'regulatory toxicity', i.e. involve testing of chemicals contained in household and other everyday products on animals. One of the biggest animal testing laboratories in Britain is Huntingdon Life Sciences which carries out thousands of experiments and pre-clinical testing for pharmaceutical companies worldwide. It has over 1,600 staff on the payroll in the UK, USA and Japan. Britain's regulations on the use of animals are some of the strictest imposed anywhere in the world. Both the USA and Japan have far fewer restrictions on animal testing.

The animal technician is there to ensure laboratory animal welfare, yet their care is subject to the limitations imposed by the animals' being live experiments. If you really care about animals, this is probably one area of work you should think twice about undertaking. The animal technician's job includes care of breeding and newborn, feeding, cage and pen cleaning, care of sick animals and keeping records of health and behaviour.

Most employers will expect applicants to have at least GCSEs at grade C in English, Maths and Sciences. A levels or a BTEC National or Higher National Certificate in Science (Animal Technology) will give you an advantage and more responsibility. There are a small number of colleges that offer Animal Technology courses. Addresses of BTEC Institutions are given below. It should also be possible to obtain the Institute of Animal Technology qualifications (leading to membership of the Institute) through a combination of at work training and open/distance/day release studies at a college or by correspondence course. These are awarded at three levels: Certificate in Laboratory Animal Technology, Membership Diploma and Fellowship Diploma, which can be gained over a minimum of five years.

Places of employment include universities, teaching hospitals, medical and veterinary colleges, pharmaceutical companies, contract research companies, and specialist animal laboratory breeders. Rates of pay vary depending on the employer but expect a minimum of £9,000 per annum for a trainee technician up to over £20,000 for a managing technician.

Useful Address

Institute of Animal Technology: 5 South Parade, Summertown, Oxford OX2 7JL. The
   IAT is the professional body for animal technicians which has about 1,400 members,
   It publishes a news *Bulletin* and a journal *Animal Technology.* It also organises
   meetings, lectures and conferences and has contacts with European and other technical
   associations. The IAT will send details of careers and training on receipt of an SAE.

WORKING ON FARMS

Agriculture has changed dramatically in the last fifty years. The demand for ever cheaper food has led to an intensive farming system and massive use of antibiotics as growth hormones (a practice potentially harmful to both humans and animals), administered routinely to livestock to help them sustain the unnatural demands made on them. These methods have produced such horrors as veal calves reared in crates unable to support their own weight as they stagger to the lorries that drive them to the abbatoir, grotesquely fat bulls which would be unable to perform their procreational duties were they required to do so (most achieve siredom by artificial insemination), intensive, egg producing farms whose chickens peck each other bald, turkeys whose legs snap under them because their artificially accelerated growth means their legs are not strong enough to support them. BSE, whether caused by organo-phosphates on the land, or by feeding ground-up infected sheep to bovines, has nevertheless come to epitomise, in the popular perception, the ultimate awful result of taking liberties with nature. Consumer concern has resulted in a demand for organically produced meat and crops which are more expensive but bought by a growing minority. There are employment opportunities both in intensive livestock farming and organically reared animals.

Compared with farming in many European countries British farming is a highly mechanised and technological industry. Livestock farming involves being outdoors in all weathers yet it is also a lifestyle that appeals to those who work in the farming industry.

Mechanisation has also meant a reduction in the number of jobs on the land and only a quarter of farms in the UK employ workers on a regular, as opposed to a temporary basis. Even so there are still over half a million people employed on farms. Working with livestock can involve raising dairy and beef herds, sheep, pigs, poultry, goats, deer and (occasionally) non-indigenous species such as ostriches, llamas and reindeer all of which are now farmed in the UK.

There are several grades of job, which involve working with livestock.

FARM MANAGER

Farm managers are responsible for the daily administration and planning of what goes on at the farm, and in making it into a profitable business. They are answerable to the tenant farmer, landowner or corporation, which ever is their employer. On a very large farm, being farm manager is likely to be a 'desk job' with very little involvement in the practical work. However, on smaller farms the farm manager mucks in with the work which may include feeding and watering animals, supervising calving, lambing etc., nursing sick animals and milking. On the administratiive side, managers take decisions on livestock breeding and hire and dismiss staff; supervision of staff may be left to a supervisor. Organising the maintenance and repair of farm buildings and equipment is also the responsibility of the manager.

There are about 8,000 farm managers employed in the UK and competition for posts is high. In addition to a higher national certificate/diploma or an agricultural degree, many appointees have a business or management qualification and several years' agricultural experience. It is possible to work your way up to farm manager from craft level (see below) gaining the necessary experience and qualifications progressively.

Training and Qualifications
Agricultural degrees generally require a minimum of five GCSEs at grades A-C and two 'A' Levels/three Highers two of which should be in scientific subjects. One year's pre-degree agricultural experience is also desirable.

BTEC Higher National Diploma in agricultural disciplines has a minimum entrance requirement of four GCSEs including two maths/science subjects and English, plus one 'A' level, or two Highers including a science.

BTEC National Diploma requires a minimum of four GCSEs and a year's agricultural experience.

Some farm managers progress from being assistant manager or unit manager, which may also be referred to as a technician or forehand. Work at this grade is normally open to those with at least one of the following qualifications:
BTEC National Diploma/Certificate or Advanced GVNQ, NVQ 3 or a City & Guilds Technician qualification. Also acceptable are a National Certificate in Agriculture (NC) a plus National Certificate in Farm Management. Entry for the National Certificate in Farm Management is for those aged 20+ already in possession of an NC in Agriculture (or equivalent) and a minimum of two years' practical experience including the disciplines covered by the the NC in Agriculture.

The Advanced National Certificate (ANC) in Agriculture is another useful qualification which can be taken after the BTEC First Diploma or National Enterprise Board (NEB) First Certificate Course in Agriculture.

FARM WORKER

The farm worker carries out farm jobs at a practical or 'craft' level. Craftsmen and women take care of livestock and do other jobs like tractor driving. Tasks connected with livestock include feeding and watering, supervising births, ensuring intake of vitamins and medicines where necessary, nursing sick animals, monitoring growth, maintaining hygienic conditions and keeping written records.

Many craft level workers tend to develop a specialisation in pigs, poultry, cows, sheep and so on. Developing a speciality can earn a higher wage than general work.

Training and Qualifications

Employment as a farm worker is acquired through a combination of on-the-job training and college courses (which can be full-time, day- or block release) towards NVQ/SVQ level two qualifications. As entry to some college courses is dependent on previous practical agricultural experience it is a good idea to help out on a local farm during school holidays or at weekends; even if this is unpaid, it will be useful towards getting access to training later on. Other qualifications include:

The BTEC First Diploma in Agriculture and NEB First Certificate Course in Agriculture one-year courses providing a general introduction to agriculture. There are no particular entry qualifications, but good GCSE passes are useful, especially in English and Maths.

The BTEC National Diploma in Agriculture is a two- or three-year, general or specialist course depending on the student's practical experience. The minimum entry requirement is 4 GCSEs plus a year's experience. Alternatively, you can enter with the BTEC First Diploma, or the National Enterprise Board National Certificate, or appropriate qualifications acquired through part-time study plus one year of practical experience.

The National Certificate in Agriculture is a one-year, general, full-time course the aim of which is to provide a basic training for those who want to work in practical agriculture. The follow-on qualification is the City and Guilds Advanced National Certificate in Agriculture (ANCA) a one-year, full-time general or specialist course. If successfully completed these courses earn credits towards NVQs levels two and three (see below).

USEFUL ADDRESSES

Lantra: c/o Royal Agricultural Centre: National Agricultural Centre, Kenilworth, Warwickshire CV8 2LG; ☎024-7669 6996. Information about careers in farming especially the Modern Apprenticeships in Agriculture scheme. Send a large sae for the leaflet on this. Lantra's remit is to deal with all land based careers included in which are small animal care, veterinary nursing, farriery and all equine careers, plus agriculture and livestock.

Edexcel Customer Enquiries Unit, Stewart House, 32 Russell Square, London WC1B 5DN; ☎customer services 0870-240 9800; e-mail enquiries@edexcel.org.uk; www.edexcel.org.uk/qualifications. Responsible for the BTEC qualification. All enquiries should be sent to this address.

Federation of City Farms & Community Gardens. (NFCF): The Green House, Hereford Street, Bedminster, Bristol BS3 4NA; ☎0117-923 1800; fax 0117-923 1900; e-mail admin@farmgarden.org.uk; www.farmgarden.org.uk.

DEFRA (Department for Environment Food and Rural Affairs): Headquarters: Nobel House, 17 Smith Square, London SW1P 3JR; ☎020-7238 6000; fax 020-7238 6591 www.defra.gov.uk/animalh.

The *Dairy Council:* 5-7 John Prince's Street, London W1M OAP; ☎020-7499 7822; fax 020-7408 1353; www.milk.co.uk

National and Scottish Vocational Qualifications

Agriculture NVQs and SVQs relating to the care of livestock are available in a range of levels:

O   Crop & Livestock Production (1,2,& 3)
O   Livestock Production (1,2 & 3)
O   Livestock Management (level 4).

There are also NVQs in hatchery production and fish and shellfish husbandry.

PAY & CONDITIONS

The Agricultural Wages Board oversees the pay levels in the agricultural industry. Pay is related to age, overtime and skill/grade. In 2003 the minimum wage for a Grade I skilled employee was £258.57 per week; overtime for the same grade was £9.95 per hour. These are the minimum rates for the top grade. More than this may be paid as employers should take into account the amount of responsibility and overtime taken on by the employee. At the other end of the scale a sixteen-year-old can expect to receive over £100 weekly. Up-to-date information on pay levels can be obtained by contacting the address below.

USEFUL ADDRESS

Agricultural Wages Board: Area 2C, Ergon House, Horseferry Road, London SW1P 2AL; ☎020-7238 5862; www.defra.gov.uk.

ORGANIC FARMING

Organic farming is regarded as the antithesis of intensive factory farming, which aims to maximise production and produce ever cheaper food. Organic farming is as much a philosophy as a farming method. There is much potential support among consumers but unless organic products are marketed well and easily obtainable (through mail order for instance), this kind of farming relies on local consumption. Ideally, to make a reasonable living organic farmers have to be shrewd business people, which does not always tally with the lifestyle and thus many organic farmers remain at small-holding level. There are however larger scale operations notably the Loseley Farm, and The Duchy of Cornwall brands and the 1,336 acre Eastbrook Farm in Wiltshire which has an on-farm butchery and sells through mail order.

Useful Addresses

Elm Farm Research Centre (EFRC): Hamstead Marshall, Newbury, Berkshire RG20 0HR; ☎01488-658298; fax 01488-658503; www.efr.com; e-mail elmfarm@efrc.com. A centre for practical and scientific research into all aspects of organic farming. Advises farmers on the commercial applications of organic systems and provides information on organic farming. Publications list on request.

Organic Farmers & Growers Ltd. (OF & G): ☎01760-755380. Acts as an advisory organisation for farmers wishing to use organic methods correctly and provides a marketing service for all types of organic products. It is an approved certifier for the organic standard and European Commission regulation (2092/91). Can help with certification for organic farmers wishing to export within the European Union.

Soil Association: Bristol House, 40-56 Victoria Street, BS1 6BY; ☎0117-929 0661; www.soilassociation.org

WWOOF: (Willing Workers on Organic Farms), P.O.Box 2675, Lewes, East Sussex BN7 1RB; ☎01273-476286; e-mail hello@wwoof.org. The British branch of an international exchange network, where food and lodging and practical experience is given in return for helping on organic farms. WWOOF provides excellent opportunities for organic training. Stays of varied length are possible. Not all hosts have animals. Send a self-addressed stamped envelope for details.

Organic Living Association (OLA): St Mary's Villa, Hanley Swan, Worcestershire WR8 OEA. Exists to promote health in farm animals and food crops by farming. Organises conferences, publishes newsletter. Membership from £4 annually (£6 airmail).

OTHER ANIMAL CARE QUALIFICATIONS

BTECS

The BTEC range of national qualifications is managed by the Edexel Foundation (Stewart House, 32 Russell Square, London WC1B 5DN; www.edexcel.org.uk/qualifications, which is the non-profit awarding body for BTEC awards, certificates and diplomas. It offers both vocational and academic qualifications. While the range of scope of subjects ranges from Aeronautics to Welding there are a number of qualifications based around animal care, management animal sciences which are useful for those who want a career working with animals:

BTEC First Diploma in Animal Care: equivalent to four GCSEs at C level.

BTEC National Diploma in Animal Management:
BTEC National Diploma in Animal Management (Care)
BTEC National Diploma in Animal Management (Science)
Equivalent to three 'A' levels.

BTEC National Certificate in Animal Management:
BTEC National Certificate in Animal Management (Care)
BTEC National Certificate in Animal Management (Science)

BTEC National Award in Animal Management:
There are versions in *Animal Rehabilitation, Exotics, Kennel & Cattery Management and Pet Store Management.* Equivalent to an 'A' Level.
BTEC Higher National Certificate in Animal Management(HNC):
Level below HND. Now being replaced by the Certificate of Higher Education.

BTEC Higher National Diploma (HND) in Animal Management:
Note that some colleges are now offering a Foundation Degree in Animal Studies, Health and Welfare etc., which is a replacement for the HND.

BTEC CENTRES
England
The following colleges offer a range of BTEC Edexel qualifications in Animal-related subjects.

Barnsley: Barnsley College, Barnsley (01226-730191; www.barnsley.ac.uk). Offers First Diploma in Animal Care, National Diploma in Animal Management. Also NVQ Level I in Animal Care.

Bath: Norton-Radstock College, Bath (01761-433161; e-mail courses@nort.coll.ac.uk). Offers First Diploma in Animal Care, National Diploma in Animal Care. Also NVQs

1&2 Caring for Animals and RCVS Veterinary Nursing.

Berkshire: Berkshire College of Agriculture (BCA), Maidenhead (01628-824444; enquiries@bca.ac.uk; www.bca.ac.uk). Offers First Diploma in Animal Care, National Diploma in Animal Care, HND in Animal Studies and Management, HND in Animal Behaviour. Also offers one year top up BA (Hons) degrees in Animal Behaviour and Animal Industry Management (accessed after HND).

Buckinghamshire: Aylesbury College, Aylesbury (01296-434111; www.aylesbury.ac.uk). Offers First Certificate in Animal Care, National Certificate in Animal Care, First Diploma in Animal Care.

Cambridgeshire: College of West Anglia (01223-860701; www.coll-westanglia.ac.uk. Offers: Foundation in Animal Care (full-time), First Diploma in Animal Care (1yr, full-time), National Award in Animal Management, National Diploma in Animal Management (2yr, full-time), National Award in Animal Management Animal Rehabilitation, HND in Animal Science.

Cheshire: Reaseheath College, Nantwich (01270-625131; www.reaseheath.ac.uk). Offers First National Diploma in Animal Care, National Award in Animal Care, National Certificate in Animal Care, National Diploma in Animal Care, HND Animal Welfare and Behaviour. Also a BSc. in Animal Behaviour.

Cornwall: Duchy College, Stoke Climsland (☎01579-372222). Offers First Diploma in Animal Care. Also several equine courses.

Cornwall: Duchy College, Rosewarne (☎01209-722100; e-mail information@corn wall.ac.uk; www.duchy.ac.uk/rosewarne). Offers National Diploma in Animal Care and Foundation degrees in Animal Science, Bird Biology and Animal Husbandry and Management. Other courses include pre-vet nursing and BVNA Nursing.

Cumbria: Newton Rigg College: Penrith (01768-863791; cumbriainfo@uclan.ac.uk; www.newtonrigg.ac.uk). Offers First Diploma in Animal Care; National Award in Animal Management (4 types: Kennel & Cattery Management, Pet Store Management, Animal Rehabilitation, Exotics), National Certificate in Animal Management; National Certificate in Animal Management (Care); National Certificate in Animal Management (Science); National Diploma in Animal Management (same fields as for National Certificate); HND Animal Science, HND Animal Conservation Science. Also offers an entry level qualification in Animal Care for people with disabilities.

Derbyshire: Derby College, Broomfield (01332-831345; freephone 0800-028 0289l; www.derby-college.ac.uk). Offers First Diploma in Animal Care and National Diploma in Animal Care.

Devon: Bicton College of Agriculture, Budleigh Salterton (01395-562300; www.bicton.ac.uk). Offers First Diploma in Animal Care, National Diploma in Animal Management, National Award in Animal Management, National Certificate in Animal Management, and Foundation Degree in Animal Science (Management and Welfare).

Dorset: Kingston Maurward College, Dorchester (01305 215000; www.kingstonmaurw ard.ac.uk). Full-time courses: First Diploma in Animal Care and National Diploma in Animal Management. Part-time courses: National Certificate in Animal Care, National Award in Kennel & Cattery Management, National Award in Pet Store Management. Short courses (either 8x3hrs or 6x3hrs): BTEC National Units in Animal Handling & Management, Animal Behaviour, Animal Health, Animal Nutrition, Animal Nursing.

Dudley: Halesowen College, Halesowen (0121-5501451). Offers First Diploma in Animal Care and National Diploma in Animal Care; both full-time.

Durham: Houghall College, Durham (0191-3861351; www.edhcc.ac.uk). Offers First Diploma in Animal Care, National Diploma in Animal Care and National Certificate in Animal Care. Other courses offered include Pre-Veterinary Nursing and NVQs levels 1 & 2 in Animal Care.

East Sussex: Plumton College, Lewes (01273-890454; www.plumton.ac.uk). Offers Introduction to Animal Care GNVQ Foundation Science, National Award in Animal

Care, First Diploma in Animal Care, National Diploma in Animal Management and HND in Animal Science.

Essex: Writtle Agricultural College, Chelmsford (01245-420705; www.writtle.ac.uk). Offers National Diploma in Animal Care, National Certificate in Animal Care and First Diploma in Animal Care. Other courses (part-time) include NVQ 2 in Animal Care, also dog grooming and canine studies.

Gloucestershire: Hartpury College, Gloucester (01452-700283). Offers First Diploma in Animal Care, National Award in Animal Management, National Certificate in Animal Management, National Diploma in Animal Management, HND in Animal Care and HND in Animal Science. Also NVQs in Animal Care, Vet nursing, BScs in Animal Care and Animal Science, and a BA in Animal Behaviour Management.

Hampshire: South Downs College, Waterlooville (023-92797979.

Hampshire: Sparsholt College, Winchester (01962-776441; www.sparsholt.ac.uk). First Diploma in Animal Management, National Diploma in Animal Management, HND in Animal Science.

Hereford & Worcester: Holme Lacy College, Hereford (01432-870316; e-mail claire-howes@pershore.ac.uk; www.pershore.ac.uk). Offers First Diploma in Animal Care, National Award in Animal Care, National Diploma in Animal Care and HNC and HND in Animal Care. Also a BSc in Animal Care Sciences. May offer one or two-day courses, depending on demand in dog grooming, training.

Hertfordshire: Oaklands College, St Albans (01727-850651; e-mail help.line@oak lands.ac.uk; www.oaklands.ac.uk). Offers First Diploma in Animal Care, National Diploma in Animal Care, HND in Animal Management. Also City and Guilds animal care and equine qualifications and BTEC Equine qualifications.

Humberside: BishopBurtonCollege,Beverley(01964-553000;www.bishopburton.ac.uk). Offers First Diploma in Animal Care, National Diploma in Animal Management (Care), National Award in Animal Management (Exotics), National Award in Animal Management (Kennels & Cattery Management), Foundation Degree in Animal Management and Behaviour.

Humberside: GrimsbyCollege,Grimsby(01472-311222;e-maillisterlm@grimsby.ac.uk). Offers First Diploma in Animal Care (full-time), National Diploma in Animal Management (full-time), National Award in Animal Management (1 yr part-time).

Kent: Canterbury College, Canterbury (01227-811111; www.cant-col.ac.uk; e-mail administration@cant-col.ac.uk). First Diploma in Animal Care, National Diploma in Animal Management, HND in Animal Management. Also does First and National Diploma in Fish Management. Other courses include NVQs in Horse Studies and Equine BTECs.

Kent: Mid-Kent College of Higher & Further Education, Chatham (01634-830633) Offers First Diploma in Animal Management and National Diploma in Animal Management.

Kirklees: Huddersfield Technical College, Huddersfield (01484-536521). Ask for the Animal Care department.

Lancashire: Myerscough College, Preston (01995-640611; www.myerscough.ac.uk). Offers First Diploma in Animal Care, National Diploma in Animal Care and HND in Animal Welfare and Management. Also a BSc in Animal Welfare.

Leeds: Park Lane College, Leeds (0113-2162000). Offers First Diploma in Animal Care, National Diploma in Animal Management and HNC and HND in Animal Management. Other courses include dog grooming and distance learning animal care.

Leicester: de Montfort University, Leicester (0116 255 1551; www.dmu.ac.uk). Does HND in Animal Science.

Manchester: North Trafford College of Further Education, Manchester (0161-886 7070; www.northtrafford.ac.uk). Offers First Diploma in Animal Care and National Diploma in Animal Care.

Middlesex: Capel Manor Horticultural and Environmental Centre, Enfield ((020-8366

4442; www.capel.ac.uk). Offers First Diploma in Animal Care, National Certificate and National Diploma in Animal Care. Other courses include equine, saddlery and BHS Stable Management.

Norfolk: Easton College, Norwich (01603-741992; www.easton-college.ac.uk). Offers First Diploma in Animal Care, National Diploma in Animal Management, HNC/HND Animal Science and Welfare (in conjunction with Anglia Polytechnic University). Other courses: NVQs in Animal Care and Vet Nursing.

Northamptonshire: Moulton College, Moulton (01604-491131). Offers First Diploma in Small Animal Care, National Diploma in Animal Care, HND in Animal Welfare and Management. Also NVQs 1 and 2 in Animal Care.

North Yorkshire: Askham Bryan College, York (01904-772277; www.askhambryan.ac.uk). Offers First Diploma in Animal Care, National Diploma in Animal Management, HND in Animal Management. Also offers a BSc (Hons.) in Animal Management.

Northumberland: Northumberland College, Kirkley Hall Campus, Ponteland, Northumberland (01661-872772).

Nottinghamshire: Brackenhurst College, Southwell (01636-817000; www.ntu.ac.uk). Offers First Diploma in Animal Care, National Certificatee in Animal Care, National Diploma in Animal Management. Also University Foundation degree in Animal Studies (equivalent of an HND)

Shropshire: Walford College, Shrewsbury (01939-262100). Offers First Diploma in Animal Care, National Award, National Certificate and National Diploma in Animal Management. Other courses include part-time dog grooming and handling.

Somerset: Cannington College, Bridgwater (01278-655000; www.cannington.ac.uk). Offers First Diploma in Animal Care, National Diploma in Animal Management, National Certificate in Animal Management, National Award in Animal Management, National Award in Fish Management, Certificate of Higher Education in Animal Science and a Foundation Degree in Animal Science.

Staffordshire: Rodbaston College, Stafford (01785-712209). Offers First Diploma in Animal Care, National Diploma in Animal Management, HND in Animal Management. Also NVQs 1 & 2 in Animal Care.

Suffolk: Otley College of Agriculture & Horticulture, Ipswich (01473-785543; www.otleycollege.ac.uk). Offers National Certificate in Animal Management, National Award in Animal Management. Other non BTEC courses include BSc in Animal Science and Welfare, and a BSc in Animal Science and Conservation.

Surrey: Merrist Wood College, Worplesdon, Guildford Surrey GU3 3PE (01483-884040; e-mail info@merristwood.ac.uk). Offers National Certificate in Animal Management, National Diploma in Animal Management, Higher National Diploma in Animal Management. Other courses include a range of equine BTECs etc.

Surrey: Nescot, Ewell (020-8394-1731; www.nescot.ac.uk). Offers National Diploma in Animal Management (Science), First Diploma in Animal Care, First Diploma in Horse Care. Also Foundation Degree in Animal Health and Welfare.

Warwickshire: Warwickshire College, Moreton Morrell Centre, Warwick (01926-318318; www.warskcol.ac.uk; enquiries@warkscol.ac.uk). Offers First Diploma in Animal Care, National Award in Animal Care, National Diploma Animal Care. Other courses including equine and pre-vet and vet nursing.

Wiltshire: Lackham College, Chippenham (01249-466800; www.wiltscol.ac.uk/ courses).Offers First Diploma in Animal Care, National Diploma in Animal Management, HNC in Animal Science (full or part-time), HND in Animal Science.

Worcestershire: Pershore and Hindlip College, Pershore (01386-552443; www.pershore.ac.uk). Offers First Diploma in Animal Care, National Award in Animal Care, National Diploma in Animal Care, HNC/HND in Animal Care. Other courses: NVQs in animal care and vet nursing.

Wales

Carmarthen: Coleg Sirgar (01554-748000; www.colegsirgar.ac.uk. Offers First Diploma in Animal Care, National Diploma in Animal Care, HNC and HND in Animal Sciences. Other courses include NVQs in Animal Care, City and Guilds Pet Store Management and a range of equine courses.

Clwyd: Llandrillo College, Colwyn Bay (01492-546666). Offers First National Diploma in Animal Care.

Clwyd: Coleg Llysfasi College, Ruthin (☎01978-790263; www.llysfasi.ac.uk). Offers First Diploma in Animal Care and National Diploma in animal Care. Other courses: Dog Grooming (35-week, one day a week).

Clwyd: Welsh College of Horticulture, Mold (01352-841000; www.wcoh.ac.uk). Offers First Diploma in Animal Care, National Certificate in Animal Management, National Diploma in Animal Management, HNC in Animal Studies, HND in Animal Studies, HND in Animal Welfare.

Dyfed: CCTA, Llanelli (01554-748000).

Dyfed: Pembrokeshire College, Haverfordwest (☎01437-765247; www.pembrokeshire. ac.uk). Offers First Certificate in Animal Care, First Diploma in Animal Care, National Certificate in Animal Management (Care), National Diploma in Animal Management (Care), HNC and HND in Animal Care.

Gwent: Coleg Gwent (01495-333333; www.coleggwent.ac.uk). Offers Nat Diploma in Animal Care, 1st Diploma in Animal Care, HNC and HND in Animal Studies. Other courses include equine and agricultural ones.

Mid-Glamorgan: Pencoed College, Bridgend (01656-302600). Offers National Award in Animal Management, National Certificate in Animal Management, National Diploma in Animal Management, HND in Animal Science. Other courses include equine and dog grooming.

Northern Ireland

Belfast: Belfast Institute of Further & Higher Education, Belfast (028-9026 5000; www .belfastinstitute.ac.uk). First Diploma in Animal Care, National Certificate in Applied Science and Animal Management, HND in Animal Management.

Higher Education-Centres for Animal Subjects HNC/HNDs and Degrees

de Montfort University: Leicester(0116-255 1551; www.dmu.ac.uk) offers HND in Animal Science, and HND in Equine Science & Sports Management at its affiliated Brooksby Melton College (01664-850850).

Nottingham Trent University, Brackenhurst College: Nottingham (0115 941 8418; www.ntu.ac.uk). Offers Foundation Science in Animal Studies, BSc (Hons.) in Animal Science.

University of Central Lancashire: Preston (01772-201201; www.uclan.ac.uk). Offers courses at its Cumbria Campus (01768-863791): BSc Animal Conservation, HND in Animal Science. Also at the linked Myerscough college (01995-642211) offers BSc Animal Behaviour and Welfare.

Other courses at Myerscough: Equine and vet nursing.

University College Northampton: (01604-735500; www.northampton.ac.uk). Offers HND Animal Welfare, HND Veterinary Studies and BSc top-up (after HND) in Animal Welfare. Other courses include HND and BSc top-up in Equine Studies. Linked to Moulton College (01604-491131), Northampton for lower BTEC qualifications.

UWE: Bristol (0117-965 6261). Offers HNDs in animal subjects and BAs and BScs all at its affiliated Hartpury College, Gloucestershire. For details see Hartpury College above.

CHOOSING A COLLEGE

Choosing where to obtain your qualifications may depend on a variety of factors including locality and where the particular course you want is available. You may go to your local college or somewhere else in the country. Colleges and campuses vary and the only way you may be able to make up your mind is to attend a college open day and look around.

Stefan Drew of the Warwickshire College gives an idea of his establishment
Colleges vary a great deal and it is often difficult to decide where to go. To help you, I would like to give you a snapshot of Warwickshire College's campus and what we offer. Start by imagining lots of space for the animals and our students. We have first class facilities and a very friendly staff. The farm and equine unit share several hundred hectares of Warwickshire countryside. We have fields of farm animals, including gambolling lambs at springtime.

There are purpose-built animal care units where students learn grooming, feeding, and care of a range of animals. This is also where trainee veterinary nurses learn about anaesthetics and post-operative care. In our woodlands, students carry out conservation experiments by putting up nesting boxes and recording data on species native to the hedgerows and ponds. There may be night use of the hides for the observation of nocturnal creatures such as badgers.

The college organises its own regular horse trials. Some of the competitors are ranked internationally and they come from all over Britain to take part in dressage, showjumping and cross-country events. We have to use over 100 of our stables to accommodate all the competing horses. We also have lecture-demonstrations by Gold Medallists and other well known equestrian figures.

In the agricultural area students learn how to plough a field and milk and monitor a dairy herd. The college has also recently opened a new library resource centre where, among other things, students can watch wildlife and other videos.

Quite a number of our students live on site in single en suite rooms. Evening meals are available in our refectory. For relaxation, students have a college union with regular discos. We welcome anyone who wants to come and look round the college,so why not come and see us yourself?

ANIMAL CARE COLLEGE

This animal care college based in Ascot is an Open Learning (Correspondence) course provider with 30 courses within the sector that provide professional OCN accredited qualifications in animal care.
Animal Care College: Ascot House, High Street, Ascot, Berkshire SL5 7JG; ☎01344-628269; e-mail animalcarecollege@cavill.org.uk; www.animalcarecollege.co.uk For details of other courses see Dogs section.

USEFUL ADDRESSES

Nescot, Faculty of Science & Technology: Reigate Road, Ewell, Epsom, Surrey KT17 3DS; ☎020-8394 3099/3111. Has a range of Animal Care and Animal Science courses at all levels from Animal Care Certificate to BTEC HND in Animal Science. The College has a Rural Studies Unit with paddocks covering nearly six acres which house a variety of livestock, ferrets and chinchillas. There is a separate section for the care of small animals.
Triple 'A' Pet Resort & Care Centre: Follingsby Lane, Washington, Tyne and Wear NE37 3JB; ☎0191-537 1344; www.Triple-a-animals.com Work placements for graduates and

students of animal sciences at a large, modern, state-of-the-art pet care centre caring for cats, dogs, small animals and birds. Services provided include grooming, hydrotherapy, dog training, and pet accommodation. The Centre has City and Guilds accreditation, providing NVQ, levels 2 and 3 in Animal Care and the 7750 Grooming qualification. Further courses are available through the College of Animal Welfare regional centre based at Triple 'A'. Has 34 full-time staff, rising to 55 during busy seasons.

WORK SCHEMES FOR AMERICANS

The Work in Britain Program allows a few thousand American students aged 18+ to work in Britain pre-arranged, or arranged after arrival, for up to six months at any time. The Scheme involves buying a Blue Card, which costs about $240 and is recognised by the Home Office for work purposes.

Applicants have to be US citizens, living in the USA and registered at a US institution at the time of application. Personal funds of not less than $800 are also required.

Further information from BUNAC USA, P.O. Box 430, Southbury, CT, 06488 (1-800-GO-BUNAC or 203-264-0901; wib@bunacusa.org).

US citizens who have been offered a full-time position in their field of study or experience in the UK, may apply for a work permit through the Association for International Practical Training (AIPT), (Career Development Exchanges, 10400 Little Patuxent Pkway, Suite 250 Columbia, MD 21044-3510; www.aipt.org).

The company Trident Transnational (Saffron Court, 14b, St. Cross Street, London EC1N 8XA; 020-7242 1515; www.trident-transnational.org) arranges internships for students from the EEA and the USA. In exchange for a fee of £140 and £420 they will send CVs around relevant companies on behalf of people who want to work for between four weeks and six months.

The Training and Work Experience Scheme (TWES) is a special arrangement within the Work Permit scheme which allows foreign nationals to do work-based training for a professional or specialist qualification, a graduate training programme or work experience. TWES permits are issued on the understanding that the individual will return overseas at the end of the agreed period and put the skills learned to use for at least two years. Further details are available from the Overseas Labour Service of the Department for Education and Employment (W5, Moorfoot, Sheffield S1 4PQ; ☎0990-210224). You can also download information from the website (www.dfee.gov.uk/ols).

Canadian Students can apply for a working holiday visa independently or, if they want the security of a package programme, they can apply to the Student Work Abroad Programme (SWAP), which is similar to the Work in Britain programme. It is operated by the Canadian Universities Travel Service (Travel CUTS) which has branches across Canada.

McTimoney College of Chiropractic

Post Graduate Diploma in Animal Manipulation
(Leading to MSc)

- 2-year mixed mode programme
- 1-year optional Research MSc
- Monthly weekend tutorials
- Self managed home study

- Ideal for Osteopaths, Chiropractors and Physiotherapists
- Training available for those without a manipulation background

For more details contact the McTimoney College of Chiropractic, Kimber House, 1 Kimber Road, Abingdon, Oxon, OX14 1BZ. Tel: 01235 523336 E-mail: chiropractic@mctimoney-college.ac.uk or www.mctimoney-college.ac.uk

Animal Welfare Organisations

Like the majority of Britain's best known charity organisations, the main animal welfare organisations were founded by good-doing, and reforming, Victorians and Edwardians. The People's Dispensary for Sick Animals (PDSA), The Royal Society for the Prevention of Cruelty to Animals (RSPCA), the Blue Cross animal clinics and the Royal Society for the Protection of Birds have grown from humble beginnings into large national organisations. Also concerned with animal welfare are the myriad of smaller, independent rescue centres and animal shelters of which there are always new ones appearing around the country. These and the RSPCA produce some of the saddest sights in animals that have to be rescued from neglect, cruelty, injury, and natural disasters especially floods. However, the other side of this is that bringing animals back from extremis to optimum condition and finding them a new, loving home can be very rewarding work.

A growing problem dealt with by animal welfare organisations is the rising number of unwanted pets. Sometimes there are genuine reasons for abandonment such as serious illness, elderly people whose pets are not allowed to share their sheltered accommodation, or even unforseen lack of means, but there are still thousands which are 'dumped' by their owners because the children lost interest in their new 'toy', or the owners didn't realise what a responsibility and expense owning an animal is, or they simply couldn't cope any more. The thing that all these organisations have in common is that they are not run for profit and are funded by the public who support their aims and concern for animal welfare.

When it comes to employment, most animal welfare organisations operate with a mixture of paid staff and volunteers. The smaller organisations may be run by one determined, dedicated and single-minded person with the help of regular and irregular volunteers. Volunteering can be an excellent way to gain experience that will impress future employers.

ANIMAL HEALTH TRUST

The Animal Health Trust (Landwades Park, Kentford, Newmarket, Suffolk, CB8 7UU; 01638-751000) is a registered charity. It is a specialised veterinary treatment and research centre dealing mainly with dogs, cats and horses. It has a fully equipped veterinary clinic including an MRI scanner. One of the major research projects involves the genetic mapping of dogs with a view to screening animals for genetically inherited diseases. The Trust also has a centre for equine studies.

Pets are referred to the centre from veterinary surgeons all over the country to be treated by its specialist vets.

The trust employs over 200 staff: vets, scientists, veterinary nurses, technicians and administrative/support staff. The trust does not have facilities for work experience. Staff vacancies are advertised in New Scientist, Nature, The Veterinary Record or local newspapers.

THE BLUE CROSS

The Blue Cross, which began life as Our Dumb Friends League in 1897, has its headquarters at Burford in Oxfordshire. It runs three animal hospitals (two in London and one in Grimsby) and an animal clinic in Wandsworth which together give over 60,000 veterinary treatments to animals whose owners cannot afford to pay for them. In addition it has 12 adoption centres including two that specialise in equines at Burford and Northiam. Every year it finds suitable homes for over 8,000 cats and dogs while the equine rehabilitation programme cares for over nearly 300 horses and donkeys. A related organisation, the Irish Blue Cross is responsible for mobile clinics in Dublin and a Horse Ambulance Service which attends equine events.

The organisation is supported by direct public contributions and fund raising. The Blue Cross pledge is that it will never destroy a healthy animal just because it has no home, and it is also committed to animal welfare and responsible pet ownership.

The Blue Cross employs thirteen qualified vets in addition to animal nurses at its three hospitals and the animals clinic in Wandsworth (see below). Nurses at the Blue Cross are expected to train for the Veterinary Nursing qualification (see previous chapter) which combines tuition in the work place from experienced staff, and formal classes attended on day-release. The Blue Cross hospitals are Approved Training Centres. A total of 50 qualified veterinary nurses are employed by Blue Cross, and about fifteen trainee VNs are employed at any one time. As well as the regular animal nursing duties, nurses at the Blue Cross become involved in finding homes for stray cats and dogs, and boarding the pets of elderly people who are in hospital.

Each of Blue Cross Adoption Centres has an experienced manager who is usually someone who has worked their way up in the organisation. There is also a Deputy Manager and a varying number (three to seven) of Animal Welfare Assistants depending on the size of the centre. Experience of working with animals is preferred; dedication and flexibility are essential. Daily duties include cleaning kennels, grooming, dog-walking if

Animal behaviourists enable owner and animal to live in harmony

applicable and feeding and administering medical treatment under supervision.

The Centre Managers for the Equine programme have equine expertise as many of the horses received have medical or behavioural problems. Rehabilitation and rehoming is a major part of the job. The horse centres also employ grooms. Prior experience with horses is preferred but not essential. Day to day care of the horses includes giving special attention to the sick and infirm ones.

A recent addition to the Blue Cross team of employees is a small number of animal behaviourists whose specialised work involves enabling owner and animal to live in harmony. Most of their work involves canines.

Blue Cross Headquarters: Shilton Road, Burford, Oxon OX18 4PF; ☎01993-825500; fax 01993-823083; www.thebluecross.org.uk

Blue Cross Adoption & Equine Centres

Bromsgrove Adoption Centre: Wildmoor Lane, Catshill, Bromsgrove, Worcs. B61 ORJ; ☎0121-453 3130; fax 0121-457 7159; www.thebluecross.org.uk/centres/ bromsgrove.htm

Burford Adoption Centre and Equine Centre: Shilton Road, Burford, Oxon OX18 4PF; adoption centre ☎01993-822483; equine centre ☎01993-822454; www.thebluecross.org.uk/centres/burford.htm

Cambridge Adoption Centre: 20 Garlic Row, Newmarket Road, Cambridge, CB5 8HW; ☎01223-350153; fax 01223-324137.

Chalfont St Peter Adoption Centre: 10 Grassingham End, Chalfont St Peter, Bucks. SL9 OBP; ☎01753-882560; fax 01753-890829.

Felixstowe Adoption Centre: 333 High Street, Walton, Felixstowe, Suffolk IP11 9QL; ☎01394-283254; fax 01394-672271.

Hertfordshire Adoption Centre: Kimpton Bottom, Near Hitchin, Herts SG4 8EU; ☎01483-832232; fax 01438 833645.

Northiam Small Animal Adoption and Equine Centre:
St. Francis Fields, Northiam, Sussex TN31 6LP; ☎01797-252243; fax 01797-252948.

Southampton Adoption Centre: Bubb Lane, West End, Southampton, Hants S030 2HL; ☎023-8069 2894; fax 023-8069-5477.

Thirsk Adoption Centre: Parklands, Station Road, Topcliffe, Thirsk, North Yorks Y07 3SE; ☎01845-577759; fax 01845-578596.

Tiverton Adoption Centre: Bickleigh, Tiverton, Devon EX16 8RS; ☎01884-855291; fax 01884-855705.

Torbay Adoption Centre: Ashley Priors Lane, Watcombe, Torquay, Devon TQ1 4SE; ☎01803-327728; fax 01803-323314.

Blue Cross Veterinary Hospitals & Clinics

The Blue Cross Animal Hospital Victoria: Sheppard House, Hugh Street, London SW1V 1QQ; ☎020-7834 4224; fax 020-7821 9083.

The Blue Cross Animals' Hospital Hammersmith:
Argyle Place, King Street, Hammersmith, London W6 ORQ; ☎020-8748 5150; fax 020-8846 9019.

Blue Cross Animals' Hospital Grimsby: 207 Cleethorpe Road, Grimsby, North East Lincolnshire, DN31 3BE; ☎01472-343278; fax 01472-269770.

The Irish Blue Cross Dublin Mobile Clinics: 8 Dartmouth Terrace, Ranelagh, Dublin 6, Ireland; ☎+353 1-4971985; fax +353 1-496 7747.

CELIA HAMMOND ANIMAL WELFARE TRUST

Celia Hammond has been rescuing animals, mainly cats, for nearly 35 years and now runs her Trust to tackle the root cause of why thousands of healthy cats, dogs, puppies and kittens have to be destroyed because of an imbalance in the number of animals born to human homes to care for them. She promotes neutering through her 'at cost' neutering and vaccination clinic opened in Lewisham, London in 1995. The clinic provides this service for pets whose owners do not qualify for free charity treatment with the PDSA but are suffering financial hardship and who cannot afford the standard veterinary charges but do not qualify for free charity treatment because:

1. They are just above the benefit level.
2. They do not live within the area covered by a charity treatment centre as these have specific geographical boundaries.
3. They are squatting or living on the streets and are neither home-owners nor have the required rent book.
4. They have more than three animals which disqualifies them for receiving treatment for additional animals with the PDSA

The CHAT also rescues animals from the London area provides veterinary treatment, neutering and accommodation for them. For elderly owners of much loved pets that have to be put down for medical reasons, the Trust provides a humane and sympathetic end for those who cannot meet the standard veterinary costs of euthanasia.

The trust also focuses on trapping, neutering and re-releasing feral cats which quickly form colonies of unapproachable felines if left to their own devices. Most charities are reluctant to deal with feral cats or routinely destroy them as do pest control firms. CHAT does not believe in killing them as a method of population control.

The Lewisham clinic employs two vets and three nurses. Volunteers are needed to help with the other work of the trust including trapping feral cats so they can be neutered. For further details contact the Trust direct.

Celia Hammond Animal Welfare Trust: High Street, Wadhurst, East Sussex TN5 6AG; ☎01892-783820/783367; fax 01892-784882; e-mail chat@ukonline.co.uk; www.celiahammond.org

Celia Hammond Animal Trust Neuter Clinic: 233-235 Lewisham Way, London SE4 1UY; ☎020-8691 2100.

THE NATIONAL ANIMAL WELFARE TRUST

The National Animal Welfare Trust (www.nawt.org.uk) was started in 1971 as a retirement home for older animals. Its brief is now wider and it cares for a range of unwanted domestic pets and livestock and injured wildlife at its centres at Watford, and near Langport in Somerset. There is also an animal rescue centre in Cornwall. The trust is aiming to expand as and when funds become available. In 2000 a site near Hungerford in Berkshire opened with a purpose-built sanctuary for animals that will not be re-homed, because of their age. The Trust always needs funds and volunteers.

There is a total staff of about 50 including a handful of office staff. The rest are employed directly caring for the animals and the high proportion of canines means many of these are kennel staff. Enthusiasm for the job is rated higher than qualifications for most of the staff, though the centre managers have a great deal of experience. Applications should be addressed to The Animal Supervisor of the Centre you wish to work for, and give some idea of your availability.

CENTRE ADDRESSES

The National Animal Welfare Trust: Tyler's Way, Watford Bypass, Watford, Hertfordshire WD2 8HQ; 020-8950 8215; e-mail watford@nawt.org.uk

The National Animal Welfare Trust: Heaven's Gate Farm, West Henley, Nr. Langport, Somerset TA10 9BE; 01458-252656.

Cornish Animal Rescue: Cornish Rescue Centre, Wheal Alfred Kennels, Wheal Alfred Farm, Hayle, Cornwall TR27 5JT; ☎01736-756005; new centre.

The National Animal Welfare Trust: Animal Retirement Home, Trindledown Farm, Wantage Road, Great Shefford, Berks RG17 7DQ. Site purchased 1997/98. No projected opening date until funds for development have been raised.

PEOPLE'S DISPENSARY FOR SICK ANIMALS

The PDSA, Britain's largest veterinary charity was started in 1917 by Maria Dickin in a small cellar in the East End of London. The PDSA's mission then as now, is to provide sick and injured pets whose owners are unable to afford it, with free veterinary services. Their other mission is to promote responsible pet ownership.

Owners, have to show that they are in receipt of a means-tested state benefit and dogs and cats represent 95% of the animals treated. All kinds of treatment are provided free, from simple medication to complex orthopaedic surgery. A 'widow's mite' donation is requested from those using the service but inevitably this falls far short of the actual costs of treatment. The PDSA's charitable veterinary services are funded entirely by public support through the generosity of animal lovers' donations and gifts in wills. The PDSA's own fund-raising activities include a productive appeals programme incorporating a popular lottery. The charity also operates a network of about 160 retail shops.

The PDSA operates 45 fully-equipped PetAid hospitals in major towns and cities. In addition, the PDSA works with over 260 private practices (known as PetAid practices), which provide free PDSA-funded treatment to owners eligible for PDSA help. Every working day the PDSA provides treatment to 4,500 sick and injured animals, at a total cost (in 2002) of about £29 million.

EMPLOYMENT

The PDSA is the largest single employer of veterinary staff in Britain. About 230 veterinary surgeons and about 250 veterinary nurses working at its hospitals. Veterinary teams are supported by animal care staff and receptionists. Overall, the Charity provides a wealth of employment opportunities in a variety of fields, either working directly with animals, or to support and promote their wellbeing. Further information about employment opportunities can be obtained either from the Human Resources department at the PDSA's head office (Whitechapel Way Priorslee, Telford, Shropshire TF2 9PQ; ☎01952-290999; fax 01952-291035; e-mail pr@pdsa.org.uk) or, by visiting the PDSA (www.pdsa.org.uk).

Veterinary Student Placements

Note that 'seeing practice' opportunities with the PDSA are available to veterinary students. Below are the PDSA veterinary centres grouped by region. Please note that you should not apply direct to the individual centre, but through the Human Resources department at the Central Office (see above), or via their website www.pdsa.org.uk.

Scottish & Northern Region:

Regional Veterinary Officer: Mr G R Dobbie, 1 Shamrock Street, Glasgow, G4 9JZ; ☎0141-333 0655.

Aberdeen: 26/30 Fraser Place, Aberdeen AB25 3TY; ☎01224 632042.

Dundee: 211 Hawkhill, Dundee DD1 5LA; ☎01382-660356.

Edinburgh: Hutchison Crossway, Gorgie, Edinburgh EH14 1RR; ☎0131-443 6178.

Glasgow: 1 Shamrock Street, Glasgow G4 9JZ; ☎0141-332 6944.

Glasgow East: Muiryfield Drive, Tolcross, Glasgow G31 5RT.
Felling, Gateshead: Stoneygate Lane, Felling, Gateshead NE10 OLX; ☎0191-438 2881.
Newcastle: 71/77 Blandford Street, Newcastle NE1 3PZ; ☎0191-516 0636.

North Central:
Regional Veterinary Officer: 18 Fawcett Street, Sunderland SR1 1RH; ☎0191-514 4353.
Batley: 50 Cross Bank Road, Carlinghow, Batley WF17 8PP; ☎01924-472958.
Huddersfield: 5 Greenhead Road, Huddersfield HD1 4EN; ☎01484-429089.
Hull: 20 Brunswick Avenue, Hull HU2 9AY; tl 01482-224452.
Leeds: 1 Leylands Road, Leeds, LS2 7QR; ☎0113 245 1172.
Middlesbrough: 148/150 Borough Road, Middlesbrough TS1 2EP; ☎01642-246224.

Eastern Region
Regional Veterinary Officer: 2-4 Mostyn Street, Leicester LE3 6DT; ☎0116-254 1905.
Derby: 186 Normanton Road, Derby DE23 6UX; ☎01332 345771.
Northampton: 151 St. Edmunds Road, Northampton NN1 5ET; ☎01604 37175.
Nottingham: Dunkirk Road, Dunkirk, Nottingham NG7 2PH; ☎0115 978 5787.
Sheffield: 14 Newhall Road, Sheffield S9 2QL; ☎0114 243 3232.

Western Region
Regional Veterinary Officer: 565 Bath Road, Brislington, Bristol BS4 3JZ; ☎0117-977 4495.
Aston: 49 Grosvenor Road, Aston, Birmingham B6 7LY; ☎0121-328 1716.
Birmingham: 456-458 Hagley Road West, Oldbury, Warley B68 ODL; ☎0121-422 2902.
Blackpool: 47 Hawes Side Lane, Blackpool FY4 4AP; ☎01253-838585.
Cardiff: 238 Bute Street, Cardiff CR1 6HZ; ☎01222-480990.
Coventry: 34 Barker Butts Lane, Coventry CV6 1DT; ☎01203 590298.
Liverpool: 36/40 Richmond Terrace, Everton, Liverpool L6 5LA; ☎0151-260 8064.
Manchester: Warwick Road South, Old Trafford, Manchester M16 OJW; ☎0161 881 0222.
Plymouth: 10 Durnford Street, Plymouth, PL1 3QL; ☎01752-266077.
Stoke-on-Trent: 5 Club Street, London Road, Stoke-on-Trent ST4 5RQ; ☎01782-413415.
Swansea: 20 Viking Way, Winch Wen Estate, Swansea SA1 7DA; ☎01792-310974.
Wolverhampton: Tuxford Close, off Hilton Street, Wolverhampton WV10 OJQ; ☎01902-459555.

London Region
Regional Veterinary Officer: Woodford Bridge Road, Redbridge, Ilford IG4 5PS; ☎020-8550 3008.
Bow: 171 Malmesbury Road, Bow E3 2DT; ☎020-8980 5011.
Croydon: 7 Hurst Road, Croydon CRO 1JT; ☎020-8686 3972.
Hendon: 4 Church Terrace, Church End, Hendon NW4 4JU; ☎020-8203 2090.
New Cross: 6 Amersham Vale, London SE14 6LD; ☎020-8691 0577.
Romford: 94 Victoria Road, Romford RM1 2PA; ☎01708-745505.
Southend: 49 York Road, Southend SS1 2DB; ☎01702-466777.
Woolwich: 2/6 Basildon Road, Woolwich SE2 OEW; ☎020-8310 4822.

Southern Region
Regional Veterinary Officer: 5 Durley Avenue, Cowplain, Portsmouth P08 8XF; ☎023-

92268164.
Bournemouth: 54 Castle Lane West, Bournemouth BH9 3JU; ☎01202-533630.
Brighton: 2 Robertson Road, Preston Park, Brighton BN1 5NL; ☎01273-566595.
Chatham: Union Street, Chatham ME4 4PZ; ☎01634-844054.
Southampton: 40/46 Mount Pleasant Road, Northam, Southampton S014 OEG; ☎023-80222622.
Southsea: 62 Middle Street, Southsea PO5 4BP; ☎023-92754429.

ROYAL SOCIETY FOR THE PREVENTION OF CRUELTY TO ANIMALS

The world's oldest, and certainly Britain's best known animal welfare organisation was founded in 1824. In 1840 when it was granted a Royal Charter, it had five inspectors each paid a guinea a week. Throughout the nineteenth and early twentieth centuries much of its energies were directed towards the cruel treatment of many working horses. Although most people think the rescue of neglected and mistreated animals and the prosecution of the perpetrators is the Society's main function, its activities are far wider and embrace virtually all aspects of animal protection and welfare including:

○ Welfare of farm animals (Freedom Food Scheme).
○ Protection of wild animals – the Society was largely instrumental in the Wild Mammals Protection Act reaching the statute book in 1996.
○ Campaigning against the testing of cosmetics on animals, the hunting of wild animals with dogs, puppy farming (i.e. indiscriminate breeding for profit), and the transportation of live meat animals abroad.
○ Campaigning for dog registration and neutering, a ban on drift net fishing which entraps sea mammals and sharks etc. needlessly, a ban on cruel whaling methods.
○ Running a programme of Animal Centre Development – building and maintaining fully equipped animal centres.

The RSPCA organisation covers England and Wales (Scotland has its own animal protection society (see below) and comprises 186 branches run by volunteers in ten different regions of which London is one. There are 106 clinics and animal centres, four veterinary hospitals and 319 inspectors. RSPCA. branches are run independently (a bit like a franchise) and give advice to animal owners.

RSPCA VETERINARY ANIMAL HOSPITALS

Birmingham Animal Hospital: Barnes Hill, Birmingham B29 5UP. Employs four vets, 11 veterinary nurses and eight ambulance drivers, a hospital administrator and a part-time administrative assistant. Supported by three clinics at Lea Hall, Wednesbury and Cradley Heath and an RSPCA kennels and cattery.
Greater Manchester Animal Hospital: 411 Eccles New Road, Manchester M5 2NN.
Harmsworth Memorial Hospital: 22 Sonderburg Road, Holloway, London N7 7QD. Employs 44 staff including five vets, 23 veterinary nurses, ten ambulance drivers, an administrator and an administrative assistant. In addition, there are three clinics attached to the hospital at Edmonton, North Kensington and Kilburn.
Putney Animal Hospital: 6 Clarendon Drive, Putney, London SW15 1AA.

RSPCA REGIONAL ANIMAL CENTRES

Blackberry Farm Animal Centre: Aylesbury, Bucks. (01296-655073).
Stapeley Grange Cattery: Nantwich, Cheshire, (☎0870 442 7102).
Great Ayton Animal Centre: Nr. Middlesbrough, Cleveland (☎01642-724016).

Bryn-y-Maen Animal Centre: Upper Colwyn Bay, Clwyd (01492-532780).
Newport Animal Centre: Llanwern, Nr. Newport, Gwent (01633-412049).
Ashley Heath Animal Centre: Ringwood, Hampshire (01425-473896).
Southridge Animal Centre: Potters Bar, Hertfordshire (0870 442 7104).
Leybourne Animal Centre: West Malling, Kent (01732-847237).
Southall Cattery: Southall, Middlesex (020-8574 2710).
Gonsal Farm Animal Centre: Dorrington, Shropshire (0870 010 4253).
West Hatch Animal Centre: Taunton, Somerset, (01823-480156).
Millbrook Animal Centre: Chobham, Surrey (01276-858792).
South Godstone Animal Centre: South Godstone, Surrey (01342-893117).
Bath Animal Home: Claverton Down, Bath, Avon (01225-466129).
Bristol Dogs' Home: St. Philips, Bristol (0117-977 6043).
Harold Hallwood Home: Warrington, Cheshire (01925-632944).
Cornwall Branch Animal Centre: St Columb, Cornwall (01637-881455).
RSPCA Shelter: Derby, Derbyshire (01332-344620).
RSPCA Animal Centre: Chesterfield, Derbyshire (01246-273358).
Little Valley Animal Shelter: Exeter, Devon (01392-439898).
Danaher Animal Home for Essex: Wethersfield, Nr. Braintree, Essex (01371-851201).
Cardiff Animal Shelter: Cardiff, Glamorgan South (029-2070 2352).
LLys Nini Animal Centre: Swansea, Glamorgan West (01792-229435).
Ranvilles Farm Animal Shelter: Fareham, Hampshire (01329-667541).
Godshill Animal Centre: Godshill, Isle of Wight (01983-840287).
Longview Kennels: Marton, Blackpool, Lancashire (01253-763991).
Animal Shelter: Near Accrington, Lancashire (01254-231118).
Animal Shelter: Oldham, Lancashire (0161-624 4725).
Animals Home: Preston, Lancashire (01772-792553).
Woodside Animal Centre: Leicester, Leicestershire (0116-233 6677).
Mayhew Animal Rescue Home: Kensal Green, London (020 8969 0178).
Southport, Birkdale & District Animal Shelter: Birkdale, Merseyside (01704-567624).
Halewood Animal Centre: Liverpool, Merseyside (0151-486 1706).
Wirral Animal Centre: Wirral, Merseyside (0151-638 6318).
Enfield Cattery: Enfield, Middlesex (020-8366 3313).
RSPCA Branch Cattery: Hyson Green, Nottinghamshire (0115-9784965).
Radcliffe on Trent Animal Shelter: Radcliffe on Trent, Nottinghamshire (0115-933 4422).
Animal Centre: Burton on Trent, Staffordshire (01283-569165).
Animal Home: Woodbridge, Suffolk (01473-623280).
Bluebell Ridge Cat Rehoming Centre: Hastings, Sussex East (01424-752121).
Animal Centre: Patcham, Brighton, Sussex East (01273-554218).
Mount Noddy Animal Centre: Eartham, Nr Chichester, Sussex West (01243-773359).
Animal Centre: Allesley, Coventry, Warwickshire (024-7633 6616).
Animal Centre: Weoley Castle, Birmingham, West Midlands (0121-427 6111).
Hull & East Riding Animal Centre: Hull, Yorkshire East (01482-341331).
Animal Home: Clifton, York, Yorkshire North (01904-654949).
South Yorkshire Animal Centre: Bawtry, Yorkshire South (01302-719790).
Sheffield Animal Home: Sheffield, Yorkshire South (0114-272 7542).
Animal Centre: Leeds, Yorkshire West (0113-245 5132).
Animal Centre: Halifax, Yorkshire West (01422-365628).
Animal Home and Clinic: Bradford, Yorkshire West (01274-723063).

WORKING FOR THE RSPCA

The RSPCA employs a range of personnel of which the Inspector is the frontline worker. Inspectors are responsible for the policing function of the Society in by trying to ensure that the statutory protection of animals (as embodied principally in the Protection of Animals Act 1911) is enforced. Inspectors provide 24-hour cover. Duties include the investigation of cruelty complaints, which come mainly from the public, and routine inspection of various types of establishments where animals are kept. Inspectors are also taught about law and how to gather and present accurate evidence for court cases, give advice, rescue animals and administer animal first aid. Inspectors have no powers to make a forced entry, however bad the conditions. They can only enter premises with the consent of the owner. If the circumstances are sufficiently suspicious, they can ask the police to get a search warrant. In cases where there has been wilful cruelty or neglect, the Society can start court proceedings. If the situation is redeemable, inspectors try to advise owners on improving care and conditions.

The society has 328 Field Inspectors and although over 2,000 applications are received annually, only a fraction of these are transmuted into trainees. Student inspectors attend a 25-week training course followed by six months probation. There are one or two inspectorate training courses annually with about 19 students per course. Application is open to those aged 22 and over, with GCSE level qualifications in English and a science subject. Applicants have to pass a medical, hold a current driving licence and be able to swim 50 metres, fully clothed. Relevant work experience with animals, and NVQs are advantageous but not essential. Good interpersonal skills, preferably in the area of handling confrontational situations are essential, and determination, are other necessary qualities. Once qualified, inspectors have to be prepared to relocate anywhere in England or Wales. Help and advice on moving are given. Further details can be obtained by sending a brief letter and an SAE to The Chief Superintendent of Training (RSPCA, Wilberforce Way, Southwater, Horsham, West Sussex RH13 9RS).

Veterinary nurse applicants wanting to work for the Society have to follow the VN course (see Chapter One for details). Veterinary Nurse vacancies with the RSPCA are advertised in the Veterinary Record. Speculative applications can also be sent to the RSPCA Animal Hospitals listed above.

Hospital and Clinic Assistants are also employed for which the most important qualities are patience, dedication and stamina. Trainees must be at least 18 and within easy travelling distance of the workplace.

Animal Care Assistants are responsible for the day-to-day care of animals at animal centres. Duties include smelly ones like cleaning the animal quarters once or twice a day and dealing with animals that have died from their injuries. More pleasant duties include working alongside the RSPCA teams to restore cured animals to the wild or find a suitable home for domestic pets. Clerical duties include keeping accurate, written records on every animal at the centre. Care assistants have to be good with both animals and people, have good GCSEs including English and Maths. The minimum age for application is 16 years.

Many RSPCA animal centres have volunteer kennel assistants and there are a few full-time positions. Contact your local branch to enquire about vacancies.

THE WILDLIFE HOSPITAL TRUST

Also known as St Tiggywinkles, the Trust takes in sick and injured wild animals and birds with the ultimate aim to return them to the wild. The Trust also established the first wildlife teaching hospital. There are ten full-time and 50 part-time staff and the Trust also acts as a consultancy and offers skills training.

Wildlife Hospital Trust: Aston Road, Haddenham, Aylesbury, Buckinghamshire HP17 8AF; ☎01844-292292; fax 01844-292640; mail@sttiggywinkles.org.uk.

ROYAL SOCIETY FOR THE PROTECTION OF BIRDS

The RSPB, founded in 1889 is an animal welfare organisation only in the broadest sense since its function is to protect birds through conserving their habitat in reserves, rather than treating and rehabilitating injured birds as the RSPCA does in its wildlife centres. The RSPB manages more than 150 nature reserves in the United Kingdom. The Society has about a million members whose subscriptions largely support its work. *Birds* the RSPB's magazine claims a readership of 1.9 million while *Bird Life* the junior members' publication is read by an estimated 250,000.

Probably the best known RSPB project of recent years is the programme to reintroduce the osprey in Scotland through its carefully managed breeding programme at Loch Garten. The society also produces reports on British birds which have declined alarmingly from a former abundance. The bittern, grey partridge, thrush and skylark are amongst the many once prolific native species which are fast disappearing through progressive elimination of their habitat.

EMPLOYMENT

The RSPB has a large staff of over 1,000 full-time, part-time and contracted staff from reserve managers to office and computer staff. The Headquarters in Bedfordshire absorbs nearly half of these and the rest are employed around the country including in the nature reserves as wardens and researchers. Every year about 100 paid, short-term staff are taken on to help run the nature reserves on contracts lasting from three months up to a year. Duties vary with the reserve, but generally include practical habitat management, surveys and species monitoring, dealing with the visiting public (leading walks, providing information etc). Being a warden is not about bird watching; these days there is a lot of office work involved. Pay is not high compared with jobs in industry and most wardens recognise that theirs is a way of life rather than a job. The RSPB also runs a volunteer wardening scheme whereby those over 16 years old can spend a minimum of a week on a nature reserve, working alongside the resident warden. Volunteers pay a contribution towards their keep.

Simon Buscuttil, who is the Area Manager for the Dungeness Estate of 2,100 acres in Kent recommends volunteering as an initial step towards a career with the RSPB

You really need to do a fair old stint as a volunteer, perhaps during a GAP year, or during university holidays. I have a degree in Philosophy, Science and Economics and this combined with my hobbies and interests gave me an entrance to the RSPB. Nowadays, it is advisable to have a conservation/management type degree of which there are many to choose from.

I used to be a warden, but now I manage the wardens. In any one month there may be 45 people working on the reserve including part-time staff and outside contractors. Here, we are using land left after gravel excavations. After the gravel company have finished extracting, they clean it up and we manage it as wetlands for waders. At certain times of year, we monitor certain types of birds – our target species at the moment are waders – and monitor them with binoculars to make sure that our programmes for them are working. One of the greatest satisfactions of the job is watching the birds coming in to land in flocks to use the habitat we have created for them.

We don't do any bird ringing ourselves. We occasionally have a project that

> *requires ringing and we call in outsiders. You have to be specially trained. The best way to learn is through the bird observatory network. You can find out about learning to ring from the British Trust for Ornithology (01842-750050) whose bird studiers are mainly volunteers and who carry out most of the studies at the bird observatories.*

The RSPB also employs about ten research biologists on a full-time basis. Their jobs involve both field work and office work. There are also short-term research appointments lasting as little as three months.

Central Addresses
RSPB Headquarters: The Lodge, Sandy, Bedfordshire SG19 2DL; ☎01767-680551.
Scottish Headquarters: 17 Regent Terrace, Edinburgh EH7 5BN; ☎0131-557 3136.
Wales Office: Bryn Aderyn, The Bank, Newtown, Powys SY16 2AB; ☎01686-626678.
Northern Ireland Office: Belvoir Park Forest, Belfast BT8 4QT; ☎01232-491547.

Wardens are employed in the following reserves:

England
SOUTH-EAST
Adur Estuary, West Sussex
Blean Woods, Kent
Dungeness, Kent
Elmley Marshes, Kent
Fore Wood, East Sussex
Langstone Harbour, Hampshire
Northward Hill, Kent,
Pulborough Brooks, West Sussex
Tudeley Woods, Kent

SOUTH-WEST
Arne, Wareham, Dorset
Aylesbeare Common, Devon
Chapel Wood, Devon
Exe Estuary, Bowling Green Marshes, Devon
Exe Estuary, Exminister Marshes, Devon
Garston Wood, Dorset
Hayle Estuary, Cornwall
Lodmoor, Dorset
Marazion Marsh, Cornwall
Radipole Lake, Dorset
West Sedgmoor, Somerset

CENTRAL ENGLAND
Church Wood, Buckinghamshire
Highnam Woods, Gloucestershire
The Lodge, Bedfordshire
Nagshead, Gloucestershire
Otmoor, Oxfordshire
Rye House Marsh, Hertfordshire
Sandwell Valley, West Midlands

EAST ANGLIA
Berney Marshes, Norfolk
Fowlmere, Cambridge,
Frampton Marshes, Lincolnshire
Havergate Island, Suffolk
Minsmere, Suffolk
North Warren, Suffolk
Ouse Washes, Cambridgeshire
Snettisham, Norfolk
Stour Estuary, Essex
Strumpshaw Fen, Norfolk (part of mid-Yare Valley Reserves)
Surlingham Church Marsh, Norfolk (part of mid-Yare Valley Reserves)
Tetney Marshes, Lincolnshire
Titchwell Marsh, Norfolk
Wolves Wood, Suffolk

NORTH-WEST
Churnet Valley Woods, Staffordshire
Coombes Valley, Staffordshire
Dee Estuary, Gayton Sands, Cheshire
Fairburn Ings, West Yorkshire
Leighton Moss, Lancashire
Marshside, Merseyshire
Morecombe Bay, Lancashire
North England
Bampton Cliffs, Humberside
Blacktoft Sands, Whitgift, Goole, Humberside
Campfield Marsh, Cumbria,
Haweswater, Penrith, Cumbria
Hodbarrow, Cumbria
Leighton Moss, Silverdale, Lancashire
St. Bees Head, Cumbria,

Scotland
Handa Island, off Sutherland
Insh Marshes, Kingussie, Highland
Killiecrankie, Pitlochry, Perthshire
Loch Garten, Nethybridge, Highland
Loch Gruinart, Isle of Islay, Argyllshire
Loch of Strathbeg, Crimongate, Lonmay, Fraserburgh
North Hoy, Orkney
      There are reserves also on Orkney and Shetland.

Wales
Conwy, Gwynedd,
Cwm Clydach, West Glamorgan,
Dinas, Gwenffrwd, Dyfed
Dyffryn Woods, Powys,
Grassholm Island off Dyfed
Gwenffrwd and Dinas, Rhandirmwyn, Llandovery, Dyfed
Lake Vyrnwy, Llanwddyn, Powys
Mawddach Valley, Gwynedd
Ramsey Iland, Dyfed

South Stack Cliffs, Gwynedd
Valley Lakes, Gwynedd
Ynys-hir, Eglwysfach, Machynlleth, Powys

Northern Ireland
Castlecaldwell, Co Fermanagh
Lough Foyle, Londonderry
Portmore Lough, Co Antrim
Rathlin Island Cliffs, Co Antrim

WOOD GREEN ANIMAL SHELTERS

In 1924 the original Wood Green Animal Shelter in London opened for unwanted strays for which little could be done except to provide them with a humane end. By the 1930s this thankless task was transformed into a service for treating sick, injured, neglected and unwanted animals by Margaret Young. After a life of doing good she died in 1993 aged 98 years. There are now three Wood Green Animal Shelters. All of them take unwanted animals and re-home them if possible. The re-homing process is quite thorough to make sure animal, and owner and environment are well matched.

The organisation employs about 185 staff of whom about 129 are directly concerned with animal care. These comprise full-time, part-time and 'weekenders'. In addition to the paid staff there are normally around 70 volunteers helping out in all departments. All applicants are interviewed and references checked. Qualified staff include veterinary nurses and trainee VNs (Wood Green Shelters is an approved training centre). For other staff an NVQ level 3 is helpful but all staff without are encouraged to work towards an animal care qualification. As those working at the Wood Green shelter in Godmanchester share the same site as the Wood Green College of Animal Welfare (01480-831177) this can be done very conveniently.

Shelter Addresses
Headquarters: Wood Green Animal Shelters, Kingsbush Farm, London Road, Godmanchester, Cambs. PE29 2NH; ☎01480-830014; fax 01480-832817; e-mail marketing@woodgreen.org.uk; www.woodgreen.org.uk. The largest of the shelters it covers 50 acres and is open 365 days a year.
Heydon: Wood Green Animal Shelters, Highway Cottage, Chishill Road, Heydon, Near Royston, Hertfordshire SG8 8PN; 01763-838329; fax 01763-838824.
London: Wood Green Animal Shelters, 601 Lordship Lane,Wood Green, London N22 5LG; ☎020-8222 2351; fax 020-8889 0245.

THE SCOTTISH SOCIETY FOR THE PREVENTION OF CRUELTY TO ANIMALS

The SSPCA. (Braehead Mains, 603 Queensferry Road, Edinburgh EH4 6EA; ☎0131-339 0222; fax 0131-339 4777; e-mail enquiries@scottishspca.org) merged with the Aberdeen Association for the Prevention of Cruelty to Animals in 1996 making the SSPCA a national Scottish organisation. Founded in 1839, the Society runs 14 Animal Welfare Centres and has a 59-strong Inspectorate who are the frontline in policing animal welfare legislation, rescuing distressed animals and advising and guiding those in charge of animals. The Society employs about the same number of kennel staff for its rescue centres. Further details of recruitment procedures can be obtained from the above address.

SSPCA Animal Welfare Centres

Ayr Animal Welfare Centre: Millview, No 4 Holding, Mainholm, Ayr KA6 5HD; ☎01292-265975.

Balmore Animal Welfare Centre: Balmore, Dounreay, By Thurso, Caithness KW14 7YB.

Bothwell Bridge Animal Welfare Centre: Bothwell Road, Hamilton ML3 0SB. One of the largest centres, it was completely rebuilt in 1997 including 80 dog kennels and 36 cat spaces.

Dundee Animal Welfare Centre: Petterden, Dundee DD4 OQD; ☎01382-380593. New centre with modern facilities.

Dunragit Animal Welfare Centre: The Kennels, Dunragit, Stranraer, Wigtownshire DG9 8PH; ☎01581-400253. Commercial boarding kennels that leases spaces to the SSPCA.

Glasgow Cat and Dog Home: 125 Kinnell Avenue, Cardonald, Glasgow G52 3RY; ☎0141-882 1688. Completely rebuilt in 1996, the Home is the busiest SSPCA centre which cares for over 6,000 dogs and cats in a year with accommodation for 100 dogs, 24 cats and 29 small animals and birds. It also has a fully equipped veterinary clinic, grooming parlour and cats' playroom. The Glasgow inspectors are also based at the home's offices.

Inverness Animal Welfare Centre: 5 Inshes, Old Perth Road, Inverness IV2 5BA; ☎01463-230206. Opened spring 2001. 10 dog kennels, 3 mother and puppy units, 20 cat spaces, pet cemetery.

Middlebank Wildlife Centre: Middlebank Farm, Masterton Road, Nr. Dunfermline KY11 5QN; ☎01383-412520. Situated just north of the Forth Bridge near Inverkeithing, the centre is the Society's specialised wildlife rehabilitation unit with a seal treatment hospital, aviaries and wildlife enclosures. A purpose-built education unit demonstrates to the public how oiled seabirds are cleaned.

Milton Animal Welfare Centre: Milton, Dumbarton G82 2UA; ☎01389-761208. Medium-size modern Centre with kennels for 43 dogs, 23 cat spaces, seven isolation units and puppy kennels. The centre also provides quarantine facilities for pets returning from abroad.

Shetland Oiled Bird Unit: Tirlandie, Gott ZE2 9SF; ☎01595-840321. Founded by the local inspector after the *Braer* disaster, the unit can also house small animals if necessary.

Stirling Animal Welfare Centre: Ladysneuk Road, Cambuskenneth, Stirling FK9 5NP; ☎01786-473388. Completely rebuilt in 1995. Well equipped small centre with seven dog kennels, 6 cat units, small animal room and vet room.

INDEPENDENT ANIMAL RESCUE CENTRES

Animals in Distress, Torbay & West Country: Animals in Distress Rescue Centre, Biltor, Edgelands Lane, Ipplepen, Newton Abbott TQ12 5UG; ☎01803-812121. Internet: www.leedham.demon.co.uk./animals/hntl.
Started in 1987, the Centre rehomes in the region of 1,000 rescued animals per year. Four full-time paid staff and about the same number of volunteers look after the animals and students from Bicton Agricultural College do work experience there.

Burstow Wildlife Sanctuary: Church Lane, Burstow, Surrey RH6 9TG; 01293-773075. Started by Penny Boyd in 1987. A unique centre in that it not only houses British wildlife, but also exotics and 100 primates. The exotics and monkeys come from different sources but include smuggled animals that have been confiscated by customs and unwanted 'pets' like the emu that was being unsuitably housed in a small pen with chickens by its former owner. Penny has two full-time permanent staff and a band of about 30 part-time volunteers including youngsters who come and work after school. Students of animal related subjects are sometimes taken on for work experience but Penny warns that a lot of the work is clearing up droppings. The Centre has a re-homing policy. Exotic animals unsuitable as domestic pets, she tries to re-home in zoos and wildlife parks.

Friends of Animals League (Foal Farm Animal Rescue and Rehoming Centre): Jail Lane, Biggin Hill, Kent TN16 3AX; ☎ 01959-572386; www.foalfarm.org.uk Contact: Sarah Hollingsworth, General Manager (manager@foalfarm.org.uk).

Foal Farm is a registered charity, established in 1960 and supported entirely by voluntary donations and legacies. Its aims are to take in as many sick, distressed or unwanted animals as possible, (usually between 300 and 400 are resident), to restore them to health and happiness and place them in good, loving (vetted homes). Each year, new homes are found for over 1200 dogs, cats, rabbits and smaller animals. Sick or injured wildlife is restored to health and released back to the wild. Sanctuary is given to cows, goats, pigs, horses, sheep and birds who are permanent residents at foal. No animal is ever destroyed, except on veterinary advice. If no home can be found, the animal remains for the rest of its natural life at Foal.

The Centre has 13 full and 8 part-time staff and also provides places for people on Duke of Edinburgh's Award Scheme, Princes Trust, those with special needs, placements for YT and NVQ training, working experience and community service. There are also a large number of dedicated volunteers who are involved in all aspects of the Centre's activities.

Last Chance Animal Rescue: (Reg. Charity no. 1002349,) Stickhill, Edenbridge, Kent TN8 5NH; ☎ 01732-865530; www.lastchanceanimalrescue.co.uk. Founded by Sylvia Wragg in 1986, LCAR takes in animals for rehoming, after they have been abandoned or mistreated. The majority are dogs and cats, but the centre also has sheep, horses, goats, fowl, rabbits, guinea pigs and pigs. The centre employs a full-time vet and other staff including dog trainers, dog walkers, home-vetters and drivers are volunteers.

Wildlife Aid: Randalls Farmhouse, Randall's Road, Leatherhead, Surrey KT22 0AL; ☎ 01372-377332. A Wildlife rescue centre run by a former London commodity broker takes in injured and orphaned wildlife of all kinds and restores them to health before releasing them back to the wild. The centre relies on the no charge services of three vets and well over 100 volunteers who care for the animals. The centre provides a distress call telephone service round the clock.

USEFUL PUBLICATIONS

Animal Rescue Directory: available from Hand to Paw (£2.95). Updated approximately every 18 months. A list of over 1,000 animal welfare organisations, mostly small ones.

Who's Who in the Environment: published by the Environment Council (212 High Holborn, London WC1V 7VW; ☎ 020-7836 2626; fax 020-7242 1180), includes animal organisations' addresses. Single volume covers England, Scotland and Wales. Also available a UK PC Disk database (£75) of 1,200 environmental organisations in Britain and Northern Ireland. Last revised 1994-96. No revision planned.

USEFUL WEBSITE

www.animalrescuers.co.uk is a comprehensive site that has information on everything to do with animals from UK wildlife centres, animal rescue organisations, directory pages by animal, and a help wanted and offered section which has details of jobs offered for volunteers and paid staff.

Working With Dogs & Cats

DOGS

There are an estimated 6.7 million pet dogs in Britain. Dogs give a lot of affection and attention to anyone who owns them and often to total strangers as well. They are able to perform many tasks useful, and in some cases essential to daily human life. They are in return dependent on humans, particularly when it comes to exercise, and unlike cats they are much less able to look after themselves generally. This leads to there being more jobs with dogs than with cats; for instance there are far more boarding kennels than catteries as a cat can always be fed by a neighbour when you are away.

Working dogs, as opposed to pet ones, perform specialised tasks for which they receive special training. In the public sector these include 'dogs in uniform' including police patrol dogs, customs drugs sniffer dogs, prison service guard dogs, army explosive and firearm detecting dogs. In the private sector there are guide dogs for the blind, hearing dogs for the deaf, dogs for the disabled, private security dogs, gun dogs, racing dogs, sheepdogs and search and rescue dogs.

KENNELS

There are over 1,500 registered boarding kennels in the UK. This is down from a figure of about 2,500 a year ago. This is because kennels are getting larger and not because business is shrinking – quite the contrary. There is a greater demand than ever from those going on holiday for short spans that do not warrant the hassle of getting a 'pet passport' to take their dog with them.

There has been a reduction in the need for quarantine kennels now that the once obligatory 6 months' quarantine has been replaced by the 'Pets Passport' which allows microchipped and rabies-vaccinated dogs, and other pet animals such as cats, to travel abroad with their owners and return with them to the UK. Before the passport for animals was introduced in 2000, three thousand pet dogs had died during quarantine in Britain (since 1973), and not one of them had had rabies. The last dog entering Britain and found to have rabies was in 1969, and before that 1922. Quarantining was unnecessarily cruel and not justifiable once modern vaccines and blood tests could guarantee a dog to be free from rabies. Quarantine kennels apart, there are still thousands of potential jobs with dogs.

Working in kennels used to be regarded (and may still be in some cases), as a lowly job with little in the way of career prospects. However there are some recognised qualifications (see below) which are available even to those not living or working near a college as it is possible to pursue the relevant qualifications through distance learning/ correspondence courses. Qualifications, together with varied experience are likely to improve career prospects. Some kennel staff quite reasonably anticipate running their own kennels, or becoming a dog trainer for the public or for private organisations. There is also the possibility of working abroad (see Part II).

Formal qualifications are not essential to work in kennels but they are likely to improve your standing with employers and merit more responsibility and higher pay. There are a couple of qualifications which can be obtained through on-the-job training lasting one to two years which include day release at college and assessment by an outside assessor. There is the National Vocational Qualification level 2, approved by the City and Guilds.

The course costs about £400. Another qualification is the CSI Small Animal Care Certificate and the National Kennelstaff Training Certificate. Most Kennel Managers would be expected to have the Canine Studies Institute Diploma of Kennel Management or an NVQ in Kennel Supervision, level 3 which, like level 2 is based on training on the job and an outside assessor. Some kennels like to employ staff straight from school and train them to their requirements, but it is advisable to work towards one of the above, nationally recognised qualifications once you have obtained a job this way.

Working in kennels is hard, physical work which involves keeping the dogs' living quarters and runs immaculate (i.e. disinfecting them and replacing the kennel bedding). The dogs also have to be groomed, and exercised outside the runs, fed, watered and inspected for illness and minor ailments. In breeding kennels, staff may have to stay up at night with a bitch in whelp, and look after the puppies until they are sold. Work usually starts early, sometimes 7am. As the kennels have to be serviced at weekends and during public holidays, staff work shifts to cover these times. As kennel work is mainly outdoors, it is not surprising that kennel owners are generally dubious of applicants who have never worked outside an office. It is advisable if at all possible to clock up experience of working with animals, perhaps on a volunteer basis in your free time at a local animal sanctuary or similar. A tour of the kennels is likely to be included in the job interview; this is not just to evoke your admiration, the interviewer will be looking closely to see how you interact with the dogs. The majority of dogs in boarding kennels are there for a week or two so there is little time to build a relationship with them. Also dogs behave differently when they are away from their normal environment and not always for the better i.e. pining, nervous aggression, constant barking, howling etc., while others will settle down into holiday mode quite happily. Kennel staff must therefore be sympathetic to their individual charges' reactions. Another most important part of the job is maintaining good customer relations.

Kennel jobs frequently (but not always) come with a accommodation in a caravan or other detached unit, or sometimes in the owner's house. Wages are not high and for school leavers can be as little as £60 a week for living out. Kennel staff with NVQ qualifications should earn more, while kennel managers who have a lot of responsibility should expect £200 plus weekly.

Many kennel staff learning the trade aspire to running their own kennels once they know the business and indeed how to run one. It is not necessary to have any qualifications to start a boarding kennels but learning management and business skills as well as having wide experience and expertise with dogs greatly improves your chances of financial success.

RUNNING YOUR OWN KENNELS

If you are thinking of running your own kennels, bear in mind that it is usually easier to buy an existing business. If you start from scratch you have to get planning permission and a licence, build the facilities and clientele etc. all of which can take years. Kennels for sale vary in price enormously depending on their size, location, facilities, clientele etc. and buying prices start at about £100,000 but generally expect to pay a minimum of double that. The trend in the business is that it is growing although the actual number of kennels is decreasing; kennels are getting bigger and more professional and all year round business is the norm (as opposed to summer only).

Running Your Own Boarding Kennels: David Cavill (3rd edition 2001) £14.99. Publication. Kogan Page (020-7278 0433; fax 020-7837-6348; www.kogan-page.co.uk). Also available from distributor: Albatross Publications, P.O. BOx 523, Horsham, West Sussex RH12 4WL (01293-871301).

Kennel Sales: Ladybird, Roman Road, Ingatestone, Essex, CM4 9AD; ☎01277-356641; fax 01277-356643; www.kennelsforsale.co.uk

The Kennels Agency: Moorfield House, Mattishall Road, Dereham, Norfolk NR20 5BZ; ☎01362-698855).

Turnpike Boarding Kennels and Cattery: Shaftesbury, Dorset (☎01737-854768). The owners Chris and Penny Rice run training weekends for those who want to run their own kennels. Cost: £250.

GUIDE DOGS ASSOCIATION

Guide Dogs for the Blind Association: Hillfields, Burghfield Common, Reading, Berkshire, RG7 3BR; ☎0870-600 2323; www.guidedogs.org.uk. The Guide Dogs Association employs kennel staff at its seven main centres in the UK and at its main breeding centre. Kennel staff are encouraged to obtain City and Guilds qualifications and some go on to be guide dog trainers (see below). Applicants must be at least 18 and be educated to at least GCSE standard (grades A-D). Must have domestic or work experience with animals and work/social experience with adults of various backgrounds. Salary starts at £8,892 per annum rising to at least £11,900 when qualified. Those interested should contact the Guide Dog Association regional centre of their choice, or the breeding centre (see below for addresses) to see if they are actively recruiting.

DOG RESCUE CENTRES EMPLOYING KENNEL STAFF

Battersea Dogs Home & British Association of Dogs' Homes (4 Battersea Park Road, London SW8 4AA; ☎020-7622 3626; fax 020-7622 6451).

Probably Britain's best known and largest dog home which began humbly enough in Holloway in 1860 as Mrs Mary Tealby's 'temporary home for lost and starving dogs'. It moved to its present site in 1871 and with many improvements since takes in about 12,000 unwanted and lost dogs and cats of London in a year. Some 42% of strays are reunited with their owners. The rehoming centre has room for up to 600 dogs and 100 cats, usually caring for around 400 dogs and 100 cats at any given time. The BDH also operates two hotlines, the Lost Cats and Dogs Line and the Behaviour Hotline for advice.

Employment: BDH employs kennel hands, four veterinary surgeons and veterinary nurse team on site. BDH also has two country rehoming centres, Battersea at Old Windsor and Battersea at Brands Hatch in Kent that are smaller in scale than the London home. The number of employees for all three centres is about 250. Volunteers are also needed at all three centres to walk the dogs and socialise dogs and cats. Further information on the work of BDH, the people who work there and for current job vacancies visit the website www.dogshome.org. Application to work at the Homes can be done online, or email jobs@dogshome.org.

Battersea Dogs Home: 4 Battersea Park Road, London SW8 4AA; ☎020-7622 6451.
Battersea at Old Windsor: Priest Hill, Old Windsor, Berkshire, SL4 2JN; ☎01784-432929; fax 01784-471538.
Battersea at Brands Hatch: Crowhurst Lane, Ash, Kent TN15 7HH; ☎01474-872855.

Other Dog Rescue Centres
Bell Mead Rescue Kennels; Priest Hill House, Old Windsor, Berkshire SL4 2JN.
Birmingham Dogs Home: New Bartholomew Street, Digbeth, Birmingham, B5 5QS; ☎0121-643 5211.
Cheltenham Animal Shelter: Gordner's Lane, Off Swindon Road, Cheltenham, Gloucestershire; ☎01242-523521.
Dog Rescue & Welfare Society (High Wycombe): Tower Farm, Oxford Road, Stokenchurch, Buckinghamshire, HP14 3TD; ☎01494-482695. Employs three kennel staff.
Dogs in Need: Chelston, Guildford Road, Chobham, Surrey GU24 8EA; ☎01276-858720.
Edinburgh Dog & Cat Home: 26 Seafield Road East, Portobello, Edinburgh EH15 1EH; 0131-669-5331.

Glasgow Dog & Cat Home: 125 Kinnell Avenue, Cardonald, Glasgow G52 3RY; ☎0141-882 1688; fax 0141-810 5533; www.scottishspca.org. Employs 20 paid staff and 20+ volunteers.

K9 Care: 23 Brookfield Road, Maerdy, Ferndale, Rhondda Cynon Taf, CF43 4TS; ☎01443-733450.

Last Chance Animal Rescue (registered charity No. 1002349): Stick Hill, Edenbridge, Kent TN8 5NH; ☎01732-865530. Has a non-destruction policy. Once a week the charity sends rescuers to Wales to collect the dogs which would otherwise be destroyed, from council pounds and rehomes thousands of them annually. LCAR employs a full-time vet and a team of about 10 staff, some of whom are part-time.

Lothian Dog Home: ☎0131-660 5849.

National Canine Defence League: West Calder, West Lothian; ☎01506-873459.

In addition to the above there are hundreds of kennels that rescue individual breeds, for details ask the Kennel Club for the Dog Rescue Directory (020-7493 2001). There are also animal rescue centres which include kennels (see the list of centres in the Animal Welfare Organisations chapter).

Manchester & District Home for Lost Dogs: (Incorporating NW Lost & Found Register), Crofters House, Moss Bk Road, Harpurhey, Manchester M9 5PG; ☎0161-205 2205. 27 full-time paid staff and 12 part-time.

Margaret Green Foundation Trust: Wingletang Rescue Kennels, Brentor Road, Heathfield, Nr Tavistock, Devon PL19 OLF; ☎01822-810215.

Margaret Green Foundation Trust: Dog Rescue & Homing Kennels, Lincoln Farm, Bere Road, Winterborne, Kingston Blandford, Dorset, DT11 9BP; ☎01929-471340. Employs 5 full-time staff. Takes work experience/trainees.

Margaret Green, Foundation Trust: Rescue Kennels for Elderly Dogs, Normandy Lodge, Winterborne Stickland, Blandford, Dorset DT11 OLY; ☎01258-450848.

Pine Ridge Dog Sanctuary: Priory Road, Ascot, Berkshire SL5 8RJ; ☎01344-882689. Employs 5 kennel staff.

Plymouth District Dog & Cat Home: Cattewater Road, Prince Rock, Plymouth; ☎01752-336679.

In addition to the above there are hundreds of kennels that rescue individual breeds. For details ask the Kennel Club for the *Dog Rescue Directory* (0870 6066 750). There are also animal rescue centres that include kennels (see the list of centres in the *Animal Welfare Organisations* chapter).

COURSES & TRAINING FOR CANINE WORK

The Animal Care College (Ascot House, High Street, Ascot, Berkshire SL5 7HG; ☎01344-622771; e-mail animalcarecollege@cavill.org.uk; www.animalcarecollege.co.uk).

The Animal Care College which specialises in open learning (correspondence) courses already mentioned in Chapter One, offers a range of animal studies courses, for beginners to experts, costing from £90 + VAT up to £290 + VAT. These courses include canine, feline and equine psychology courses at introductory, intermediate and advanced levels. Examples of canine courses from the prospectus are:

Certificate in Pet Dog Ownership: for novice owners. £140 + VAT.

Diploma of Kennel Management: for kennel proprietors and managers. As the range of study areas is so wide, students can tailor a course to their own needs. Subjects include: planning and design, building regulations and local authority requirements, staff and training, health, safety, book-keeping and accountancy, VAT, and associated profitable enterprises.

Fit for Life – Training the Family Dog: (£140 + VAT).

Intermediate Canine Psychology: (£265 + VAT).

Certificate in Showing Dogs: (£265 + VAT).

Judging Diploma: for those with at least five years' experience of showing dogs.
Grooming Theory: (£265 + VAT).
National Small Animal Care Certificates: suitable for those in their first year of kennel work and those wanting a career change.
The Anatomy & Physiology of Cats and Dogs: £176 plus VAT.
The Dog Breeding Diploma: £265 + VAT).

Bicton College School of Animal Care (East Budleigh, Budleigh Salterton, Devon EX9 7BY; ☎01395-562300; fax 01395-567502; enquiries@bicton.ac.uk; www.bicton.ac.uk).
Bicton College offers a part-time (one day a week course running from September to June) in Canine Studies, £350. Other canine courses revolve around grooming.

MICROCHIPPING

Britain is one of the few countries to allow non-veterinarians to carry out microchipping of cats and dogs. The idea is that they are innoculated against rabies and can travel relatively freely between Britain and other countries without having to undergo quarantine when they return to Britain. The microchip enables the dog to be easily identified and its credentials checked.

It is possible to attend a microchipping workshop lasting less than a day in order to learn how to do this. Courses are attended by rescue centres, breeders, groomers and dog trainers. One company offering such a course is Pet Chip Company Ltd (020-7625-2828; e-mail info@pet-detect.com), which charges £25 for rescue centres and £60-75 for others exclusive of VAT. The microchip training is held by an experienced vet. Microchipping three of your own animals is included in the price and a Certificate is awarded on completion.

DOG TRAINER

Although there are hundreds of private dog trainers practising in Britain it is an unregulated trade with no standard qualifications throughout the profession. In essence, anyone can advertise themselves as a dog trainer and offer dog and owner training classes or one-to-one training. The profession is represented by the British Institute of Professional Dog Trainers which runs its own Instructor's Course for those who have basic dog training experience. The Animal Care College (see above) also runs an Instructor course. The Institute has over 600 members not all of whom are professional dog trainers (i.e. hold the Institute's Instructor qualification). The UK Registry of Canine Behaviourists registers only those trainers who have a very high standard of expertise. Either of these organisations will advise anyone wishing to become a dog trainer/canine behaviourist. It is important however that candidates have some previous experience of working with canines before embarking on an Instructor course.

Useful Addresses
The British Institute of Professional Dog Trainers: Bowstone Gate, Disley, Cheshire SK12 2AW; ☎01663-762772; www.bipdt.net Offers training for instructors.
Mr John Rogerson: Northern Centre for Animal Behaviour, The Tavern, Ferry Hill, Co. Durham. Considered one of the UK's leading animal behaviourists. Offers courses relating to dog training and behaviour.
Mrs Sheila Bailey: Derbyshire Canine Centre, White Lea Farm, Castleton, Hope Valley S33 8WB; ☎01433-620415; sheilabailey@mac.com www.checkthenet.co.uk/canine. Runs vocational courses relating to training and behaviour.
Mrs Philippa Wiliams: Leadon View Cottage, Buttersend Lane, Hartpury, Glos; ☎01452-7000023; www/dogsworldwide.com. Offers courses relating to dog training

and behaviour.

Wormley Boarding & Training *Kennels/Cattery:* Broxbourne, Hertfordshire; ☎01992-451666; www.DOGTraining.uk.com. Specialised residential training for dogs, and also training for handlers. Trained and partly-trained dogs for sale. At time of press had staff vacancies.

DOGS FOR THE DISABLED

Dogs for the Disabled is relatively new and small charity that sets up partnerships between highly trained dogs and disabled people in order to give greater independence and confidence to the human side of the partnership. About 30 dogs a year are trained to a very high standard to carry out daily tasks that are very difficult for the client (usually a wheelchair user). Tasks include picking up dropped items, fetching the post, milk, mobile phone etc. activating light switches and alarms, helping load and unload front loading washing machines, entering supermarkets, removing items from shelves and handing the money/purse to the cashier, opening and closing doors, assisting with dressing by fetching clothes and through use of a special harness, help a person who has difficulty balancing, to walk. The charity has about 150 dogs working around the country. Each dog takes about 7 months to train and once it has been allocated, a follow-up service is provided to give ongoing support and help with any problems. As you might expect, there is a waiting list of clients. As the dog, its food and insurance are provided free to the disabled person the organisation is unlikely to expand without a substantial increase in funds.

There are about eight to ten full time dog trainers working for Dogs for the Disabled. New ones are occasionally taken on as apprentices and they receive two years of tutelage with an experienced instructor before they are allowed to train dogs on their own. Places are likely to be oversubscribed, but likely applicants should be a minimum of 18 years, have at least a good level GCSE education and previous experience of working with disabled people. A connection with dogs beyond just owning one is also required and a driving licence is essential.

Dogs for the Disabled is a member of the umbrella group, Assistance Dogs UK, the other members of which are listed below.

Dogs for the Disabled: The Frances May Centre, Blacklocks Mill, Banbury, Oxfordshire, OX17 2BS; e-mail info@dogsforthedisabled.org; www.dogsforthedisabled.org

CANINE PARTNERS

A similar organisation to Dogs for the Disabled, the CPI trains mainly labradors and golden retrievers to work in partnership with wheelchair users. Dog trainers work from the CPI Training Centre (Unit E2, The Brickyards, Steep Marsh, Nr Petersfield, Hants GU32 2BN; ☎01730-894830).

Alison Whittock who is 25, worked as a trainer of assistance dogs for Canine Partners for Independence. When she was still at school, she helped out at her local kennels as a kennelmaid. She then 'switched to horses' and did NVQs in equine management. She worked in studs, trained horses, and worked as a riding instructor before coming into dog training.

Alison Whittock comments on training dogs   ·

The most important ability to bring to this job is an understanding of animals. In fact, I have found that training dogs is very similar to training horses. Some people come into this kind of work after studying animal husbandry at college and working in a rescue or other type of kennels. CPI recommends that potential trainers also attend some dog behaviour/training courses; for instance Brinsbury College (01798-877400) near here runs such courses.

We also take people on work experience from college and we have puppy

walkers, who socialise our dogs by caring for them in their own homes before they are trained as assistance dogs.
We have four to six dogs in advanced training (which takes four months), at any one time. A typical day begins at 9am collecting the dogs from their kennels about ten miles away. Then we take them to a local common ground and exercise them and do some obedience practice for two hours. We return to the Centre for a half-hour break and then begin working with the dogs attached to wheelchairs. We have some volunteer disabled people to occupy the chairs and give their general comments on how they think the dog is doing. On site we teach the dogs to press lift buttons with their feet or noses, open and close doors, and we have our own pedestrian crossing for more button pressing, and a mock-up supermarket check out to teach the dogs how to take their owner's purse and hand it to the cashier. Once we think they are ready, we take the dogs into the real town with the wheelchairs and disabled volunteers to practice some more.
I'm also in charge of ordering all the equipment and food for all our dogs including those with puppywalkers. One of the nicest things is working in my office with the dogs lying under the desk knowing that having them there is part of my job.

Other Members of the Assistance Dogs Group

Support Dogs: The John Fisher Centre, Trianco House, Newton Chambers Road, Thorncliffe Park Estate, Chapeltown, Sheffield, South Yorkshire S35 2PH; ☎0114-257 7997; fax 0114-240 2821; e-mail sptdogs@aol.com; www.support-dogs.org.uk. Trains clients' own dogs to act as assistance dogs and seizure alert dogs for people with epilepsy.

PRO Dogs National Charity: National Head Office, 4-6 New Road, Ditton, Kent ME20 6AD; ☎01732-848499; fax 01732-842175; e-mail reception@prodogs.org. Volunteers take their own pet dogs to visit the elderly, sick and disabled who benefit psychologically from the contact with an animal. Volunteers with suitable dogs can volunteer their services once a week, fortnight or month. Also promotes responsible dog ownership to school-age children.

GUIDE DOG TRAINER/MOBILITY INSTRUCTOR

The Guide Dogs For the Blind Organisation (Hillfields, Burghfield, Reading RG7 3PG; ☎0118-9835555; fax 0118-9835433; www.gdba.org.uk) is a recognised charity providing specially trained dogs to act as 'the eyes' of a person who cannot see for themselves. The Guide Dogs for the Blind Association was founded in 1931 and gives many blind people the mobility they would not otherwise have. In order for this to happen the dog has to be trained to be guide and owner and dog have to be matched, and trained to work together. The GDBA is responsible for nearly 7,000 dogs including breeding stock, puppies, dogs in training, at work and retired. There are over 4,300 working dogs and 2,500 at any one time are breeding stock with 1,000 puppies being produced every year.

Guide dogs do not begin training until they are a year old. As puppies, they go to 'puppy walkers' who volunteer to look after them from the age of six weeks, and gradually accustom them to busy streets, getting on and off buses and to other dogs. When they are returned to the Association, they are sent to one of the regional centres' kennels where they are allocated to a guide-dog trainer for about six months. Following this, they are ready to be handed on to a Mobility Instructor who provides the final advanced skills training. The trained dogs are then paired with their new blind owners and trained as a duo for four weeks.

Guide Dog Trainer

The guide dog trainer's job is an extremely important one as these dogs have to take on an astounding amount of responsibility. Guide dogs are often, but not exclusively, labrador/ retriever types bred for temperament and intelligence. After the young adult dogs arrive at the centre the trainer lets them relax and enjoy themselves for a couple of weeks while he or she assesses their potential and suitability. The dogs have to be taught to walk down the middle of a pavement and to obey directional commands (forward, back etc.). They have to be taught to sit at every kerb, crossing the road only when there is no approaching traffic. They are introduced to the harness they will wear when they are working and they learn that when not in harness, they are off-duty and can behave like any other pet dog. The trainer's final test for his charge is to don a blindfold and put the dog through its paces.

Basic entry requirements for Guide Dog Trainer are three GCSEs at grades A-C including maths, English and a science. Accepted candidates spend the first two months of their training learning basic dog care skills in kennels, followed by eleven months working towards their City and Guilds Guide Dog trainer qualification. The trainees are paid while they are training. Applicants should contact the centre of their choice directly (see list below) to see whether they are actively recruiting. Speculative applications without a prior enquiry are not accepted.

Guide Dog Mobility Instructor

Mobility instructor work involves working with people as much as dogs. The instructor handles the future guide dog a few months prior to introducing it to its new owner. The Instructor builds on skills already acquired, for instance, teaching the dog how to use its shoulders to manoeuvre an owner safely through a crowd. The Instructor then matches up dogs and owners taking into account the temperament of the dogs and the age and lifestyle requirements of the future owners. Each instructor takes on the training of four dog/person duos and encourages the owners to develop confidence in their dog. He or she gradually introduces the pairs to gradually more complicated situations. The owners are taught how to avoid undoing their dog's careful training. Finally, when dog and owner have departed for their new domestic life, the instructor provides follow-up and support by periodically visiting the owners and helping sort out any problems.

Entrance requirements for mobility instructors are five GCSEs grades A-C including Maths, English a science subject plus ideally, a social science subject. The minimum age is 18 years.

Applicants for Apprentice Guide Dog Mobility Instructors should be addressed to the head office address (see above).

The regional centres of The Guide Dogs for the Blind Association

North West: Nuffield House, Lowndes Street, Bolton, Lancashire BL1 4QA. (☎01204-495111).

Wales and South West: Cleve House, Exwick Lane, Exeter, Devon. (☎01392-272967.

Scotland: Princess Alexandra House, Dundee Road, Forfar, Scotland (☎01307-463531).

Midlands: Edmonscote Manor, Warwick New Road, Leamington Spa (☎01926-337244).

North East: Freda Valentine House, 65a Highfield Road, Middlesbrough (☎01642-232666).

London & Home Counties: Redbridge House, 7 Manor Road, Woodford Green, Redbridge, Surrey (☎020-8506 1515).

Guide Dogs Association Breeding Centre

Tollgate House, Banbury Road, Oakley Wood, Bishops Tachbrook, Warwickshire (☎01926-651226).

HEARING DOGS FOR DEAF PEOPLE

The idea of training dogs to help deaf people was adopted from America where the programme took off under the direction of the American Humane Association in the 1970s. In 1982 a pilot scheme was launched in the UK. In 1984 nine, specially trained dogs were placed with deaf owners. By 1996 the organisation had placed its 400th trained dog and expanded from one centre in Lewknor, Oxfordshire to two others: the Beatrice Wright Training Centre at Cliffe, North Yorkshire and the International Training Centre, Grange Farm, Saunderton in Buckinghamshire. The charity sends experienced staff to other countries to instruct dog trainers there in hearing dogs training.

Hearing dogs for Deaf People trains carefully selected dogs to alert severely or profoundly deaf people to everyday sounds such as the doorbell, telephone, smoke and baby alarms and cooker timer. The deaf person decides which sounds they would like the dog to respond to. A deaf hospital radiographer has had her dog trained to respond to her bleeper. The idea is that the dogs respond in a different way to each sound, communicate by touch and then lead their owner to the source of the sound or, lie down to indicate danger. The benefits to deaf people of a trained hearing canine companion are immense. It helps their self confidence and esteem and helps them feel more relaxed and less isolated in their silent world. It gives them a new interest and purpose for living and makes it easier to engage with the hearing world, and encourages visitors to call more frequently. A great number of these hearing dogs have come from rescue centres, so they too get a new and fulfilled life. To date, the Charity has placed nearly 900 dogs around the UK.

Dog Trainer for Hearing Dogs

Rescue dogs make up a large proportion of hearing dogs, others are donated by breeders. Although Hearing Dogs for Deaf People is a small charity it does offer its own training scheme, but applicants are expected to have to have previously acquired the necessary basic skills before applying. Many applicants come from full-time employment with animals such as veterinary nursing or professional kennel work. It is necessary to show some practical experience of training dogs – membership of Dog Clubs and attendance of dog-training classes with your own dog. Registering your dog as a PAT (Pets As Therapy) dog and making regular visits to ill and lonely people provides other helpful experience. Formal education should be a minimum good GCSE standard. A full driving licence is necessary. Some graduates with relevant degrees (Zoology, Psychology, Animal Science) have also been taken on as trainers.

Hearing Dogs for Deaf People also advises that applicants should attend a course incorporating dog behaviour or dog training.

Hearing Dogs for Deaf People: The Grange, Wycombe Road, Saunderton, Princes Risborough, Bucks HP27 9NS; ☎01844-348100; fax 01844-348101; e-mail jenny.moir@hearing-dogs.co.uk; www.hearing-dogs.co.uk

DOG GROOMER/CANINE BEAUTICIAN

Apart from poodles, which require an elaborate pom-pom coiffure, it used to be mainly the long-haired breeds like Afghans, setters, Old English Sheepdogs etc. which needed the attentions of a dog groomer. However, along with the cult of celebrity has come the cult of celebrity dogs. These tend to be toy breeds like shih tzus, yorkies and other diminutive canines. Where celebrities set the trend others will follow and many smaller breeds are getting the full grooming treatment as well.

There has been a boom in grooming salons over the last few years. The Pet Care Trust, which oversees qualifications and standards in pet maintenance, estimates there to be over 2000, most of them independent establishments, and the rest attached to other pet-related premises (veterinary, petshops, kennels etc). In addition there are hundreds of

Poodles require an elaborate pom pom coiffure

self-employed mobile groomers.

The dog groomer normally positions the animal on a table and hand clips the delicate areas around the face, between the pads etc. This is usually followed by shampooing, rinsing and drying under a special stand dryer, followed by a final comb through or brushing. Groomers, sometimes called canine beauticians, may also offer other services such as claw trimming and dental cleaning. The only non-beauty treatment offered may be spot of ear cleaning and parasite control. A groomer may deal with up to half a dozen dogs a day and the charges vary, starting at about £15 for a toy breed and over three times that for an Old English Sheepdog.

Peter Young, owner of Peter's Posh Pets grooming salon (020-7602 1357) in west London, helped formulate the City and Guilds Pet Grooming qualification. Peter says that cost is usually based on the amount of time spent on a dog. He also points out that dog grooming can also promote dog health, as groomers are liable to pick up some problems, which require veterinary attention.

Dog Groomers also prepare dogs for showing and competitions. Believe it or not, there are doggie fashions when it comes to how they should look and serious groomers tend to follow the fads. They can keep up with them by consulting the trade magazine *Grooming Times* and or by going to grooming seminars.

This job is one which enables the practitioner to be either self-employed or an employee in a grooming parlour. One of the largest employers of dog groomers is the UK's largest franchise of pet stores, Pets at Home. According to head office about 20 of its 145 outlets offer grooming services. Jobs are usually advertised locally but you can also apply to the headquarters in Cheshire (Pets at Home, Epsom Avenue, Stanley Green Trading Estate, Handforth, Cheshire SK9 3RN; ☎0161-486 6688) by ringing up and asking for an application form. You can also e-mail job enquiries (jobopportunities@petsathome) or check on their website www.petsathome.co.uk.

Other entrepreneurial grooming exponents provide a mobile service visiting owners' homes. Of course, there is nothing to prevent owners grooming their own dogs, but fortunately for dog groomers, many prefer to pay them to do it instead.

Potential groomers can work towards the NVQs Level 2 and 3 in Dog Grooming.

Useful Addresses

Animal Care College: Ascot House, High Street, Ascot, Berkshire SL5 7JG; ☎01344-28269; fax 01344-22771. Open learning Grooming Theory for City and Guilds and NVQ Level 3.

The Pet Care Trust: Bedford Business Centre, 117 Mile Road, Bedford, MK42 9TW; ☎01234-273933; info@petcare.org.uk; www.petcare.org.uk) can provide a list of centres offering pet grooming qualifications as well as the address of your nearest dog groomer.

City and Guilds Dog Grooming Training Centres

Canine Comforts: 6, St. James Terrace, Suffolk Parade, Montpellier, Cheltenham GL50 2AA; ☎01242-226600; www.canine.co.uk. Offers a range of courses including City and Guilds 775 and Assessment for Kennel Management and Animal Husbandry.

Dunragit Grooming: Auchterless, The Walled Garden, Dungragit, Stranraer, Scotland DG9 8PH; ☎01581-400613.

Dog Studio: Unit 3, Goosey Wick Farm, Charney Bassett, Wantage, Oxon. OX12 OEY; ☎01367-718478.

Pankington Kennels: Hatton, Lincoln LN3 5LS; ☎01673-858622.

Salon 2000 Training Centre: 2 Henry Street, Keighley, West Yorkshire BD21 3DR; ☎01535-661776.

Scotgroom: Milton Bank, 23 Lanark Road, Carluke, South Lanarkshire, Scotland ML8 4HE; ☎01555-770333.

Other Useful Addresses

Askham Bryan College: York. New dog grooming course. Ring 01904-772200 or 01904-772277; or look on www.askhambryan.ac.uk for details.

Bicton College: East Budleigh, Budleigh Salterton, Devon, EX9 7BY; ☎01395-562300; fax 01395-567502; e-mail enquiries@bicton.ac.uk; www.bicton.ac.uk. Like The Animal Care College, Bicton offers its own courses and qualifications. Basic Dog Grooming and Basic Dog Clipping and Stripping, both 4-day courses, are aimed at the private dog-owner, or those training for the industry.

Brinsbury College: West Sussex College of Agriculture, North Heath, Pulborough RH20 1DL; ☎01798-873832. Runs three part-time courses: Dog Groomers Foundation Course, Intermediate Dog Grooming and Intensive Dog Grooming.

British Dog Groomers Association (part of the Pet Care Trust): Bedford Business Centre, 170 Mile Road, Bedford MK42 9TW; ☎01234-273933; fax 01234-273550. Has a list of grooming training centres (see above) which are members of the British Dog Groomers Association.

Derby College Broomfield: freephone 0800 028 0289; ☎01332-831345; www.derby-college.ac.uk. Offers NVQ Levels 1 and 2 Dog Grooming.

Coleg Llysfasi: Ruthin, Clwyd, Wales; ☎01978-790263; www.llysfasi.ac.uk; Dog Grooming, 35 weeks, one day per week from September to June.

Easton College: Norwich, NR9 5DX; ☎01603-742105; fax 01603-741438. Courses in Introductory Dog Grooming and Grooming Parlour Management NVQ Levels 1 and 2.

Kistor Canine Beauticians: 363 Torquay Road, Preston, Paignton, S Devon fax 01803-213430. Kistor is a training centre for NVQ 2 and 3 in Animal Care, which includes grooming. In depth training is given in this element. Also provides one or two day assessment courses towards the City and Guilds 775/1 Dog Grooming exam.

Lackham College: Lacock, Nr. Chippenham, Wiltshire SN15 2NY; ☎01249-466800; www.wiltscol.ac.uk/courses. BTEC NC/Diploma in Dog Grooming.

Leeds: Park Lane College, Leeds (0113-216200). Part-time, 2 years, half-day per week.

Mid-Glamorgan: Pencoed College, Bridgend (01656-302600). Offer Open College Network (OCN) Dog Grooming course at levels 2 and 3. Each course is a half-day or evening for 10 weeks.

Mucky Pups: North Harrow, Middlesex; ☎020-8863 7220; (other salon in Hendon). Offers one-to-one training covering every aspect of the grooming business. Courses last from one day to as long as it takes for beginners to learn the trade. Business may soon be under new ownership.

Otley College of Agriculture & Horticulture: Ispwich (☎01473-785543; www.otleycollege.ac.uk) offers a part-time, 10 weeks (one day a week) course in dog grooming, which is a module from one of its other courses.

Triple 'A' Animal Hotel and Care Centre: Follingby Lane, West Bolton, Washington, Tyne and Wear NE37 3JB; ☎0191-537 1344; e-mail sue.sloane@petcareco.com ; www.triple-a-animals. A recognised NVQ centre which offers NVQs 2 and 3 in Grooming and NVQ 2 and 3 in animal care.

Walford College: Shrewsbury, Shropshire (01939-262100). Dog Grooming 10 weeks, 2hrs a week. College Certificate.

Warwickshire College: Royal Leamington Spa & Moreton Morrell, Moreton Morrell Site, Moreton Morrell, Warwick; ☎01926-318333; fax 01926-318300. Offers part-time Dog Grooming course (one day a week for eight weeks), or Dog Grooming as part of an NVQ in Animal Care.

Writtle Agricultural College: Writtle Agricultural College, Chelmsford (01245-420705; www.writtle.ac.uk). Dog Grooming 2 year, one day a week City and Guilds. Also does own course College Certificate in Dog Grooming, 1 year, half-day per week.

DOGS IN UNIFORM

In order to become a dog/handler, trainer for the dogs of the armed forces, the police, H.M. Customs and Excise, the Prison Service, the Atomic Energy Authority or the Ministry of Defence Police, it is necessary first to join the service involved and then ask for transfer to the dog section. Since working with dogs is usually one of the more

The dog is supposed to hang on to the suspect's clothing without actually biting him

enjoyable aspects of uniformed work, there is usually a long waiting list for transfers.

In the case of the regional police forces, dog handlers have to undergo full police training and several years' service before they can request to be assigned dog work. Police dogs live with their handlers and their families which is essential to ensure that they are friendly with the public in general. Even so, it is not unusual to read in the press of a police dog being too enthusiastic in its work. The dog is supposed to detain the suspect, by hanging on to clothing by its teeth if necessary until the handler catches up with the handcuffs to make an arrest. Biting the suspect (however deserving) is not allowed but sometimes happens anyway.

Women handlers are in the minority; out of 254 in the Metropolitan Police force seven are female. This is in part due to the controversial test which includes press-ups which, the majority of female applicants have failed. The other tests are: lifting an 80lb weight over your head (which shows ability to lift a dog) and a speed and agility test involving a running slalom between cone markers. The press-up test has been the subject of an industrial tribunal dispute brought by a woman PC who failed it.

PRIVATE SECURITY DOGS

A number of private security firms use dogs to patrol the clients' premises which can be a private building, or a building/construction site. Patrolling with dogs is only one of a number of jobs security personnel perform and unlike police dog handlers, the dogs do not usually live at home with them. Larger companies like K9 of Oxford which has about 20 dogs, employ someone to look after the kennels. It may be possible to progress to dog trainer once you have the necessary experience.

Like police dogs, security dogs' working lives can be hazardous. Patrolling building and construction sites which are dangerous in themselves, or confronting characters up to no good sometimes leads to injuries.

DOG WARDEN

Dog wardens are employed by local authorities to deal with dogs causing problems. Dog wardens educate local communities to reduce dog fouling in towns, parks, seaside resorts etc. and ensure pet dogs are properly controlled. Unattended dogs, which may be lost or strayed, are picked up by the warden and taken to kennels. If the owners can be traced the warden will return the dog to its home and if necessary advise the owners of their responsibilities. This is a job that requires good person-to-person skills as well as an understanding of dogs. Wardens also co-operate with the police and animal welfare societies as needed. A driving licence is essential and most people come to the job having already had a basic training and proven experience of working with dogs and or a qualification in animal care such as the NVQs 1,2, and 3 already mentioned.

There is no standardised, national qualification in dog wardening at the time of press. However, Sue Bell of the National Dog Warden Association says that this will change shortly and that the best place to get further details is from her (e-mail admin@ndwa.co.uk). The qualification is likely to be overseen by Lantra, the organisation for land-based careers (0845-707-8007; www.lantra.co.uk).

Jobs may be advertised in the local press. Bicton College (01395-562300) in Devon has been running dog-wardening courses for some years as has the Animal Care College in Ascot (01344-628269).

Further information

National Dog Warden Association: Sue Bell, Secretary, National Dog Warden Association, c/o Tewkesbury Borough Council, Council Offices, Gloucester Road, Tewkesbury, GL20 5TT; ☎01684-295010.

GREYHOUND RACING KENNELHAND/TRAINER

The body that overseas greyhound tracks in the UK is the National Greyhound Racing Club. There are 31 greyhound tracks in England licensed by the NGRC and one in Scotland. There is also independent greyhound racing not governed by the strict rules and regulations of the NGRC but which has to obtain a licence from the local authorities where the racing takes place.

Greyhound racing offers a number of job and career possibilities including kennel hand and professional trainer.

Each kennel is likely to have its own version of the daily routine care of greyhounds, which involves feeding, exercise, grooming and training. Kennel hands accompany the greyhound(s) in their particular care to the racetrack and liaise with the racecourse staff and the vet who is in attendance there. There are pre-race procedures to be followed (weighing, veterinary examination, and parading). Promotion within the greyhound business is usually on merit and ability. It is possible to progress to trainer after about two years' experience as a top kennel hand. The best way to find out about opportunities working with greyhounds is probably from the manager of your nearest greyhound track.

According to one estimate, 30,000 greyhounds are bred for racing each year in Britain and Ireland. Despite the popularity of the sport there is terrific wastage as not all dogs are suitable for racing. Unfortunately, thousands of reject puppies are destroyed annually. Even those that show the required prowess are generally raced out by the age of five. While some owners and trainers are caring enough to find good homes for their retired dogs, many alas, adopt the more expedient policy of destruction or selling on to other countries (Spain is one) where the attitude to animals and lack of legal protection is marked and the results unpleasant: dogs may be raced to death, used for vivisection etc. Anyone thinking of working with greyhounds might be able to work for improvements in this aspect of the industry.

USEFUL ADDRESSES

National Greyhound Racing Club: Twyman House, 16 Bonny Street, London NW1 9QD; ☎020-7267 9256; fax 020-7482 1023; e-mail mail@ngrc.org.uk; www.ngrc.org.uk. Oversees the rules and regulations.
British Greyhound Racing Board: ☎020-7292-9900. Deals with the commercial side of greyhound racing.

Race Courses Subject to the Rules of the NGRC

Birmingham: GRA Ltd., Hall Green Stadium, York Road, Hall Green, Birmingham B28 8LQ; ☎0870-840 7362; fax 0870-840 7390.
Birmingham: Perry Barr Greyhound Club Ltd: Perry Barr Stadium, Aldridge Road, Perry Barr, Birmingham B42 2ET; ☎01213-562324; fax 01213-568393.
Brighton & Hove: Coral Stadia Ltd., Brighton & Hove Stadium, Nevill Road, Hove, Sussex BN3 7BZ; ☎01273-204601; fax 01273-820763.
Crayford: Ladbroke Racing Ltd., Crayford Stadium, Stadium Way, Crayford, Kent DA1 4HR; ☎01322-522262/557836; fax 91322-524530.
Glasgow: Shawfield Greyhound & Leisure Co Ltd., Shawfield Stadium, Rutherglen, Lanarks G73 1SZ; ☎01416-474121; fax 01416-477265.
Harlow: Leaside Leisure Ltd., Harlow Stadium, The Pinnacles, Roydon Road, Harlow, Essex CM19 5DY; ☎01279-639248; fax 01279-444182.
Henlow: Henlow Ltd., Henlow Greyhound Stadium, Bedford Road, Lower Stondon, Beds SG16 6EA; ☎01462-851850; fax 01462-815593.
Hull: Hull Greyhound Racing Ltd., Hull Greyhound Stadium, Craven Park, Preston Road, Hull HU9 5HE; ☎01482-374131; fax 01482-799590.

London: GRA Ltd, Catford Stadium, Adenmore Road, London SE6 4RJ; ☎020-8690 8000/2240; fax 020-8690 2433.

London: Walthamstow Stadium Ltd., Chingford Road, London E4 8SJ; ☎020-8498 3311; fax 020-8523 2747.

London: GRA Ltd., Wimbledon Stadium, Plough Lane, London SW17 OBL; ☎020-8946 2054; fax 020-8947 0821.

Manchester: GRA Ltd., Belle Vue Stadium, Kirkmanshulme Lane, Gorton, Manchester M18 7BA; ☎01612-238000; fax 0870-840 7275.

Mildenhall: Mildenhall Stadium, Hayland Drove, West Row, Bury St. Edmunds, Suffolk IP28 8QU; ☎01638-711777; fax 01638-510967.

Milton Keynes: Gaming International plc, MK Stadium Ltd, Milton Keynes Stadium, Ashland, Bletchley, Milton Keynes, MK6 4AA; ☎01908-670150; fax 01908-670504.

Newcastle: Team Greyhounds (Brough Park) Ltd., Brough Park Stadium, The Fossway, Byker, Newcastle-upon-Tyne NE6 2XJ; ☎01912-652665; fax 01912-651452.

Nottingham: Nottingham Greyhound Stadium Ltd., Colwick Park, Nottingham NG2 4BE; ☎01159-103331; fax 01159-103330.

Oxford: GRA Ltd, Oxford Stadium, Sandy Lane, Cowley, Oxford, OX4 5LJ; ☎01865-778222; fax 01865-748676.

Peterborough: Peterborough Sports Stadium Ltd., First Drove, Fengate, Peterborough PE1 5BJ; ☎01733-296930; fax 01733-296932.

Poole: Poole Stadium Ltd, Wimborne Road, Poole, Dorset BH15 2BP; ☎01202-677449; fax 01202-677980.

Portsmouth: GRA Ltd, Portsmouth Stadium, Target Road, Tipnor, Portsmouth, Hants PO2 8QU; ☎023-9266 3232; fax 023-9267 3165.

Reading: Gaming International plc., Reading Stadium, Bennet Road, Smallmead, Reading, Berkshire RG2 OJL; ☎01189-863161; fax 01189-313264.

Romford: Coral Stadia Ltd., Romford Stadium, London Road, Romford, Essex RM7 9DU; ☎01708-762345; fax 01708-744899.

Rye House: Carter & Bailey Ltd., Rye House, Stadium, Rye Road, Hoddesdon, Herts EN11 OEH; ☎01992-469000; fax 01992-469069.

Sheffield: Sheffield Sports Stadium Ltd., Owlerton Stadium, Penistone Road, Sheffield S6 2DE; ☎01142-855888; fax 01142-333631.

Sittingbourne: Cearnsport Ltd, Central Park Stadium, Church Road, Eurolink, Sittingbourne Kent ME10 3SB; ☎01795-438438; fax 01795-430337.

Stainforth: Meadow Court Stadium Ltd., Station Road, Stainforth, Nr. Doncaster DN7 5HS; ☎01302-351639; fax 01302-351650.

Sunderland: The Regal Sunderland Stadium Ltd.,Sunderland Greyhound Stadium, Newcastle Road, Sunderland, Tyne and Wear SR5 1RP; ☎01915-367250; fax 01915-191153.

Swindon: Gaming International plc., Swindon Stadium, Lady Lane, Blunsdon, Nr Swindon, Wilts SN2 4DN; ☎01793-721253; fax 01793-723038.

Wolverhampton: Ladbroke Racing Ltd., Monmore Green Stadium, Sutherland Avenue, Monmore Green, Wolverhampton, WV2 2JJ; ☎01902-456663; fax 01902-871164.

Yarmouth: Norfolk Greyhound Co. Ltd.: Yarmouth Stadium, Yarmouth Road, Caister on Sea, Gt. Yarmouth, Norfolk NR30 5TE; ☎01493-720343; fax 01493-721200.

NCDL (NATIONAL CANINE DEFENCE LEAGUE)

The UK's largest dog charity was founded in 1891 to protect dogs from 'torture and ill-usage of every kind'. In its early years, the NCDL was instrumental in the creation of the Protection of Animals Act 1911 and for conducting anti-vivisection campaigns. Since then it has a run a variety of dog protection campaigns which make fascinating historical reading such as providing AA patrols in the 1920s with humane pistols to dispatch dogs badly run over by cars. It has its headquarters in Wakely Street, London and runs 16 animal shelters nationally. A total of about 300 people work for the NCDL plus a further 100 office staff in London. The charity employs Managers for its animal shelters, kennel staff and animal behaviour experts.

Re-homing Centre Managers: Oversee the day-to-day running of the centre. Need to have thorough knowledge of kennel work, administration, staff supervision and book-keeping. Need to liaise with related professionals, give the public advice on adoption, and maintain close contacts with the local media.

Assistant Re-homing Managers: Most duties similar to centre manager but less administration and daily management. Must be able to take charge when the Centre Manager is away.

NCDL London: 17 Wakeley Street, London EC1V 7RQ; ☎020-7837 0006; fax 020-7833 2701; www.ncdl.org.uk; e-mail info@ncdl.org.uk

Canine carers: Experience is preferred, but not essential as training is given. Need to be dedicated to the wellbeing of the dogs in their care. Duties include caring for number of dogs, cleaning kennels and run areas, feeding, grooming, exercising and providing any necessary treatments under the supervision of a senior staff member.

Volunteers: volunteers are always needed to help the kennel staff with their duties and for dog walking. Volunteers have to be aged 16+ to comply with NCDL's insurance terms.

Work Placements: Some of the larger re-homing centres can offer work placements. Applicants should make their requests and give reasons in writing to the re-homing centre manager.

The NCDL centres advertise vacancies in the local press. Applicants should apply in writing to the Re-homing Centre Manager.

NCDL Re-homing Centres

NCDL Ballymena: Fairview, 60 Teeshan Road, Ballymena, Co Antrim BT43 5PN Northern Ireland; ☎028-2565 2977; fax 028-2563 8463.

NCDL Bridgend: Court Colman, Pen-Y-Fai, Bridgend, Mid-Glam CF31 4NG; ☎01656-725219; fax 01656-725274.

NCDL Canterbury: Radfall Road, Chestfield, Whitstable, Kent CT3 3ER; ☎01227-792505; fax 01227- 793988.

NCDL Darlington: Hill House Farm, Sadberge, Near Darlington, Co Durham DL2 1SL; ☎01325-333114; fax 01325-333048.

NCDL Dumfries: Dovecotwell, by Glencaple, Dumfries DG1 4RH; ☎01387-770346; fax 01387-770346.

NCDL Evesham: 89 Pitcher's Hill: Wickhamford, Evesham, Worcs WR11 6RT; ☎01386-830613; fax 01386-832617.

NCDL Ilfracombe: Hazeldene, West Down, Ifracombe, North Devon EX34 8NU; ☎01271-812709; fax 01271-814098.

NCDL Kenilworth: Honiley, Kenilworth, Warwickshire, CV8 1NP; ☎01926-484398; fax 01926-484196.

NCDL Leeds: Eccup Lane: Adel, Leeds, West Yorkshire, LS16 8AL; ☎01132-613194; fax 01132; 300886.

NCDL Merseyside: Whiston Lane, Huyton, Liverpool L36 6HP; ☎0151-480 0660; fax 0151-4806176.

NCDL Newbury: Plumb's Farm, Hamstead Marshall, Newbury, Berks RG20 OHR; ☎01488-658391; fax 01488-657211.

NCDL Roden: Roden Lane Farm: Roden, Telford, Shropshire TF6 6BP; ☎01952-770225; fax 01952-770416.

NCDL Salisbury: 45 Amesbury Road, Newton Tony, Wiltshire SP4 OHW; ☎01980-629634; fax: 01980-629706.

NCDL Shoreham: *Brighton Road:* Shoreham by Sea, West Sussex BN43 5LT; ☎01273-452576; fax 01273-440856.

NCDL Snetterton: North Farm Kennels: North End Road, Snetterton, Norfolk NR16 2LD; ☎01953-498377; fax 01953-498325.

NCDL West Calder: Bentyhead, Hartwood Road, West Calder, Fife EH55 8LE; ☎01506-873459; fax 01506-873275.

SEARCH AND RESCUE DOGS

Most of us are probably aware that dogs are sometimes employed to find survivors under rubble, or snow, as they are able to use their acute sense of smell to detect the living. Probably the best known example is the St. Bernard, which was used as long ago as the 17th century by the monks of the St. Bernard Hospice to rescue lost travellers, or those buried under avalanches in the Swiss Alps. The advantage of dogs over human searchers is one of speed, which can be crucial if a person is injured.

The organisation for search and rescue dogs in Britain, the Search and Rescue Dogs Association (SARDA) is much younger than the St. Bernard tradition, having been in operation only since 1996. It is a volunteer organisation whose members are civilian mountain rescue teams who train their own pet dogs for rescue work. Not all dogs are suitable. Breeds with the appropriate stamina include German shepherds, labradors and collies. SARDA already has hundreds of members and has four national branches covering England, Scotland, Wales and Northern Ireland. Only 26 of the 700 members of Scotland's mountain rescue teams have fully trained search and rescue dogs but the number will almost certainly increase, given their effectiveness in the right conditions.

Dog and handler usually have a year of extensive training to make them equipped to operate in an open search area. Another year is required to specialise in specific search situations (e.g. rubble, buildings or water rescue). Volunteer dogs and handlers give up regular free-time (evenings and weekends) for training.

Neither the civilian, mountain rescue service nor SARDA receive any government funding, and like the Lifeboat Institution depend on volunteer operatives and public donations.

It is normally the police who co-ordinate mountain, hill and moorland rescues, which often include an RAF rescue helicopter. The dogs' training includes being winched aboard and lowered from a helicopter wearing a special harness. The harness is also adapted to carry lights for night work, but not unfortunately a flask of brandy for grateful survivors. As SARDA dogs spend most of their time as family pets, the harness also acts as a signal to the dog that it is on duty. Dogs are not suitable for all rescue situations for instance on steep rock faces or in hot, still weather which dulls their sense of smell.

Useful Addresses

Search & Rescue Dog Association: Nikki Lyons, The Cottage, Egypt Lane End, Golberdon, Nr. Callington, Cornwall.

SARDA: Honorary Secretary of the Highland section of SARDA, Alwyn Jones, SARDA, Toux Croft, Fetterangus, Mintlaw, Aberdeenshire AB42 8LX.

Casualty Search Dogs: 126 Main Road, Sheepy Magna, Atherstone, Warwickshire, CV9 3QY; ☎01827-717280. A stamped, addressed envelope is appreciated. All members are volunteers who offer their services and dogs. All members are qualified First Aiders as well as search dog specialists and are on call to the emergency services 24-hours. Also operates The Search Dog School (SAR) to assist other organisations who require dogs and handlers for search and rescue, as well as other types of search training (e.g. arson detection).

Useful Publications

Dogs Monthly: Ascot House, High Street, Ascot, Berks; ☎01344-628269; fax 01344-

622771; www.dogsmonthly.co.uk. Colour magazine that describes itself as 'the magazine for serious dog owners.' Small classified section. £2.95 from newsagents or £35 per year subscription and postage.

Dogs Today: Pet Subjects Ltd., Pankhurst Farm, Bagshot Road, West End, Woking, Surrey GU24 9QR; ☎01276-858880; fax 01276-858860.

Kennel Gazette: The Kennel Club Publications Dept, 1-5 Clarges Street, London W1Y 8AB; ☎0870-6066 750. Monthly magazine of The Kennel Club first published in 1880. Can be ordered through newsagents or direct from the KC Publications Dept.

Our Dogs: 5 Oxford Road Station Approach, Manchester M60 1SX; ☎(subscriptions) 0870-731 6503; www.ourdogs.co.uk. This newspaper celebrated its 100th anniversary in 1995. All the dog show news and gossip for breeders.

THE KENNEL CLUB

The Kennel Club (1 Clarges Street, Piccadilly, London W1J 8AB; 0870 606 6750; fax 020-7518 1058; info@the-kennel-club.org.uk; www.the-kennel-club.org.uk), which was founded in 1873 is the body that oversees breeding standards and promotes all round improvement in dogs from educating the public on how to care for them, to investigating genetic problems like deafness in dalmations and hip dysplasia in German shepherds. The Kennel Club Charitable Trust started in 1989 to carry out research projects.

The Kennel Club has a computerised database of pedigree records – some four million of them, and its headquarters in Clarges Street houses Europe's largest canine library (which is open to the public and researchers). Although it does not provide any job finding services the KC will send out leaflets on careers with dogs as well as providing specific information that could be useful to the job seeker, such as a list of breeders of a particular breed in your area. It will also send out copies of the Dog Rescue Directory to those wanting to adopt a rescue dog. It includes hundreds of dog rescue centres around Britain and Northern Ireland including Breed rescue centres which rescue particular breeds as well as the general dog rescue centres.

Perhaps the best known face of the Kennel Club is the annual Crufts Dog Show held at the National Exhibition Centre in Birmingham, which can be a useful place to make contacts for working with breeders. The Kennel Club also organise the Discover Dogs event at Earls Court, London, where visitors can meet over 180 different breeds of pedigree dog as well as see many dog displays by crossbreeds and pedigrees alike.

FREE ENTERPRISE

Dog walker

If you have a way with dogs but prefer being in control of your own work then there are some free enterprise possibilities, particularly in affluent urban areas whose dog-owners are at work all day. Over the last five to ten years the demand for professional dog-walkers who are paid to exercise dogs for their owners has increased to the point where it can be a fairly lucrative form of employment for the committed dog-walker who has built up a full schedule of clients. Some dog walkers charge £9 per walk. Costs vary depending on your catchment area and how far you have to travel to pick up and put back. The set-up costs are minimal: a few strategically placed adverts or flyers to bring in the first few clients; and then word-of-mouth should do it. Ideally, the dog-walker should have a large van suitable for doggy transport in order to provide a collection service from the owners' homes. Access to a large park or other suitably vast open space where a pack of dogs can be allowed to hare about without causing irritation to other park users is also necessary.

Suzy Crabtree, an educational psychologist, who turned full-time dog walker eight years ago, has just written a book on the subject named for her own dog Baggins (*Baggins' Gang*, published by Aurum, £14.99) in which she endeavours to pass on her expertise in readable form. Suzy says there are several criteria for a good dog walker:

- Ideally, you should be a dog owner yourself.
- You need extensive experience of dogs
- You need to know about different breeds' characters
- You should be known to vets as a responsible person (not least, so they can post your flyers/recommend you in their surgeries)

Suzy will also take her charges as boarders when necessary.

Dog-sitting
Dog sitters usually stay in the owner's home while they are away. See also *Animal Sitting* in *Other Opportunities*.

Dog Day Care Centre
Whilst it is commonplace for working people to leave their offspring with a child-minder, an American variation sees yuppies dropping off their canine companions at a home-from-home dog centre complete with an indoor 'playroom' and outside exercise yard. The indoor room is likely to have a range of toys including balls, things to chew, and of course a stereo system and television (for the dogs); some even have small swimming pools. Even in America, this idea was deemed crazy a decade or so ago, but now dog-care centres are to be found in every major US city. On a rational note, it *is* probably kinder to a dog to take it to a day-centre where it can mix with other dogs and humans, rather than leave it mewed up on its own all day in its owner's apartment.

Proprietor's of dog day-care centres need suitable premises and usually some veterinary experience; perhaps a veterinary nurse qualification, or one of the other qualifications mentioned in this section or in the Professions and Qualifications chapter. It will be interesting to see if the idea catches on in Britain. The nearest British equivalent is probably Elmwood Exclusive Hotel for Dogs, a boarding kennels with-a-difference in Berkshire, which provides the pampered pets of pampered owners with furnished rooms, television and their customary tipple or nibble be it caviar, champagne or some other delicacy.

The dog hotel provides a furnished room, TV and champagne

USEFUL WEBSITE
Jobswithdogs.co.uk a website linked to *K9 Magazine,* and, gives information on the latest jobs.

CATS

While it is the case that the number of cats in Britain has increased to an estimated 7.2 million and that they have taken over from dogs as the most common pet, the number of jobs concerned with them has not increased. The reason for this is probably obvious. Cats are perceived as the most suitable pet by the increasing number of single people living on their own, or for households where both adults are working. Cats can amuse themselves and it is not rare for them to convince two households simultaneously that they are its owners.

Whilst virtually every veterinary practice and animal rescue centre is bound to have its share of feline clients, there are nonetheless some organisations that specialise in cats exclusively.

CAT-ONLY VETERINARY PRACTICES
There are only a handful of cat-only practices in the UK:

Bristol and Edinburgh Veterinary Schools – Feline Centres: the Feline Advisory Bureau (see below) funds a lecturer and a resident in feline medicine at the Bristol Veterinary School which has a Feline Centre dedicated to treating cats. There is a similar arrangement at Edinburgh.

Other cat clinics
The Feline Clinic: 258 Derby Road, Bramcote, Nottingham NG9 3JN; e-mail info@ashvet.co.uk; www.ashvet.co.uk
Nine Lives Veterinary Practice for Cats: 2068 Stratford Road, Hockley Heath, West Midlands B94 6NT; enquiries@vetsforcats.com; www.vetsforcats.com.

CATS' PROTECTION
Cats' Protection, the UK's largest cat dedicated organisation, was founded in 1927 (as the Cats' Protection League), and has the same aims that it started out with, namely: to rescue and re-home if possible stray and unwanted cats, to promote neutering of all felines except breeding stock and to educate the public about how to care for cats. Its administrative headquarters are at 17 Kings Road, Horsham, West Sussex RH13 5PN, and it runs 13 purpose built rescue shelters around Britain, each of which has a small, paid team of staff which re-home about 8,000 cats and kittens a year between them.

Main CPL Shelters & Locations
Axhayes Shelter, Exeter; Josephine Fryer Shelter, New Malden; Amy Ellison Shelter, Warrington; Mabel Jenkins Shelter, Birmingham; Barnjet Shelter, Crawley Down; Nerea de Clifford Shelter, Haslemere; Bredhurst Shelter, Sittingbourne; North London Shelter, Archway; Bryncethin Shelter, Bridgend; Riverside Shelter, Kings Lynn; Cardyke Farm Shelter, Glasgow; Ryde Shelter,Isle of Wight; Dundonald Shelter, Northern Ireland.

The paid shelter staff are normally locals who tend to stay long-term, so employment opportunities are limited. If you wish to try, a list of shelters is available from the above address or telephone 01403-221900. However, about 90% of CPL staff, are volunteers. There are estimated to be about 5,000 of them looking after cats at the 250 voluntary branches nationwide doing everything from answering the telephone, to fostering rescue cats in special garden pens; not to mention fund raising.

The CPL magazine The Cat comes out bi-monthly and subscriptions are £12 annually (£6 for senior citizens). The CPL website is www.cats.org.uk; e-mail cpl@cats.org.uk.

USEFUL ADDRESSES & PUBLICATIONS

The Cat Fancy: The Governing Council of the Cat Fancy, 4-6 Penel Orlieu, Bridgwater, Somerset; www.gccfcats.org; e-mail gccf-cats@compuserve.com. The Cat Fancy is the feline equivalent of the Kennel Club.

Feline Advisory Bureau: Taeselbury, High Street, Tisbury, Wiltshire SP3 6LD; ☎0870-742-2278; fax 01747-871873; information@fabcats.org; www.fabcats.org;. A registered charity that uses its funds for the benefit of all cats. FAB funds several post-graduate posts at Bristol and Edinburgh Veterinary Schools including two lectureships in Feline Medicine. FAB publishes over 60 information sheets on feline health and welfare, information for cat owners, breeders and anyone wishing to set up a cat rescue centre or boarding cattery.

The FAB Boarding Cattery Manual: 2002, editor Claire Bessant. £28.50 + £2.50 postage from the Feline Advisory Bureau. Includes free *FAB Standard for Construction & Management of Boarding Catteries*.

The FAB Standard for Construction and Management of Boarding Catteries: 2002, available from the Feline Advisory Bureau £7.50 plus £1 postage. Comes free if you order the Boarding Cattery Manual.

The FAB Rescue Manual: by Anne Haughie. Published autumn 1998. Covers practical aspects of rescue from setting up a shelter to mangagement, staffing, homing, cat care and fundraising. £15 + £1.50 postage. Available from the Feline Advisory Bureau (see above).

Cat Action Trust 1997: Charity no. 801245; P.O.Box 1639, London W8 7ZZ; www.cat77.org.uk (020-8993 7041) volunteers always needed to rescue and re-home feral cats. Also campaigns on behalf of ferals to get them domesticated and neutered rather than destroyed. All adult feral cats are neutered and returned to site.

Manual of Canine and Feline Behavioural Medicine: published 2002 by the British Small Animal Veterinary Association (☎01452-726700), price £66 to non-members.

Other Cat Rescue Centres Which May Take Volunteers
Blue Cross: Chalfont St (01753-882560).
Blue Cross: Cambridge (01223-350153).
Caring for Cats: South Ockenden (01708-854567).
Cat Rescue/Re-home: Colchester (01206-864284).
Cats-R-Us: Shildon (01388-774610).
Disley Cat Sanctuary: Disley (01298-816200).
Furness Cat Shelter: Barrow in Furness (01229-431557)
Humane Society: Wilmslow (01625-520802).
Ingleside Feline Sanctuary: Bristol (01179-602360).
Nine Lives Cat Rescue: Romsey (01794-340743).
Feline Friends: 362 New North Road, Hainault, Ilford IG6 3DY;(020-8500 0984).

Working With Horses

The horse industry is a multi-billion dollar one worldwide, yet few of those working with horses can expect to get rich from it except a privileged few; mainly celebrity jockeys and show jumpers. Working with horses is regarded more as a way of life, a passion, and even an obsession, for the majority of those involved in it. However, decent working conditions and reasonable accommodation can make life much pleasanter, and a first class training in a well-known establishment can advance your prospects. It is still possible to be exploited for love of the horse, so when negotiating with an employer you should always ask for a contract that states the terms and conditions of your employment. Many of the leading showing, show jumping and event yards take on working pupils who progress through their BTEC qualifications while working with the horses. It is important that you get fair treatment and rewards and The British Horse Society will provide a sample *Working Pupil Contract* on request. Conditions have improved significantly in recent years, with reasonable wages paid by most employers, less primitive living conditions and a range of graded, nationally and internationally recognised qualifications to train towards.

It is often said that girls are fascinated by horses until they discover boys. Judging by the number of women riders (72%) compared with men (28%) a large number retain their love of horses, though probably not exclusively. Nonetheless a recent survey of women found that faced with the choice, 80% would dispose of their partners before their horse. The female majority is also reflected in the world of jobs and careers with horses of which the two most common are grooms and riding instructors/ride leaders which are dominated by women. Racing is however, a traditionally male realm, particularly race-horse training (there are about 20 women – famous ones include Jenny Pitman (now retired) and Venetia Williams – out of a total of 645 licence holders). Of the stable staff (i.e. lads) about 40% are female.

There are also the horse-related trades that necessitate contact with horses such as farrier and saddler, both of which can bring in a reasonable living, and less specialised jobs like horse box driver.

HOW TO FIND A JOB

Vacancies can be found through word of mouth, agencies and in the horse magazines particularly the internationally available Horse and Hound (subscriptions ☎01444-445555) and for racing jobs, *The Racing Post* (☎ 020-7293 3092; www.racingpost.co.uk) newspaper. A glance at the job page of the latter revealed adverts for a horse box driver, assistant trainers, stable staff and trainers' secretaries, as well as jobs abroad.

AGENCIES

Agencies that specialise in finding jobs for stable staff also advertise in the equine press. They charge the employer a finding fee but not the job seeker.

Career grooms: 16e Randolph Crescent, London W9 1DR; ☎0207-289 6385; fax 0207-289 6385; fax 08701 385750; e-mail info@careergrooms.co.uk; www.careergrooms.co.uk. Recruitment specialists for the equestrian community mainly in the UK and Europe and some work further afield. Website offers temporary, permanent and contract work. Equestrian staff can register online for free and search and apply for jobs online and be notified of new jobs as they arrive.

Country File Employment Agency: Abernant Glas Farm, Glanamman, Ammanford SA18 2YG; ☎01269-851441. Run by Caroline Carpenter who has over five years' experience of finding jobs for stable staff countrywide. Experience is valued over qualifications. About 300 vacancies are filled annually.

Nags 'n' Nannies: (☎01244-535449 fax: 01244-534399; e-mail nagsnannies@aol.com; www.nagsandnannies.co.uk)

Spectrum: (☎01903 506127).

World of Experience: 52 Kingston Deverill, Warminster, Wiltshire, BA12 7HF; ☎01985-844022; fax 01985-844102; e-mail office@equijobshop.com; www.equijobshop.com. Specialises in jobs with horses and has requests for general stable staff, grooms, riders, instructors, stable managers etc. The jobs are mainly in Britain, with some in 20+ other countries worldwide.

TYPES OF STABLES

There are an estimated 565,000 horses in the UK of which 88% are owned by individuals) i.e. not in riding schools or yards. An estimated 2.6 million people ride every year and two million of these are regular horse riders. Horse riders and owners spend a whopping 900 million pounds a year on their beasts, and horse and rider accoutrements, which makes it a huge industry with a vast employment spin off.

There are several types of equine establishment which all have different nuances arising from the usage of the horses in them:

- Equitation Centres/Riding Schools
- Livery Stables (can be combined with the above)
- Competition (Eventing/Showjumping/Dressage) Stables
- Racing Stables
- Stud Farms
- Hunt Stables
- Polo Stables

There are also working possibilities in Horse and Donkey sanctuaries where the pace is more relaxed as they are not primarily commercial or competitive.

Circuses also employ grooms to look after horses and ponies (see Circuses for further details).

EQUINE QUALIFICATIONS

Once you have decided that you are going to work with horses it is advisable to combine it with getting qualifications. The basic ones are National Vocational Qualification (NVQ) Level 1 or British Horse Society (BHS) Stage 1 and 2. The next qualifications should be selected to be appropriate to the direction you want your career to take.

NVQS.

NVQs are awarded through City and Guilds organisation (☎020-7294-2468). They are available in Horse Care (Levels 1,2, and 3). Level 1 gives a very basic level of competence for those working under supervision. Level 2 is aimed at those able to carry out routine work without direct supervision and report back to a more senior person; it also includes competence to exercise fit horses and gives a sound basis of knowledge. Level 3 is aimed at providing the capability to run a small yard alone and includes efficient planning of work. It also provides competence to teach novice riders up to level 2. Each NVQ comprises a number of compulsory units and a free choice of other units.

BTECS

The BTEC qualifications are awarded by Edexcel Foundation (☎020-7393 4500; www.edexcel.org.uk/qualifications):

National Diploma in Equine Management
A two-year, full-time course which you can enter with four GCSEs at grade C or higher. Alternatively, you can enter with intermediate GNVQ, or evidence of practical experience. Modules include equitation, ground schooling, teaching practice, stud practice and equine science. Specialialist options in stud, rehabilitation and theory and teaching. The content is about 40% academic and 60% practical. Holders can go into stud assistant, riding instruction, veterinary nursing and equine welfare work.

Higher National Diploma in Equine Management
The BTEC HND lasts two years plus a year industrial placement in year two. For entry you need Maths, English and a science subject at GCSE and four A level points/relevant GNVQ/National Diploma or two Scottish Highers at grade B or three C grades at Irish Higher level. One of these should be Biology. Evidence of equestrian ability is also needed.

science for equine students, business information systems, equine veterinary science, managing people and horse anatomy and physiology are just some of the modules included in the course which is 50% practical and 50% academic.

It can lead into equine business management, teaching, training etc. or, as access to the third year of an equine science degree or a degree in equine sports science.

BSC HONS, EQUINE SCIENCE

BScs in Equine Science are being offered by an increasing number of colleges including Brinsbury College, Sussex (☎01798-873832) and the Abingdon and Witney College (☎01993-703464) both of which run their courses in conjunction with a University, London (Wye College) and Oxford Brookes respectively. Also Warwickshire College 01926-318000.

Courses last four years including a foundation year. Entry is with high A level grades, preferably in maths and sciences. In the case of Wye College, students must complete assignments and projects in order to enter the second year of the course.

The course is geared to produce scientists with good vocational skills who can carry on to M.Sc or Ph.D level, and work in the sporting, leisure and service sectors of the horse industry.

BRITISH HORSE SOCIETY QUALIFICATIONS

For over 50 years, the BHS, Britain's largest equine charity has promoted the welfare of the horse. However, its mission statement 'For the sake of the horse' gives little indication of its all pervasive activities in all matters affecting horses and riders.

1. It campaigns for the continuance of existing horse routes and lobbies Government for greater provision and better upkeep of riding and carriage-driving routes.
2. It monitors the health and welfare of horses countrywide and provides practical advice on horse care in order to prevent mistreatment through ignorance. It also provides information on breeds and breeding and operates a rescue programme for neglected and mistreated horses and ponies.
3. It administers riding clubs countrywide to promote instruction and fun and competitions.

4. It promotes greater safety for horse and rider by setting recommended standards of clothing and accessories designed to give as much protection as possible from injury and runs campaigns to educate motorists and riders to reduce risks of accidents between them on the roads.
5. Perhaps the best known face of the BHS is education and training section which oversees the range of BHS exams for instructors (see below), stable managers and grooms as well as those offering riding holidays. BHS qualifications are recognised in 29 countries worldwide. The training section also offers careers advice, refresher courses and a range of seminars and conventions.

The British Horse Society Training Office: Stoneleigh Deer Park, Kenilworth, Warwickshire CV8 2XZ; ☎01926-707700; fax 01926-707800; www.bhs.org.uk; e-mail enquiry@bhs.org.uk. Can provide a list of about 25 colleges offering BHS approved equine studies courses around the UK.

ASSOCIATION OF BRITISH RIDING SCHOOLS EXAMS

The ABRS was founded in 1954 and has members all over the world. In response to demand, the ABRS devised a series of exams for teachers and grooms. The exams for grooms (called assistant stable managers in the USA) take the candidate from basic groom up to senior manager level (able to run a yard and supervise staff). The Initial Teaching Award requires the holder to teach a basic group ride, private lesson, and give a lecture. The Advanced Teaching Diploma expects the holder to teach up to Grand Prix level. If you are sufficiently knowledgeable and experienced you will not have to do level 1 before you enter for level 2, or 3 (the Diploma). For details of ABRS affiliated schools abroad, see Parts II and III.

The Association of British Riding Schools: Queens Chambers, 38-40 Queen Street, Penzance, Cornwall TR18 4BH; ☎01736-369440; fax 01736-351390; e-mail office@abrs.org; www.abrs.org.

Useful Addresses

Capel Manor: Horticultural and Environmental Centre, Bullsmoor Lane, Enfield, Middlesex EN1 4RQ; ☎020-8366 4442; fax 01992 717544; www.capel.ac.uk The London School Animal Care Equine and Saddlery (ACES). offers a wide range of full and part-time courses at NVQ level 1, First and National Diploma level in Animal and Horse Management. Cordwainers Diploma in Saddlery and HND Saddlery Technology are unique to Capel Manor.

Hayfield International Ltd: Hazlehead Park, Aberdeen, Scotland AB15 8BB; tel/fax 01224-321132. An international equitation centre which has a useful website (www.equiworld.net), which has a special section listing all of the UK riding and training centres and provided a job-search and advice section for employers and young people.

Oaklands College: Oakfields Campus, Hatfield Road, St.Albans, Herts. AL4 OJA; ☎01727-850651; fax 01727-847987. Offers BTEC National Diploma in Horse Studies and HND in Equine Studies.

Warwickshire College for Equine Studies: Moreton Hall, Moreton Morrell, Warwick CV35 9BL; ☎01926-318000. Has been running equine courses since 1974. These range from day-release up to HND and degree level (BA and BSc) in Equine Studies.

Most Agricultural colleges offer the BTEC National Diploma in Equine Studies. A list of higher education establishment offering HNDs and degrees in equine studies can be found in the *Official UCAS Handbook* which is available in public libraries.

GROOM/ASSISTANT STABLE MANAGER

Most jobs with horses are as grooms, with duties varying slightly depending on the type of stables (racing, eventing, stud, show/dressage, private employer) and the experience of the groom. In the stable the groom feeds, waters, grooms, mucks out, rugs and beds down his or her charges and usually exercises them. Whatever the type of stable, the routine is likely to start very early in the morning. The groom must also be able to fit all kinds of tack correctly and maintain its condition by preventing rotting and seeing that any weak stitching gets repaired.

The job also requires knowledge of common horse ailments and injuries and the ability to follow veterinary instructions on administering treatments. Other skills include the ability to remove broken, loose or twisted shoes.

Being a groom is hard physical work and apart from grooming (which takes up to 45 minutes to do properly) there is a lot of lifting and carrying (mainly bales and pails), bending and yard cleaning. It can be a pleasure to be outdoors in the warmer months but in winter it can be cold and pretty spartan.

RIDING INSTRUCTOR

The BHS examinations are held at centres around the country. The first level of award is the Preliminary Teaching Certificate for which the minimum entry age is 17 years 6 months.

The preliminary teacher then has to log 500 hours of teaching experience, one quarter of which can be stable management teaching before obtaining the BHS Assistant instructor certificate. The next stage of the ladder is the Intermediate Instructor's Certificate, which requires a higher standard of equestrianism and the ability to work without supervision. The final stage, BHS Instructor's Certificate is the standard professional qualification in this area. The minimum age for entry is 22 years and to achieve full instructor status two examinations have to be passed:
The BHS Stable Manager's Examination (also a qualification in its own right but below
    BHS Instructor)
The BHS Equitation and Teaching Examination
    The BHS qualification is recognised in 29 countries. For further details contact the BHS Training Centre.

Some Colleges offering Equine Qualifications
Abingdon & Witney College: Holloway Road, Witney, Oxon, OX28 6NE; e-mail inquiry@abingdon-witney.ac.uk Courses: BTEC First Diploma in Horse Care, BTEC National Diploma in Horse Management, HNC/HND Equine Management, BSc (Hons) Equine Science International Thoroughbred Management in conjunction with Oxford Brookes University. Also National Certificate in Horse Care, NVQs in Horse and Racehorse Care and BHS courses.
Berkshire College of Agriculture: Hall Place, Burchetts Green, Maidenhead, Berks SL6 6QR; ☎01628-824444; fax 01628-824695; e-mail: enquiries@bca.ac.uk; www.bca.ac.uk. Courses: BTEC First Diploma in Horse Care, National Certificate in Horse Care, BTEC National Diploma in Horse Management, CGLI Advanced National Certificate in Equine Business Management, HND National Diploma in Equine Studies with Management, HND in Equine Sports Performance (full or part-time), BA (Hons) Equine Sports Performance, BA (Hons) Equine Industry Management. Also BHS courses.
EquiStudy at Equine Open Learning College: Moreton Hall, Moreton Morrell, Warwick

CV35 9BL; ☎01926-651085; fax 01926-318300; e-mail equistudy@warkscol.ac.uk
A division of Warwickshire College and Moreton Morrell. Enables students to work at
their own pace towards an HNC/HND in Equine Studies, Foundation Degree in Equine
Studies, BA (Hons) in Equine Studies or Equine and Business Management. Also BHS
exam preparation and range of other equine courses.

Merrist Wood College: Worplesdon, Guildford, Surrey GU3 3PE; ☎01483-884000;
fax 01483-884001; Student Services 01483-884040; e-mail info@merristwood.ac.uk;
www.merristwood.ac.uk. Courses: First Diploma Horse Care, National Cert. in
Equine Studies (1 year), National Diploma in Horse Management (2 years), National
Certificate in Advanced Riding and Coaching Skills, HND in Equine Management.
Also part-time BHS courses.

Oaklands College: St Albans Smallford Campus, Hatfield Road, St. Albans, Herts., AL4
OJA; ☎01727-737 080; e-mail help.line@oaklands.ac.uk; www.oaklands.ac.uk.

Royal Agricultural College, Cirencester; Cirencester, GL7 6JS; ☎01285-652531; fax
01285-650219; e-mail admisssions@royagcol.ac.uk; www.royagcol.ac.uk. Courses:
BSc (Hons) Equine & Agricultural Management. MSc/MBA Equine Business
Management, MSc Applied Equine Science.

Walford College: Baschurch, Shrewsbury, Shropshire SY4 2HL; ☎01939-262100.
Courses: BTEC HND/BSc in Equine Studies jointly with the University of
Wolverhampton.

Warwickshire College: Moreton Morrell, Warwick CV35 9BL; ☎01926-318318. Full-
time courses: BTEC First Diploma in Horse Care, BTEC National Cert. and National
Diploma in Horse Management, HND Equine Studies or Science, HNC/HND Equine
Sports Coaching, HND Equine Sport Science, BA (Hons) Equine Studies, BA (Hons)
Equine and Business Management, BSc (Hons) Equine Science, BSc (Hons) Equine
and Human Sports Science.

RACING

In 1992 formal training structures were introduced into the industry which consequently
is a well-regulated area of work, with standard recommended pay rates and qualifications
for yard and stud staff, principally NVQs levels 1 to 3 specially geared to Racehorse
Care (Level 2) and Racehorse Care and Management (Level 3). Racehorse Trainers also
have to obtain a formal qualification before they can gain licences or permits. Permitted
trainers are limited to training horses for themselves and near family, while Licensed
ones can train horses for other owners.

Sarah Lawrence had ridden ponies since she was a child and after winning a donkey
derby thought she might go into racing when she left school. Her mother had learned of
the British Racing School at Newmarket and her school's career office got the necessary
papers to apply.

Sarah Lawrence recalls her training course

*There were thirteen boys and girls on our 9-week residential course and although
we worked a long day I thought the school was very well run and apart from
two who dropped out the pupils' riding ability progressed rapidly. There were
76 horses at the school with other beginners' courses and those for apprentice
jockeys and amateur riders being run at the same time. Although I had ridden
previously, others had not, but by the end of the nine weeks we were all cantering
in groups on racehorses.*

*The accommodation and food were excellent and days out to Newmarket Races
were arranged. Sunday was an easy day when parents and family visited. At the
end of the course everyone was assessed, getting a Certificate for NVQ Level*

> One. *A few of the pupils had come from racing yards, and went back to them while the rest of us all had jobs arranged for us by the school.*
>
> *I had made friends with another pupil Vicky Plowman and we asked to be placed together if possible, in the Lambourn (Berkshire) area.*
>
> *Places were found for us at a small (about 20 horses) yard 3 miles from Lambourn run by Ed James and we arrived together just before Christmas. We shared a cottage together right next to the yard. Vicky is only working part-time now as her parents have bought the local shop, but I am still there full-time and really enjoy the work. It is a very friendly yard, training mostly steeplechasers and hurdlers; I ride plenty of work and schooling and hope eventually to become a conditional (junior) jockey.*
>
> *When I take a horse racing I often see friends from the Racing School and several of those working in flat racing yards have already got their apprentice jockey licences. I really enjoy working in racing and would strongly recommend the British Racing School to anyone thinking of racing as a career. Even if you don't make it as a jockey there are always opportunities for travelling lads/girls, box drivers or head lads or girls, or even secretaries. If you like the outdoors and horses and do not mind hard work, it is a great life; lots of laughs and a real thrill when you watch the horse you look after winning races.*

Stable staff working for NVQs at levels 2 and 3 can choose either a racing or breeding option. The former provides competency in all aspects of preparing, handling and caring for horses at stables and the racecourse. The latter provides a wide range of skills needed for work in a thoroughbred stud, including managing stallions, caring for mares and foals and maintaining stud documentation.

There are about 4,000 full time racing stable employees and a further 1,725 who are employed part-time. Most stable staff are expected to ride out (i.e. exercise their charges), and for this a weight limit of 9½ stone is preferred for flat yards, though in National Hunt yards 10½ stone will be usual. Some training yard staff may not have not have ridden before starting their training and it is certainly no bar to a job or career in racing. Once you are engaged by a yard there is the possibility to progress to the supervisory positions of Head Lad or Travelling Head Lad. The latter often drives the horsebox and sometimes travels abroad. Those who show talent can apply to be an Apprentice Jockey (flat) or Conditional Jockey (jump) as the first step to a jockey career. Since 1997 there has been a policy of encouraging stable lads/lasses to ride as amateurs under Rules which has made race riding a little less exclusive. An amateur has to attend a one-day training session at the British Racing School and obtain a Jockey Club permit. Amateurs who wish to ride against professional jockeys in jumping races have to attend a longer, three-day course at the School in Newmarket.

Only a few jockeys reach the pinnacle of the profession and enjoy a celebrity lifestyle and its lucrative spin-offs. But even those working short of star status can have a successful career riding hundreds of races a year. The current pay rate is £75.60 for a flat race and £103.25 for a jumping race, plus 7-10% of win and place prize money. A number of top jockeys go on to become trainers once they retire (a.k.a. hang up their boots) from riding but their talent rarely commends itself to this sphere. It is possible to apply for a job as an Assistant Trainer once you have racing stable or jockey experience as a way of learning the trade before setting up independently.

A recommended way of entering the industry as a 'lad' is to apply to the British Racing School or the Northern Racing College or the British Horseracing Training Board (BHTB). Alternatively, you can contact trainers direct although you will still have go to school. Most candidates start training at ages 16 to 18 years, but there are possibilities also for those in their early twenties.

Graduates of the Abingdon and Witney College, based at Witney (01993-703464), are also very well thought of as potential employees. The College has its own thoroughbred stud and offers courses geared to training, breeding and administration in the thoroughbred industry.

Kate Corbett took a three-year BTEC National Diploma sandwich course in Equine Studies at Abingdon and Witney College. Although primarily based around horses, the course covered a challenging range of husbandry matters as well as accounts, RSA typing, bookkeeping and computers.

Kate Corbett remembers her varied course

We did a huge variety of work covering agriculture generally, livestock, soil analysis, grasses, gallops, haymaking, stable design etc.

The College have their own farm and stud farm and we prepared yearlings and foals for the autumn Bloodstock sales and learnt to break in young racehorses.

The middle year was spent on work experience away from the college. I did three months working for Martine Head on their stud farm near Deauville in France; it was a great thrill to see the yearlings we had prepared go to the Deauville sales and fetch fabulous prices. After this I went to America for 9 months, working for a racehorse trainer called Steve Dimauro. We started off wintering at Gulf Stream racecourse in Florida and after a few months the horses moved north to New York State to race at Belmont Park and Aqueduct before going on again to Saratoga for the summer. The hours were very long, but it was a brilliant experience; I rode out on the racecourses every morning and usually led a horse up at the races in the afternoon, before going back for evening stables. The College at Witney was really good at finding jobs for their students who, during the year out, were scattered all over the world.

After my final exams back in England, I worked for a trainer in Lambourn, Berkshire for a couple of years as a work rider, secretary, and generally dogsbody. It was good fun and I actually got to ride in a few races as an amateur jockey. Eventually, I bottled out of another winter riding out in the freezing cold and landed a job with the publishers Raceform Ltd. who compile the official form book for Flat and National Hunt racing in Britain. So I am still working with horses but not quite so hands on!

Other graduates of the Abingdon and Witney Equine Studies courses include Michael Caulfield, Director of the UK Jockeys Association, Richard Phillips, the well-known racehorse trainer and comedian, and jockey Rupert Wakley. Note: the BTEC courses at Abingdon and Witney college are now two years while the sandwich programme is now a four-year BSc (Hons) course in Equine Science with a year abroad working in the racing industry.

THE JOCKEY CLUB

The Jockey Club, racing's independent regulating body, has its origins in the 1750s when it was responsible for organising challenges; a term still used for some races today. Two hundred and fifty years later the Jockey Club oversees almost every aspect of racing in Britain. Its regulations govern Flat and National Hunt racing, Point-to-Pointing and Arab Horse racing. It is also responsible for issuing licences to the UK's 59 racecourses and their staff and riders and trainers, dealing with disciplinary matters and carrying out security investigations, as well as overseeing race meetings on the day. Media attention and literary fiction tend to concentrate on the security and investigative role of the Jockey Club. Where huge sums of money are at stake (as they often are in racing), corruption, and malpractice inevitably arise in the form of riding sharp practices, race fixing and nobbling (horse doping). A year rarely passes without a high profile investigation into allegations linked to these misdemeanors. Despite such sensations, The Jockey Club maintains that racing in Britain is cleaner than in most other countries. During the last few years the regulatory arm of the JC has been especially busy in the area of education standards and training for the industry. All levels of employee up to and including trainers, now have to have formal qualifications and a recognised training which includes courses in Business Skills and Staff Management (for trainers), before a licence can be issued.

Apart from regulating the expertise standards of those involved in the sport, the Jockey Club is itself an employer. Not all racecourse staff are JC employees and not all JC employees work directly with horses; many are administrative posts. JC employees whose work is close to horses include Veterinary Officers and Veterinary Technicians. The VOs job is to check horses' identity on arrival at the racecourse and monitor them throughout the day, both before and after racing. Vet Technicians collect urine samples for testing. These are sent to the Horseracing Forensic Laboratory in Newmarket. Starters are also involved with horses, checking saddle girths before ensuring a fair start. The starting stall handlers, employed by Racetech, load the horses into the stalls for flat racing.

STUD WORK

While bloodstock may rate lower than armaments or pop music on Britain's biggest earners list, it is nevertheless number six and is therefore very important. There are about 5000 people employed at the 550 thoroughbred studs in Britain. There are two main categories of breeding establishments, Public ones which stand stallions for a fixed fee to visiting mares during the stud season (generally February to July) and Private ones which specialise in housing brood mares and foals for a particular owner. There is however some 'self pollinating' where the same breeder owns both types of establishment. In Britain and Ireland combined there are approximately 20,000 thoroughbred mares and 700 stallions actively producing. A stud can be a few dozen acres or several hundred, and can be owned by a Sheikh or an ex-stable lad. A fashionable stallion (i.e. one from an illustrious stud, whose offspring have distinguished themselves) can make its owner £25,000 richer per servicing. The main foaling season is from mid-January to June. From August to October stud staff prepare stock for the yearling sales and it is the turn of mares and foals to be sold in November and December.

It is not necessary to have riding experience for stud work. The British Stud Staff Training Scheme (c/o Caroline Turnbull, National Stud, Newmarket, Suffolk, CB8 OXD; ☎01638-663464), developed by the National Stud and the Thoroughbred Breeders' Association, runs courses twice a year for 16-18 year olds who wish to enter the breeding industry. Graduates enter a National Traineeship programme, and following an induction course held at the National Stud, are placed on suitable studs where they undergo on-the-job training towards their NVQ Level 2 in Racehorse Care – Breeding Option. Progress is monitored by the BSSTS, judged on a continuous assessment basis by on-site Assessors and the qualification is usually achieved within 12 to 18 months. The opportunity to go on to a Modern Apprenticeship, including NVQ Level 3 is also offered.

Additionally, the Abingdon and Witney college runs one and two-year courses that are recognised by the breeding industry.

The National Stud also runs an intensive Diploma course for older applicants who have had a least a year of full-time experience.

Useful Racing Addresses

Abingdon and Witney College: Holloway Road, Witney, Oxon OX28 6NE; ☎01993-703464; e-mail inquiry@abingdon-witney.ac.uk. The only UK college specialising in thoroughbreds. Has its own stud farm. Range of equine courses and a degree in equine sciences run jointly with Oxford Brookes University. Courses include British Horseracing & Training Board NVQ Racehorse Care levels 1-3. Helps all its graduates get jobs and has many alumni working in the industry in Britain and around the world.

The British Horseracing Training Board (BHTB): (formerly the Racing & Thoroughbred Breeding Training Board), Suite 16, Unit 8, Kings Court, Willie Snaith Road, Newmarket, Suffolk CB8 7SG; ☎01638-560743; e-mail info@rtbtb.keme.co.uk. The BHTB is the awarding body for NVQs and Key Skills qualifications for working in horseracing. It also coordinates a training programme at well known racing establishments including the Northern Racing School. Produces a free publication *Careers in Horse Racing* (latest edition 2000) outlining the different jobs and careers available.

British Racing School: Snailwell Road, Newmarket, Suffolk CB8 7NU; ☎01638-665103.

The Jockeys' Association of Great Britain Ltd.: 39A Kingfisher Court, Hambridge Road, Newbury, Berks. RG14 5SJ; ☎01635-44102; www.jagb.co.uk

The Jockey Club: 42 Portman Square, London W1H OEN; ☎020-7486 4921; e-mail info@thejockeyclub.co.uk; www.thejockeyclub.co.uk.

Northern Racing College: The Stables, Rossington Hall, Great Northern Road, Doncaster DN11 OHN; ☎01302-865462; e-mail info@nrcdonc.demon.co.uk; www.northernracingcollege.co.uk

The National Stud: Newmarket, Suffolk CB8 OXE; ☎01638-663464.

The National Trainers Federation: 9 High Street, Lambourn, Hungerford, Berkshire RG17 8XN; ☎01488-71719; www.racehorsetrainers.org

The Stable Lads' Association: 74 High Street, Swadlincote, Derbyshire DE11 8HS; ☎01283-211522.

The Thoroughbred Breeders' Association: Stanstead House, The Avenue, Newmarket, Suffolk CB8 9AA; ☎01638-661321. Offers a four-week residential course at the National Stud in Newmarket to prepare school leavers for work placements with training to NVQ Level 2.

Warwickshire College: Moreton Morrell, Warwick CV35 9BL; ☎01926-318000; fax 01926-318300. Offers a range of equine courses from NVQ to degree level including BA (Hons) Business and Management for the Horseracing Industry.

HORSEBOX DRIVER

The movement of the industry's horseflesh provides a reasonable living for the forty or so companies that transport racehorses to and from race meetings and studs. Many yards and studs have their own horsebox and employ a full-time box driver. A good knowledge of horses and riding ability may be required.

In addition to the yards, a number of companies specialise in transporting horses around the country or abroad. Most such companies are small and therefore the employment potential is not vast. The best time to approach potential employers is probably during the summer when they are busiest and most likely to take on extra drivers. Permanent jobs can be landed through an initial temporary position, or by word-of-mouth. Jobs are sometimes advertised in the Racing Post or the local press. Company box drivers are usually expected to have some experience of handling horses and a clean HGV licence is the essential requirement. A groom with yard experience accompanies the horses en route. In the case of international travel by air, a small pool of flying grooms regularly accompany horses in transit, rather than the box driver. Drivers need to be flexible about spending time away from home and working unsocial hours.

Addresses of UK-based Transporters

British Bloodstock Agency (BBA): Queensberry Mews, High Street, Newmarket, Suffolk CB8 9AE; ☎01638-665021; www.bbashipping.com Founded 1911. Involved in the worldwide movement of horses.

Centurion Horse Transport: Centurion Stables, 16 Swaffham Road, Reach, Cambridgeshire, CB5 OHZ; ☎01638-743440. National service.

Eric Gillie Ltd. Potsclose Cottage, Nr Kelso, Roxburghshire TD5 8BN; ☎01573-430252; fax 01573-430210. Started 1975. Nationwide service.

Michael John Hinchcliffe: Postdown Farmhouse, Seven Barrows, Lambourn, Hungerford, Berkshire, RG17 8DH; ☎01488-73224; fax 01488-73328. Started 1985. Racing studs, airports etc.

Horseferry Transport Ltd: Carousel, Beechenlea Lane, Swanley, Kent BR8 8DR; ☎01322-664848; Started 1983. National and international.

Howard Forrest Horse Transport: New Road Farm, Tingrith, Milton Keynes MK17 9EN; ☎01525-717546. Started 1980. Specialises in studs, agencies and airports.

Bob Jones Ltd: Boydon End House, Wickhambrook, Newmarket, Suffolk; ☎01440-820664; fax 01440-820958. Started in 1979. Transport with quarantine livery for over 50 horses.

9*Lambourn Racecourse Transport Limited:* Baydon Road, Lambourn, Hungerford, Berkshire RG17 8NT; www.racehorsetransport.co.uk; ☎01488-71710; fax 01488-73208. Founded 1930. Largest fleet of horseboxes in Europe. Racing, sales and regular trips to Ireland and Europe.

M.C. International Horse Transport: Wits End, Dullingham Ley, Newmarket, Suffolk CB8 9XG; ☎01638-507278. Started 1986. National and International.

Newmarket Horse Services: Priory Stables, 22 Church Street, Exning, Newmarket, Suffolk, CB8 7EH; ☎01638-578140. Started 1985. Specialise in international transport particularly Scandinavia and Germany.

John Parker International Ltd. Little Owl Barn, Hedlinge, Hythe, Kent CT21 4JJ; ☎01303-266621; fax 01303-269400. To and from Europe, USA and Canada.

Parkes International Transport Ltd.: Oxford Road, Chieveley, Berkshire RG20 8RU; ☎01635-247742; fax 016356-247114. Started 1994.

Rapido Horse Services (UK Ltd): The Old Station Yard, Newmarket, Suffolk CB8 9BA; ☎01638-665145; fax 01638-660848. Most kinds of horse transporting and mostly international.

Janet Savill, International Horse Transport: 12 Oxford Street, Exning, Newmarket, Suffolk CB8 7EW; ☎01638-578150; e-mail janet.savill@ntlworld.com. Started 1991. Organises all kinds of horse transport for racing, dressage, ponies, showjumpers to Europe and Scandinavia. Does the paperwork so has no horseboxes herself, but has lots of contacts amongst horse transporters.

Shelley Ashman International Ltd: New Barn Farm, Bucklebury Village, Reading, Berks. RG7 6EF; ☎0118-9714714. International horse transport worldwide; www.shelleyashman.co.uk.

Ventureneed Horse Transportation: Atalanta House, Beggarbush Hill, Benson, Oxfordshire OX10 6PL; ☎01491-825035; www.ventureneed.net.

TNT Aviation Services: Felstead House, 2/6 Frances Road, Windsor SL4 3AA; ☎01753-844484. Started 1986. Air transport for horses worldwide.

Wardall Bloodstock Shipping Ltd: Manor Farm Stud, Nr Salisbury, Wiltshire SP5 5JY; ☎01722-780777. Only does the paperwork for import export of horses, but knows lots of contacts for international transporters.

Weyhill Horse Transport Ltd: Fyfield Stud, Fyfield, Andover, Hants. SP11 8EW; ☎01264-773033.

Whiteoaks Horse Transport: Kirby House, Woolsthorpe-by-Belvoir, Nr Grantham, Lincolnshire; fax 01476-870382.

HORSES IN UNIFORM

MOUNTED POLICE

There are limited opportunities to work with horses in the Police Force. Out of the 51 regional police forces in the UK, only about 17 still use mounted police, in twos and fours rather than dozens. There are about 340 active duty police horses in total. The Metropolitan Police (i.e. London) have the largest contingent of 120 horses. The area covered by this force was originally restricted to anywhere within a day's ride of Charing Cross. Nowadays, police forces around the country 'hire' horses and riders from other ones when needed for football matches, marches etc. It costs £375 to hire a Metropolitan horse and rider for one shift. Nevertheless, four-hoofed transport lasts better than four-wheeled: a panda car lasts on average eighteen months compared to a horse's seventeen years.

For riot control and public order duties, horses wear protective gear, and it is estimated a handful of them can be as effective in pushing back a crowd as 50 officers on foot.

Although both horses and riders are highly trained, the riders are police officers first and foremost, and an interest in police work is your most important asset as an applicant.

As the number of police horses is likely to keep on declining, the best bet is probably the Met, though you may soon have to be emblazoned with logos if a new proposal which would allow sponsorship of police horses by private companies is approved.

Further information about training as a police officer and thence to mounted duties, can be obtained from The Metropolitan Police Mounted Branch, (Imber Court, East Molesy, Surrey).

HORSE SUPPORT STAFF

According to the Training Manager of the Metropolitan mounted division, there are 29 civilian horse staff working with the Metropolitan Police. All the mounted units have civilian support, i.e. grooms and horse trainers. Metropolitan Police horse trainers work at Imber Court, the headquarters of the Metropolitan police mounted branch. Recruitment of civilian horse care/training staff is carried out first internally and then advertised to the public. Further information about working with the Metropolitan Police as horse support staff can be obtained by writing to The Personnel Manager (Metropolitan Police Public Order OCU, Room 733, New Scotland Yard, Broadway, London SW1H OBG). Note that you will be expected to have previous experience and qualifications relevant to working with horses.

ARMY

The army has two mounted units both of which are familiar to fans of British pageantry and ceremonial occasions: The Household Cavalry Mounted Regiment and the Kings Troop Royal Horse Artillery. As with the mounted police, mounted soldiers are soldiers first and horsemen second. Note that despite the historical examples of Joan of Arc, and Catherine the Great of Russia, women are not eligible. Although soldiers involved in either unit are trained for and may be used in modern combat, there is a progressive career structure in riding instruction, horse management and equestrianism, which is useful when carried on to civilian life. Farriery and saddlery can also be learnt in the army.

Kings Troop, Royal Horse Artillery: Ordnance Hill, St. John's Wood, London NW8 6PT; (☎ 020-7414 4603).

Household Calvary Mounted Regiment: Hyde Park Barracks, Knightsbridge, London; (☎ 01753-755213).

FARRIER

The farrier, is the chiropodist and cobbler of the equine world who makes or shapes horseshoes, trims and prepares horses' feet for shoeing and fits and nails the shoes to the hooves. Evidence of horses being shod goes back at least to Roman times making it an ancient manual skill and one which is unlikely to decline as long as recreational riding and equine sports remain popular.

The skill of the farrier is evidenced by his or her ability not only to make and fit shoes correctly, but also to devise compensatory or corrective shoes if the horse's action or feet are defective. The job is not without other challenges: some horses shoe better than others while not a few have quirks and a minority have vices (i.e. they kick). Dealing with all these variables successfully brings with it a certain job satisfaction. Communicating well with owners is another skill the trade requires. Farriers charge anything from £30 to £50 for shoeing a horse all round and make a decent living being self-employed or working as one of several for a farriery firm or partnership.

Many horses have quirks and a minority have vices

Farriers have to be licensed by the licensing body, The Farriers Registration Council. Farriers can do this once a three to four-year apprenticeship has been successfully completed leading to the Diploma of the Worshipful Company of Farriers, the body, which oversees the training and competence standards of farriers in the UK.

Apprentices can start at the age of 16 and there is no upper limit. Those under 21 years of age must have a least four GCSE passes including English language. Apprentices also have to undergo a medical examination. Most farriers are men but it is hoped that the 35 women currently registered will encourage others to take up the craft. Although farriery is physically strenous there is no convincing reason why women should find it unsuitable, though they might develop rather pronounced arm muscles in the course of their work.

A would-be apprentice has to find an Approved Training Farrier (ATF) who is willing to offer them an apprenticeship and the ATF then has to propose them to the Farriers Registration Council. There are about 300 ATFs to an annual intake of 300-320 apprentices. As demand for places is greater than supply, be prepared to send off a lot of application letters before you get an affirmative reply. There are no women AFTs at the time of press. The Farriery Training Service (FTS) is the Managing Agency set up by the FRC to oversee the training of farriery apprentices in Britain but it also accepts applications from ATFs and Apprentices worldwide. Farriery training costs about £6,500 plus the cost of a farrier tool kit (forge and shoeing tools) and personal protective equipment (leather apron, steel-capped boots and safety glasses). Apprentice salaries range from £3,600 for the first year up to £7,100 in the fourth year.

Every two years the National Association of Blacksmiths arranges an international exchange programme with the USA and Europe. For the addresses of farriery associations abroad, see individual country sections.

Useful Addresses

The Farrier Registration Council: Sefton House, Adam Court, Newark Road, Peterborough, PE1 5PP; ☎01733-319911; fax 01733-319910; e-mail frc@farrier-reg.co.uk; www.farrier-reg.gov.uk. Farriery Training Service: ☎01733-319770. Established under the Farriers (Registration) Act 1975, to license the trade.

The National Association of Farriers, Blacksmiths and Agricultural Engineers: Avenue B, 10th Street, N.A.C. Stoneleigh, Warwickshire, CV8 2LG; ☎024-7669 96595; nafbaehq@nafbae.org.uk; www.nafbae.org The National Association founded in 1905 is the 'trade union' for the trade, which protects the interests of its members and provides free legal advice and insurance at discounted rates. A comprehensive list of farriery and blacksmithing books is available from the Association as is *Forge,* the trade magazine. The Association also organises events and seminars of interest to anyone dealing with horses. For information on farrier exchanges with Europe and the USA, see *Parts II and III.*

The Worshipful Company of Farriers WCF: 19 Queen Street, Chipperfield, Herts WD4 9BT; ☎01923-260747; fax 01923-261677; e-mail theclerk@wcf.org.uk; www.wcf.org.uk. The WCF was established in London in 1356 to oversee farriery within the Cities of London and Westminster. For more than 100 years it has been responsible for maintaining the standards of farriery through its examinations board.

It is possible to attend a one-year Equine Studies with Blacksmithing course at one of three approved colleges. The successful completion of such a course does not guarantee future acceptance at an ATF, but if accepted it is likely that the apprenticeship will last the minimum three years and two months rather than the maximum four years and two months.

Approved Colleges for Equine Studies with Blacksmithing and Other Courses

Oatridge Agricultural College: Ecclesmachan, Broxburn, West Lothian EH52 6NH; ☎01506-854387; info@oatridge.ac.uk; www.oatridge.ac.uk. Equine Studies with Blacksmithing.

Herefordshire College of Technology: Folly Lane, Hereford HR1 1LS; ☎01432-352235; e-mail enquiries@hereford-tech.ac.uk; www.hereford-tech.ac.uk.

Warwickshire College: Moreton Morrell, Warwickshire CV35 9BL; ☎01926-651367. BTEC First Diploma in Horse Studies Pre-Farriery Training and BTEC National Certificate in Blacksmithing. Also, Equi Study, the correspondence course branch of Moreton Morrell, offers a course The Horse's Foot as part of its Horse Care Series.

PHYSIOTHERAPIST

As with chiropractors that treat animals, physiotherapists have to complete training in human physiotherapy before extending to animals. After spending two years in general practice as a Chartered Physiotherapist, practitioners become eligible for certified courses run by The Association of Chartered Physiotherapists in Animal Therapy. There follows a period of training as an animal therapist under direct veterinary supervision until competency has been established. All animal physiotherapists work only with veterinary approval and after veterinary referral.

Equine physiotherapy is in demand, particularly for competion horses. Like any top athletes they are vulnerable to the strains resulting from the heavy demands on their physiques. Most therapists work on a mobile basis visiting animals in situ. A few therapists operate from their own homes and can lodge animals for a recovery period if necessary.

The Association of Chartered Physiotherapists for Animal Therapy (ACPAT): Membership Secretary, Morland House, Salters Lane, Winchester Hampshire, S022 5JP; tek 01962-844390. Write to The Secretary for further details.

The Chartered Society of Physiotherapy: 14 Bedford Row, London WC1R 4EB; ☎ 020-7306 6666; www.csp.org.uk.

SADDLER

Although the saddler works more with leather than animals, saddlery-making is nevertheless a job connected with horses. It is also a possibility for those with some kinds of disability which preclude them from working with horses directly. Like farriery, saddlery-making is an enduring craft that goes back centuries, and good saddlery that is properly looked after will outlast the horse or owner for whom it is made. Items made by saddlers include various designs of saddle and bridlework, and also driving harness, which still has its uses despite the demise of horse transport. Ideally a saddle should be custom-made to fit a particular horse, but the huge expense makes this a luxury that only some can afford. The majority of horses and ponies make do with an 'off the peg' saddle that is either new or secondhand, and which fits requirements adequately. However, a saddler's training provides the ability to make saddle for any horse that is difficult to fit because of injury etc. In recent years there has been an increase in tack made from synthetic materials, but this is unlikely to cause a decline of the saddler's craft as leather tack remains the best and most popular kind and inevitably, it requires periodical repairs for wear and tear, however well it is looked after.

TRAINING

The two routes for entry into the trade are via an apprenticeship with a Master Saddler under the Millennium Aprenticeship Scheme, or college-based training. Under both schemes the student will work towards the City and Guilds saddlery qualifications which are available at three levels. Saddlery-making can be studied full and part-time at Cordwainers@Capel Manor College and Walsall College of Art and Technology. There are also some private sources of training.

Useful Addresses

Cordwainers@ Capel Manor College: Bullsmoor Lane, Enfield, Middlesex EN1 4RQ; ☎ 020-8366 4442.

Society of Master Saddlers: Kettles Farm, Mickfield, Stowmarket, Suffolk IP14 6BY; 01449-711642.

Wallsall College of Art and Technology: Shelley Campus, Scarborough Road, Walsall WS2 2TY; ☎ 01922-720889.

Equistudy: Moreton Morrell, Warwick CV35 9BL; ☎01926-318000; fax 01926-318300; e-mail equistudy@warkscol.ac.uk Equi Study is a division of Warwickshire College and offers a study at home programme that includes saddlery and horse-clothing studies (note: not saddle making but saddlery theory and correct practice).

EQUINE RESCUE CENTRES

Another possibility for work is at one of the many rescue centres around the country. Some of the best known are listed below. Others can be found through the Yellow Pages under a*nimal welfare societies.*

Bob Westacott was the former Chief Equine Welfare Officer for the Redwings Horse Sanctuary. He came to the job after 20 years in the Household Cavalry and then as a civilian government equine advisor to the Sultan of Oman. He worked for the British Horse Society in horse welfare before moving to Redwings in 1993.

Bob Westacott describes his work at Redwings Horse Sanctuary

My work was mainly looking at horses and assessing them. Redwings gets calls from members of the public and Redwings supporters. We also have a network of about 100 welfare officers nationwide and anyone of them can telephone and ask for the Chief Equine Welfare Officer to visit a case which meant going anywhere in England, Scotland, Wales or Northern Ireland to look at a horse. You could be asked to go to Lowestoft or Scotland. There are about 60 to 100 call-outs in a year. Redwings is one of the few organisations that guarantees to 'have a look' if there is an adverse report on the condition of a horse.

When I got to the call out place, I might try to see the owner. I always carried a copy of my birth certificate to show them, as I got called a lot of different things! Redwings representatives have no power to enter private property, confiscate horses or anything like that. They are here to educate the public and offer advice where necessary.

Another part of my job was touring schools, clubs etc. giving slide shows and talks about good horse husbandry and how to spot if a horse has problems. Some people will call Redwings if they see a horse standing in a muddy field, because they think it is being mistreated. The Redwings Horse Sanctuary is a retirement home for horses that are no longer usable, but which still have quality of life. This does not stop people calling Redwings to ask us to take their horses for all sorts of reasons. I really would like to emphasise to these people that a horse is for life, not for just as long as it suits you.

Redwings prefer to have a few paid employees to look after their equines, rather than a lot of volunteers. There are usually one to three volunteers helping out in any one year, and on open days when the public visit, we have a lot of teenage volunteers helping groom the horses etc. which is great.

Useful Addresses

Blue Cross Equine Centre: Shilton Road, Burford, Oxon OX18 4PR; ☎01993-822483; www.thebluecross.org.uk. The Blue Cross animal charity has several horse protection centres in the UK. Each employs a centre manager, deputy centre manager and grooms. It is not essential for grooms to have prior experience of looking after horses although it is preferred. Jobs for grooms are advertised in the vacancies section of the above website. You should send your application to the Human Resources Department at the above address.

International League for the Protection of Horses: Anne Colvin House, Snetterton,

Norwich NR16 2LR; ☎0870 870 1927; fax 01953-498373; e-mail claines@ilph.org; www.ilph.org. Founded in 1927, the ILPH aims for the worldwide protection and rehabilitation of all kinds of equines including donkeys and mules. It has five recovery and rehabilitation centres in the UK and employs 16 full-time field officers who inspect horse sales and investigate reports of cruelty or neglect. Rehabilitated horses are loaned to new homes where their ongoing progress in monitored by regular visits. Human Resources manager is Elaine Sawyer.

Redwings Equine Welfare & Protection Agency: Redwings Horse Sanctuary, Hapton, Norwich, NR15 1SP; ☎01508-481000; fax 0870 4581947; www.redwings.co.uk; another sanctuary is the Open Day Centre, Caldecott Hall, Fritton, Norfolk N31 9EY (only Redwings centre open to the public). A third sanctuary is Redwings at Pigotts Farm, Tasborough, Norfolk. The current Chief Equine Welfare Officer is Nicholas de Brauwere. Jobs at the Redwings equine centres are advertised locally as the centres are fairly remote.

Ada Cole Memorial Sanctuary: Nazeing, Nr. Harlow, Waltham Abbey; 01992-892133; e-mail adacole@totalise.co.uk; www.adacole.co.uk Has about 60 horses. Always needs volunteer grooms.

Bransby Rest Home: Lincoln. Has about 250 total donkeys, horses and ponies. (01427-788464; www.bransbyhorses.co.uk). Volunteers always needed to help the 10 permanent staff.

Equine Cruelty Helpline: Port St Mary (01624-833922).

ILPH *Equine Rehabilitation Centre:* Lingfield. (01342-832420; e-mail iang@ilph.org; www.ilph.org). Has 40+ horses.

Fforest Uchaf Rescue Centre: Pontypridd. Horses, ponies and donkeys. (01443-480327; e-mail roy@pitponies.co.uk; www.pitponies.co.uk).

Home of Rest for Horses: Princes Risborough (01494-488464).

Hopefield Sanctuary: Brentwood. Horses and goats (01277-201110).

Horse & Pony Protection: Basildon (01268-584603).

Horse & Poney Protection: Tintern. (01291-689371).

Horse & Pony Rescue: Birmingham (0121-458 5689.

Horse & Pony Rescue: Newmarket. (01638-750713).

Humane Education Society: Equine Home (01625-520802).

Lockwood Donkey Sanctuary: Godalming. (01428-682409).

Luest Horses and Ponies: Camarthen. Horses and donkeys.(01550-740661.

Only Foals & Horses Rescue & Sanctuary: Accrington. (01254-235559.

Phyllis Harvey Sanctuary: Leeds. Horses and donkeys. (01132-676122).

Raleagh Equine Rescue: Crossgar, Northern Ireland. (01238-563110.

Redwings Horse Sanctuary: Hall Lane, Frettenham, Norwich NR12 7RW; ☎01603 737432; fax 01603-738286; www.redwings.co.uk Rescue home for ponies, donkeys and mules.

Remus Memorial Sanctuary: Ingatestone. (01277-356191).

Rest Home for Horses: Douglas (mainly older horses). (01624-67494).

Shetland Rescue: Liverpool. Shetland Ponies. (0151-425 4627).

USEFUL PUBLICATIONS

British Equestrian Directory: directory of all the trades associated with horses. Published by the British Equestrian Trade Association and the Equestrian Management Consultants. 2002 edition £12 including postage. Note that the next edition is likely to be on CD-Rom. Obtainable from the British Horse Society bookshop (01926-707762; www.britishhorse.com).

BHS Guide to Careers with Horses: 40 pages. £3.50 + 50 postage.

Working with Horses: Jenny Morgan. How To books 1999. £9.99.

Seasonal Work Opportunities

The following employers offer seasonal work with horses:

Cantreff Trekking Centre: Brecon, Powys LD3 8LR; ☎01874-665223.
Situated in the Brecon Beacon mountain range. Lots of riding involved and contact with people of all ages from many countries.
Pony trekking guides: Wages negotiable. Hours depend on the length of the treks, with possibility of overtime. Work is 6 days a week. Minimum age is 18. Pony Club B or BHS Stage I, also Riding and Road Safety qualifications essential. Must be experienced rider and able to get along well with people. Period of work 1 June or 1 July to 1 September. Applicants must be prepared to work the specified length of time. Interview essential. Applications from March to M. Evans.

Grand Western Horseboat Co.: The Wharf, Canal Hill, Tiverton, Devon EX16 4HX; ☎01884-253345; www.horseboat.co.uk.
This company runs horse-drawn barge trips along a peaceful canal with plenty of wildlife and nature. Needs a crew member for the horse-drawn barge and the work includes working with heavy horses, steering, roping and teamwork. Work is from 4 days a week; more in high season. Applicants should be aged 25+ and hold a driving licence and be of neat appearance. No accommodation. Apply from 1 April.

Grange Trekking Centre: The Grange, Capel-y-ffin, Abergavenny, Gwent NP7 7NP; ☎01873-890215.
A small, informal, family-run centre situated in a very rural area, high in the beautiful Black Mountains of Wales. Remote area with breathtaking scenery; eight miles to the nearest shops and no public transport.
Trek leader and Assistant leader: for a variety of work including mucking out, trek leading, tack cleaning, maintenance and dealing with customers. Some training available. Salary and hours negotiable. Free accommodation in caravan with shower block. Must be over 18 and qualifications preferable. Also the possibility of looking after two little girls for a few hours each day.

Mrs G S Rees: Cross Farm Racing, Sollom, Tartleton, Preston, Lancashire PR4 6HR; ☎01772-812780; fax 01772-812799.
Small, friendly yard situated in the Lancashire countryside, but near to Southport and Preston.
Stable staff: for racehorses. Wages of £176 per week, plus overtime when going to the meetings. To work 40 hours per week Mon-Fri and Saturdays until 1pm, plus one weekend in three to be worked. Must have experience and be a capable rider. Weight should be under 9st. 7lbs.

Knowle Farm Riding Centre: Timberscombe, Minehead, Somerset TA24 6TZ; ☎01643-841342; fax 01643-841644; e-mail knowlemnr@aol.com.
Knowle Manor is a residential riding holiday centre based in Exmoor National Park. Set in 80 acres of grounds with indoor heated swimming pool, trout lake, croquet and badminton areas.
R*iding instructor:* 5 days a week. £160+ per week. Must be qualified.
Ride leaders: 40 hours per week approx. £144+ per week. Experience essential. Riding and Road Safety qualifications.
   Work is from July to the end of August or preferably until September/October. Apply from February onwards.

KRB Thoroughbreds Ltd: Spigot Lodge, Leyburn, North Yorkshire DL8 4TL; ☎01969-625088; fax 01969-625099; e-mail karl@karlburke.co.uk.
Yard hand: to take care of racehorses. £200 per week.
Grooms: wages negotiable according to experience. Work involves grooming and riding racehorses.
   Minimum period of work is three months. Accommodation is available for £50 per week. Suitably qualified foreigners with fluent English are welcome.
   Applications at any time to Kathryn Warnett, Secretary at the above address.

Northfield Farm: Flash, near Buxton, Derbyshire SK17 OSW; ☎01298-22543; fax 01298-27849; e-mail northfield@btinternet.com.
BHS approved riding centre and working farm, located in a small village. 30 horses used including Andalusian stallion at stud.
Trek Leaders: must be competent riders, good with people and preferably car drivers. Needed from April to September for £90-£100 per week plus free board and lodging. Five and a half days per week. Riding and Road Safety Test and First Aid qualification also preferred.
Apply from March. No applications before March please.

Northumbria Horse Holidays. East Castle, Annfield Plain, Stanley, Co. Durham DH9 8PH; ☎01207-230555.
A horse-riding skills centre that offers fully catered holidays for riders of all abilities.
Post Trail Leaders: from £164 per week. Good horse and riding skills and pleasant personality.
Riding Instructors: from £200 per week. Must have BHS Certificate or foreign equivalent.
   Work period is from Easter to the end of October. Minimum period of work two months.

Panama Sports Horses. The Stables Cottage, Gisburn Park, Gisburn, Lancashire BB7 4HU; (tel/fax 01200-445687); e-mail work@panamasportshorses.co.uk).
Yard staff: to work all summer looking after horses, assisting at shows and carrying out general yard work. Wages are negotiable depending on age and experience. Accommodation is available.
   For further details and for applications, contact Ailsa Richardson.

R A Fahey. Manor Farm, Butterwick, Malton, North Yorkshire Y017 6PS; ☎01653-628001; fax 01653-628959. The following summer staff are needed for racing yard:
Stable staff: to care for/ride out racehorses. Five and a half days per week plus alternate weekends.
Work riders: to work 7am-12.30pm, 3.30pm-5.30pm and Sat 7am-12.30pm.
   Staff needed from May to September. Overtime paid when attending race meetings. Some bonuses based on racehorse success. If riding, must be very capable and light weight. Age 16+.
   Applications to J H Hardy.

Rhiwiau Riding Centre. Llanfairfechan, North Wales LL33 OEH; ☎01248-680094; fax 01248-681143; e-mail rhiwiau@aol.com; www.rhiwiau.co.uk.
Instructor/ride leader: to work from 8am-5.30pm, 5 days per week. Wages of £100 per week with full board provided. Must be aged over 18 and wither a BHS Preliminary Teaching or BET qualification.
   Period of work is June to September. Applications to Ruth Hill.

Rookin House Equestrian and Activity Centre. Troutbeck, Penrith, Cumbria CA11 OSS; ☎01768-483561; fax 01768-483276; e-mail deborah@rookinhouse.co.uk.

Equestrian centre offering trekking, hacking and lessons. Also multi activity centre.
Trek Leaders: wages from £150 per week, to work 40 hours per week. Applicants should be over 18, hold Riding and Road Safety qualifications. Accommodation is available at £20 per week. Overseas applicants with fluent English and work permit welcome.

Snowdonia Riding Stables. Waunfawr, Caernarfon LL55 4PQ; ☎01286-650342; e-mail riding @snowdonia2000.fsnet.co.uk.
A trekking centre/riding school with approximately 50 horses including dressage/event horses, young stock and liveries.
Trek Leaders: work includes care of horses, yard work, trek leading and light maintenance work. Wages negotiable. 40 hours per week. Applicants must be over 18 with good riding ability. Staff are required from mid-July to mid-September. Applications from overseas welcome. Self-catering accommodation in caravans is provided free of charge.
Mrs R Thomas at the above address from spring onwards.

Tal y Foel Riding Centre. Dwyran, Anglesey LL61 6LQ; ☎01248-430377).
A friendly BHS approved centre on the shores of the Menai Straits. Facilities include indoor and outdoor manège, cross-country training course, four miles of grass tracks, liveries, lessons and treks.
Yard staff/ride leaders: £75 per week plus free accommodation in a caravan. To work from June to August. Minimum period of work is 8 weeks. Must be qualified in riding and stable management. Overseas applicants welcome if available to be interviewed.

Tyn-Morfa Riding Centre. Rhosneigr, Anglesey LL64 5QX; ☎01407-810072.
A riding centre situated on the west coast of Anglesey at Rhosneigr within minutes of some of Anglesey's best beaches. It is one of north Wales's oldest riding establishments and beach riding is a speciality.
Trek leaders or assistants: to escort rides on the beach. Wages negotiable according to age and experience. 8am-5pm, 6 days per week. Free board, and lodging in a caravan. Applicants should be aged 18+, be able to ride well and be responsible enough to take charge of rides. Season begins mid-May.
Applications from 1 April to Mr C P Carnall.

West Anstey Farm Exmoor. Dulverton, Somerset TA22 9RY; ☎01398-341354.
A working farm and stables adjoining open moorland four miles from Dulverton, the nearest town. Lovely riding country of moorland, fields and woods.
Riding Assistants: must be capable to take out rides and lead beginners when necessary. Hours vary depending on schedule of activities. Minimum age 16. Must be fairly light, a good rider with experience of going on riding holidays or of conducting treks and caring for ponies, horses and people. Sense of fun, helpfulness and a cheerful disposition essential. Must also be willing to help indoors when necessary.
Pocket money and board and lodging provided. Accommodation is all female. Minimum work period is 8-10 weeks.

Woodlands Stables. Woodlands Lane, Market Rasen, Lincolnshire LN8 5RE; ☎07971-940087.
Stables with 25 horses in training for flat and jump races.
Stable hands: to ride and take care of horses and for general stable work. Wages from £125-£200 per week depending on experience. To work from 7am-4pm with 3 hours for lunch. Minimum period of work is 3 months. Positions are available all year. Applicants should weigh under 10 stone, not smoke, ride well and live in. Accommodation cost is £10 per week. Interview necessary. Apply to Mr. Chapman.

Zoos, Safari Parks, Aquaria & Circuses

ZOOS

Wild animals are still exhibited in zoos in environmentally deprived conditions with scant attention paid to their physical and psychological wellbeing. A number of European zoos have recently been exposed to criticism for their poor animal care and welfare records. Cramped sterile cages for powerful, agile beasts naturally designed to forage vast expanses, and inadequate veterinary care for the ailments and problems associated with captivity, produce distressing sights like big cats pacing up and down in tiny cages, and prey and predator housed within sight of each other. These do nothing to attract the public and have helped to give some zoos a bad reputation. There are however many excellent zoos and some, like Edinburgh, have gone to enormous lengths to provide environmentally appropriate enclosures for their species, where their lives if not natural, are at least relatively fulfilled. Indeed, for some species, zoos are a lot safer than the wild where their lives are liable to be 'nasty, brutish and short'.

It may be some comfort, whatever your opinion of zoos in general, that Britain has a better reputation for zoo standards than some of its European neighbours, thanks to statutory legislation and inspections. Italy and Greece, neither of which have licensing, conditions in 1998 were singled out as particularly appalling.

When it comes to consideration of the animal world's welfare it often seems that Britain takes the initiative. In 1998 Britain led a campaign for the adoption of an EU directive to establish minimum conditions for zoos throughout the European Union and to enhance the very important species conservation role that zoos and safari parks fulfill through their breeding programmes.

In the last thirty years conservation has probably become the most important function of zoos, as they can provide controlled environment breeding programmes which are the final hope for the growing number of species hovering on the verge of extinction. Equally vital is the role of zoos in education and raising awareness of the irreplaceable richness and variety of the world's wildlife and what can and should be done to preserve it. Britain is at the forefront of breeding and conservation projects. Increasingly, animals are bred in captivity with the aim of releasing them back into their native habitats.

Britain has over 200 zoos, which is more than most other European countries (Italy for instance, has 80). Sixty British and one Irish zoo belong to the Federation of Zoological Gardens of Britain and Ireland. This federation was founded in 1966 by seven zoos: Bristol, Chester, Dublin, Edinburgh, London, Paignton, Dudley, which together established their own system of standards and inspections. These became the basis of the Zoo Licensing Act of 1981, which regulates British zoos and covers all aspects of animal husbandry as well as safety regulations for staff and the visiting public. However, what was acceptable in 1981 is not necessarily so in 2003 and conditions are subject to regular review and progress as wider knowledge about animals and what improves their well-being is put into practical usage.

The Zoo Licensing Act covers a wide range of establishments including zoological gardens, safari/wildlife parks, aquariums/vivariums, wildfowl and wetland reserves, bird centres and even butterfly farms. All zoos have their own particular character, which derives in part from who owns or runs them. This can be a zoological society, charitable trust, local authority or private owner or business.

Employment

The 80 largest zoos in Britain employ about 2,500 people between them, i.e. an average of 32 employees per zoo. However, many small zoos, often privately run, employ a handful of staff while the largest employer Chester employs about 165 permanent staff plus an additional 150 in high season. Only 47 of these are keepers who work directly with the animals. Large zoos also employ a range of other staff which may include all or some of the following, depending on the individual establishment: gardeners, grounds staff, maintenance/transport personnel, catering and retail staff, administration staff, education staff, marketing and public relations staff. They may also employ vets, veterinary nurses and laboratory and stores staff.

The majority of temporary jobs related to zoo-keeping are work experience schemes lasting a minimum of one month. These are open to school students age sixteen or above and are most suitable for those considering an animal studies related career. Zoology and Veterinary university students who require practical experience with animals as part of their studies are also taken on. Larger zoos are the most likely to accept job experience trainees from abroad. Conditions vary for these, but those coming from abroad should be prepared to be self-funding.

ZOO KEEPER

Zoo keeping is considered a vocation rather than a temporary or seasonal job. Most zoos will expect applicants to have some previous experience of animal husbandry although the amount of experience and qualifications required varies greatly. Chester for instance, expects a minimum of a Diploma in Animal Management and four years' experience for permanent keeper applicants. However, despite the competition for zoo-keeping posts, Nicholas Gould, Editor of *International Zoo News* is encouraging about access prospects:

> *the zoo world is not a closed shop – more like a club which anyone really interested can join*

The ideal way to 'join the club' would be to take part in the zoo volunteer scheme, which many zoos have. This was the route followed by John Partridge, Asssistant Currator at Bristol Zoo (where he has worked for 27 years). John worked as an unpaid volunteer at Barry Zoo (now defunct) while he was still at school, moved to Bristol zoo when he had gained experience, and worked his way up to his current post. Bristol Zoo has its own volunteer scheme which also works like a probation period:

> **John Partridge on Bristol Zoo's volunteers**
> *Bristol zoo volunteers come for one or two days a week. They get experience and we get to assess their aptitude. A lot of people don't stay long because the work is physically hard. After they have been a volunteer for about seven months, if there is a vacancy, they may get the job. Bristol zoo is very supportive towards its staff and will pay the costs of the City and Guilds Certificate in Animal Management which is a correspondence course.*

There are other routes to zoo-keeping if the direct approach is unsuccessful: for instance, it is possible to be engaged for a seasonal job in another department and charm your way into the animal section in one brief season if you are seen to be a natural Doctor Dolittle. Getting your face, your aptitude and your ambition known are the first steps. At Knowsley Safari Park that most of the ranger staff had no 'appropriate' qualifications or experience when they arrived and were trained on the job by senior staff.

> **John Hall on working at Knowsley Safari Park**
> *Last summer, one of the temporary summer staff working in the service area stayed on as an apprentice ranger. The atmosphere at Knowsley is unique and relaxed. The first job an apprentice keeper usually gets is to hold open gates. It takes five or six years to progress to dealing with the lion enclosure.*

The keeper's job is a varied one, although one did describe it as 'shovelling the food in at one end and shovelling it up at the other' there is a lot more to it than that. Cleaning the animal quarters is certainly an inescapable part of the job (the animals at Paignton Zoo produce three tonnes of droppings a day) but there is a whole range of other aspects to exotic animal management. Food preparation has become a precision science in the last dozen years and the zookeeper is responsible for ensuring his or her charges get a balanced diet including supplements where necessary. Keepers may also be expected to replicate natural feeding patterns. For instance big cats are fed fresh meat every four days at Port Lympne Wildlife Park because that is how they feed in the wild. The zoo keeper is also responsible for ensuring that the animals behave as naturally as possible and do not show signs of boredom or behave repetitively, which was a common feature of zoos twenty or so years ago (and still is in some countries). This is done by devising games and making the animals 'work' for their food by hiding it, placing it in receptacles (for chimps) so the lids have to be removed, providing stone nesting rings for penguins etc. All these techniques come under the heading of behavioural and environmental enrichment and are a developing area in which input from, and monitoring by, the keeper is very important.

Animal guardians also have to be observant enough to notice any changes in their charges' behaviour or appearance that may indicate illness or discomfort.

Another area of keeper concern is the design of the enclosures themselves, which have both to display the animals naturally to the public and provide the animals with protection from adverse weather such as extreme heat or cold. The safety of the enclosures for both beasts and public is equally important and barriers and fences have to be checked for weaknesses, and wear and tear. Pranksters have to be stopped from climbing barriers or feeding the animals with unsuitable or idiotic titbits.

> **John Partridge on the highs and lows of the keeper's work**
> *One of the worst aspects is waking up on a mid-winter morning when it is minus five outside and realising that you still have to go out there to feed the animals. It's not too bad at Bristol because we have only 12 acres, but somewhere spread out like Whipsnade or Marwell must be much worse.*
> *The best part of the job is undoubtedly your relationship with the animals themselves. You get to see them as individuals and it is inevitable that you develop special relationships with some of the 'higher' animals.*

It is perhaps obvious, but still worth stating that keepers should be a fountain of knowledge about their particular species including its geographical distribution, typical behaviour in various situations, dietary needs and habits, status in the wild, gestation period, the number of young etc. and that they can transmit their fascination to the public when required. In both safari parks and zoos keepers may have to remove any plants and weeds that may be harmful or poisonous to the animals. In small zoos keepers may also double up as a gardener/groundsperson. Communication with zoo visitors is also part of the job. Dealing with visitors' curiosity about the animals often means answering the same questions many times. Larger zoos are likely to have an education department and gifted and qualified keepers who may sometimes also be zoologists, may find themselves required to take the podium lecturing and educating the public of all ages.

Communicating with zoo visitors is also part of the job

SAFARI PARKS

Safari parks have been described as zoos where the humans are in cages (i.e. cars) and the animals are free. People who find zoos unappealing because of the confinement of the animals, often feel that a safari park is the next best way to see wild animals apart from their native habitats. The zookeeper in a safari park is transformed into a wildlife ranger which is essentially the same thing, but it sounds more exciting and they might get to drive around in a zebra-striped 4x4. Safari parks tend to be somewhat more informal than zoos, which are more inclined to stress their scientific credentials. In addition to animal care duties, wardens or rangers in safari parks will patrol the park making sure that the public is safe and not behaving irresponsibly by disembarking from their vehicles or picnick-ing in the lion enclosure. The rangers also rescue anyone having a vehicular or nervous breakdown.

USEFUL ADDRESSES

Association of British Wild Animal Keepers (ABWAK): c/o Laura Gardner, Leeds Castle, Maidstone, Kent ME17 1PL; www.abwak.co.uk. Send a stamped addressed envelope with request for careers information.

Cannington College: Cannington, Bridgwater, Somerset TA5 2LS; ☎01278-655123; fax 01278-655055; e-mail enquiries@cannington.ac.uk; www.cannington.ac.uk Offers a range of courses, from BTEC First Diploma in Animal Care through to Foundation degree or Certificate of Higher Education in Animal Science. Veterinary nursing courses, herpetology and equine care and management also available. Courses

Rangers make sure no one is picknicking in the lion's enclosure

can be studied on either a full or part-time basis at the main campus at Yeovil, or the centres within Bristol and Paignton zoos

Federation of Zoological Gardens of Britain and Ireland: Regent's Park, London NW1 4RY; ☎020-7586 0230; e-mail fedzoo@zsl.org; www.zoofederation.org.uk. Send s.a.e. for a list of Federation member zoos.

University of Edinburgh: Royal (Dick) School of Veterinary Studies, Division of Veterinary Clinical Studies, Animal Behaviour and Welfare Group, Easter Bush Veterinary Centre, Easter Bush, Roslin, Midlothian EH25 9RG; ☎0131-651 6259; fax 0131-651 3913. At the time of press, details of new short courses applicable to zoo staff were unavailable. The department also offers an MSc in applied animal behaviour and animal welfare.

Zoo Volunteer Scheme: The Co-ordinator, Bristol Zoo Gardens, Clifton, Bristol, Somerset, BS8 3HA; ☎0117-970 6176; www.bristolzoo.org.uk.

Zoological Society of Glasgow and the West of Scotland: Glasgow Zoo, Calderpark, Uddingston, Glasgow G71 7RZ; ☎0141-771 1185; fax 0141-771 2615; www.glasgowzoo.co.uk. Dedicated to conservation and education and to the creation of good zoological parks in the west of Scotland.

AQUARIA

MARINE & FRESHWATER BIOLOGISTS

Marine biologists concentrate on the plants and creatures in the oceans and freshwater biologists on lakes and rivers. Two of the main areas of scientific concern are pollution and depleted fish stocks resulting from over fishing. The work can be in the field and/ or the laboratory. There are many other speciality niches for marine and freshwater biologists but these two main areas produce the majority of commercial employment opportunities for instance with the Natural Environment Research Council or the Ministry of Agriculture, Fisheries and Food. Freshwater biologists also work for water companies and environmental agencies. There are normally more people qualified in marine and freshwater biology than there is employment for them and government appointments are decreasing along with departmental budgets.

To qualify as a marine/freshwater biologist you can either study for a first degree in the subject or take a first degree in biology followed by a higher one in marine/freshwater biology. Details of 23 first degree and combined courses in marine/freshwater biology can be obtained from a careers office or a degree course guide such as that published by the Careers Research Advisory Council (CRAC).

Working in Aquaria

Probably the most appealing job for a marine biologist, and the one most relevant to this book is as an aquarist at an aquarium, ocean park or other places where captive marine life is managed. The very talented can end up as the curator of such an establishment. Juan Romero is the General Curator of the National Marine Aquarium in Plymouth which he describes as 'the Marine Biology capital of Europe.' He came to the National Marine Aquarium when it was 'just a building site at the end of 1997' after an international upbringing and career: he is Spanish, born and raised in Venezuela, studied marine biology in Montpellier, France, worked with the late Jaques Cousteau, which gave him a fascination with sharks, worked for a goverment body in the United States and was curator at the Genoa aquarium in Italy.

Juan Romer on his current post and aquarium work

Conservation work is my main love and I was attracted by the job offered me here because the National Marine Aquarium is the only aquarium that is a charitable trust run for conservation, education and research. I would say that a curator's job is 50% office-based doing administration, and in my case, 25% aquarist work and 25% conservation. In the USA this job would be called Director of Husbandry Operations. There is a trend now for aquaria to deal with both underwater and above water creatures like reptiles and penguins and to create real environments for them – like here, we have real trees, grass and flowers growing. Eventually we may have some types of birds too.

I have half a dozen hands-on aquarium staff ranging from those with years of experience but no specialist qualifications, to Ph.D students. We also take work experience people, often as part of a course in animal care, who come for a minimum of four weeks and preferably six. Trainees who come to us from other EU countries through the Leonardo da Vinci programme, which also funds their stays of about nine months.

An aquarist must be practical; it's a practical job which needs lots of common sense and a love of animals as well as basic science qualifications.

Apart from dedicated aquaria, a number of zoos have a marine section. Typically, an aquarium will have a main section, which is on show to the public and an off show part where quarantine, breeding programmes and conservation projects are carried out. British aquaria are generally small scale compared those in the USA and Japan.

Useful Addresses & Publication

Anglesey Sea Zoo: Brynsiencyn, Isle of Anglesey, North Wales, LL61 6TQ; ☎01248-430411; fax 01248-430411; e-mail fishandfun@seazoo.demon.co.uk; www.angleseyseazoo.co.uk

Anglesey Sea Zoo operates with a base of volunteers, mainly marine biologists who help generally in the zoo, caring for the fish and communicating with the public and helping them to understand more about marine life. The zoo has a breeding and conservation policy and volunteers should be familiar with the range of specimens, species and habitats on display.

Full training will be given, but volunteers are expected to commit for a reasonable period of time. Most stay for a whole season, volunteering for 1 or 2 days a week, but alternative periods will be considered.

Volunteers from abroad will be given consideration if their English is good. A reasonable degree of fitness is essential and a driving licence is recommended, as the zoo is quite remote. No accommodation but daily expenses paid after trial period.

For other aquaria, see under *Directory of Zoos and Aquaria.*

Aquarium Sciences and Conservation: Chapman and Hall, 2-6 Boundary Row, London SE1 8HN. Periodical.

British Marine Life Study Society: 14 Corbyn Crescent, Shoreham-by-Sea, Sussex BN43 6PQ; ☎01273-465433. Publishes the newsletter *Glaucus.*

Institute of Biology: 20 Queensbury Place, London SW7 2DZ; ☎020-7581 8333.

Marine Biological Association: The Laboratory, Citadel Hill, Plymouth, Devon PL1 2PB.

SEA LIFE CENTRES

The Sea Life Centres are a chain of aquariums and marine sanctuaries owned by Merlin Entertainments Group. There are nine in Britain (including, the National Seal Sanctuary in Cornwall). There are also Sea Life centres in Belgium, Finland, Germany (3), France, The Netherlands and Spain.

The head office of the Sea Life Centres and Sanctuaries is: Merlin Entertainments Group Ltd.(3 Market Close, Poole, Dorset, BH15 1NQ; ☎01202-666900; fax 01202-661303; www.sealife.co.uk and www.sealsanctuary.co.uk.

Birmingham National Sea Life Centre: (☎0121-643 6777). Overlooking the city's canal network. Over 60 Marine and fresh water displays of different creatures. Has a 360-degree transparent walkthrough tunnel through a display of sharks, stingrays and giant skates.

Blackpool Sea Life Centre: (01253-621258). Includes a giant tropical shark display (black-tipped reef, sand tiger, brown etc.). Seahorse conservation centre.

Brighton Sea Life Centre: (☎01273-604234). Special feature: convalescence facility for endangered sea turtles.

Hunstanton Sea Life Sanctuary: Southern Promenade, Hunstanton, Norfolk PE36 5BH; ☎01485-533576; fax 01485-533531; e-mail Hunstanton@merlinentertainments.biz; www.sealsanctuary.co.uk). Aquatic life (fish, penguins, otters and seals; specialising in the rehabilitation of seal pups). Employs 20 staff.

Great Yarmouth Sea Life Centre: Marine Parade, Great Yarmouth, Norfolk NR30 3AH; ☎01493-330631; fax 01493-330442; www.sealife.co.uk. Tropical and British marine life. Has an ocean display with a variety of tropical sharks from two-foot juveniles, to nine-foot specimens of nurse shark. 12 staff. Voluntary experience is a useful asset when considering work in this field.

National Seal Sanctuary: Gweek, Near Helston, Cornwall; ☎01326-221361; www.sealsanctuary.co.uk. Includes a Seal Hospital with intensive care and isolation units, special treatment cubicles, convalescents' pools and more for the rehabilitation of sickly pups. When rehabilitated they are released back into the wild.

Oban Scottish Sea Life Sanctuary: (☎01631-720386; www.sealsanctuary.co.uk). In addition to being an aquarium, Oban Sea Life is Scotland's largest marine mammal rescue centre, which cares for dozens of sick, injured and orphaned seal pups every year. It operates a 'rear and release' programme for rescued common seal pups.

Scarborough Sea Life Centre: (☎01723-373414). Aquarium and resident and rescued seal pups; also otter sanctuary and sea turtle convalescence facility.

Weymouth Sea Life Park & Marine Sanctuary: (☎01305-761070): Aquarium with thousands of sea creatures. A special feature is the Tropical Shark Lagoon which is a sanctuary set up to take in sharks which have outgrown their tanks or which are homeless. Also a seal sanctuary for resident adult seals which are unable to be returned to the wild, an otter sanctuary with a successful breeding record and a penguin sanctuary.

DIRECTORY OF ZOOS AND AQUARIA

Banham Zoo: The Grove, Banham, Norfolk NR16 2HE; ☎01953-887771; fax 01953-887445.

Birdland: Rissington Road, Bourton-on-the-Water, Cheltenham, Gloucestershire GL54 2BN; ☎01451-820480; fax 01451-822398; e-mail sb.birdland@virgin.net.

Blackpool Zoo Park: East Park Drive, Stanley Park, Blackpool, Lancashire FY3 8PP; ☎01253-830830; fax 01253-830800; Covers 32 acres. Employs 17 keepers and 2 trainee keepers. Specialises in marsupials. Contact the Zoo Manager for details.

Blue Reef Aquarium, Portsmouth: (☎023-92875222; e-mail bluereefaquarium@portsm outh.co.uk; www.bluereefaquarium.co.uk).

Bristol Zoo Gardens: Clifton, Bristol, BS8 3HA; ☎0117-9747300; fax 0117-9736814; e-mail info@bristolzoo.org.uk; www.bristolzoo.org.uk. World famous Bristol Zoo is a private, non-profit organisation in 12 acres. Amongst the avian attractions is a walk-in aviary where visitors can stroll amongst exotic plants and free flying birds. Total staff of 140 (includes non-keeping staff).

Camperdown Wildlife Centre: Camperdown Country Park, Coupar Angus Road, Dundee, DD2 4TF, Scotland; 01382-432 661; fax 01382-432660.

Chessington World of Adventures: Human Resources Dept., Thorpe Park and Chessington World of Adventures, P.O. Box 125, Chessington KT9 2WL; ☎01372-725050; fax 01372-731570; www.chessington.com. Started as a private collection of wild animals in 1931, became a zoological gardens in 1935 and added a theme park in 1987. Closes to the public in winter. The zoo specialises in primates and invertebrates. About 165 staff.

Chester Zoo: Upton-by-Chester, Chester, Cheshire CH2 1LH; ☎01244-380280; fax 01244-371273; e-mail info@chesterzoo.co.uk; www.chesterzoo.org. 109 acres. 187 staff of which about 47 are keepers (30 mammal, 12 bird, 5 aquarium/reptile).

Chestnut Centre Conservation Park: Castleton Road, Chapel-en-le-Frith, Derbyshire SK23 6PE; ☎01298-814099; fax 01298-816213; www.ottersandowls.co.uk. Founded in 1984. Owl and otter haven covering several acres in the Peak District national park. Five types of Otter including giant Amazon otters which grow two metres long and several types of owl. Employs two full-time animal keepers and occasionally takes work experience trainees. Trainees must stay a minimum of two weeks and be enrolled on an animal-related course at college or university.

Churnet Valley Wildlife Park: Spinks Lane, Kingsley, Cheadle, Staffordshire, ST10 2BX; tel/fax 01538-756702.

Colchester Zoo: Stanway Hall, Maldon Road, Colchester, Essex CO3 5SL; ☎01206-330253; fax 01206-331392; e-mail admin@colchester-zoo; www.colchester-zoo. Privately owned zoo covering 24 acres. Has fifty staff and specialises in primates and cats.

Cotswold Wildlife Park: Burford, Oxfordshire, OX18 4JW; ☎01993-823006; fax 01993-823807; www.cotswoldwildlifeparkc.co.uk

Curraghs Wildlife Park: Ballaugh, Ramsey, Isle of Man IN7 5EA; ☎01624-897323; www.gov.im/wildlife. 40 acres and 185 acres bird and botanical. Ten staff. Specialises in otters.

Drayton Manor Family Theme Park: Tamworth, Staffordshire B78 3TW; ☎01827-252400; fax 01827-288916; e-mail info@draytonmanor.co; www.draytonmanor.co.uk

Dudley & West Midlands Zoological Society: 2 The Broadway, Dudley, West Midlands

DY1 4QB; ☎01384-252401; fax 01384-456048. Non-profit zoological society. 46 acres. Specialises in Arabian gazelle. 50 staff.

Drusillas Zoo Park Ltd: Alfriston, East Sussex BN26 5QS; ☎01323-874100; fax 01323-874101; e-mail drusilla@drusilla.demon.co.uk; www.drusillas.co.uk DZP began in 1922 as tea-rooms with a small menagerie of exotic animals as a gimmick. In 1997 the then private owner sold it to another private owner, former millionaire businessman Laurence Smith, who runs it with his family. The zoo is small by zoo standards and specialises appropriately in small species of which there are nearly 60 on site including, lemurs, meerkats, monkeys, wallabies, otters, pythons, crocodiles and fruit bats. The zoo employs 14 keepers.

Edinburgh Zoo: Murrayfield, Edinburgh, EH12 6TS; ☎0131-334 9171; fax 0131-314 0382; e-mail aalabaster@rzss.org.uk; www.edinburghzoo.org.uk. Owned by the Royal Zoological Society of Scotland, a registered charity promoting the conservation of endangered animals through breeding, education, and by inspiring the visitors. 82 acres. 180 staff.

Exmoor Zoological Park: Bratton Fleming, Nr. Barnstaple, North Devon EX31 4SG; ☎01598-763352.

Flamingo Land: Kirby Misperton, Malton, Yorks YO17 OUX; ☎01653-668287; fax 01653-668280; e-mail zoo@flamingoland.co.uk; www.flamingoland.co.uk. 99 acre zoo in a 358 acre park. Number of staff working directly with animals about 20.

Folly Farm: Begelly, Kilgetty, Pembrokeshire SA68 OXA; ☎01834-812731; fax 01834-813148; www.folly-farm.co.uk.

Glasgow Zoo: Calderpark, Uddingston, Glasgow G71 7RZ, Scotland; ☎0141-771 1185/6; fax 0141-771 2615. 49 acres. 32 staff. Specialises in reptiles and education.

Harewood Bird Garden: Harewood House, Harewood, Leeds LS17 9LQ; tel/fax 0113-2813723; fax 0113-2181034; e-mail birdgdn@harewood.org; www.harewood.org. Harewood (pronounced Harwood) was started in 1969 and is a general collection of 500 birds from 120 species. The centre employs 4 full-time keepers, a gardener and an administrator. This last maintains the records of the rare species (which include Mauritius pink pigeons and Bali starlings) breeding programmes. There are usually one or two trainees on work experience programmes and one to three university students working on projects related to zoology, animal behaviour etc. They pay their own expenses including accommodation.

The Hawk Conservancy: Weyhill, Near Andover, Hampshire SP11 8DY; ☎01264-773850; fax 01264-733722; e-mail info@hawk-conservancy.org; www.hawk-conservancy.org. Six staff.

Howletts (Canterbury) & Port Lympne (Hythe): The John Aspinall Wild Animal Parks, Port Lympne, Hythe, Kent CT21 4PD; ☎01303-264647; fax 01303-264944; e-mail info@howletts.net; www.howletts.net. Howletts and Port Lympne zoos are part of the same charitable foundation founded by John Aspinall for the breeding of rare and endangered animals with the aim of introducing them back into the wild. Howletts has 31 keeping/animal staff plus 62 other staff. A few staff are taken on annually for which there are dozens of applications. Head keepers are either qualified or very experienced. Apprentice keepers need enthusiasm and a genuine interest in the animals more than a raft of qualifications and they will be trained on the job. Zoology students and young people on work experience schemes are also welcomed. Howletts specialises in primates, especially gorillas. Other animals include African elephants, tigers, monkeys, wolves, bongo, bison and dhole. For details of Port Lympne, see below.

Jersey Wildlife Preservation Trust: Les Augrès Manor, Trinity, Jersey JE3 5BP, Channel Islands, British Isles; ☎01534-864666; fax 01534-860001; e-mail jerseyzoo@durrell.org; www.jerseyzoo.org. A non-profit trust which specialises in the breeding and study of rare and endangered species. 27 acres. 90 staff total (all departments).

Kirkleatham Owl Centre: Kirkleatham Village, Redcar TS10 5NW; 01642-480512; fax 01642-492790; www.jillsowls.co.uk. Started in 1991, the Centre is small and family-run with a varying owl population of owls from around the world, and rescued injured owls. The centre is open every day except Monday, all year round. Takes non-residential volunteers for work experience.

Knowsley Safari Park: Prescot, Merseyside L34 4AN; ☎0151-430 9009; fax 0151-426 3677; e-mail safari.park@knowsley.com; www.knowsley.com Knowsley covers 550 acres and its animal collection includes: antelope, elephants, buffalo, camels and lions. It has over a dozen wildlife rangers and occasionally takes trainees on animal husbandry courses, or in a gap year before studying zoology etc.

Linton Zoological Gardens: Hadstock Road, Linton, Cambridgeshire CB1 6NT; ☎01223-891308; 01223-891308.

Liverpool Museum Aquarium, National Museums and Galleries on Merseyside: William Brown Street, Liverpool L3 8EN; ☎0151-478 4314; fax 0151-478 4249; e-mail Denis.murphy@nmgm.org; www.nmgm.org.uk. Curator of aquarium is Denis Murphy.

London Zoo: (Part of the Zoological Society of London which also owns Whipsnade Wild Animal Park), Regent' Park, London NW1 4RY; ☎020-7722 3333; fax 020-7586 5743; www.zsl.org. Site covers 36 acres. The largest zoo in terms of species and staff (270 total of which about 50 are keepers) in Britain. A possible route to keeping is through summer (April to September) employment when a number of paid extra keepers are taken on. Some weekend work is expected but two days off in the week are given. Applicants must have an animal qualification or some experience of working with animals.

Lotherton Hall Bird Garden: Towton Road, Near Aberford, Leeds, LS25 3EB; ☎01132-813723.

The Lions of Longleat: Longleat Park, Warminster, Wiltshire BA12 7RJ; ☎01985-844328. Owned by the Marquess of Bath. 296 acre park and lake. Open March to October. About 400 mammals and twelve reptiles. 30 staff employed.

Marwell Zoological Park: Colden Common, Winchester, Hants SO21 1JH; ☎01962-777407; fax 01962-777511; e-mail marwell@marwell.org.uk; www.marwell.org.uk. 100 acres. Charitable Trust. Large collections of hoofed animals, big cats, primates, and many bird species. 30-35 keeper staff. Applicants should be over 18 and either on, or about to embark on a recognised course of animal-related study. Applications to the Deputy Curator to the above address or e-mail.

Mole Hall Wildlife Park: Widdington, Saffron Walden, Essex, CB11 3SS; ☎01799-540400; fax 01799-542 408; e-mail enquiries@molehall.co.

National Birds of Prey Centre: Newent, Gloucestershire GL18 1JJ; ☎01531-821581; fax 01531-821389; e-mail jpj@nbpc.demon.co.uk; www.nbpc.co.uk. Has an average of 300 birds and 85 species. Specialises in owls and raptors. Employs 7-8 bird staff. Work experience available.

National Marine Aquarium: The Barbican, Plymouth, Devon, PL4 OLH; ☎01752-220084; www.National-Aquarium.co.uk. A senior aquarist is responsible for others each of whom is responsible for a tank. The most important task each day is to feed the one thousand or so fish and other marine life at the aquarium. Work begins at 8am. The other important part of the job is observation – aquarists look out for any signs of disease or other problems in their assigned tank. They are also responsible for maintenance and dealing with questions from the public. Diving is part of the day-to-day work. For maintenance as well as selective feeding of fish. Senior aquarists are involved in conservation and research programmes.

Natureland Seal Sanctuary: North Parade, Skegness, Lincs PE25 1DB; tel/fax 01754-764345; e-mail natureland@ffbdial.co.uk; www.skegnessnatureland.co.uk. Specialist in rehabilitation of rescued, orphaned Common and Grey seal pups and the captive breeding of seals and tropical marine fish. Employs 8 staff. Has work experience weeks for veterinary students and those studying animal care.

New Forest Otter, Owl and Wildlife Conservation Park: Deerleap Lane, Longdown, Ashurst, Southampton, Hampshire S04 4UH; ☎02380-292408; fax 02380-293367.

Norfolk Wildlife Centre & Country Park: Great Witchingham, Norwich, Norfolk NR9 5QS; ☎01603-872274; ☎01603-872274. Private organisation, The Philip Wayre Wildlife Trust. Small staff of 4. Specialises in endangered European species of European mammals and birds and rare domestic breeds.

The Owl Centre: Muncaster Castle, Ravenglass, Cumbria CR18 1RG; ☎01229-717393; fax 01229-717107; admin@owls.org.

Paignton Zoological & Botanical Gardens: Totnes Road, Paignton, Devon TQ4 7EU; ☎01803-557479; fax 01803-523457. 30 ha. Educational and scientific charity. 150 staff of which about a third are keepers. Cannington College (see useful addresses above) also has a centre at the zoo for the instruction and training of those doing a National Diploma in Animal Management.

Paradise Park: Hayle, Cornwall TR27 4HB; ☎01736-753365; fax 01736-751028; e-mail info@paradisepark.org.uk; www.paradisepark.org.uk Home of the World Parrot Trust. Specialises in parrots and exotic birds. 18 Staff. Has a waiting list for those wanting work experience/volunteers.

Paradise Wildlife Park: White Stubbs Lane, Broxbourne, Hertfordshire EN10 7QA; ☎01992-470490; fax 01992-440525; www.pwpark.com.

Port Lympne Wild Animal Park: Lympne, Hythe, Kent CT21 4PD; ☎01303-264647; fax 01303-264944; e-mail info@howletts.net; www.howletts.net. Part of the John Aspinall Charitable Foundation for the breeding of endangered animals for release back into the wild. The Wildlife Park centres upon an historic mansion built by Sir Herbert Baker in 1915 and 395 acres of enclosures. 64 staff are employed about 33 of whom deal directly with the animals which include black rhinoceroses, Indian elephants, lions and wolves.

Sea Aquarium Weston-super-Mare: (☎01934-641603). Located on its own pier, shows everything from seahorses to sharks.

Seaquarium Rhyl: (☎01745-344660; www.seaquarium.co.uk). Has over 70 species of native sea creatures from seahorses and sharks to octopus and stingrays.

St Andrews Aquarium: (☎01334-474786; e-mail info@standrewsaquarium.co.uk; www.standrewsaquarium.co.uk). Specialises in displaying the sea creatures of the Scottish coastline including outdoor seal pools, as well as a tropical collection.

Southport Zoo & Conservation Trust: Princes Park, Southport, Merseyside PR8 1RX; ☎01704-548894; fax 01704-538102; e-mail: info@southportzoo.co.uk; www.southportzoo.co.uk. Southport Zoo covers about six and a half acres. Specialises in small animals; the largest inmates are lions and chimpanzees. Other animals include snow leopard and fishing cats (from S.E. Asia), penguins, parrots and small monkeys. There are eight keepers, six of whom are part-time and two trainees. Apart from the trainees, applicants are expected to have at least two years zoo experience. Applications should be addressed to Tony Lewis, The Curator.

Tilgate Nature Centre: Tilgate Park, Crawley, West Sussex RH10 5PQ; ☎01293-521168; e-mail Tilgate@crawley.gov.uk

Tropical World: 1 Park Cottages, Roundhay Park, Leeds LS8 1DF; ☎0113-2661850; fax 0113-2370077.

Twycross Zoo: East Midlands Zoological Society Ltd, Twycross, Atherstone, Warwickshire CV9 3PX; ☎01827-880250; fax 01827-880700; www.twycrosszoo.com Private zoological society registered as an educational charity. Specialist in primates and education. 60 staff employed.

Underwater World, Hastings: (☎01424-718776; www.underwaterworld-hastings.co.uk). Includes a marine nursery with early life cycle of sharks, rays, cuttlefish, seahorses and more.

Whipsnade: Whipsnade Wild Animal Park, Whipsnade, Dunstable, Bedfordshire LU6 2LF; ☎01582-872171; fax 01582-872649. 260 ha. Owned by the Zoological Society of London which also owns London Zoo (see above). Specialises in herd animals. 80 staff employed.

The Wildfowl & Wetlands Trust – Martin Mere: Fish Lane, Burscough, Nr. Ormskirk, Lancs. L40 OTA; ☎01704-895181; fax 01704-892343; www.wwt.org.uk. Covers 400 acres of which 30 acres is given over to a captive breeding programme for rare waterfowl. There are only four full time wardens, the rest of the staff are volunteers and work experience trainees. The centre relies heavily on volunteers.

The Wildfowl & Wetlands Trust: District 15, Washington, Tyne and Wear NE38 8LE; ☎0191-416 5454; fax 0191-416 5801. Covers 100 acres, 70 acres of which are reserve and the rest birds in captivity. There are nine staff in order of seniority: wardens (3), senior warden (1) and grounds manager (1). There is a low turnover of staff and new appointments tend to be taken from those who have provided their services for years as volunteers.

Wildwood Centre: Wealden Forest Park, Herne Road, Herne Bay, Kent CT6 7LQ; enquiries@wildwood.co.uk.

Woburn Safari Park: Woburn, Bedfordshire MK17 9QN; ☎01525-290407; fax 01525-290489; e-mail info@woburnsafari.co.uk; www.woburnsafari.co.uk One of Britain's best known animal parks includes a 142 hectares safari park. As well as the safari park there is a free ranging deer park and a zoological park. The total collection for the three sites is nearly 2000 animals including the famous African lions and Bengal tigers as well as monkeys, birds, reptiles, invertebrates and deer. The collection manager is Dr. Jake Veasey and the Head Deer Keeper is Callum Thomson. Staff employed; 60-130 inclusive of seasonal staff. Site open to the public March to October inclusive and weekends only in winter.

The World Owl Centre: Muncaster Castle, Ravenglass, Cumbria CA18 1RQ; ☎01229-717393; 01229-717107; e-mail admin@owls.org; www.owls.org One of the best owl collections in the worlds. Has over 50 species/subspecies. Headquarters of the World Owl Trust. 10 staff.

TRAINING ANIMALS FOR ZOOS

If you want to train animals to perform, but a life on the road in a circus does not appeal, it is possible to train animals for zoos. For example London's Whipsnade zoo has sea lion 'demonstrations'. The sea lions are trained every day during the winter and in summer perform three times a day for the public and receive fishy rewards from their trainers.

Useful Publications

Publications in which zoo jobs are advertised include *Cage and Aviary Birds, International Zoo News* (tel/fax 01243-782803), and *Ratel* the journal of the Association of British Wild Animal Keepers (12 Tackley Road, Bristol BS5 6UQ). Other useful publications include:

International Zoo Yearbook: A list of zoos in the United Kingdom and around the world can be found in the *International Zoo Yearbook* published regularly by the Zoological Society of London (2003 edition £67). Details about availability and back volumes from Dept IZY, ZSL Scientfic Books, The Zoological Society of London, Regent's Park, London NW1 4RY, UK; ☎020-7449 6281; fax 020-7449 6411; e-mail yearbook@zsl.org; www.zsi.org The Yearbook can be consulted in major city libraries: National Library of Wales (Aberystwyth), The British Library (Legal Deposit Office, Boston Spa), University Library (Cambridge), Trinity College (Copyright Office Dublin), National Library of Scotland (Edinburgh), Bodleian Library (English

Accessions Section, Oxford) or at the Library of the Zoological Society in Regent's Park (☎020-7449 6411); e-mail fionafisken@zsl.org; www.zsl.org.

Quantum Verzeichnis: publishes directory *European Zoos and Conservation Organisations* covering 37 countries. Also has information on species survival groups worldwide, international animal organisation directors and much more. For further information contact Quantum (Schützenhofstrasse 30, 26315 Oldenburg, Germany; ☎+49 441-2182-705; fax +49 441-2182-708; e-mail quantum@t-online.de).

USEFUL WEBSITES

www.zoos-worldwide.com: worldwide zoo directory.
www.safaripark.co.uk: directory of UK safari parks.
www.csbg.org: Global Zoo Directory.

CIRCUSES

OVERVIEW

In the nineteenth century, the only forms of entertainment for many people were the travelling shows, circuses and fairs. Nowadays, the spectacle of animals and humans performing in a giant tent has to compete with the sophisticated array of virtual thrills provided by incessant technological advancement. The 'Greatest Show on Earth' has also been a victim of changes in tastes and perceptions with regard to animal performances. Animal action groups working undercover with one circus in Britain exposed cruel training methods and poor animal husbandry both on the road and in 'winter quarters'; the perpetrator was convicted. This is however one circus among the fifteen or so of the 20 British and Irish ones which have animal acts. It is worth pointing out that in the rest of Europe, where the circus is regarded as as art form and receives subsidies, there are many more performing animals, and in Switzerland which has very stringent animal welfare laws, a circus trainer or presenter is respected and attracts a popular following. Perhaps it has taken circuses too long to take account of what the public deems is acceptable in the treatment of animals, particularly wild ones. This is due in large part to circuses being considerably bound by their traditions. In many ways the life of circus animals for the first three-quarters of the 20th century was little different from the 19th century, i.e. scant considerations were given to adequate exercising and mental stimulation outside the circus ring. Suggestions have been made for improvements especially by the animal behaviourist Dr. Marthe Kiley-Worthington in a report she produced in 1990. To some extent her recommendations have been implemented although there is still much more to be done, especially with regard to the husbandry standards for animals in winter quarters. Big cats, camels, elephants, chimpanzees, giraffes, zebras etc., once the staple exotica of circuses, are now considered in a respectful way and the emphasis is now on 'appropriate animal acts to enhance the species and display the animals' abilities.' For instance, an elephant can pick up a small object, the size of a marble from the ground with its trunk, while the natural agility of a lion means it can walk a parallel tightrope between pedestals. As to the whip, it is a traditional circus accoutrement but not apparently strictly necessary. It is not for whipping the animals but for cueing them i.e. the position of the whip acts as a semaphore. However, arm and hand signals can work just as well as some animal presenters demonstrate. There are also presenters with older, experienced animals who can cue them with voice alone.

It is interesting to note that the antis do not mention that circus animals (like some humans) are natural performers and thrive on the attention, nor that circus animals are called by name, a custom that has virtually disappeared from the farming world. It also appears as with humans, some animals are born comedians. A female trainer with a troupe of llamas intended to present a regular synchronised liberty act with individual star turns but soon found the llamas had invented their own tricks which transformed it into a comedy turn. The act was presented to the audience as a serious animal act but then the beastly clowning took over. A llama supposed to jump over poles, went under them; another supposed to trot around the ring stopped regularly and investigated the audience; yet another rolled in the sawdust (repeatedly if the audience clapped hard enough), and another llama jumped out of the ring and trotted happily about the aisles. Occasionally the act appeared to be going smoothly before chaos broke out again. The audience found the act delightful and hilarious and the animals had more or less invented it themselves. This incident is documented in Dr. Marthe Kiley Worthington's book (see below).

Unlike race horses or greyhounds, circus animals are not normally put down when they are too old to perform, mainly because of the strong empathy between trainer and animal. However, those that are retired do not always appreciate it. There are endless stories of circus elephants pining once they are retired from the ring and the attention. The apparently sound argument for not using endangered animals (e.g. tigers, lynxes) in circuses as it may encourage trading in them and further deplete their populations in the wild is refuted by the fact that in 1990 54% of carnivores were 'circus born' and a further 40% came from zoos.

In the interests of good public relations, some circuses, including Zippo's have invited the RSPCA to inspect their animals without incurring any complaints from that respected organisation. The other general defence of circus animal acts comes from the Circus Friends Association which publishes the scientific study by Dr Marthe Kiley-Worthington *Animals in Circuses and Zoos: Chiron's World*, which examines the training of animals in circuses. Originally commissioned by the RSPCA, this study concluded that circuses were not inherently cruel to animals. Besides the arguments both for and against animals in circuses there is the fact that trainers working with them rarely abuse them because they will never perform well or willingly. It is probably a old wives' tale that animals never forget if someone really abuses them and that they wait patiently for an opportunity to get their own back like a kind of Nemesis with jaws and claws.

An opposing view of circuses is taken by the reputable charity Born Free (01306-712091), which campaigns to keep and protect wildlife in the wild, and through its Zoo Check programme campaigns against environmentally impoverished conditions and poor treatment and concern for animals in zoos. Born Free is unambiguous on the matter of animals in circuses, it wants 'the banning of all animals in circuses', citing physical and psychological suffering caused to animals forced to live and perform in circuses. It has published a report into the welfare of circus animals, copies of which are available to the public.

The circus tradition tends to run in families; either dynasties like the Smarts, Fossetts and Chipperfields who own the circuses, or for performers themselves. There is no doubt that there are fewer animal acts, at least in British circuses, than there were thirty years ago, and some circuses like the modern 'Le Cirque du Soleil' are without any animals at all. Those that still occur include lion-tamers, bareback riders, liberty (i.e. riderless) horses, elephants, llamas, zebras, camelids and novelty dogs and birds.

A circus life usually involves touring during the summer (although some circuses may stay on a fixed pitch for the season). When touring, the animals are moved around the country in 'beast wagons' looked after by their keepers/grooms and trainers. Out of season circus animals are housed in winter quarters which have received the brunt of the criticism of circus animal ill treatment and neglect. The winter quarters are where the circuses also store all their equipment so they tend to be rather untidy places generally unsuited to the keeping of wild animals.

EMPLOYMENT

Even these days, running away to join a circus is not entirely a fantasy and being a lion-tamer is not beyond the realms of possibility. According to Bob Fossett of Bob Fossett's circus, it can be as easy as 'just asking someone nicely' as your first step towards the sawdust ring. The Association of Circus Proprietors recommends joining either a travelling or resident circus as an animal groom or tent/ring person and then get to know one of the performers who may be prepared to give you training. Details of the addresses of these circuses can be obtained from the Association of Circus Proprietors and then you should approach the circuses direct.

Dr Marthe Kiley-Worthington studied circuses in Britain and the USA and discovered that all kinds of people work in circuses and enjoy the sense of belonging

Ex-criminals to bank managers or lawyers, may join the circus for short periods of time to help in lowly capacities – such as ring boys and grooms. Despite the hard work and often primitive living conditions, this way of life is very attractive to someone from outside the circus one's background and status outside the circus become irrelevant, what matters is your commitment to it. It is possible in a relatively short time to work one's way up from being a tent hand, ring boy or groom, to being an 'artiste' and then to being hired by other circuses, maybe in other lands because the circus will often give a chance to a young person who would like to try his or her own animal training abilities there is constant recruitment of people joining circuses.

Another characteristic is that the circus people live all the time with their animals. The result is familiarity with, and treatment of each animal as an individual.

Some trainers are victims of their animals' affection

Professional circus animal trainers are few and far between. Britain has about six who make their living training animals and then hiring them out to circuses. A trainer, will either present the act in the ring themselves or they will train a presenter to do this for them or for other circuses. The replacement presenter usually spends a few weeks training with the trainer and the animals before going on the road with the act. The presenters have to undertake not to train the animals to do any new tricks because generally they lack the expertise to do this properly. In any case, there is a tendency for trainers to complain when the animals are returned to them that they have developed bad habits which require further training to iron them out. Training is a very demanding and time-consuming job. It requires great patience and skill to know when an animal has had enough and how to build confidence in an animal. It is a profession much admired amongst circus folk who know just what goes into it; but it is generally unlauded elsewhere.

Lion-taming is probably the most macho of all animal acts with its undeniably high thrill quotient. In a steel cage, alone with the huge wild beasts, the tamer works them with only the quality of his or her relationship with each one of them to sustain authority. Trainers of big cats run a high risk of being mauled and scarred for life somewhere on their body during their generally long careers. Interestingly, some tamers are victims of 'affection' from their animals – a playful swipe with a giant paw is fine between tigers but not if one's playmate is human. The big cats are the only type of animal that show reluctance to enter the ring and sometimes have to be prodded with a broom handle to leave their cages.

Marion Fossett was one of the first lady lion-tamers. She made her first circus appearance aged 10, as a general member of the company. She worked with different animals including elephants, leopards and horses before moving on to lions. She began taming lions in the 1940s touring Ireland with Jeserich's Circus, which is no longer in existence.

Marion Fossett describes her lion-taming career and offers some advice

I became a lion-tamer literally by accident. The existing lady lion tamer was injured by one of lions and didn't want to work with them any more. I had seven lions and I was so busy thinking of the next trick they were going to do that I didn't have much time think about being nervous. The only moment I didn't like was when I entered the cage they set up in the ring for the lions, and heard the door click shut behind me. My scariest incident in four years of being a lion-tamer, was when all the lights in the big-top went off when the generator failed. The lions got off their pedestals and started to wander around the cage. Some quick-thinking member of the audience got their car and drove it up to the tent, raised the tent wall and shone their headlights on the cage. It was like being rescued by a knight in shining armour.

Two of the lions I hand-reared when they were rejected by their mothers. Although I could take more liberties with them than the others, I had to very careful not to make the other lions jealous. They are like dogs or children in that respect. I used a whip with no lash for pointing a cue to the lions but I never used cruelty; it would have been counter-productive.

If a woman wanted to be a lion-tamer today, it is still possible. It is almost better if you have no animal experience so you can learn from the beginning. You need to be relaxed and let the lions get to know you. They watch every move you make. I never did anything as stupid as to put my head in a lion's mouth. I know a few people who lost their heads that way. I used to ride on a lion to finish my act.

One way to work up to presenting an animal act in the ring is to join in a lowlier position. For instance, there are no qualifications necessary to join a circus as a groom or stock person. Some such staff are permanent employees but the majority tend to be casuals. Ideally, those who are genuinely interested in animals should be employed but this is not always the case. Most circuses are now aware that the public take a great interest in the animals and how they are treated, and are trying to create a good and professional impression, and to train and supervise the animal staff properly. However, since trainers are often the proprietors, mechanics, and organisers as well it is always a problem for them to find a regular time for training purposes. It would help to have one of the animal management qualifications mentioned in the zoo section above, but this will not be insisted upon.

Entering the circus as an animal keeper or groom is a lot cheaper than starting your own act. Don Stacey, the veteran circus journalist worked in circuses before taking up the pen. Some years ago he decided with a partner to train a troupe of stallions for the circus ring. Six years later he worked out that it had cost £100,000 to get the act to performance level. This is perhaps as good an indication as any, how expensive animal acts can be and how much circuses invest in them.

There are a handful of circus schools in Britain, none of which gives instruction on working with circus animals. Among the recommendations in the Kiley-Worthington report was that such a school should be set up to teach animal husbandry systems and that it would attract students from other areas such as zoos, stables, kennels etc. However, the focus of the school would be on handling and training which is where dealing with circus animals differs from other kinds of work with animals.

USEFUL ADDRESSES

Associations
The Association of Circus Proprietors: P.O. Box 131, Blackburn, Lancashire BB1 9DT; ☎01254-672222. Association to which about 14 British circuses belong. The secretary is Mr Malcolm Clay. If asking for any information, please send a stamped addressed envelope.

Circus Friends Association of Great Britain: Fir Tree Cottage, Little Hormead, Buntingford, Herts SG9 OLU; ☎01763-289543. Association founded 1934 at Olympia, London. Publishes *King Pole* magazine (see useful publications below).

The National Association of New Circuses: 1, Moorgate Rise, Kippax, Leeds LS25 7RG. Can advise on training establishments.

Tenting Circuses With Animals
Bobby Roberts Super Circus: P.O. Box 12, Oundle, Peterborough PE8 5AY. Registered office: Five Tops Ltd., Brook Farm, Polebrook, Peterborough PE8 5LS; ☎01832-273644. Managing Director: Bobby Roberts Junior. Touring telephone number 0860-787745.

Circus Atlas: Gate 2, Brook Farm, Polebrook, Peterborough PE8 5LS; ☎01832-275665; tel/fax 01832-275379; on tour 0850 050794, 0802 495195. Directors: Gabi Donnert, Beverley Donnert, Bernie Hasler, Lynda Hasler.

Circus Carousel: Proprietor: Peter Hill, 27 Tillyard Croft, Selly Oak, Birmingham B29 5AH. Touring telephone number: 0589 125134.

Circus King: Honington Junction, Honington, Grantham NG32 2PD. Directors: Jeffrey and Elli Hoffman.

Circus Markus: Telephone on tour 0860 210991. Directors: Rodney and Shirley Mack.

Gerry Cottle's Circus: Office: 7 Merton Park Parade, Kingston Road, London SW19. Telephone on tour 0836 509579.

John Lawson's Circus: 1 Simmonds Road, Wincheap, Canterbury, Kent CT1 3RA; ☎01223-770406. Proprietors: Daniela De Reszke, Vonni De Reszke, Niven Lawson. Telephone on tour 0860 498833.

Papprhiann Circus: Plasynghraen, Llanefyl, Welshpool, Powys SY21 OJB; ☎01938-820511. Directors: Heidi Rhiann, Jozsef Papp.

Peter Jolly's Circus: Circus Caravans, Ridgeway Farm, Edgton, Craven Arms, Shropshire SY7 8HW; ☎01588-680239. On tour: 0831 460637, 0850 687503.

Ray Smith's Circus Mystique: Proprietor: Ray Smith. Telephone on tour 0836 734748.

Santus Circus: The Santus Family.

Sir Robert Fossett's Circus: Manor Farm, Towcester Road, Milton Malsor, Northampton NN7 3AZ; ☎01604-858369.

Uncle Sam's Great American Circus: Honington Junction, Honington, Grantham NG32 2PD. Proprietor: Peter Hoffman.

Zippo's Circus: Zippo's Circus Productions Ltd., 174 Stockbridge Road, Winchester, Hants. SO22 6RW; ☎07050 247287; fax 07050 244867. Mobile 070500 94776. Director: Martin Bourton.

Circus Animal Acts

Chipperfield Enterprises Ltd.: White House, Southcombe, Chipping Norton, Oxfordshire; ☎01608-643885; fax 01608-642031. Directors: R.J. Chipperfield, J Chipperfield.

Evelyn Darnell & Her Horses: 155 Westhorpe Road, Gosberton, near Spalding, Lincolnshire PE11 4EN; ☎01755-840990.

Joan Rosaire & Her Golden Horses: Melbourne, Coxes Farm Road, Billericay, Essex; ☎01277-624972.

Tommy Roberts Jnr.'s Liberty Horses: Brook Farm, Polebrook, Peterborough PE8 5LS.

Circus Schools

Circomedia: Academy of Circus Arts and Physical Theatre, Unit 14, The Old School House, Kingswood Foundation, Britannia Road, Kingswood, Bristol BS15 2DB; tel/fax 0117-9477288.

Playbox Theatre: Head Office, 74 Priory Road, Kenilworth, Warwickshire CV8 1LQ; ☎01926-512388. Artistic directors: Mary McGill, Stewart McGill. Training in transdisciplinary arts, circus movement, Commedia Dell'Arte, dance, theatre.

The Circus Space: London's Centre for the Circus Arts. Coronet Street, Hackney, London N1 6HD; ☎020-7613 4141. Registered charity number 1001839.

Greentop Community Circus Centre: St Thomas Church, Holywell Road, Brightside, Sheffield, S9 1BE; ☎01442-560962

Norwich Circus Centre: 194 Nelson Street, Norwich NR2 4DS; ☎01603-613445. Offers courses in circus skills.

Zippo's Academy of Circus Arts (ZACA): 174 Stockbridge Road, Winchester, Hants S022 6RW; ☎01962-877600. ZACA is linked to Zippo's Circus. Manager Verena Cornwell.

USEFUL PUBLICATIONS

Animals in Circuses and Zoos: Dr. Marthe Kiley-Worthington (1995) Aardvark Publishing (Fir Tree Cottage, Little Hormead, Buntingford Herts SG9 0LU; ☎01763-289543). Price £12.50 plus £2. 240 pages. A fascinating read and the only scientific study of animals in circuses.

King Pole: quarterly magazine (March, June, September and December plus one special issue) published by the Circus Friends Association of Great Britain. Lots of circus news and information. The annual subscription £23 payable to the Circus Friends Association (Membership Secretary, 20 Foot Wood Crescent, Shawclough, Rochdale, Lancs OL12 6PB). A single issue can be ordered for £5 from CFA Merchandising, 31 Crown Avenue, Pitsea, Basildon, Essex SS13 2BE. Annual subsribers get an additional special issue *King Pole Extra* based around a special topic.

World's Fair: Show, exhibition, fair and circus newspaper, 75p weekly from newsagents. Carries occasional job offers.

Other Opportunities

PET SHOPS

Britain's reputation as a nation of animal fanciers is highlighted by the number of pet shops nationwide, estimated at 3,500, selling a general range of animals, plus several hundred more specialist aquatic outlets. These between them employ about 15,000 people, while the peripherals, feed stuffs, equipment and accessories give employment to many more.

A sign of how thriving the industry is, might be seen in the burgeoning of the UK's first one-stop pet supermarket chain which burst on to the UK market from the USA in 1997 and was taken over by Pets at Home in 1999. Pets at Home has 145 stores throughout England, Wales, Scotland and Ireland and they are run as franchises. Pets at Home stores sell a range small animals including snakes, rabbits, hamsters, gerbils and guinea pigs (but not puppies or kittens as there are so many of these in rescue homes awaiting adoption). The bulk of jobs involve small animal husbandry. Some stores offer veterinary services, and about 20 offer grooming services. Management jobs have to be applied for through the head office, but for other jobs it is possible to apply on spec to the stores direct. You can find your nearest Pets at Home by logging on the website www.petsathome.co.uk and typing in your postcode. Enquiries about jobs can also be e-mailed to jobopportunities@petsathome.co.uk from where they will be forwarded to the appropriate store. Alternatively, you can phone Pets at Home and ask for an application form for work. Jobs are advertised in the local press and at the time of press it seemed likely they would also soon be listed on the website.

The addresses of independent pet shops can be found in any Yellow Pages.

Working in a pet shop covers various duties:
1. You will need to know the specific care required by a variety of small animals including their feeding, housing, cleaning, grooming and checking for ailments.
2. Not only will you need to be knowledgeable about individual animals but also the range of associated products stocked by the store including feeds, treatments, equipment and accessories and their uses. If the store stocks a choice, you will need the ability to compare the advantages and disadvantages of one product against another.
3. In the end, working in a pet shop is about commerce, and in particular retailing and the ability to deal courteously with customers is paramount, as is never missing an opportunity to make a sale.

QUALIFICATIONS & TRAINING

The only qualification aimed specifically at those working in pet shops is the City and Guilds Pet Store Management Certificate 776. Below are some centres providing this course. However, City and Guilds have increasingly encouraged pet stores to train their own staff in-house using the City and Guilds syllabus, and then apply to a City and Guilds centre for taking the exam.

NVQs 1 & 2 in Animal Care have a pet shop (retailing) component. The NVQ 3 has a Pet Shop Management option, and which is about 40% of the course.

Alternatively, The Pet Care Trust provides a correspondence course based on three or four hours of study a week for about six months leading to the City and Guilds exam which is held annually in June. Applicants can register as an external candidate in order to take the exam at their local college. The course costs £168 (£148 for Trust members).

Useful Addresses

Carmarthen: Coleg Sirgar ☎01554-748000; www.colegsirgar.ac.uk. Offers City and Guilds Pet Store Managementm.

Cumbria: Newton Rigg College, Penrith ☎01768-863791. Offers BTEC National Award in Pet Store Management.

Holme Lacy College: Holme Lacy, Herefordshire, HR2 6LL; ☎01432-870316; fax 01432-870566. Offers courses in NVQ Level 3, Pet Care and Supply.

Wiltshire: Lackham College, Chippenham, Wiltshire, SN15 2NY; ☎01249-466800; www.wiltscol.ac.uk/courses). Offers City and Guilds in Pet Store Management.

Pershore College of Agriculture: Worcestershire; ☎01386-552443. Offers City and Guilds in Pet Store Management.

Pets at Home Ltd: Senior Personel & Training Administrator, Epsom Avenue, Stanley Green Trading Estate, Handforth, Cheshire SK9 3RN; ☎0161-486 6688; fax 0161-485 4846; www.petsathome.co.uk Has 145 stores nationally. Usually based just out of town on trading estates. See above for job opportunities.

Pet Care Trust: Bedford Business Centre, 170 Mile Road, Bedford, MK42 9TW; ☎01234-273933; www.petcare.org.uk. Correspondence course in City and Guilds Pet Store Management.

Warwickshire College: Royal Leamington Spa & Moreton Morrell, Moreton Morrell Site, Warwick, CV35 9BL; ☎01926-318333; fax 01926-318300. NVQ Level 3 in Animal Care with Pet Shop Management option.

THE ANIMAL RECEPTION CENTRE, HEATHROW AIRPORT

The Reception centre, usually referred to as ARC, is a 24-hour quarantine holding centre for animals travelling by air to the UK, or in transit to a third country. Robert Quest, the centre manager, says that over half a million creatures pass through the centre annually. Most individual animals are dogs and cats (7,000) and competition horses (1,000). The dogs and cats wait at the centre for not more than 48 hours for collection by their quarantine kennels (which may be phased out in the next few years). There are also very large consignments of agricultural stock, for instance 20,000 chicks in one go, or of reptiles and birds for the pet trade. Guests also include exotic wild animals, Mr Quest reckons the strangest was a South African aardvark, a nocturnal termite-eater with a tubular snout and extendible tongue. Despite the huge number of clients, the centre employs a modest thirteen full-time animal assistants plus four other staff. Mr Quest says he gets two or three applications for jobs a week and the suitable ones get filed for future reference. Staff turnover is fairly low and on average, he might employ one or two new member of staff a year. He sometimes takes young people on work experience schemes. The work is in shifts and employees must have a minimum GCSE in Maths and English as there is a lot of documentation (e.g. checking licences and getting paperwork done and to the airline concerned) for each consignment in addition to caring for the animals themselves. Staff have to have an annual rabies inoculation (in the arm). Anyone interested in working at ARC can write to Robert Quest (Animal Reception Centre, Beacon Road, Heathrow TW6 3JF).

ANIMAL SITTING

Another possibility is house and animal sitting. Owners usually contact sitters through one of the handful of agencies specialising in providing experienced staff. Animal sitters have to be very competent with animals, at the very least dogs and cats. Some sitters are also skilled with horses, goats, poultry and other types of non-companion animals. To work for an agency you will need impeccable references and will be thoroughly vetted (!) as you will usually be in sole charge of someone's home as well as their animals. Also the work is not for everyone. According to one very experienced sitter who did this kind of work for four years, 'you have to like your own company and be prepared to go anywhere in the country for days or weeks at a time. It is quite an isolated existence.'

Useful Address
Animal Aunts: Smugglers, Green Lane, Rogate, Petersfield, Hampshire GU31 5DA; ☎01730-821529; fax 01730-821057; e-mail office@animalaunts.co.uk

WALTHAM PET CENTRE

The Waltham Pet Centre in Leicestershire is where a leading brand of British pet food manufacturers try new products on a testing panel of dogs and cats. Described by one former employee as 'doggie and moggie heaven', the lucky animals live a life of pampered and well-regulated luxury as they indicate their approval or disapproval of the latest recipe. There is more to it than that of course: Waltham is one of the world's top research centres into pet animal and equine nutrition and wellbeing. It is also becoming increasing involved in the science of captive wild (i.e. zoo) animals' dietary needs and wellbeing. The centre's staff include animal carers and animal scientists. Further details from The Personnel Department, Waltham Centre for Pet Nutrition, (Waltham-on-the-Wolds, Melton Mowbray, Leicestershire LE14 4RT; ☎01664-415400; fax 01644-415440; e-mail mailbox@wcpn.demon.co.uk; www.waltham.com).

ANIMALS IN SHOWBIZ

AGENT

If you have ever wondered who supplies the moggies and canines that feature in dog and cat food advertisements, or the dogs and cats and exotics for atmosphere shots in movies and T.V. dramas, it is most probably one of the UK's 120 or so animal agencies which are recognised by the Animal Consultants and Trainers Association. For owners it is a question of applying to an agency. You should bear in mind that agencies are likely to receive dozens of applications from hopefuls in a week from which only a few are suitable. The majority of pets cannot handle the noise and lights of a studio, let alone a couple of rostrum cameras whizzing round them. Most agencies will require head and body photographs. The agencies audition pets and once your animal is in the system, work opportunities should be on-going, if not continuous. Specially trained animals command a higher fee than those, which are not. Daily fees are from £50, while product icons such as the Old English Sheepdog in a well-known paint advertisement can command up to £1,500 a performance. However, having an animal in showbiz is more of a thrill than a money-spinner; you will still need a day job.

Alternatively you could start your own agency which is likely to be more lucrative, but only once you have become established.

Amongst the best known agencies are Animals Galore (208, Smallfield Road, Horley,

Surrey RH6 9LS; 01342-842400) run by Cindy Newman, and the Olive Tate Animal Agency (020-8303 0683).

AMAZING ANIMALS

Amazing Animals is the only company licensed (under the *Dangerous Wild Animals Act 1976)*, in the UK to train zoological animals. They supply all kinds of animals wild and domestic for film, TV, commercials, natural history, still photography and live promotional events industry. Their recent coups include the 'flying' pigs for the Zürich banking television commercials. They have supplied wild animals for the BBC's *Extreme Animals* and also for the TV vet Steve Leonard. The company regularly takes work experience candidates, usually proposed by their colleges. They will also consider applications from others with varying degrees of experience with animals including zoo keepers. Staff working directly with the animals number about 15 including keepers, handlers and trainers. Apply direct to Jim Clubb, Director, Amazing Animals Ltd, Heythrop Zoological Gardens Ltd., Heythrop, Chipping Norton, Oxfordshire OX7 5TU; ☎01608-683389; fax 01608-683420; e-mail jclubb@amazinganimals.co.uk; www.ama zinganimals.co.uk.

RABBITS

After dogs and cats, rabbits are the third most acquired pet in Britain and their abandonment has risen accordingly as households discover that they are not loveable, fluffy bunnies all the time and that they can bite and scratch, mainly because they do not like being cuddled all the time. There is a growing tendency to keep them as pets for the whole household in the manner of cats and dogs. The campaigning organisation promoting this idea is the British House Rabbits Association which says they can be housetrained to use a litter tray, come when their name is called and respond appropriately to a 'no' command.

Rabbits can be taught to come when their name is called

   Rabbit abandonment, mainly to rescue centres, was running at the rate of 24,000 a year in 1997 and is most usually the result of rabbits being bought as pets for the children, who become bored with them a few weeks later. Britain's first all-rabbit sanctuary was Cotton Tails in Bristol, and many animal shelters around the country have a rabbit section. There are also rabbits in pet shops and pet supermarkets. It is therefore quite difficult to find jobs working just with rabbits although if you live near any of the sanctuaries below, or ones you can find on the internet (try www.UKRabbitandCavyRescue/rescuelists) it might be worth asking if they need any volunteer help.

Rabbit Sanctuaries

Chin-up Sanctuary: Pwllheli. Chinchillas. Note that these are South American rodents with beautiful dense fur not rabbits. They are similar in size to rabbits and are farmed for their fur. This sanctuary rescues them from the cruel conditions on fur farms.(01766-810799).

The Cotton Tails Rabbit and Guinea Pig Rescue: 108 Staple Hill Road, Fishponds, Bristol BS16 5AH; ☎0117-9866806.

Cat & Rabbit Rescue: Chichester. (01243-641409).

Bright Eyes (formerly The Rabbit Charity): Hornsey. (☎0208-8888 0001; e-mail info@bunny.org; www.bunny.org.uk. The Rabbit Charity merged with Cottontails Brighton in 2002. The new organisation deals with rabbits and hares nationally and has rabbit welfare, rescue and public education programmes.

Rabbit Rescue: Leek. Domestic and wild rabbits. (01538-381117).

Rabbit Sanctuary: Watford (01923-447446; e-mail sally.machell@ntlworld.com).

VOLUNTEERING/WORK EXPERIENCE WITH ANIMAL PROJECTS

Apart from organisations already mentioned there are other animal projects, charities and trusts that are privately run with a particular aim or philosophy towards animals. These organisations encourage volunteers, sometimes requiring them to pay a fee towards funds for their project; others take students doing animal care and similar courses for work experience.

Claire Tuck, was just finishing a 2-year National Diploma in Animal Care at Merrist College, Guildford. Before that she did one-year of NVQs 1&2.

Claire Tuck describes her fortnight's summer work experience at Monkey World in Dorset

My course was 50/50 written and practical experience. The college has lots of contacts for work experience and because I said I wanted to work with exotic animals they suggested Monkey World, an ape rescue centre in Dorset. There were four of us there on work experience and it was the busiest time of year for visitors. We ran the domesticated animals section. We started at 8.30am by letting out all the animals and birds that had been shut up for the night. Then we fed them all and cleaned out the guinea pigs. We also had to protect the baby guinea pigs from the hawk, and the children from the goats, which butted.

Monkey World has a philosophy of keeping the wild animals as wild as possible so there is minimal handling of the monkeys. There was one baby chimp, which arrived having been mistreated. It was lovely to watch how the other chimps protected her because she was the smallest and weakest. There was even one, Charlie, who behaved a bit like a bodyguard. Under their care, and the keeper's attentions you could see her gaining confidence with her own kind.

The afternoons were spent logging any deliveries and giving a scripted talk to the visitors about the animals. There was a regular keeper on hand to answer any difficult questions that we didn't know the answers to.

From about 3pm to 4pm we cleaned the animal food kitchen and did other odd jobs. From 5pm it was feeding time again and then we put all the animals to bed at 6pm.

There was no accommodation provided, but we stayed at a fantastic local b&b.

The good thing about work experience is that it helps you decide what you are really interested in and you find out what you don't want to do. For instance, I had previously worked in a veterinary surgery and I didn't enjoy that nearly as much. Now I know that I really want to work with wild animals, preferably in Africa.

Bardsey Island Bird and Field Observatory: Steve Stansfield, Warden, BBFO, Cristin, Bardsey off Aberdaron, via Pwllheli, Gwynedd LL53 8DE Wales; e-mail steve@bbfo.f reeserve.co.uk.
Volunteer programme for assistant wardens on bird island 2 miles off the tip of the Lleyn Peninsula. Contact the warden for details. No phone, and mail can be delayed by bad weather.

Bee World and Animal Centre: Stogumber Station, Taunton TA4 3TR; ☎01984-656545. Employs a bee helper and two animal helpers during the summer for eight weeks or less. Pays a very small wage but offers good work experience.

Beale Park: The Child-Beale Trust, Lower Basildon, Reading, Berkshire RG8 9NH; ☎01734-845172; fax 01734-845171; e-mail bealepark@bun.com; www.bealepark.co.uk.
Beale Park is a charity dedicated to the conservation of the land it owns and rare breeds of animals and birds. It is open to the public in the form of a natural world theme park of 300 acres which includes ancient water meadows and 45 acres of woodland. Animals graze the meadows while birds are housed in spacious bird enclosures, which are part of a captive breeding programme. Peacocks, golden pheasants and owls are amongst the birds kept, and llamas and highland cattle are amongst the free grazing animals.
20-30 volunteers per year work at Beale Park helping with animal and bird care and maintenance, the gardens, grounds, organic farm, education (environmental) and administration. Volunteers can be taken on for a few days, weeks or all year. Expenses and pocket money are paid but accommodation is not readily available.
Anyone interested should contact the Beale Park office at the above address.

Hessilhead Wildlife Rescue Trust: Gateside, Beith, Ayrshire, KA15 1HT; ☎01505-502415; e-mail info@hessilhead.org.uk; www.hessilhead.org.uk.
A wildlife rescue and rehabilitation centre in Scotland. Offers training courses on first aid for injured wildlife, work experience for animal care and veterinary students. About 20 volunteers/trainees annually. Applicants do not need special skills and although experience with animals is advantageous it is not essential as training is given. Volunteers help with a range of jobs involving rescue, daily care and cleaning of wild birds, animals, treatment and handrearing, assessment for release and post-release monitoring. Minium stay 2 weeks; maximum 6 months mostly in the period April to October. Accommodation with heating and cooking facilities. Donation to the Trust for accommodation is appreciated. Contact Gay Christie at the above address.

Mole Hall Wildlife Park: Widdington, Saffron Walden, Essex CB11 3SS; tel/fax 01799-540400; e-mail: enquiries@molehall.co.uk; www.molehall.co.uk.
Employs two or three animal wardens during summer. Minimum age 16. Pocket money and accommodation provided in return for 40 hours a week.

The Monkey Sanctuary Co-operative Limited: Murrayton, Nr. Looe, Cornwall PL13 1NZ; ☎01503-262532; www.monkeysanctuary.org; e-mail info@monkeysanctuary.or g.
The Monkey Sanctuary was established in 1964 near Looe in Cornwall. It is the first place where the Woolly Monkey has survived and bred outside its natural habitat of the South

American rain forests. As well as serving as a conservation centre, the Sanctuary also rescues ex-pet monkeys. It is open to the public from Easter to the end of September.

Most of the several dozen volunteers taken on every year are needed during these periods to help with various duties including preparing food for the monkeys, performing domestic tasks and attending to the public. During the winter volunteers are still needed mainly for maintenance work, gardening and cleaning the monkey enclosures. Volunteers stay for periods of two to four weeks depending on availability. There is no direct contact between volunteers and moneys.

Longer-term staff such as keepers with relevant experience of primate rehabilitation may occasionally be needed. All staff live on site as a community.

Applicants must be fluent in English, in good health and over 18 years old. Board and lodging are provided.

For further information contact the Volunteer Co-ordinator at the above address sending an s.a.e.

Monkey World, Ape Rescue Centre: Longthorns, Wareham, Dorset BH20 6HH; ☎01929-462537; fax 01929-405414; e-mail apes@monkeyworld.org; www.monkeyworld.org.
Takes on trainee keepers associated with a university for a minimum of six-nine months. Monkey World does not take volunteers or work experience people. Trainees would be expected to help with various aspects of animal husbandry including, cleaning, food preparation and keepers' talks. Trainees would start on the domestic animal sections (guinea fowl, donkeys, pigs etc) prior to working with primates. Applications to the Head Keeper or Dr. Alison Cronin, Scientific Director.

Moray Firth Wildlife Centre: Spey Bay, Moray, IV32 7PJ.
The Whale and Dolphin Conservation Society takes on seasonal volunteers to work at the Moray Firth Wildlife Centre in Spey Bay, Scotland. Volunteers normally need to be able to commit to six months. Accommodation is provided and a contribution is made towards expenses. The work is varied and included research (shore and boat-based), interpretation (working with the public in the centre's exhibition), awareness-raising events around Scotland, helping with WCDS school visits. For more information e-mail ellie@wdcs.org or send a CV and covering letter to the above address. For details of voluntary and paid opportunities with WDCS, visit www.wdcs.org.

The National Seal Sanctuary: Gweek, Nr. Helston, Cornwall TR12 6UG; ☎01326-221361; fax 01326-221210; www.sealsanctuary.co.uk.
Established for more than four decades, the Sanctuary is situated on the upper reaches of the Helford river, approximately six miles from Helston, and is a well-known marine animal rescue centre. As well as caring for seals and sea lions, it is also a retirement and rescue haven for a variety of other creatures including otters, which through no fault of their own have become homeless. The sanctuary's permanent residents include Patagonian and Californian sea lions.

Volunteers are taken all year round but the busiest time for seal rescues is during the autumn and winter. Volunteers must be over 18 and able to stay at least two weeks. Potential volunteers should write to Tamara Cooper, National Seal Sanctuary at the above address.

Operation Osprey: The Royal Society for the Protection of Birds (RSPB), Grianan, Tuylloch, Nethybridge, Inverness-shire PH25 3EF.
One of the RSPB's many special projects, Operation Osprey involves protection and conservation work for one of Scotland's rarest species of which there are about 100 nesting pairs. Volunteers are needed for one-week stints from March through to early

September for Osprey nest site protection and surveillance and providing information to the public. Tented accommodation and food are provided and volunteers pay a weekly contribution of £20. Longer stays by negotiation after the initial week.

Sea Life Surveys: Ledaig, Tobermory, Isle of Mull, Argyll PA75 6NR; tel/fax 01688-400223; www.sealifesurveys.demon.co.uk.
Sea Life Surveys carries out whale and dolphin surveys with the aim of studying and monitoring the species, number and behaviour of cetaceans (minke and killer whales, harbour porpoise, common and Risso's dolphin) and sharks, seals and seabirds of the Inner Hebrides for the Hebridean Whale and Dolphin Trust. Volunteer work takes place mostly at sea and includes observing, recording cetacean dive times, plankton sampling, bird and seal counts and inputting computer data. Periods of two to seven days from April to October. Costs £145-500 all inclusive of meals and accommodation.

USEFUL WEBSITES

www.veggies.org.uk – styles itself 'the website for everyone interested in animal welfare'. The site includes an *Animal Contacts Directory* of organisations based in the UK, but which are involved with the welfare of animals in other countries through volunteers or campaigns. There is also a *Jobs and Volunteers* section where UK rescue centres advertise for volunteers or have jobs to offer. Also listed are zoos and UK wildlife centres and much more.

www.uksafari.com/wildlifehospitals.htm – list of wildlife hospitals in the UK and Northern Ireland.

www.nhbs.com – the website of the Natural History Book Service Ltd, suppliers of enviromental books and a unique resource for naturalists, biologists, scientists, conservationists, environmentalists and anyone with an interest in environmental subjects. Includes mainstream literature and thousands of specialist titles. Books can be mail-ordered direct from the website.

Directory of UK Animal Organisations

Advocates for Animals: 10 Queensferry Street, Edinburgh, EH2 4PG; ☎0131-225 6039. Campaigns for the increasingly stringent reforms in using animals in scientific tests especially in reducing the number of animal experiments and in finding alternative methods of testing without using animals. Works in alliance with the British Veterinary Association.

Animal Actors UK: same address etc. as *The National Ferret School* (see below).

Animal Aid Society: The Old Chapel, Bradford Street, Tonbridge, Kent TN9 1AW; ☎01732-364546; fax 01732-366533. Campaigns against vivisection and factory farming. Publishes *Outrage* magazine bi-monthly. Branches and contacts countrywide. Membership by subscription.

Animal Concern: P.O. Box, 5178, Dunbarton G82 5YJ; ☎01389-841639; e-mail animals@jfrobins.force9.co.uk; www.animalconcern.com. Pressure group which campaigns on behalf of animals. Also has an animal concern advice line 01389-841111; also at the same address is Save Our Seals Fund www.saveoursealsfund.org.

Animal Procedures Committee (APC): The Home Office, 50 Queen Anne's Gate, London SW1H 9AT; ☎020-727 32915; fax 020-7273 2029; e-mail apc.secretariat@homeoffice.gsi.gove.uk; www.apc.gov.uk. Independent statutory committee that advises the Home Secretary on the administration of the Animals (Scientific Procedures) Act 1986 which applies to all animal experiments in the UK.

Association of British Wild Animal Keepers (ABWAK): c/o Laura Gardner, Leeds Castle, Maidstone, Kent ME17 1PL; www.abwak.co.uk. Send a stamped addressed envelope with request for careers information.

The Barn Owl Centre: Brockworth Court, Brockworth, Gloucester GL3 4QU; ☎01452-865999; fax 01452-865906; e-mail info@thebarnowlcentre.co.uk; www.barnowl.co.uk Actively supports the welfare of birds whether wild or captive origin. All birds housed at the Centre are of captive origin and specially trained. Supports wild barn owls through conservation projects and supports captive bred owls and Harris hawks and their keepers through educational courses and practical experience. Does not breed owls or hawks.

The Barn Owl Trust: Waterleat, Ashburton, Devon, TQ13 7HU; ☎01364-653026; e-mail info@barnowltrust.org.uk; www.barnowltrust.org.uk The Barn Owl Trust is a wildlife conservation organisation. Activities include: practical and advisory work with farmers and landowners, educational work, scientific research, and the provision of information for the public, conservation groups, and professionals.

The Bat Conservation Trust: 15 Cloisters House, 8 Battersea Park Road, London SW8 4BG; ☎020-7627 2629; fax 020-7627 2628; www.bats.org.uk. Dedicated to the care of bats and their habitat. Publishes *Bat News (*quarterly) members' newsletter.

Birdlife International: Wellbrook Court, Girton Road, Cambridge, CB3 ONA; ☎01223-277318; www.birdlife.net. Linkage of worldwide bird organisations.

British Chelonia Group: Dr R Avery, The School of Biological Sciences, University of Bristol, Bristol BS8 1UG. Can supply tortoise, terrapin and turtle information.

British Divers Marine Life Rescue (BDMLR): c/o Limehouse, Regency Close, Uckfield, East Sussex TN22 1DS; tel/fax 01634-281680; info@bdmlr.org.uk; www.bdmlr.org.uk. Active in the rescue, treatment and rehabilitation of all types of marine wildlife affected by pollution, injury etc. Operates a 24-hour rescue and response service for marine mammals, injured, stranded etc.

British Falconers' Club: Home Farm, Hints, Near Tamworth, Staffordshire B78 3DW; tel/fax 01543-481737; e-mail admin@britishfalconersclub.co.uk; www.britishfalcone rsclub.co.uk Primarily a sporting club for falcon owners, but can tell you where the nearest falconry or hawk preservation societies are to you.

British Goat Society (BGS): 34-36 Fore Street, Bovey Tracey, Newton Abbot, Devon TQ13 9AD; ☎01626-833168; e-mail secretary@allgoats.com; www.allgoats.com. Disseminates knowledge and information about goats and their managment. Publishes *Yearbook of the BGS* and journal several times a year. For other publications, please request a list.

British Hedgehog Preservation Society (BHPS): Hedgehog House, Dhustone, Ludlow, Shropshire, SY8 3PL; ☎01584-890801; e-mail bhps@dhustone.fsbusiness.co.uk; www.software-technics.com\bhps Educates and provides information about caring for sick and injured hedgehogs.

British Herpetological Society (BHS): c/o The Zoological Society of London, Regent's Park, London NW1 4RY; ☎020-8452 9578; e-mail pat.pomfret@binternet.com. Deals with all areas of interest in reptiles including conservation of British native species in wild, and other species, particularly in a zoological setting.

British Horse Loggers Association (BHLA): c/o FCA Head Office (☎01467-651368; www.fcauk.com/Horseloggers.htm). Started in 1992 to promote and develop the use of draught horses in forestry in the UK.

British Llama and Alpaca Association: c/o Candia Midworth, Bank Way House, Effingham Common, Leatherhead, Surrey KT24 5JB; fax 01372-451131; www.llama.co.uk and www.alpaca.co.uk Publishes *Camelids Chronicle*, a quarterly magazine, and gives advice on buying and keeping llamas. Handbook available (£2) incorporating membership form, bi-annual conference, seminars and workshops (for members). Some owners and breeders will accept veterinary students, or those wishing to make a career with camelids, for work experience.

British Marine Life Study Society (BMLSS): Glaucus House, 14 Corbyn Crescent, Shoreham-by-Sea, Sussex BN43 6PQ; ☎01273-465433; e-mail bmlss@acompuserve.com). Formed in 1990 to study the flora and fauna of the sea and shores of Britain and to publish and disseminate information and promote conservation projects. Publishes *Glaucus (*www.glaucus.co.uk*)*, journal concerned with the marine life of the British Isles, *Shorewatch* a quarterly newsletter, and *Torpedo* an electronic bulletin.

British Naturalists' Association (BNA): P.O. Box 5682, Corby, Northants, NN17 2ZW; tel/fax: 01536-262977; e-mail Brit.Naturalists@btinternet.com. Founded in 1905, the Association supports campaigns and schemes for the protection of wildlife and areas of natural beauty.

British Trust for Ornithology: The National Centre for Ornithology, The Nunnery, Thetford, Norfolk IP24 2PU; ☎01842-750050; fax 01842-750030; www.bto.org. Promotes the wider understanding and appreciation of birds through scientific study and research carried out to high standards using members and cooperating with others engaged in relevant research. Also works constructively with those whose activities affect birds' environment and conservation. Also, works to protect and preserve permanently lands and habitats which are suitable for bird and flora and fauna generally.

British Union for the Abolition of Vivisection (BUAV): 16 Crane Grove, Islington, London N7 8LL; ☎020-7700 4888; e-mail info@buav.org; www.buav.org. Since its founding in 1898, BUAV has campaigned for an end to all animal experiments.

British Veterinary Association Animal Welfare Foundation (BVAAWF): 7 Mansfield Street, London W1G 9NQ; ☎020-7636 6541; www.bva-awf.org.uk Founded in 1984 with the aim of identifying problems of animal welfare and finding practical solutions based on science and free from political, commercial or emotional prejudice.

Butterfly Conservation (membership): Manor Yard, East Lulworth, Nr. Wareham, Dorset, BH20 5QP; www.butterfly-conservation.org.

Compassion in World Farming (CIWF): Charles House, 5a Charles Street, Petersfield, Hants GU32 3EH; ☎01730-264208; e-mail compassion@ciwf.co.uk; www.ciwf.co.uk A non-profit organisation that campaigns for the abolition of factory farming and the animal suffering associated with it.

The Donkey Sanctuary: Sidmouth, Devon EX10 0NU; ☎01395-578222; fax 01395-579266; e-mail thedonkeysanctuary@compuserve.com; www.thedonkeysanctuary.org.uk. Registered charity that prevents the suffering of donkeys worldwide through the provision of high quality, professional advice, training and support on donkey welfare. In the UK and Ireland permanent sanctuary is provided to any donkey in need of refuge. Since its founding in 1969, it has helped more than 8,600 donkeys. It has over 150 paid full-time staff. No part-time.

Earthkind: Humane Education Centre, Bounds Green Road, London N22 4EU; ☎01202-682344. Campaigns for the well-being of all animals domesticated and wild through education and action. Owns the boat *Ocean Defender* a rescue boat for marine wildlife.

FAWN: (stands for Farm Animal Welfare Network), P.O.Box 40, Huddersfield HD9 3YY; ☎01484-688650. Campaigns against cruelty to farm animals.

Federation of City Farms & Community Gardens. (NFCF): The Green House, Hereford Street, Bedminster, Bristol BS3 4NA; ☎0117-923 1800; fax 0117-923 1900; e-mail admin@farmgarden.org.uk; www.farmgarden.org.uk.

Fund for the Replacement of Animals in Medical Experiments (FRAME): Russell & Burch House, 96-98 North Sherwood Street, Nottingham, NG1 4EE; ☎0115-958 4740; fax 0115-950 3570; e-mail frame@frame.org.uk; www.frame.org.uk. Researches and develops practical alternatives to using live animals for medical experiments and toxicity tests. Provides informed and balanced information affecting government legislation on animal experiments and liaises with scientists in the private and public sectors to find ways of reducing the number of animals used in experiments. Over two and a half million animals were used in the UK in experiments in 2000 (the latest figure available at the time of press).

Hawk and Owl Trust: Zoological Society of London, Regent's Park, London NW1 4RY; tel/fax 01582-832182; e-mail hawkandowltrust@aol.com; www.hawkandowl.org. The Trust works to conserve wild birds of prey and their habitats.

Hebridean Whale and Dolphin Trust (HWDT): Marine Discovery Centre, 28 Main Street, Tobermory, Isle of Mull, Argyll PA75 6NU; (☎01688-302620; 01688-302728; www.activitypoint.co.uk). There are always volunteer opportunities with the HWDT Trust in administration, on boats and to carry out research and education projects.

Humane Research Trust: 29 Bramhall Lane South, Stockport, SK7 2DN; ☎0161-439 8041. Works for medical research that does not involve cruelty to animals.

Humane Slaughter Association (HSA): The Old School, Brewhouse Hill, Wheathampstead, Hertfordshire AL4 8AN; ☎01582-831919; fax 01582-831414. Since 1911, the HSA has worked exclusively to ensure that the best welfare standards are developed and used worlwide for the care of food animals during transport. The charity takes a practical and technical approach, providing constructive advice, educational materials and training for those involved in livestock handling and slaughter and contributes funds to appropriate research and equipment.

The League Against Cruel Sports (LACS): 83-87 Union Street, London SE1 1SG;

☎020-7403 6155; fax 020-7403 4532; info@league.uk.com; www.league.uk.com Formed in 1924 the League campaigns for the protection of wildlife from acts of cruelty, particularly bloodsports. The League also buys land in the West Country for animal sanctuaries; currently it has 38 sanctuaries totalling 2,500 acres.

Lord Dowding Fund for Humane Research: 261 Goldhawk Road, London W12; ☎020-8846 9777; campaigns@animaldefenders.org.uk and campaigns@navs.org.uk; www. animaldefenders.org.uk; www.ldf.org.uk. Wants to find alternatives to using animals for scientific research. At the same address are the National Anti-Vivisection Society (NAVS). Animal Defenders which seeks a ban on animal circuses.

The Mammal Society: 15 Cloisters House, 8 Battersea Park Road, London SW8 4BG; ☎020-7498 4358; fax 020-7622 8722; e-mail enquiries@mammal.org.uk; www.mammal.org.uk The Mammal Society is the voice for British mammals and the only organisation solely dedicated to the study and conservation of all British mammals. Current activities of the Mammal Society include organising surveys of British mammals; producing books and fact sheets, holding meetings, conferences and field activities and running a youth group called Mammalaction. It also provides quality training in mammal identification.

The Marine Connection: P.O. Box 2404, London W2 3WG; e-mail info@marineconn ection.org; www.marineconnection.org. The Marine Connection are a London-based dolphin and whale charity that believe one of the most effective methods of protecting these marine mammals and their environment is through education. The Marine Connection work worldwide, saving dolphins and whales in areas such as Africa, Peru and the UK. By teaching people how to respect the world's oceans, it helps save marine life. The charity is happy to help answer, marine mammal questions.

Marine Conservation Society: 9 Gloucester Road, Ross-on-Wye, Herefordshire, HR9 SBU; ☎01989-566017; e-mail info@mcsuk.org; www.mcsuck.orgHollybush, Chequers Lane, Eversley, Basingstoke, Hants RG27 ONY; ☎01989-566017; fax 01989-567815.

National Anti-Vivisection Society (The NAVS): Ravenside, 261 Goldhawk Road, London W12 9PE; ☎020-8846 9777; 020-8846 9712; info@navs.org.uk; www.navs.org.uk. Founded in 1898 the NAVS campaigns for the prohibition of all experiments on animals but supports reform measures that cause reduction, rather than cessation as a step along the way to its aims. Currently NAVS is campaigning for an end to the secrecy surrounding animal experiments. Also funds research into ways of carrying out medical research without using animals.

National Birds of Prey Centre, Newent, Gloucestershire GL18 1JJ; ☎0870-990 1992; fax 01531-821389; e-mail jp@nbpc.demon.co.uk; www.nbpc.co.uk. The NBPC is involved in the conservation of about 60 species of birds of prey, which includes a captive breeding programme. The centre has eleven full-time and five part-time staff and needs volunteers for general maintenance of the centre's environment.

National Federation of Badger Groups (NFBG): 15 Cloisters Business Centre, 8 Battersea Park Road, London SW8 4BG; ☎020-7498 3220; fax 020-7627 4212; e-mail susan.symes@nfbg.org.uk; www.badger.org.uk

National Ferret Welfare Society: c/o Patrick Smith, Argyle Cottage, St. John's Street, Bridgwater, Somerset TA6 5JA; ☎01278-421855; www.n-f-w-s.co.uk or www.nfws.net

National Ferret School: Holestone Gate Road, Holestone Moor, Ashover, Derbyshire S45 OJS; ☎0870 220 1608; fax 0870 220 1609; e-mail james@honeybank.co.uk.

National Rabbit Aid: 108 Staple Hill Road, Bristol BS16 956; ☎0117-9563148. Can provide a list of rabbit rescue centres.

The National Fancy Rat Society: P.O.Box 24207, London SE9 5ZF; www.nfrs.org

The National Hawking School: same address etc. as *National Ferret School* (see above).

Non-animal Medical Research: 81 Beresford Avenue, Skegness PE25 3JQ.

Orkney Seal Rescue (OSR): Dyke End, South Ronaldsay, Orkney, KW17 2TJ; ☎01856-831463; fax 01856-831463; e-mail SelkieSave@aol.com. OSR runs a seal rescue centre that cares for about 50 seals a year. Also works to encourage public awareness of seals and to study and monitor their behaviour in the interests of improving their welfare.

Parrot Society: 108b Fenlake Road, Bedford, MK42 OEU; ☎01234-358922. Concerned with the study and conservation of parrots worldwide.

People's Trust for Endangered Species (PTES): 15 Cloisters House, 8 Battersea Park Road, London SW8 4BG; ☎020-7498 4533; fax 020-7498 4459; e-mail enquiries@ptes.org; www.ptes.org. The Trust aims to protect creatures in the wild, which are threatened with extinction. It acts by funding scientific research, field work to protect populations in immediate danger, raising public awareness of species in danger, and purchase of land to pursue these aims when possible. Works both in Britain and abroad.

Petsearch (UK): 35 Church Lane, Melksham, Wilts SN12 7EF; ☎01225-705175; ukpetsearch@freeuk.com; www.ukpetsearch@freeuk.com. National database register for lost and found animals and birds. Will put you in touch with your nearest Petsearch helpline.

Proteus Reptile Rescue: 5 Oakland Road, Handsworth, Birmingham, B21 ONA; ☎0121-523 9500; www.proteus.uk.net Gives advice on reptiles, and rescues those bought as pets whose owners find they have bitten off more than they can chew (or perhaps the reptile has). Needs donations to support its growing number of abandoned reptiles.

Rare Breeds Survival Trust (RBST): National Agricultural Centre, Kenilworth, Warwickshire CV8 2LG; ☎024-7669 6551; fax 024-7669 6706; e-mail enquiries@rbst.org.uk; www.rbst.org.uk RBST is a registered charity formed to maintain and increase existing stocks of rare farm breeds, which would otherwise disappear completely. Publishes *The Ark* monthly magazine.

Respect for Animals: P.O. Box 6500, Nottingham NG4 3GB; ☎0115-952 5440; fax 0115-9560753; e-mail info@respectforanimals.org; www.respectforanimals.org Respect for animals was founded in 1993 with the aim of abolishing the consumer market for products, which result from cruelty to animals. It concentrates on informing the consumer. Currently it is campaigning against the horror behind the international fur trade.

Sea Mammal Research Unit (SMRU): Lynn Doig School of Biology, Gatty Marine Laboratory, University of St. Andrews, St. Andrews, Fife KY16 8LB; (www.biology.st-and.ac.uk/sch-smru.html) Part of the Natural Environment Research Council. Provides scientific advice to government departments on the conservation and management of sea mammals, especially seals.

Sea Watch Foundation: 36 Windmill Road, Headington, Oxford OX3 7BX; ☎01865-764794; www.seawatchfoundation.org.uk. Monitors environmental threats to whales, dolphins and porpoises.

Scottish Society for the Protection of Wild Birds (SSPWB): Foremount House, Kilbarchan, Renfrewshire, PA10 2EZ; ☎01505-702419. Conducts regular research surveys and manages the Lady Isle Nature Reserve, off Troon, a seabird reserve in the West of Scotland.

Scottish Wildlife Trust (SWT): Cramond House, Cramond Glebe Road, Edinburgh, EH4 6NS; ☎0131-312 7765; fax 0131-312 8705; www.swt.org.uk Manages over 100 wildlife reserves and practises conservation and education.

Tortoise Trust: BM Tortoise, London WC1N 3XX; e-mail tortoise trust@aol.com and ttrust@tesco.net; www.tortoisetrust.org and www.ttinstitute.co.uk Offers advice and carries out practical rescue and conservation. Provides free leaflet on tortoise care and online training courses.

Universities Animal Welfare Trust: c/o James Kirkwood, The Old School, Brewhouse Hill, Wheathampstead, Herts, AL4 8AN; ☎01582-831818. UFAW is a science-based charity, which accepts that humans use animals for food, experimental research and other things, but does not accept that this entitles us to treat animals in any way but humanely. UFAW funds research into the behaviour and needs of animals, and from this produces the best advice on how to care for and manage different species. Has a range of publications, which report on its research. Publishes scientific quarterly journal *Animal Welfare.* Also produces a booklet *Careers with Animals.*

Whale & Dolphin Conservation Society: Brookfield House, 38 St. Pauls Street, Chippenham SN15 1LY; e-mail info@wdcs.org; www.wdcs.org.

Wildfowl & Wetlands Trust – Caerlaverock (WWT): Scottish Centre of the WWT is at Eastpark Farm, Caerlaverock, Dumfriesshire, DG1 4RS; ☎01387-770200; fax 01387-770200.

Wildfowl & Wetlands Trust – Martin Mere: Burscough, Lancs L40 OTA; 01704-895181; fax 01704-892343; e-mail: karen.halsall@www.wwt.org.uk; www.wwt.org.uk Wetland reserve (Ramsar, SSSI and SPA site)and captive breeding programme for rare and endangered wildfowl. Centre run by 20 full time staff, 20 part-time and over 100 volunteers (min.age 16 years). Volunteers required all year to work with visitors – education, information, children's activities. Some grounds work available.

Wildfowl & Wetlands Trust (WWT): Penclacwydd, Llwynhendy, Llanelli, Dyfed SA14 9SH; ☎01554-741087; fax 01554-741087.

The Wildfowl & Wetlands Trust: Slimbridge, Gloucestershire GL2 7BT; ☎01453-890333; fax 01453-890827. Aims to preserve wetlands and save them and their particular wildlife through research, conservation and raising awareness of appreciation. WWT has eight wetland and wildlife centres open to the public. Publications list on request.

The Wolf Trust: (replaces the now defunct Carnivore Wildlife Trust); www.wolftrust.org.uk Focuses on the protection, conservation and welfare of foxes and wolves) threatened by extinction or mistreatment.

World Pheasant Association: 7-9 Shaftesbury Street, Fordingbridge, Hampshire SP6 1JF; ☎01425-657129; (www.pheasant.org.uk). Specialist group responsible for the international conservation of galliformes (game birds) which include pheasants, turkeys, grouse, quails, francolins, partridges, curassows (S. & Central American birds) and megapodes (found in Australia). Volunteers needed for research overseas on ecology, behaviour and habitat.

World Society for the Protection of Animals (WSPA): 39 Albert Embankment, London SE1 7TP; ☎020-7793 0540; fax 020-7793 0208. Registered charity, which promotes the conservation and protection of animals worldwide. Cooperates with over 300 member animal welfare societies in over 60 countries. Also runs Libearty, the world campaign for bears.

Zoological Educational Services: same address etc. as *The National Ferret School* see above.

Part II

Europe

WESTERN EUROPE

Austria – Belgium – Denmark – Finland –
France – Germany – Greece – Iceland –
Ireland – Italy – Luxembourg –
The Netherlands – Norway – Portugal –
Spain – Sweden – Switzerland

EASTERN EUROPE & RUSSIA

Bulgaria – Croatia –
Czech Republic –
Estonia – Hungary – Latvia –
Lithuania – Poland – Romania – Russia
Slovakia – Slovenia – Ukraine

Europe-wide Organisations

FINDING A JOB

For vets, veterinary nurses, zoo keepers, farriers, racing staff etc. the first point of call should be their own professional association. In the case of racing stable staff, the racing authority of the foreign country can be the starting point. Professional associations will be able to provide some assistance such as the addresses of their corresponding organisations in other countries and advice on getting qualifications gained in Britain recognised in other countries. Some professional organisations such as the UK's Worshipful Company of Farriers organise their own exchange schemes with European countries.

It is possible to contact potential employers direct and many useful addresses are given below in the individual country sections. If practicable, it is advisable to make a brief telephone enquiry to the organisation you wish to apply to in order to find out the name of the person to whom you should address your application.

VETERINARY

Addresses of veterinary associations are given under individual countries below. The following addresses are pan-European for vets interested in wildlife and zoo medicine.

The European Association of Zoo and Wildlife Veterinarians (EAZWV): P.O. Box 23, 3097 Liebfeld-Berne, Switzerland; ☎+41 31 300 20 30; fax +41 31 30 20 31; e-mail secretariat@eazwv.org; www.eazwv.org.

European Association of Zoos and Aquaria (EAZA): c/o Amsterdam Zoo, P.O. Box 20164, 1000 Amsterdam, The Netherlands; ☎+31 20 5200753; fax +31 20 5200754; e-mail info@EAZA.net; www.EAZA.net

HORSES

For jobs with horses in Europe, the internationally distributed British magazine *Horse and Hound* which is available through newsagents or by postal subscription (01444-445555; fax 01444-445599) usually carries some adverts for jobs abroad in each issue. Also try the UK tabloid newspaper *Racing Post* (☎020-7510 3000; www.racingpost.co.uk), especially the Saturday and Wednesday issues. Stable staff can also register with agencies that specialise in placing equestrian staff with foreign stables. These usually charge the employer for the service rather than the job seeker.

Stable Staff Agencies

Career grooms: 16e Randolph Crescent, London W9 1DR; ☎0207-289 6385; fax 0207-289 6385; fax 08701 385750; e-mail info@careergrooms.co.uk; www.careergrooms.co.uk. Recruitment specialists for the equestrian community mainly in the UK and Europe and also further afield. Website offers temporary, permanent and contract work. Equestrian staff can register online for free, search and apply for jobs online, and be notified of new jobs as they arrive.

Hayfield International Ltd: Hazlehead Park, Aberdeen, Scotland AB15 8BB; tel/fax 01224-321132. An international equestrian centre which operates a useful website www.EquiWorld.Net/ which is linked to 6000 other equestrian websites in the UK, Europe and worldwide and has a job section.

Nags 'n' Nannies: ☎01244 535449; fax 01244 538244.

One the largest agencies is *A World of Experience*, Equestrian Employment Agency (52 Kingston Deverill, Warminster, Wiltshire; ☎01985-844102/844022 Mon-Fri 9am-5pm; fax/answerphone 01985-844102; email office@equijobshop.com); www.equijobshop.com).

This agency, which has been in business since 1988 deals with about 900 temporary and permanent vacancies a year in Britain and other countries; about a third of these are outside Britain. Vacancies are with all types of employers including private owners, families, commercial and competition yards. Also, jobs for head grooms and sole charge grooms, schooling/competition riders, stable managers, instructors, stud staff and working pupils.

Of the vacancies outside Britain, the majority are in Germany and Switzerland and the rest in other European countries (Austria, Belgium, Denmark, France, Greece, Ireland, The Netherlands, Spain and Portugal) and there are occasional vacancies in the USA, Canada, Middle East, Far East, Australia and New Zealand.

SOURCES OF INFORMATION

The information departments of foreign embassies can provide data related to a specific request, e.g. a list of riding establishments or the addresses of zoological organisations or animal protection agencies. They cannot however help with finding jobs.

Chambers of Commerce can also provide specific information. Their main function is to facilitate trade, but amongst their registered members there may be animal practitioners and other animal related businesses, so they might be useful for contact addresses. Usually this will be in the form of the Chamber's list of members for which you will have to pay; Chambers of Commerce are located in cities and major towns in every country which is why they are a good source of information about a particular locality. Their addresses can be obtained from telephone directories.

The internet can also be a valuable tool. You can search for a particular type of organisation in the country of your choice. Many organisations from animal shelters to ecological organisations have their own websites, or you can simply carry out a general search under animal organisations, zoos, etc. Needless to say the density of internet connections varies among countries. The USA has by far the greatest number of websites while Italy has fewer than most European countries.

USEFUL ORGANISATIONS

Europarc Federation: Kröllstr. 5, Postfach 11 53, 94475 Grafenau, Germany; ☎+49 8552 96 10 0; fax +49 8552 96 10 19; e-mail office@europarc.org; www.europarc.org The Europarc Federation is an umbrella organisation of about 500 European national parks, nature parks and biosphere reserves. The Federation represents their interests and works to promote the exchange of practical experience in protected area management.

Quantum Conservation: publishes directory *European Zoos and Conservation Organisations* covering 37 countries. Also has information on species survival groups worldwide, international animal organisation directors and much more. Their websites include:

www.zoos.org – lists links to zoo homepages.

www.Conserve.org – a searchable database of al environmental and species conservation information.

Also publishes the directory of zoos and conservation organisations in Europe.For further information contact Quantum at Schützenhofstrasse 30, 26315 Oldenburg, Germany; ☎+49 441-2182-705; fax +49 441-2182-708; e-mail quantum@t-online.de.

USEFUL PUBLICATIONS

Eurovet Guide: Les Editions du Point Vétérinaire, 9 rue Alexandre, B.P. 233, 94702 Maisons-Alfort cedex – France; ☎+33 1 45 17 02 32; fax +33 1 45 17 02 74; www.po inteveterinaire.com Information and contacts in 37 European countries. Was intended to be a biennial publication but at the time of press there is no update in progress (1st edition 1998-99). 520 pages, 5000 addresses, 125 congress dates. All kinds of data from who to contact for an Erasmus scholarship to veterinary clinics throughout Europe that accept students wanting to see practice, or an assessment of the veterinary system in each country mentioned. Price about 50 euros (about £31) plus 9 euros postage and packing.

LANGUAGES

It would be impractical in most cases not to have some knowledge of the language of the country where you are working. Exceptions might be if you were working at riding stables that catered for English-speaking tourists, or employed temporarily in some Scandinavian countries where English is learned to a high standard by nearly everyone. Even so you would have to learn the national language eventually if you were planning to stay on.

It is relatively easy to find a language course for most European languages i.e. French, German, Spanish, Serbo-Croat, Italian etc, at a local college, or as a home-study pack. These will give you a basis for communicating in the language, but will not provide the specialised vocabulary that animal jobs require. You may be able to get a list of terms from the relevant professional association in the country you are going to.

Western Europe

Thanks to the European Union, to which fifteen western European countries (Switzerland and Norway are exceptions) belong, it is now relatively easy for the citizen of one member state to go and work in another EU state for a few months or a few years. The EU has reduced red tape for workers wishing to move around the Union and there is an inherent obligation to accord all citizens of EU countries the same rights at work as the nationals of whichever member country they are working in. Furthermore, it is not essential to arrange a job in advance; an EU national can go to any EU country looking for work and stay for up to three months before requiring a residence permit. Once you have decided to stay on in another EU country, it is relatively easy to get a residence permit.

Not only has the bureaucracy surrounding residence and work been simplified but also the problem of getting qualifications and experience acquired in one EU country recognised in another one been tackled. The EU has instituted two main EU directives for the mutual recognition of education and training (see details below). This means in theory, qualifications obtained in one member state are valid in all the others.

For Americans, Australians, South Africans and other non-EU nationals wanting to work in Western Europe, the process is more complicated and generally involves obtaining work permits through the relevant embassy before leaving the home country. There is also the possibility of arranging an exchange or internship, or working a temporary assignment through an officially recognised organisation which will organise the work permit for you (see below).

MUTUAL RECOGNITION OF QUALIFICATIONS IN THE EU

Since 1989 professional qualifications awarded after at least three years of higher education (e.g. veterinary) have been mutually recognised in the EU. A copy of the 1989 directive governing the professions in Europe is contained in the Department of Trade and Industry's booklet *Europe Open for Professionals* (Kingsgate House, 66-67 Victoria Street, London SW1E 6SW; ☎ 020-7973 1992).

All qualifications that take less than three years to obtain (i.e. all the professions not covered by the 1989 directive) have been mutually recognised since 1992/1994. These include qualifications achieved after post-secondary education involving courses of 1-3 years (defined as diplomas); awards made on completion of a course following a minimum school leaving age qualification (defined as certificates); and work experience. This means that National and Scottish Vocational Qualifications (NVQs and SVQs) and their equivalents are recognised in the EU. The organisation in Britain responsible for providing information on the comparability of academic qualifications of all kinds is the National Academic Recognition Information Centre (NARIC) which can be contacted at ECCTIS 2000 Ltd. (Oriel House, Oriel Road Cheltenham, Glos GL50 1XP; ☎ 01242-260010; fax 01242-258600).

It is important to note that mutual recognition of qualifications may in some instances be subject to certain conditions such as proficiency in the language of the state where you wish to practise, and your length of experience. Further details of the qualifications covered by this directive can be obtained from the above address.

Prospective job seekers are advised to consult the association relevant to their profession for the exact conditions of acceptance and registration in another EU country. If their British association does not have the details they should have the address of their counterpart organisation in the country where work is being applied for and should contact them direct. Alternatively, details are obtainable through one of the 40 or so European Documentation Centres (EDCs) in the UK. To find the address of your nearest one, contact the Commission of the EC (Information Centre, 8 Storey's Gate, London SW1P 3AT; ☎020-7973 1992).

CERTIFICATES OF EXPERIENCE

If you have experience but no formal qualifications, you can apply for a European Community Certificate of Experience. For EU citizens in the UK, this is issued by the British Chambers of Commerce on behalf of the Department of Trade and Industry. In Britain, those wishing to practise their trade or profession in another EU state can contact the Department of Trade and Industry (Certificates of Experience Unit), Kingsgate House, 66-74 Victoria Street, London SW1E 6SW; ☎020-7215 4004; fax 020-7215 4489) requesting an application form for a European Community Certificate of Experience (form EC2/GN). The form will be accompanied by a copy of the Directive applicable to the job. The applicant should check where he or she meets the terms of the Directive before completing the application form. To be eligible for a Certificate, you must normally (but not exclusively) have had managerial or self-employed experience for a number of years in the job concerned. The DTI charges £80 for a certificate and a smaller fee for an update/revision. The charge is to cover the costs of checking and authenticating the information submitted by the applicant.

EU WORK EXPERIENCE SCHEMES

One of the problems for those leaving school or university is that when they begin to look for work, they find that they are up against those with a proven track record, who understandably find greater favour with employers than those with no experience in the work place. The EU has come up with various schemes for young people aimed at giving them invaluable work experience in other EU countries. The most ambitious of these is LEONARDO which includes vocational training and placements in other EU countries for students, graduates and those on an advanced course of vocational training that is not degree level and young workers and apprentices. The upper age limit is 28 years. Among other strands of Leonardo are the intensive work experience placements in another EU country. Work placements last three weeks to twelve months. There is a separate strand, Youthstart, for young people under 20 years, in particular the unemployed and the unqualified.

The Leonardo scheme in the UK is organised through the Central Bureau for Educational Visits and Exchanges (10 Spring Gardens, London SW1R 2BN; ☎020-7389 4004). Applications have to be submitted through the college where the applicant is studying and are on a reciprocal basis. You cannot apply direct to the Central Bureau as an individual.

For young people between 16 and 19 from an EU country who want to have work experience in the UK, the EU runs the European Work Experience Scheme. For details contact the EWE Project Coordinator (Unit One, Red Lion Court, Alexander Road, Hounslow, Middx TW3 1JS) or telephone 020-8572 2993; www.ewep.com.

STUDENT EXCHANGE ORGANISATIONS FOR NON-EU NATIONALS

The following organisations are mentioned because they have the authority to arrange short term working visas for non-EU nationals to work in Europe.

Council on International Educational Exchange (CIEE): 205 East 42nd Street, New York, NY 10017; ☎212-822-2600/1-888-Council). The CIEE runs work abroad programmes for students in the following western European countries: Britain, Ireland, France and Germany for which a fee of US$225 is charged for administration and working visas. American students can contact their nearest branch or ask for the leaflet *Work Abroad*.

Student Work Abroad Programme (SWAP): Student Services Australia, STA Travel (P.O.B. 399, Carlton South, Victoria 3053; 03-9348 1777/fax 9347 8070). SWAP can arrange working visas for the UK and Germany.

Student Work Abroad Programme: the Canadian branch of SWAP is operated from Travel CUTS (part of the Canadian Federation of Students) offices, or contact the head office (243 College Street, Toronto, Ontario M5T 2Y1. Similar coverage of countries to Council, plus Finland.

COUNTRY GUIDE

Austria

Austria is wedged between the countries of western and eastern Europe and is historically and culturally committed to both areas. It is a member of the EU and has accepted thousands of economic migrants from former Yugoslavia and other eastern European countries. The Austrian population is approximately eight million.

Vets & Veterinary Nurses
The veterinary school in Vienna is one of the largest in Europe and is currently producing too many vets for the falling animal population of the country. There are approximately 1,300 veterinary practices in Austria, mostly run by individuals and with family helpers rather than qualified veterinary nurses.
Registry body for foreign vets: Bundeskammer der Tierärzte Österreichs, Biberstrasse 22, 1010 Vienna; ☎+43 1 512 17 66; fax +43 1 512 1470; e-mail oe@tierarztekammer.at; www.oe.tierarztekammer.at.
Austrian Association for Homeopathic Veterinary Medicine: Österreichische Gesellschaft für Veterinärmedizinische Homöpathie, Mariahilfer Str 110, 1070 Vienna; ☎+43 1 526 75 75; fax +43 1 526 7575-4; www.homoepathie.at/vet.
Austrian Society of Veterinary Families & Veterinary Nurses: Rotenmuehlgasse 13, 1120 Vienna; ☎+43 1817 84 68; fax +43 1 813 29 83; e-mail: maria.pimpel@telecom.at.

Dogs
The Austrian dog population is estimated at 600,000.
Austrian Breeders and Trainers/Canine Association: Hundezucht- und Abrichtevereine,

Österreichischer Kynologenverband, 1230 Mauer, Vienna; ☎+43 1 88870 92; fax +43 889 26 21.

Horse
Austrian racing authorities:
Austrian Racehorse Owners Club: Freudenau 65, 1020 Vienna; ☎+43 1 728 9535; fax +43 1 728 9517; e-mail austrian-racehorse@galopp-freudenau.at.
Pferdezentrum Stadl-Paura: Stallamweg 1, 4651 Stadl-Paura; ☎+43 7245 21700; www.pferdezentrum-stadlpaura.at.
Austrian Riding Association: Bundesfachverband für Reiten und Fahren in Österreich, Geiselbergstrasse 26-32/512, 1110 Vienna; ☎+43 1 749 9261 91; e-mail office@fena.at; www.fena.at.
Spanische Hofreitschule (Spanish Riding School): Michaelerplatz 1, 1010 Vienna; ☎+43 1 5339031; fax +43 1 533 903240.
The Austrian farriers Association:
Bundesanstalt für Pferdezucht: Stallamtsweg 1, 4651 Stadl Paura.

Zoos & Aquarium
Das Haus des Meeres (Aquarium and Vivarium): Esterhazy Park, Fritz-Grünbauplatz 1, 1060 Vienna; ☎+43 1 587 1417; fax +43 1 586 0617; e-mail haus--des--meeres@gmx.net; www.haus--des--meeres.at.
Salzburg-ANIF: Zoo Salzburg: 5081 Anif, Salzburg; ☎+43 662 820176; fax +43 662 8201 1766; e-mail office@salzburg-zoo.at; www.salzburg-zoo.at
Innsbruck: Alpenzoo Innsbruck: Weiherburggasse 37, 6020 Innsbruck; ☎+43 512 292323; fax +43 512 293089; e-mail alpenzoo@tirol.com; www.alpenzoo.at.
Wien: Schönbrunner Tiergarten, Maxingstr 13b, 1130 Vienna; ☎+43 1 877 92 92; fax +43 1 877 96 41; office@zoovienna.at; www.zoovienna.at.

Animal & Bird Welfare, Protection & Conservation
Zentralverband der Tierschutzvereine Österreichs (Association of Austrian Animal Welfare Organisations): Khlesplatz 6, 1120 Vienna; ☎+43 1 804 7774; fax +43 1 804 77774-52.
Graz: Tierheim des Landestierschutzvereines für Steiermark, Grabenstr 113, 8010 Graz; ☎+43 316 68 42 12.
Österreichischer Katzenschutzverein (Austrian Cat Protection Society: Katzenheim Freudenau, 1020 Vienna; ☎+43 1 218 9567.
Salzburg: Tierheim des Tiershutzvereines für Stadt und Land Salzburg, Heim 1, Karolingerstr 13a, 5020 Salzburg; ☎+43 662 83 23 22. Animal rescue centre for stray cats and dogs from the streets and animals that cannot be looked after any longer by their owners as well as animals with terminal illnesses and any small animal wild or domestic. Seven paid staff including a vet and eight unpaid helpers. Helpers should have a recognised animal qualification and speak German and be prepared to stay a reasonable length of time as it takes at least three weeks to learn everything about the place.
Salzburg: Österreichischer Tierschutzverein, Neutorstr. 18/17, 5020 Salzburg; ☎+43 662 84 32 55.
Wels: Welser Tierheim Tier-und Umweltschutzverein, Tierheimstr 40, 4600 Wels; ☎+43 7242 430 12. Animal sanctuary and environmental protection organisation.
Wien: Tierheim.at is an animal rescue centre at Franzengasse 6, 1050 Vienna; www.tierheim.at. fax +43 662 1 81501 69. Animal protection organisation.
Wien: Tierheim Am Mühlwasser, Am Mühlwasser 231, 1220 Vienna; mobile ☎0664 181 43 48. Animal rescue home.
Wien: Österreichischer Tierschutzverein (Austrian Association for the Protection of

Animals), Mariahilfer Strasse 162/8; 1150 Vienna; ☎+43 1 8973346; fax +43 1 897
3482; e-mail oetv.wien@chello.at; www.tierschutzverein.at.
Wien: Österreichischer Pferdeschutz und Allgemeiner Tierschutzverband, Schmidtgasse
13, 1080 Vienna; ☎+43 1 408 75 78. Horses and other animals protection
organisation.
Vienna: Birdlife Österreich – Gesellschaft für Vogelkunde (Austrian Society for
Ornithology and the Protection of Birds): Museumsplatz 1/10/8, 1070 Vienna; ☎+43
1 523 4651; fax 43 1 523 465150; www.birdlife.at The Austrian society for the
protection of birds.

Circus
Circus Elfi Althoff-Jakobi: 2115 Merkersdorf 37-38, Ernstbrunn; ☎+43 2576 7066; fax
+43 2576 70664; www.zirkus.at
Circus Louis Knie: St. Veiter Strasse 41, 9020 Klagenfurt; ☎+43 463 590077; fax +43
463 590079; www.oenc.at

Austrian Embassies
Australia: 12 Talbot Street, Forrest, ACT 2603, Canberra; ☎02-6295 1533; fax 02 6239
6751; www.austriaemb.org.au
Canada: 445 Wilbrod Street, Ottawa, Ontario K1N 6M7; ☎613 789 1444; fax 613-789
3431; www.austro.org
UK: 18 Belgrave Mews West, London SW1X 8HU; ☎020-7235 3731; fax 020-7344
0292; www.austria.org.uk
USA: 3524 International Court, NW Washington, DC 20008; ☎202-895 6700; fax 202-
895 6750; www.austria.org

[rhr]*Belgium*

Belgium

Belgium, the smallest European country, is about the size of the state of Maryland, has
three distinct regions: the Flemish region, the Brussels capital region and the Walloon
Region, which have similarities with American states or German Länder. The three
official languages, Dutch, French and German correspond to these regions.

Over the last decade of the 20th century, Belgium has been tightening its laws
dealing with animal welfare. In January 1996 a law forbidding the sale of dogs and
cats in markets was introduced. In February 1997 a law was passed affecting animal
sanctuaries, boarding kennels and catteries, commercial animal establishments and
breeding establishments. The law includes regulations for the minimum dimensions for
housing cats, dogs, birds, reptiles and aquarium fish. All are now subject to veterinary
inspections and approval under the law.

Half of all Belgian households keep domestic pets and if you include aquarium fish,
pets outnumber Belgians of whom there are just under ten million. Aquarium fish are the
most popular (and presumably the least troublesome) creatures (3.5 million) followed
by aviary birds (3 million). There are also one million pet rodents owned by Belgian
fanciers.

Vets.
The Belgian veterinary association has 4,800 members (of whom 750 work outside
Belgium) and 2,900 veterinary practices evenly spread around the country; even villages
are likely to have a practice. The main veterinary organisations in Belgium are:
Administration de la Santé Animale, Inspection Générale des Service Veterinaires: World

Pets outnumber the Belgians

Trade Centre 3, 4th and 5th Floors, Boulevard Simon Bolivar 30, 1000 Bruxelles; ☎+32 2/208 32 11; fax +32 2/208 36 12.

Ordre des Vétérinaires Médicines Belges: 31 rue de la Croix Rouge, Boîte 7, 5100 Jambes; ☎+32 81/30 87 88; fax +32 81/30 89 99. National veterinary organisation of Belgium.

Union Professionnelle Vétérinaire: 41 Avenue Fonsny, 1060 Brussels; ☎+32/2 538 17 54; fax +32 2 53732 54/.

Dogs & Cats

Since 1994 Belgium has had an obligatory dog registration scheme so that inoculation can be controlled and owners can be traced immediately, for instance if a dog strays. Each animal has to have an tiny microchip (known as *une puce)* inserted under the skin, or a tattoo so it can be registered with the central register (Registre National Belge ☎02/ 673 52 30). Changes of ownership have to be notified within eight days. The canine population is 1.7 million (slightly more than cats at 1.6 million).

Antwerp International Cat Club: Ravelsbergstraat 59, 2100 Deurne; ☎03/336.10.82.

Belgium Cats Lovers/Felin's Fan Club: Vrankenstraat, 3890 Ginelom Try des Mäles 39, 5190 Jemappe-sur-Sambre; ☎011/48.58.69; fax 011/48.70.03/.

Société Royal Saint-Hubert: Avenue de l'Armée 25,1050 Brussels; ☎+32 2/733.45.90. The Belgian kennel club organisation that records pedigrees of Belgian dogs, organises expos, competion shows and breeder selection days. Can also advise on microchipping dogs and cats for identification. Can also provide a list of clubs that organise dog training (dressage pour chiens) classes.

Union Royale Belge des Clubs Berger Belges: Rue Monçai 23, 5580 Ave et Auffe; ☎+32 84/38.84.44. Dog breeding organisation for one of Belgium's main national breeds.

Horses

Horse riding and equestrian sports are as popular in Belgium as elsewhere. There is no official figure for the number of horses but estimates vary from 60,000 to 100,000. The native breeds include the draught horses (*chevaux de trait*), the Belgian and the Ardennes. Anyone wanting to work on a stud farm with these magnificent animals could try contacting the Société Royale Le Cheval de Trait Belge or the Société Royale Le Cheval de Trait Ardennais (see addresses below).

A federation for horse racing was set up in April 1998 under the Ministries of Finance and Agriculture. There are two kinds of racing, trotting races and galloping races. Equine matters and regulations come under the Ministry of Agriculture (Ministre de l'Agriculture et des Petites et Moyennes Entreprises, rue Marie Therese, Brussels, ☎+32 2/21106 11; fax 02/219 61 30) from which all details of regulations concerning everything to do with horses, (racing, riding establishments etc.) can be obtained.

Racing Authorities
Jockey Club de Belgique: 53 Chausée de la Hulpe, 1170 Brussels; ☎+32 2 672 72 48; fax +32 2 672 54 77.
Société Royale d'Encouragement de Belgique: Chausée de la Hulpe 53, 1170 Brussels; ☎+32 2 673 67 92; fax +32 2 660 45 05.
Hippodroom d'Ostende: Ostende Racing Society, 48 rue du Sport, 8400 Ostende; ☎+32 59 80 60 55; fax +59 80 78 24..
Société des Steeple-Chases de Belgique: 115 Franklin Roosevelt, 1050 Brussels; ☎+32 2 675 19 00; fax +32 2 675 15 01.

Horse-Ball, a kind of volleyball on horseback, is popular. It is exceptionally difficult and skilful since it involves keeping the ball in the air and passing it between riders towards a goal. If the ball falls to the ground, a rider must pick up the ball from a moving horse using only one hand. The Belgian Horseball Federation might be a useful contact for the addresses of stables (☎647.92.97).

Addresses of Equestrian Training Centres:
BLOSO Dressuurschool: Mevr. Gekhiere, Kloosterweide 6,1744 Sint Ulriks Kapelle; ☎+32 2/452 75 47.
Mlle Ch. Duchêne, Directrice: Rue du Haras 16, 5340 Gesves; ☎+32 83/67.74.11.
Gemeenschapsonderwijs: Sint Martinusstraat 3, 3740 Bilzen; ☎+32 89/41.16.18.
VILO 'Ter Borcht': Baronielaan 29, 8860 Meulebeke; ☎+32 51/48.88.91.
Other Equine organisations:
Le Cheval de Sport Belge: Av. Brassine 38, 1640 Rhode St Genese; ☎+32 2/358 55 38. Competition horse organisation.
Fédération Royale Belge des Sports Equestres: Ave Houba de Strooper 156, 1020 Brussels; ☎478.50.56. Can supply a list of riding stables nationwide.
Société Royal le Cheval de Trait Belge: 49 Avenue de Suffrage universel, 1030 Brussels; ☎+32 2/215 93 48.
Société Royale le Cheval de Trait Ardennais: 50 rue des Aubépines, 6800 Libramont; ☎061/23.04.04; fax 061/23.04.09. The Trait Ardennais is one of the native Belgian heavy draught horses.
Antwerp Polo Club: the club, located in Kapellen (ten minutes from Antwerp and 45 minutes from Brussels) was revived in 1986 after a lapse of several decades and has a modest number of players numbered in tens rather than hundreds and over 200 polo ponies. For work with the ponies try contacting the club +32 3/485.64.46.
U.N.P.M.F.B.: The Belgian Farriers Association, Rue de la Lasne 26, 1380 Lasne; tel/fax +32 2 633 26 10. There are about 130 farriers who are members of the Association. Not all farriers are members of the association or have been examined and approved. Approved farriers display a turquoise logo. The main farriery school is in Brussels and it takes 100 students a year, one or two of whom are foreigners.

Zoos, aquaria, safari parks etc.
There are about 20 zoological and safari parks, bird parks, a deerpark, dolphinarium and aquaria. There are also some privately owned specialised collections. The most important are:

Aquarium Dubuisson de l'Université de Liège: Institut de Zoologie, 22 quai van Beneden, 4020 Liege; ☎+32 43/66 5021; +32 43/66-5010; e-mail aquarium@ulg.ac.be; www.ulg.ac.be/aquarium.

Antwerp Zoo: Koningin Astridplein 26, 2018 Antwerp; ☎+32 3/202-4540; fax +32 3/202-4547; e-mail info@zooantwerpen.be; www.zooantwerpen.be.

Bellewaerde Park: Meenseweg 497, 8902 Ieper; tel; +32 57/46-8686; fax +32 57/46-7595; www.bellewaerdepark.be. Amusement and animal park.

Boudewijn Park: Alfons de Baeckestraat 12, 8200 Brugge; ☎+32 50/38-3838; fax +32 50/38-2343; e-mail info@boudewijnpark.be; www.boudewijnpark.be. Dolphinarium and amusement park.

Deigne-Aywaille Safari Park: Fange de Deigne 3, 4920 Deigne-Aywaille; ☎+32 43/60-9070; fax +32 43/60-9108; e-mail: zoo.mosa@pophost.eunet.be; www.mondesauvage.be.

Dierenpark Planckendael: Leuvensesteenweg 582; 2812 Muizen-Mechelen; ☎+32 /15/41 4921; fax +32 15/42 422935; e-mail info@planckendael.be; www.planckendael.be. Extension of Antwerp Zoo particularly aimed at children with its collection of smaller animals such as pygmy chimpanzees and a children's petting farm.

Olmense Zoo: Bukenberg 45, 2491 Olmen-Balen; ☎+32 14/309882; fax +32 14/302346; e-mail olmensezoo@glo.be; www.olmensezoo.be.

Gent Zoological Park: Twaalf Roeden 10, 9042 Gent; ☎+32 9/253-0790; fax +32 9-253-2108; e-mail munrozoo@busmail.net and munro@vt4.net.

Limburgse Zoo: Marcel Habetslaan 58, 3600 Genk; ☎+32 8/381844.

National Sealife Blankenberge: Koning Albert 1 laan 116, 8370 Blankenberge; ☎+32 50424 200; fax +32 50424 424; www.sealife.co.uk.

Paradiso Park: Domaine de Cambron 1, 7940 Cambron-Casteau; ☎+32 68/250 820; fax +32 68/455-405; info@paradisio.be; www.paradisio.be. Inclues 7000 square metres free flying bird hall. Council subsidised.

Réserve d'Animaux Sauvage: rue Joseph Lamotte 2, 5580 Han-zur-Lesse/Rochefort; ☎+32 84/37-7213 ; fax +32 84/37-7712; e-mail grotte-de-han@grotte-de.han.be; www.grotte-de-han.be. A safari park located in the Ardennes region containing the main wild animals: wild boar, deer, wolves, bison, tarpan, lynx and brown bears, which once populated the Ardennes and other European forests. Nearby is another tourist attraction, the Han Grottos.

Zwin Vogelpark: Ooievaarslaan 8, 8300 Knokke-Heist; ☎050/60 70 86; e-mail kirs.struy@pandora.be. A bird sanctuary in the largest salt marsh in Belgium, home to several thousand breeding birds. Affiliated to a bird-zoo (special breeding programmes for storks and eagle owls).

Other zoological enterprises:
- Amo Safari, Amougi (safari park)
- Aviflora, Ingelmunster (bird park)
- Crête des Cerfs, Bouillon (deer park)
- Dieren park Lochristi, Lochristi (animal park).
- North Sea Aquarium, Ostende.
- Sea Life Centre, Ostende. Council subsidised.
- Schickler, Schelle (animal park)
- Stockmanshoeve, Sijsele (pets)
- Vlindertuin, Knokke; ☎050/61.04.72 (butterfly park).
- Wazoo, Sint-Niklaas

New laws are being formulated to govern zoological parks taking into account that the menagerie aspect has been supplanted by a serious approach to their educational, environmental, research and conservation roles. At the time of press the exact content of the new law was still being formulated.

Farmwork
The organic farming movement is growing in Belgium. Potential volunteers have to apply through the organisation Nature et Progrés (rue de Dave 520, 5100 Jambes; ☎0811-30 36 90) for a list of organic producers in the French-speaking part, and the organisation Velt (Uitbreidingstraat 392c, 2600 Berchem; ☎03-281 74 75) for the Flemish-speaking part.

Animal & Bird Protection, Welfare & Conservation
Association Nationale des Sociétés de Protection Animale: National Association of Animal Protection Organisations, Boulevard Jules Graindor 5, 1070 Brussels; ☎+32 2 524 2915.
AVES: rue de la Cambre/Terkamerenlaan 16, 1200 Brussels; ☎02/771 81 13. Bird watching organisation.
Croix Bleue de Belgique: 170 rue de la Scierie, 1190 Brussels; ☎+32 2/376 32 62; fax +32 2/376 32 60. Animal protection and welfare society similar to Britain's Blue Cross animal charity.
Gaia: Gaia is an association that aims to defend animals' rights. (☎+32 2/245 29 50).
Vlaamse Vereniging voor Dierenbescherming: 95 Langdorpsestraat, 3200 Aarschot; ☎+32 16/56.77.07. Animal protection organisation.
Ligue Royale Belge pour la Protection des Oiseaux: FAO Roger Arnhem, rue de Veeweyde 43, 1070 Brussels. The Royal League for the Protection of Birds will help with all matters to do with birds including advice if you find a wounded or ringed bird (☎+32 2/521 28 50).
Réserves Naturelles et Ornithologiques de Belgique (RNOB)/Belgische Natuur – en Vogelreservaten (BNVR): rue Royale Ste-Marie 105, 1030 Brussels; ☎+32 2 245 55 00; fax +32 2 245 39 33. Belgian bird protection and conservation organisation which is a member of the worldwide organisation Birdlife International.
Société Royale Protectrice des Animaux: Royal Society for the Protection of Animals, Avenue d'Itterbeek 600, 1070 Brussels.

Organisations needing volunteers:
Natuur 2000: Bervoetstraat 33, 2000 Antwerp; ☎03-231 26 04; www.home.planetin ternet.be/n2000. The Flemish association of young environmentalists, Natuur 2000, needs volunteers for their bat reserve cum nature education centre located in a former WW1 fortress near Antwerp. Natuur 2000 also organises summer conservation camps for which a registration fee is payable to cover food and accommodation, insurance and local transport. They also need office volunteers with computer skills, for their centres in Antwerp and Ostend.

Belgian Embassies & Consulate
Australia: Consulate, Trelawny Street, Woollahra, NSW 2025; ☎02-9327 8377.
Canada: 4th Floor, 80 Elgin Street, Ottawa, Ontario K1P 1B7; ☎613-236-7267; fax 613-236 7882.
UK: 103-105 Eaton Square, London SW1W 9AB; ☎020-7470 3700; fax 020-7259 6213; www.belgium-embassy.co.uk.
USA: 3330 Garfield Street, NW Washington, DC 20008; ☎202-333 6900; fax 202-333 3079.

Denmark

Only Belgium and the Netherlands (just) are smaller EU countries than Denmark. Denmark consists of the province of Jutland (Jylland), which projects into the North Sea, and the Danish archipelago of over 400 islands, many of them tiny and uninhabited. The two largest islands are Zeeland (Sjoelland) on which the capital Copenhagen is situated (a mere half hour away from Sweden) and Funen (Fyn). Zealand and Funen are linked by bridge. Denmark is home to a population of 5.2 million. The huge Arctic island of Greenland and the Faroe Islands between Iceland and Scotland are also Danish territories.

Vets & Veterinary Nurses
There are 2,346 veterinarians registered as practising with the Danish Veterinary Association. The number of practices (600) emphasises the fact that most work together in group practices of anything from two to eight practitioners. The contact for details of the Danish Veterinary Profession is Den Danske Dyrlaegeforening (Rosenlunds Allé 8, 2720 Vanløse; ☎+45 38 71 08 88). However, foreign vets register with the Danish Veterinary and Food Administration: Veterninaer-og Fødevaredirektoratet (Rolighedsvej 25, 1958 Frederiksberg C; ☎+45 33 95 60 00; fax +45 33 95 60 01; www.vfd.dk).

There are 260 members of the Danish Veterinary Nurses Association (c/o Christoffers Alle 86 st.mf.,2800 Lyngby; ☎+45 44 98 13 43; fax +45 44 44 35 27).

Dogs
The Danes keep fewer dogs than cats (600,000 of the former compared with 900,000 of the latter). The Danish Kennel Club can provide most types of information and can be found on the internet at www.dansk-kennel-klub.dk or at the following address: Dansk Kennel Club, Parkvej 1, 2680 Solrød Strand; ☎+45 5618 8100.

Horses
There are an estimated 34,000 horses in Denmark (saddle and race horses).

Racing authority:
Danish Jockey Club: Foreningen til den Aedle Hesteavis Fremme, Hestesportens Hus, Box 20, 2920 Charlottenlund; ☎+45 39 96 20 20; fax +45 39 96 20 44.

Equine & Farriery organisations:
Dansk Ride Forbund: (Danish Riding Union): Langebjerg 6, 2850 Naarum; ☎+45 45 80 43 44. The Danish riding association could provide a list of riding schools.
Foreningen Hestens Vaern (Horses): Gammel Hovegade 8,2, 2970 Horsholm; ☎45 86 87 74; fax 45 76 87 75.
Association of Danish Blacksmiths: Farriers Committee, Magnoliavej 2,5250 Odense SV. The Association of Blacksmiths has about 90-100 practising farriers amongst its 1000+ members, of which 25 are certificated farriers and the rest are blacksmiths (i.e. metal workers) who also shoe horses. The farriery course lasts 4 years and includes studies at agriculture and veterinary school. There are not usually enough applicants to take up all the places as apparently young Danes are not interested in this type of work. Under animal welfare law passed in 1998, all farriers must now be formally trained.

Zoos, Aquaria & Safari Parks
The most important zoos are Copenhagen, which has a worldwide reputation, and Aalborg.
Aalborg Zoologiske Have: Molleparkvej 63, 9000 Aalborg; ☎+45 96 31 29 29; fax +45

98 13-1933; fax +45-9813-1933; e-mail hju@aalborg-zoo.dk; www,aalborg-zoo.dk.
Akvarium & Museum: 8600 Silkeborg; ☎89 21 21 89; fax 89 21 21 88.
Copenhagen Zoo: Sdr. Fasanvej 79, Frederiksberg; 2000 Copenhagen; ☎+45 75/82
0137; fax +45 36/44 2455; e-mail lla@zoo.dk; www.zoo.dk.
Danmarks Akvarium: Charlottenlund Aquarium, Kavalergaarden 1, 2920 Charlottenlund;
☎+45 39/62 3283; fax +45 39/62-0416; e-mail danmarks@akvarium.dk;
www.danmarksakvarium.dk.
Esbjerg Aquarium: Fiskeri-og, Sofartsmuseet, Tarphagevej 2, 6710 Esbjerg V; ☎+45 76
1220-00; fax +45 76 122010; e-mail: svend.tougaard@fimus.dk; www.fimus.dk.
Frydenlund Fuglepark og Opdraetscenter: Skovvej 50, 5690 Tommerup; ☎64 76 13
22 & 65 90 21 87.
Givskud Zoo: Gemeinnützige Stiftung, Løveparkvej 3, 7323 Givskud; ☎+45
75.73.02.22; fax +45 75.73.03.21; e-mail: info@givskudzoo.dk; www.givskudzoo.dk.
Safari park and zoo.
Jyllands Park Zoo: Haunstrupvej 13, 6920 Videbaek, Haunstrup; ☎+45 97 16 61 20;
fax +45 97 16 62 31;e-mail info@jyllandsparkzoo.dk; www.jyllandsparkzoo.dk.
Knuthenborg Safari Park: Knuthenborg Park, 4941 Bandholm; ☎53 88 80 88.
Nykobing Zoologisk Have: O[ob]stre Alie, 4800 Nykøbing F; ☎54 85 20 26.
Odense Zoo: Sdr Boulevard 320, 5000 Odense C; ☎+45 66.11-1360; fax +45 65-90-
8228; e-mail: odensezoo@odensezoo.dk; www.odensezoo.dk.
Terrarium Vissenbjerg: Kirkehelle 5, 5492 Vissenbjerg; ☎+45 64.47.18.50; fax +45 64
47 18 57; e-mail:lizard@email.dk; www.reptil-zoo.dk

Farmwork
VHH: c/o Inga Nielsen, Asenvej 35, 9881 Bindslev. The Danish WWOOF (international
organic farm organisation). Volunteers can work for keep. Choice of farms 25. Check
whether or not they have livestock from their details on the list obtainable from the
above address for a fee of £5 (US$10).

Animal & Bird Welfare, Protection and Conservation
Dansk Ornitologisk Forening (DOF – Birdlife DK): Vesterbrogade 140, 1620
Copenhagen V; ☎+45 3131 4404; fax +453131 2435; e-mail: dof@post2.tele.dk. The
Danish ornithological society and member of Birdlife International.
Dyrevennernes Landsforening (Friends of Animals Association): Teglvaerksbakken 12,
2900 Hellerup; ☎39 65 67 20.
Dyrevaernforeningen Kattens Vaern: Dronning Olgas Vej 4, 2000 Frederiksberg; ☎38
88 12 00; fax 38 88 12 05. Cat protection organisation.
Dyrevaernsforeningen Svalen: Advokathuset, Kongevejen 54, Postboks 39, 2840 Holte;
☎42.42.16.16; fax 42.42.56.55. Swallow protection organisation.
Dyrevaernsforeningernes Faellesrad (Council for the Protection of Animals): Sekretariat,
Advokathuset, Kongevenjen 54, Postboks 39, 2840 Holte; ☎42 42 16 16.
Faroese Ornithological Society: Føroya Fuglafrødifelag, Postssmoga 1230, 110
Torshavn, Faroe Islands; ☎+298 18 588; fax +298 18 589.
*Foreningen Til Dyrenes Beskyttelse Danmark (Protection of Animals):*Kontor,
Alhambravej 15, 1826 Frederiksberg C; ☎21 22 32 22.
*Nordisk Samfund Til Bekaem Pelse af Misbrug af Dyr (Nordic Association Against
Animal Cruelty):* Blichers Alle 32, 6700 Esbjerg.

Danish Embassies
Australia: Hunter Street, Yarralumla ACT 2600; ☎02-6273 2195.
Canada: Suite 450, 47 Clarence Street, Ottawa, Ontario K1N 9K1; ☎613-234 0704;
fax 613-234 7368.
UK: 55 Sloane Street, London SW1X 9SR; ☎020-7333 0200; fax 020-7333 0270; e-

mail lonamb@um.dk; www.denmark.org.uk
*USA:*3200 Whitehaven Street, NW Washington, DC 20008, USA; ☎202-234 4300; fax 202-328 1470.

Finland

Suomi, as the Republic of Finland calls itself, has been independent from Russia only since 1917. It is the fifth largest European country and the least densely populated (5.1 million inhabitants) and is located in Europe's north-eastern corner, on the 'roof of Europe', at about the same latitude as Iceland. One third of its area lies within the Arctic Circle. It shares a long border with Russia, and its northern extremity is part of Lapland – a huge wilderness that includes swathes of Norway and Sweden, and which has a distinctive culture and tradition of its own. Ten per cent of Finland is water, made up of a myriad of lakes, many of them interlinked and forming navigable water routes. Finland joined the EU in 1995.

Among native species are brown bears, golden eagles, flying squirrels, elk, lynx, wolverine, deer, seals, beaver capercaillie and whooper swans. There are an estimated 450,000 dogs, 1.5 million cats and 50,000 horses in the country.

Trainee schemes

Finland actively encourages trainees to come to Finland for short-term paid work. The International Trainee Exchange programme in Finland is administered by CIMO, the Centre for International Mobility (P.O.B. 343, 00531 Helsinki; ☎+358 9 7747 7033/fax +358 9 7747 7064). Students and graduates who want on-the-job training in their field (including veterinary and agriculture) lasting between one and 18 months should apply directly to CIMO. Short-term training takes place between May and September, while long-term training is available year round. Applications for summer positions must be in to CIMO by the end of January. CIMO point out that there are very few veterinary placements but they would try to help anyone who asked for one. There are also possibilities for veterinary nurses. VNs can apply direct to animal hospitals in Finland and then approach CIMO for the necessary documentation.

This programme is open to people from Europe and outside Europe. Even for the latter, red tape is relatively straightforward. Applicants should write to CIMO for a list of cooperating organisations in 13 countries which will be able to help trainees to obtain the necessary work and residence permit before entering Finland. American applicants should contact InterExchange (161 6th Avenue, New York NY 10013; ☎212-924 0446;e-mail interex@earthlink.net).

To qualify as a trainee, you must have studied for at least one year, preferably with a year's related experience. Wages for trainees are on a par with Finnish remuneration for similar work.

Vets & Veterinary Nurses

There are about 1400 Finnish veterinarians more than half of them women. There are fewer private practitioners in Finland (230) than in most other European countries as private vets have been established only since the 1970s. They deal almost exclusively with small animals and equines. Up to the 1970s municipally appointed vets carried out regular veterinary work as well as governmental concerns like overseeing animal welfare and food hygiene. Employment prospects for newly qualified vets are better than in many countries.

Foreign vets have to register with the Ministry of Agriculture and Forestry (Veterinary and Food Department, PL232, 00171 Helsinki; ☎+358 9 160 33 99; fax +358 9 160 33 38).

Other veterinary organisations:
Finnish Veterinary Association: Suomen Eläinlääkäriliitto r.y., Mäkelänkatu 2c, 00500 Helsinki; ☎+358 9 701 13 88; fax +358 9 701 83 97; e-mail: kirsti.liukkonen@sell.fi; www.sell.fi.
Finnish Veterinary Nurses Association: Klinikkaeläinhoitajat, P.O. Box 99, 100131 Helsinki. Has 140 members.
Finnish Association of Self-employed veterinarians: Suomen Yksityiset Eluainkäärit, c/0 Tikkurilan Ell.asema, Vernissakatu 6, 01300 Vantaa; ☎+358 9 857 21 13; fax +358 9 857 14 77.
Finnish Association of State Veterinarians: Valtion Virkaeläinläärit, Mäkelänkatu 2c, 00500 Helsinki; ☎+358 9 701 13 88; fax +358 9 7010 83 97.

Dogs
The Finns keep an estimated 450,000 dogs. Further information on dogs and potential employers can be obtained from The Finnish Kennel Association (Suomen Kennel-Liitto, Kamreerintie 8, 02770 Espoo; ☎+358 9 887 300; fax +358 9 88730331).

Horses
There are an estimated 50,000 horses in Finland.
Main Racing Organisation: Hippos, Tulkinkuja 3, 02600 Espoo; ☎+358(0)9-511001; www.hippos.fi
Main Recreational Riding Organisation: Suomen Ratsastajainliitto (Finnish Riders' Association): Radiokatu 20, 00093 Helsinki; ☎+358(0)9-2294 510; fax +358(0)9-1496864: e-mail ratsastus@ratsastus.fi
Finnish Farriers Association: Suomen Kengitysseypat R.y., Vermon Ravirata, 00370 Helsinki.

Zoos
Finland has only one major zoo, Helsinki Zoo, at Korkeasaari-Högholmen, 00570 Helsinki; ☎+358(0)9 169591; fax +358(0)9 169 5991; e-mail seppo.turunen@hel.fi; www.hel.fi/zoo. Projects there include snow leopard and forest reindeer. The zoo houses a large variety of species from the tundra to the tropics.
There is also a smaller zoo, The Animal Park of Ähtäri, located in southern Ostrobothnia in the west of Finland, specialising in animals from the northern latitudes. Its address is Karhunkierros 130, 63700 Ähtäri; ☎(06) 5393 555; fax (06) 5393 611; e-mail ahtarinelainpuisto@ahtarinelainpuisto.fi; www.ahtarinelainpuisto.fi

Farmwork
WWOOF Finland: c/o Anne Konsti, Partala Information Services for Organic Agriculture, Huttulantie 1, 51900 Juva; ☎15-321 2380; e-mail anne.konsti@mtt.fi. You have to pay a fee of US$10 for the list of organic farms.

Animal & Bird Protection and Conservation
Birdlife Suomi – Finland: Annankatu 29A, P.O. Box 1285, 00101 Helsinki; ☎+358 9 685 4700; +3589 685 4722; e-mail: (birdlife@surfnet.fi).
Elainsuojeluliitto Animalia: Porvoonkatu 53, 00520 Helsinki. Animal protection organisation.
Finnish Animal Protection Association (SEY): Kotkankatu 9, 00510 Helsinki; ☎+358 9 877 1200; fax +358 9 877 1206.

Finnish Embassies
Australia: Darwin Avenue, Yarralumla ACT 2600; ☎02-6273 3800.
Canada: Suite 850, 55 Metcalfe Street, Ottawa, Ontario K1P 6L5; ☎613-236 2389; fax

613-238 1474.
UK: 38 Chesham Place, London SW1X 8HW; ☎020-7838 6200; www.finemb.org
USA: 3301 Massachusetts Avenue, NW Washington, DC20008; ☎202-298 5800; fax
202-298 6030.

France

France is the largest country in the EU and is linked to the United Kingdom by the
Channel Tunnel between Calais and Dover. The French passion for gastronomy has
resulted in practices long considered decadent by animal lovers; consuming wild song
birds, eating frogs' legs and force-feeding geese in order to produce *paté de foie gras*
(now threatened by an EU ban), are some widely known examples.

Work Scheme for Americans
There is a scheme through which American students with a working knowledge of
French (normally a minimum of 2 years' study at university) are allowed to look for a
job in France at any time of year and work for up to three months with an *autorisation
provisoire de travail.* This scheme is organised by the CIEE (205 East 42nd Street, New
York, NY10017; 1-888-COUNCIL). Eligible Americans already in France can apply to
the CIEE office in Paris (112,ter rue Cardinet, 75017 Paris; ☎+33 (0)1 58 57 20 66).

Vets
With a population fast approaching 60 million it is not surprising that the French have
enough domestic and agricultural animals to keep most of their 17,000 registered vets
in business. Approximately 2,700 are retired and a further 2,274 are not practising for
other reasons including unemployment. There are about 8,000 vets in private practice
and 5,435 veterinary practices.

The market for small animal work in cities is all but saturated and vets have had to
diversify by selling more pet products including food and medicines and by offering
boarding and grooming services.

Conseil Supérieur de l'Ordre National des Vétérinaires: 34 rue Bréguet, 75011 Paris,
 France; ☎+33 1 47 00 12 27; fax +33 1 47 00 09 25. Foreign vets have to register
 with this body.

Other veterinary organisations:
French Association of Veterinary Riders: Association Française de Vétérinaires Cavaliers
 (AFVC), 4ter place de l'Eglise, 78125 Saint Hilarion; ☎+33 4 74 05 37 50; fax +33 4
 74 05 37 59. New organisation started in 1997. 10 members.
*French Association of Small Animal Clinics: Association Française des Cliniques
 Vétérinaires* (petits animaux) AFCV, Maison des Vétérinaires, 10 Place Léon Blum,
 75011 Paris; ☎+33 1 55 50 71 90; fax +33 1 5550 63 59.
Association Française des Vétérinaires de Parcs Zoologiques: 53 Ave. de Saint Maurice,
 75012 Paris; ☎+33 1 44 75 20 00; fax +33 1 43 43 54 73. Zoo vets association.
East-West Veterinary Cooperation and Exchange: Coopération et Echanges Vétérinaires
 Est-Ouest (CEVEO), 45 Cours Aristide Briand, 69300 Caluire; ☎+33 4 78 08 30 92;
 fax +33 4 78 08 30 92.
Vétérinaires Sans Frontières (VSF): 14 avenue Berthelot, 69361 Lyon Cedex 07; ☎+33
 4 78 69 79 59; fax +33 4 78 69 79 56; e-mail: (VSF@globenet.gn.apc.org); http:
 //vetonet.crihan.fr/www/vsf.html). Sends experienced vets to developing countries to
 help mainly with post crises agricultural animal projects in the long term.

Useful Publication

Roy Veterinary Surgeon's Directory: Roy Annuaire Vétérinaire, Les Editions du Point
   Vétérinaire, 9 rue Alexandre, B.P. 233, 94702 Maisons-Alfort, France; ☎+33 1 45 17
   02 25; fax +33 1 45 17 02 74. Listing of all French veterinarians, veterinary suppliers,
   veterinary associations and bodies, professional journals and calendar of forthcoming
   events.

Cats & Dogs
It is somewhat startling for the acknowledged 'nation of animal lovers' (i.e. Britain)
to discover that France has the statistical edge in the number of pets (*animaux de
compagnie*). There are between eight and ten million dogs (compared with Britain's
6.7 million) and 8.2 million cats (compared with 7.2 million in Britain). Of these
150,000 cats and dogs are found wandering as strays annually, and a further 100,000 are
abandoned by their owners on the doorsteps of animal charities.

Recent legislation to protect animals is based on the Law of 10 July 1976 which
guaranteed animals the protection of the law against ill treatment. The 1989 Law of 22
June established standards for the conditions of establishments where cats and dogs are
housed or sold. The French government is formulating measures to reduce the number of
stray dogs through obligatory registration and tagging either with a microchip under the
skin or a tattoo, which will identify the animal through a national register. A law under
proposal also aims to ensure that anyone who breeds, sells, boards, trains or grooms
companion animals for a living has a recognised relevant qualification. France also
intends to follow Belgium in banning the sale of animals at markets and fairs.

Horses
France has an estimated 350,000 horses and the lowest percentage of shod horses (30 to
40%) in the EU. Horse sports are as popular in France as Britain. There are two types of
racing trotting and galloping.

Racing organisations and officials
France Galop: 46 Place Abel Gance, 92655 Boulogne Cedex; ☎+33 149 10 2030; fax
   +33 1 47 619332. Supervises seven racecourses in the Paris area (Auteil, Chantill,
   Enghien, Evry, Longchamp, Maisons-Lafitte, Saint-Cloud).
Société des Steeple-Chases de France (Auteil): 7 rue de l'Amiral d'Estaing, 75116 Paris;
   ☎+33 1 47 23 54 12.
Ministère de l'Agriculture, Service de Haras, des Courses et de la Equitation: Ministry
   of Agriculture horse breeding, racing and equitation service, 14 Ave de la Grand
   Armée, 75017; ☎+33 1 43 59 20 70; fax +33 1 45 61 91 11.
Syndicat des Eleveurs de Chevaux de Sang de France (Breeders Association): 257
   Avenue Le Jour se Leve, 92100 Boulogne, Paris; ☎+33 1 47 61 06 09; fax +33 1
   4761 0474.
Syndicat des Proprietaires de Chevaux de Courses au Galop: Racehorse Owners
   Association, 70 avenue des Champs-Elysees, 75008 Paris; ☎+33 1 45 62 85 48.
Association des Entraineurs de Chevaux de Courses au Galop: 18 bis, avenue du General
   Leclerc, 60501 Chantilly; ☎+33 3 44 57 25 39; fax +33 3 44 57 58 85. Association
   of racehorse trainers.
Association des Jockeys: 43 Avenue de Saint-Germain, 78600 Maisons Laffitte; ☎+33
   1 39 62 05 28; fax +33 1 39 62 00 33.
Association de Formation et d'Action Sociale des Ecuries de Courses (AFASEC): 10
   Avenue Desaix, B P 74, 78600 Maisons-Lafitte; ☎+33 1 39 62 05 05; fax +33 1 39
   62 33 69. Training centre for stable lads and jockeys. Selection training period every
   August. Annual intake of recruits in September. The centre takes boys aged 14 or 15.
   No particular school qualifications but weight limit of 99lbs.

Chantilly Racecourse & Training Centre: 16 Avenue du General Leclerc, 60500 Chantilly; ☎+33 44 57 21 35; fax +33 44 57 02 54 (racecourse).

Training Centre Maisons-Lafitte: Centre d'Entrainement de Maisons-Lafitte, 7 Avenue Mme Lafitte, 78600 Maisons-Lafitte; ☎+33 1 962.25.90.

Horse protection organisation:
Federation des Amis du Cheval: 3 rue de Lyon, 75012 Paris.

Useful Addresses

Association Française d'Information et de Rechèrche Sur l'Animal de Compagnie (AFIRAC): 7, rue Pasteur-Wagner 75011 Paris; ☎01 49 29 12 00; fax 01 48 06 55 65. The French Association for Information and Research in Companion Animals studies the relationship between companion animals and man.

Association Ouvrière des Campagnons du Devoir: 82 rue de l'Hotel de Ville, 75180 Paris Cedex 04; ☎+33 1 44782250; fax +33 1 44 71 1019. French farriers association.

Syndicat National des Marecheaux-Ferrants: 31 cité d'Antin, 75009 Paris; ☎+33 1 61 48 78 55 15; fax +33 1 61 48 74 83 77. French blacksmiths trade union.

Syndicat National des Professionnels du Chien (SNPC): Rue des Paulines, B.P. 09, 63390 Saint-Gervais d'Auvergne; ☎+33 (0)4 73 85 83 67; fax +33 (0)4 73 85 84 34; Minitel: 36 15 CHIENDOG. Membership association for dog trainers (*les dresseurs de chien*), dog groomers/beauticians (*les toiletteurs*), and those involved with security dogs (*les professionnels de la sécurité par chien*).

Animal & Bird Welfare, Protection and Conservation

Conseil National de la Protection Animale: 10 Place Leo Blum, 75011 Paris.

Collectif d'Action Pour la Libération Animale: B.P.9-6034, 35060 Rennes Cedex 3.

Fondation Brigitte Bardot:, 45 rue Vineuse, 75116 Paris; ☎+33 1 45 05 14 60; fax +33 1 45 05 14 80; www.fondationbrigittebardot.fr Primarily a fund raising organisation that campaigns on behalf of various animal rights. The Paris headquarters employs 20 people. The foundation also sponsors a home in Normandy for elderly animals of all kinds and a reception home for dogs and cats in the Paris suburbs.

Fonds Mondial Pour la Nature (WWF): 151 boulevard de la Reine, 78000 Versailles; ☎+33 1 39 24 24 24; fax +33 1 39 53 04 46; www.panda.org/, organises conservation programmes in France and internationally.

Ligue pour la Protection des Oiseaux (LP0): La Corderie Royale, B.P. 263, 17305 Rochefort Cedex, France; ☎+33 546 82 12 34; fax +33 546 82 12 50; e-mail: lpo_ birdlife@mail.a2i-micro.fr The League for the Protection of Birds was founded in 1912 and has 80 paid staff. Publications include *l'Oiseau* and *Ornithos*.

Société Protectrice des Animaux (SPA): 39 boulevard Berthier. 75017 Paris; ☎+33 1 43 80 4066; fax +33 1 47 63 74 76. France's animal protection society.

Zoos, Aquaria, Safari & Birdparks

France has nearly 50 zoos, aquariums and bird parks:

Amiens: Parc Zoologique de la Ville d'Amiens, 139 rue du Faubourg de Hem, 80000 Amiens; ☎+33 322-696100; fax+33-322-696109; e-mail zooamiens@wanadoo.fr.

Amnéville: Parc Zoologique du Bois de Coulange, Centre Thermal et Touristique, 57360 Amnéville; ☎+33 387 702560; fax +33 387 714145; e-mail zoo.amneville@wanado o.fr; www.zoo-amneville.com.

Antibes: Marineland Antibes, ave. Mozart, 06600 Antibes; ☎+33 493-334949; fax +33 493-333865.

Arcachon: Musee Aquarium d'Arcachon, 2 rue du Professeur Jolyet, 33120 Arcachon; ☎+33 556-223903; fax +33-556 835104; www.multimania.com/aquafree/ arcachon.htm.

Asson: Zoo d'Asson, 64800 Asson; ☎+33 559 710334; fax +33 559 710155; e-mail asson.zoo@caramail.com. Includes primates, birds and kangaroos.

Biarritz: Aquarium du Musée de la Mer, Esplanade du Rocher de la Vierge, 64200 Biarritz; ☎+33-559 223334; fax +33-559 227530; e-mail musee.mer@wanadoo.fr; wwww.museedelamer.com.

Brest Cedex: Océanopolis – Aquarium de Brest, 29275 Brest Cedex; ☎+33 2983-44040; fax +33 2983 44069; e-mail oceanopolis@oceanopolis.com; www.oceanopolis.com.

Champrepus: Parc Zoologique Champrepus, Hotel Mahé, 50800 Champrepus; ☎+33 233-613074; fax +33 233-617143.

Cleres: Parc Zoologique de Cleres, 76690 Cleres; ☎+33 235-332308; +33-235 331166; e-mail alain.hennache@wanadoo.fr. Specialists in pheasants.

Courzieu: Parc Animalier de Courzieu: 69690 Courzieu; ☎+33 474 709610; fax +33-474 708663; info@parc-de-courzieu.fr; www.parc-de-courzieu.fr.

Dompierre sur Besbre: Le Pal, 03290 Dompierre sur Besbre; ☎+33 4704 26810; fax +33 4704 20152.

Doué la Fontaine: Parc Zoologique des Minières, Route de Cholet, 49700 Doué la Fontaine; ☎+33-241 591858; fax +33 241 592586; e-mail info@zoodoue.fr; www.zoodoue.fr.

Fréjus: Parc Zoologique de Fréjus; 83600 Fréjus; ☎+33 494 407065.

Jurques: Parc Zoologique de la Cabosse: Carbonel, 14260 Jurques; ☎+33 23177 8058; fax +33 23177 7764.

La Flèche: Zoo de la Flèche, Le Tertre Rouge, Route de Savigne, 72200 La Flèche; ☎+33-243 481919; fax +33 243 481918; e-mail zoo.de.la.fleche@wanadoo.fr.

Le Guerno: Parc Zoologique de Branféré, 56190 Le Guerno; ☎+33 297 429466; fax +33 297 428122; e-mail contact@branfere.com; www.branfere.com.

Les Epesses: Fauconnerie du Puy du Fou, B.P. 25; 85590 Les Epesses; ☎+33 25157 6844; fax +33 25157 3888; e-mail fauconnerie@puydufou.tm.fr. Falcon centre.

Les Mathes: Zoo de la Palmyre, 17570 Les Mathes; ☎+33 546 224606; fax +33 546 236297; e-mail admin@zoo-palmyre.fr; www.zoo-palmyre.fr.

Lille: Parc Zoologique de Lille, Avenue Mathias Delobel, 59800 Lille; ☎+33 3285 20700; +33 32057 3808; e-mail zoolille@mairie-lille.fr; www.nordnet.fr/zoolille.

Lyon: Jardin Zoologique de la Ville de Lyon, Parc de la Tete d'Or, 69006 Lyon; ☎+33 472 823500; fax +33 472 823 509; eric.plouzeau@mairie-lyon.fr.

Montpellier: Parc Zoologique de Lunaret, 50 Avenue d'Agropolis, 34090 Montpellier; ☎+33 467 632763; fax +33 467 414557;.

Mulhouse: Parc Zoologique de Mulhouse, 51 rue du Jardin Zoologique, 68100 Mulhouse; ☎+33 389 318511; fax +33 389 318526; e-mail zoomulhouse@hrnet.fr.

Obterre: Parc de la Haute Touche, Museum Natonal d'Histoire Naturelle, Laboratoire de Conservation des Especes, 36290 Obterre; ☎+33 254 0222040; fax +33 254 392433; www.parcdelahautetouche@yahoo.fr. National Natural History Museum, Species conservation laboratory.

Ozoire-la-Ferriére: Parc Zoologique du Bois d'Attilly, 77330 Ozoir-la-Ferriére; ☎+33 160 027080; fax +33 164 403927.

Paris: Menagerie et Vivarium du Jardin des Plantes: Musee d'Histoire Naturelle, 57 rue Cuvier, 75231 Paris; menagerie ☎+33 140 793794; Fax +33 140 793793; ☎vivarium +33 140 793765. Zoo and vivarium.

Paris: Parc Zoologique de Paris, 53 Avenue de Sainte-Maurice, 75012 Paris; ☎+33 144 752000; +33 143 435473; e-mail pzp@mnhn.fr.

Paris: Aquarium du MAAO: 293 avenue Daumesnil, 75012 Paris; ☎ +3314474-8525/ 8480; fax +33 14343 2753; fax +33 14343 2753; e-mail aquarium.maao@culture.fr.

Peaugres: Safari de Paugres, 07340 Peaugres; ☎+33 475 330032; fax +33 475 337797; e-mail: safari@safari-peaugres.com; www.safari-peaugres.com. Safari park.

Plaisance du Touch/Toulouse: African Safari, 41 rue des Landes, 31830 Plaisance du Touch/Toulouse; ☎+33 561 864503; fax +33 561 067018; e-mail african.safari@free.fr;

www.zoo-africansafari.com. African safari park.

Pont-Scorff: Parc Zoologique de Pont-Scorff, Kerruisseau, 56620 Pont-Scorff; ☎+33 29732 6086; fax +33 29732 5706; e-mail xavier.zoo@wanadoo.fr.

Rive de Gier: Espace Zoologique de St Martin la Plaine, 42800 Rive de Gier; ☎+33 477 751868; fax+33 477 836099; e-mail zoo.st.martin@wanadoo.fr; www.espace-zoologique.com.

Rocamadour: Rocher des Aigles, 46500 Rocamadour; fax +33 56533-6906.

Romaneche-Thorins: Touroparc, cidex 944, 71570 Romaneche-Thorins; ☎ +33 385 355153; fax +33 385 355234; e-mail: Touroparc@wanadoo.fr; www.touroparc.com

Roscoff: Aquarium et Musée Charles Pérez, Station Biologique de Roscoff, Place George-Teissier, B.P. 74, 29682 Roscoff Cedex; ☎ +33 2 98292305; fax +33 298 292380; e-mailjoly@sb-roscoff.fro/Aquarium.

Sigean: Reserve Africaine de Sigean, Route Nationale 9, 11130 Sigean; ☎ +33 468 482020; fax +33 468 488085; ra.sigean@wanadoo.fr; www.reserveafricainesigean.fr. African safari park.

St Aignan: Zoo Parc Beauval, 41110 St Aignan; ☎+33 254 750556; fax +33 254 326594; e-mail infos@zoobeauval.com; www.zoobeauval.com. 3900 animals. 22 hectares.

Strasbourg: Strasbourg Zoo de l'Orangerie, Parc de l'Orangerie, 67000 Strasbourg; ☎& fax +33 388616288.

Thoiry: Parc Zoologique de Thoiry, 78770 Thoiry; ☎+33 134 875225; fax +33 134 875412; www.thoiry.tm.fr.

Trégomeur, St. Brieuc: Jardin Zoologique de Bretagne Moulin de Richard, 22590 Trégomeur, St Brieuc; ☎+33 296 790107; fax +33 296 793242.

Upie: Jardin aux Oiseaux, 26120 Upie; ☎+33 47584 4590; fax +33 47584 3926; e-mail   lejardin-aux-oiseaux@vallee-drome.com;   www.vallee-drome.com/jardin-aux-oiseaux. Bird garden.

Villars les Dombes: Parc des Oiseaux, 01330 Villars les Dombes; ☎+33 474 980554; fax +33 474982774; e-mail info@parc-des-oiseaux.com; www.parc-des-oiseaux.com. Bird park.

Villiers en Bois: Zoorama Européen de la Foret de Chizé, 79360 Villiers en Bois; ☎+33 549 771717; fax +33 549 771718; e-mail cenes@wanadoo.fr; www.zoorama-cenes.org. Zoo of European animals.

Zoo & Aquarium Associations:

Association Nationale de Parcs et Jardins Zoologiques privés (ANPJZ); c/o Zoo Parc Beauval, 41110 St. Aignan; ☎+33 254 750556; fax +33 254 326594. Association of privately owned animal parks and zoos.

Union des Conservateurs d'Aquarium (UCA): 293 avenue Daumesnil, 75012 Paris; fax +33 3 014343 2753. Union of aquarium keepers.

French Embassies
Australia: Perth Avenue, Yarralumla, ACT 2600; ☎02-6216 0100.

Canada: 42 Sussex Drive, Ottawa, Ontario K1M 2C9 Canada; ☎613-789 1795; fax 613-562 3704.

UK: 21 Cromwell Road, London SW7 2EN; ☎020-7838 2000; www.ambafrance.org.uk

USA: 4101 Reservoir Road, NW Washington, DC 20007; ☎202-944 6000; fax 202-944 6072.

Germany

Germany is made up of sixteen Länder or states, six of which were in former East Germany, and it has the largest population (83.5 million) in the EU. Former Chancellor Kohl was responsible for driving ahead the reunion of east and west Germany in 1991 which has put tremendous financial and social pressure on what was the strongest EU economy; a situation probably exacerbated by Germany's acceptance of thousands of eastern European economic refugees who poured across into Germany at the beginning of the 1990s.

Work Experience Scheme for Americans
The CIEE has two programmes for Germany. American students who have studied some German at college can work for up to three months between mid-May and mid-October, or students who can fix up a career-related internship can work for up to six months at any time of year. Details can be obtained by calling 212-822 2600. CIEE's office in Germany is at Oranienburger Strasse 13-14, 10178 Berlin (☎+49 (0)30 2848 590).

Vets
Not unexpectedly for such a densely populated country, Germany has the most qualified vets (30,897) in the EU with over 4,750 of these retired and another 4,683 not practising for various reasons. There are 8,262 practices the majority of them mixed and small animal. There are 3,615 practice assistants.

The main problem for the German veterinary profession is unemployment among new graduates because of near saturation of demand. Additionally German veterinary teaching is very scientifically based which although it provides a wide range of professional possibilities it does not provide for practical experience. Many students work as volunteers in clinics to get the necessary practical experience.

Foreign vets from the EU need a licence to work in Germany. Vets working there short-term need a permit (Erlaubnis). The contact organisation is:
Bundesministerium für Gesundheit und Soziale Sicherung: D53108 Bonn; ☎+49 1888 441-0; fax: +49 1888 441 4900.

Horses
Germany has an estimated 600,000 horses and racing, showjumping and dressage all have an enthusiastic following.

Racing authorities & riding clubs
Direktorium für Vollblutzucht und Rennen e.V: Rennbahnstrasse 154, 50737 Köln.
Hauptverband für Traberzucht und -rennen e.V.: Postfach 2360, D41554 Kaarst.
Deutsche Reiterliche Vereinigung e.V.: Postfach 110265, 48204 Warendorf.

Zoos, Aquaria, Wildlife & Bird Parks
VDZ Verband Deutscher Zoodirektoren e.V.: Hubertusallee 30, 42117 Wuppertal; fax 0202-741888; e-mail info@zoodirektoren.de; www.zoodirektoren.de German association of Zoo Directors.
Deutsher Wildgehege Verband e.V.: Geschäftsstelle: Wildpark Schwarze Berge, Am Wildpark 1, 21224 Rosengarten – Vahrendorf; ☎040-79688265.; e-mail info@wildgehege-verband.de.

Germany has over 100 zoos, aquaria, wildlife and bird parks and single species sanctuaries, many of which are small-scale. Those listed below are the largest:
Augsburg: Zoologischer Garten Augsburg: Brehm 1, 86161 Augsburg; ☎0821-555031; fax 0821-5627299; e-mail info@zoo-augsburg.de; www.zoo-augsburg.de.

Bendorf-Sayn: Garten der Schmetterlinge Schloss Sayn: 56170 Bendorf-Sayn; ☎02622-15478; fax 02622-15479; e-mail schmetterlinge@sayn.de; www.sayn.de.

Berlin: Zoologischer Garten Berlin: Hardenbergplatz 8, 10787 Berlin; ☎030-2540 10; fax 030-2540 1255; e-mail info@zoo-berlin.de & info@aquarium-berlin.de; www.zoo-berlin.de.

Berlin: Tierpark Berlin-Friedrichsfelde: Am Tierpark 125, 10307 Berlin; ☎030-515310; fax 030 515406; www.tierpark-berlin.de.

Bochum: Tierpark + Fossilium Bochum: Tierpark Bochum, Klinikstrasse 49, 44791 Bochum; ☎0234-950-2900; fax 0234 950 29 70; e-mail tierpark.bochum@t-online.de; www.tierpark-bochum.de.

Bremerhaven: Zoo am Meer: H.-H.-Meier Strasse 5, Direkt am Weserdeich, 27568 Bremerhaven; ☎0471-42071; fax 0471-42072; e-mail info@oo-am-meer-bremerhaven.de; www.zoo-am-meer-bremerhaven.de.

Cottbus: Tierpark Cottbus: Kiekebuscher Strasse 5, 03042 Cottbus; ☎0355-714159; fax 0355-722103.

Darmstadt: Vivarium Darmstadt: Schnampelweg 4, 64287 Darmstadt; ☎06151-13 3391; fax 06151-13-3393; e-mail vivarium@stadt.darmstadt.de; www.stadt.darmstadt.de/darmstadneu/info/freizeit/vivarium.

Dortmund: Zoo Dortmund: Stadt Dortmund, Mergelteichstrasse 80, 44225 Dortmund; ☎0231 5024 392; fax 0231-712175; e-mail zoo@dortmund.de; www.dortmund.de/zoo.

Dresden: Zoo Dresden: Tiergartenstrasse 1, 01219 Dresden; ☎0351-4780 60; fax 0351-4718-625; e-mail zoo@zoo-dresden.de; www.zoo-dresden.de.

Duisburg-Kaiserberg: Zoo Duisburg: Mülheimer Strasse 273, 47058 Duisburg-Kaiserberg; e-mail info@zoo-duisburg.de; www.zoo-duisburg.de.

Erfurt: Thüringer Zoopark Erfurt mit Aquarium: Kommunaler Eigenbetrieb der Landeshauptstadt Erfurt Zum Zoopark 8-10, 99087 Erfurt; ☎0361-7518821; fax 0361-7518822; e-mail zoo-erfurt@t-online.de; www.zoopark-erfurt.de.

Frankfurt: Zoo Frankfurt: Alfred-Brehm Platz 16, 60316 Frankfurt; ☎069-212 33727; fax 069-212 37855; e-mail info.zoo@stadt-frankfurt.de; www.zoo-frankfurt.de.

Gelsenkirchen: Ruhr-Zoo Gelsenkirchen: Bleckstrasse 64, 45889 Gelsenkirchen; ☎0209-954 50; fax 0209-954 51/22; e-mail info@ruhr-zoo.de; www.ruhr-zoo.de.

Görlitz (Neisse): Naturschutz-Tierpark Görlitz: Zittauer Strasse 43, 02826 Görlitz; ☎03581-407400; fax 03581-407401; e-mail Naturschutz-Tierpark-Goerlitz@t-online-de; www.tierpark-goerlitz.de.

Halle/Saale: Zoologischer Garten Halle: Fasanenstrasse 5a, 06114 Halle/Saale; ☎0345 5203 300; fax 0345 5203 444; e-mail zoo.halle@t-online.de; www.zoo-halle.de.

Hannover: Zoo Hannover: Adenauerallee 3, 30175 Hannover; ☎0511-28074 163; fax 0511 28074 122; e-mail info@zoo-hannover.de; www.zoo-hannover.de.

Heidelberg: Tiergarten Heidelberg: Tiergartenstrassse 3, 69120 Heidelberg; ☎06221-645510; fax 06221-645588; e-mail info@zoo-heidelberg.de; www.zoo-heidelberg.de.

Hoyerswerda: Zoo Hoyerswerda: Stadtverwaltung Hoyerswerda, Burgplatz 5, 02977 Hoyerswerda; ☎03571-456450; fax 03571-456455.

Karlsruhe: Zoologischer Garten Karlsruhe: Ettlingerstr. 6, 76137 Karlsruhe; ☎0721-133 6801; fax 0721-133 6809; e-mail zoo@karlsruhe.de./Zoo.

Köln: Zoologischer Garten Köln: Riehler Strasse 173, 50735 Köln; ☎0221-77850; fax 0221 7785 111; e-mail info@zoo-koeln.de; www.zoo-koeln.de.

Leipzig: Zoo Leipzig: Pfaffendorferstr. 29, 04105 Leipzig; e-mail office@zoo-leipzig.de; www.zoo-leipzig.de.

Magdeburg: Zoologischer Garten: Am Vogelgesang 12, 39124 Magdeburg; ☎0391 280 900; fax 0391-280 9012; e-mail callithrix@aol.com; www.magdeburg.de./kultur/zoo.html.

München: Münchener Tierpark Hellabrun: Tierparkstrasse 30, 81543 München; ☎089-

625 080; fax 089-625 0832; e-mail office@zoo-munich.de; www.zoo-munich.de.

Meereszentrum Fehmarn: Gertrudenthaler Strasse 12, 23769 Burg auf Fehmarn; ☎04371/44 16; www.meereszentrum-fehmarn.de(aquarium).

Münster: Allwetterzoo Münster: Sentruper Strasse 315, 48161 Münster; ☎0251-89040; fax 0251-8904990; e-mail info@allwetterzoo.de; www.allwetterzoo.de.

Neunkirchen/Saar: Neunkircher Zoologischer Garten: Zoostrasse 25, 66538 Neunkirchen/Saar; ☎06821-913633; fax 06821-9113625; e-mail zoo@zoo.nk.de; www.zoo-neunkirchen.de.

Neumünster: Tierpark Neumünster: Geerdtsstrasse 100, 24537 Neumünster; ☎04321-51402; 04321-53162; e-mail tierpark-neumuenster@t-online.de; www.tierparknms.de.

Neuwied: Zoo Neuwied: Förderverein Zoo Neuwied, Waldstrasse 160, 56566 Neuwied; ☎02622-90460; fax 02622-904629; e-mail info@zooneuwied.de; www.zooneuwied.de.

Osnabrück: Zoogesellschaft Osnabrück: Am Waldzoo 2-3, 49802 Osnabrück; ☎0541-951050; fax 0541-9510522; e-mail zoo@zoo-osnabrueck.de; www.zoo-osnabrueck.de.

Rheine: NaturZoo Rheine: Salinenstrasse 150, 48432 Rheine; ☎05971-1614; fax 05971-1614820; e-mail info@naturzoo.de; www.naturzoo.de.

Rostock: Zoologischer Garten Rostock: Rennbahnallee 21, 18059 Rostock; ☎0381-20820; fax 0381-4934 400; e-mail post@zoo-rostock.de; www.zoo-rostock.de.

Saarbrücken: Zoologischer Garten der Landeshauptstadt Saarbrücken: Graf-Stauffenberg Strasse, 66121 Saarbrücken; ☎0681-980 440; fax 0681-980 4438; www.saarbruecken.de/sbnet/zoo.

Sea Life Timmendorfer Strand: Kurpromenade 5, 23669 Timmendorfer Strand; ☎04503/3 58 80; www.sealife-timmendorf.de

Sea Life Dortmund: Westfalenpark, Florianstr. 24, 44139 Dortmund; ☎0231 95 8 07 30; www.sealife.de.

Sea Life Konstanz: Klein Venedig, Hafenstrasse 9, 78462; ☎07531 128270; www.sealife.de.

Schwerin: Zoologischer Garten Schwerin: Zoo Schwerin, Waldschulenweg 1, 19061 Schwerin; ☎0385-395510; fax 0385 3955130; e-mail info@zoo-schwerin.de; www.zoo-schwerin.de.

Straubing: Tiergarten der Stadt Straubing: Stadt Straubing, Lerchenhaid 3, 94315 Straubing; ☎09421-21277; fax 09421-830439; e-mail stadt@straubing.de; www.straubing.de.

Stuttgart: Zoologisch-Botanischer Garten Wilhelma: Postfach 501227, 70376 Stuttgart; ☎0711-54020; fax 0711-5402222; e-mail info@wilhelma.de; www.wilhelma.de.

Vogelpark Walsrode: Am Rieselbach, 29664 Walsrode; ☎05161 6 04 40; www.vogelpark-walsrode.de.

Waldtierpark Bretten: ☎07252 72 56; www.tierpark-bretten.de

Wuppertal: Zoologischer Garten Wuppertal: Hubertusalle 30, 42117 Wuppertal; ☎0202-27470; fax 0202-741888; e-mail direktion@zoo-wuppertal.de; www.zoo-wuppertal.de.

Idea Schmetterlings-Paradies: Wirsbergerstrasse 12, 95339 Neuermarkt; ☎09227 90 25 25; www.schmetterlingspark.de.

Safari Parks
Senne Grosswild Safariland: Mittweg 16, 33758 Schloss Holte-Stukenbrock; ☎05207/ 952425; fax 05207-952426; e-mail buero@safaripark.de; www.safaripark.de

Serengeti-Safaripark Hodenhagen: 29691 Hodenhagen; ☎05164-531; fax 05164-2451; e-mail info@serengeti-park.de; www.serengeti-park.de.

Organic Farming
Aspiring volunteers for organic farms should contact WWOOF's German branch (Postfach 210 259, 01263 Dresden; info@wwoof.de) has over 150 members. Membership fee gives access to the addresses of 170 farmers.

Animal & Bird Welfare, Protection And Conservation
BNA-Bundesverband für Fachgerechten Natur- und Artenschutz e.V.: Postfach 11.10 76707 Hambrücken; ☎07255-2800; fax 07255-8355; e-mail gs@bna-ev.dc; www.bna-ev.de

Deutscher Tierschutz e.V: Bundesgeschäftstelle, Baumschulenallee 15, 53115 Bonn; 0228-604960; fax 0228-604 9640; e-mail bg@tierschutzbund.de; www.tierschutzvebund.de.

International Fund for Animal Welfare (IFAW) Deutschland; Postfach 10 46 23 20032, Hamburg; ☎+49 40 866 5000; fax +49 40 866 500 22; e-mail info-de@ifaw.org.

Pro Wildlife: Gräfelfinger Str. 65, 81375 Munich; ☎089.81299-507; e-mail mail@prowildlife.de; www.prowildlife.de.

WWF-Deutschland: Rebstöcker Str. 55, 60326 Frankfurt; ☎069 79144-0; fax 069 6117221; www.wwf.de

Akademie für Tierschutz (Animal Protection): Einrichtung des Deutschen Tierschutzbundes e.V., Spechtstr.1, 85579 Neubiberg; ☎+49 89 600291 0; fax +49 89 600291-15; e-mail: Akademie.fuer.Tierschutz@muenchen.org.

Bund gegen den Missbrauch der Tiere (League against the mistreatment of animals): Hauptgeschäftsstelle, Viktor-Scheffel-Strasse 15, 80803 München; ☎+49 89 383952-0; fax+4989 383952-23; e-mail: joprinz@metronet.de.

Conserve: Geschäftsstelle, Heeder Dorfstrasse 44, mail conserve@t-online.de; www.conserve-links.org. Online databank including addresses of nature organisations worldwide and conservation projects which need volunteers.

Deutsche Gesellschaft Tiere & Nature: German organisation for animals and nature, Danzigerstr 35, 20099 Hamburg; ☎+4940 247544.

Gesellschaft zur Rettung der Delphine e.V.: Komwegerstr. 37, 81375 Munich; ☎+49 89/74 16 04 10; fax 74.16 04 11; e-mail: delphine@t-online.de Organisation for Dolphin Rights.

Gesellschaft zum Schutz der Wölfe (Organisation for the Protection of Wolves): von Goltstein-Strasse 1 53902 Bad Münstereifel; ☎+49 2191665802; fax +2191 665802.

Natureschutzbund Deutschland (NABU): German Society for the Protection of Nature, Herbert-Rabius Str 26, 53225 Bonn; ☎+ 49 228 9 75 61 0; fax +49 228 9 75 6190; e-mail: 100726.2535@compuserve.com.

PETA (Deutschland) E.v.: People for the Ethical Treatment of Animals, German branch, Postfach 311503, 70475 Stuttgart.

Animal & Bird Rescue Centres *(Auffangsstationen):*
Eickeloh: Auffangstation, Brinkstrasse 2, 29693 Eickeloh; ☎+49 51 164 429; Owls and birds of prey.

Güttingen: Tierärztliches Institut Güttingen, Groner Landstrasse 2, 37073 Güttingen; ☎+49 551-391. Veterinary Institute & bird rescue.

Metelen: Biologisches Institut Metelen (NRW); Forschungseinrichtung für Biotop- und Artenschutz, Samberg 65, 48629 Metelen; ☎+49 2556-7077/8;fax +49 2556-1000. Research organisation and wild animal sanctuary.

NABU-Artenshutzzentrum Lieferde: Hauptstrasse 20, 38542 Leiferde; ☎05373-6677; fax 05373-1260; e-mail NABUArtenschutzzentrum@t-online.de (birds and reptiles).

Norden: Seehundaufzucht- und Forshungsstation, Dörper Weg 22, 26508 Norden; ☎+49 4931-8919. Seal rearing and bird sanctuary; also research station.

Statliche Vogelshutzwarte Seebach: Lindenhof 3, 99998 Weinbergen; ☎03601-440662;

fax 03601-440664; e-mail vswseebach@TLUJena.Thuerringen.de Contact Herr
Kaiser (birds and reptiles).
Tierschutzzentrum Pritzwalk GmbH & Co KG: Johann-Sebastian-Bach-Str. 4, 16928
Pritzwalk; ☎03395-301301; fax 03395-311890 (Birds, Reptiles and Amphibians).
Vogelpark Biebesheim: Anglerweg, 64584 Biebesheim; ☎06258-81865. Contact. Herr
Zimmermann (birds only).
Wildtier-und Artenschutzstation e.V: Hohe Warte, 31553 Sachsenhagen; ☎05725-
708730; fax 05725-708740; www.wildtierstation.de (birds and reptiles).

German Embassies
Australia: Empire Cct, Yarralumla, ACT 2600; ☎02-6270 1911.
Canada: P.O. Box 379, Postal Station A, 14th Floor, 275 Slater Street, Ottawa, Ontario
KIP 5H9; ☎613-232 11-1; fax 613-594 9330.
UK: 23 Belgrave Square, London SW1X 8PZ; ☎020-7824 1300; fax 020-7824 1345;
www.german-embassy.org.uk.
USA: 4645 Reservoir Road, NW Washington; DC 20007; ☎202-298 4000; fax 202-298
4249.

Greece

Although part of western Europe through membership of the EU, the Greeks do not really
consider themselves Europeans. Geographically, mainland Greece reaches towards the
Orient over its border with Turkey. There is a festering territorial dispute with Turkey
over the island of Cyprus, the northern part of which was invaded by Turkey in 1974.
Apart from southern Cyprus (which remains Greek), there are dozens of Greek islands
of which the biggest are Crete, Lesbos and Rhodes; the others are often referred to by
their group names: the Cyclades, Sporades, Dodecanese etc. The total Greek population
is 10.5 million.

Unfortunately, Greece has one of the poorest reputations for animal welfare in the EU.
Some Greek zoos and abbatoirs in particular have had damning criticism levelled at them
by organisations concerned with animal welfare.

Vets
There are 2,300 practising vets in Greece. In keeping with Greece's perceived reputation
as one of the last bastions of male chauvinism in western Europe, the profession is over
80% male. Sheep and goats are the most numerous animals (9.1 million and 5.6 million
respectively) and small ruminants provide about half the job prospects for vets in the
state sector and private practice the other half. There are about 800 private veterinary
practices. There are very few veterinary specialists in Greece and those who wish to
specialise usually have to go abroad to complete their studies. This means that there are
possible openings for foreign specialists. The main barrier for foreigners would therefore
seem to be a language one.

The Ministry of Agriculture is responsible for checking foreign vets' credentials; their
address is Acharno 2, 10176 Athens; ☎+301 822 44 24 or +30 1 822 7345; fax: +30 1
822 91 88; e-mail: vetserv@ath.forthnet.gr.

Horse Racing
Jockey Club of Greece: 18 Filikis Eterias Square, 10673 Athens; ☎+30 1 36 26 873;
fax +30 1 3636568.

Animal & Bird Welfare, Protection & Conservation

Animal Welfare Society of Lesbos ('Pan'): 22, Mitilini, 81100, Lesbos.

Animal Welfare Society of Thessaloniki ('Argos'): P.O. Box 11052, Pc 54110 Thessaloniki.

Hellenic Ornithological Society (HOS): Vas Irakleioou 24, 106 82 Athens, Greece; tel/fax +30 1 822 8704; ☎+30 1 822 87047; e-mail: birdlife-gr@ath.forthnet.gr; www.ornithological.gr has a version in English.

Animal Projects needing Volunteers:

Aegean Wildlife Hospital in Paros: The Wildlife Hospital was started in 1995 and treats and rehabilitates wildlife that is injured or exhausted from migration. Currently planning a larger establishment also on Paros. The Hospital has trained vets and volunteers. The latter can help with feeding and rehabilitation and environmental education. Prospective volunteers can apply to the Hospital direct, and should be self sufficient as regards finding and funding their own lodging and food.

Contact, Aegean Wildlife Hospital, Paros 844 00, Greece; tel/fax 011-302 842-2931; e-mail awh@paroshome.com; www.greektravel.com/greekislands/paros/birds.html

Archelon-Sea Turtle Protection Society of Greece: Solomou 57, 10432 Athens, Greece; ☎+30 210 5231342; fax +30 210 5231342; e-mail stps@archelon.gr; www.archelon.gr. The STPS is a non-profit organisation that runs conservation projects in Greece and takes 350-400 international volunteers annually. Summer fieldwork lasts from early May to late October takes place on Zakynthos, Crete and Peloponesus where the most import loggerhead nesting beaches are. At the Sea Rescue Centre volunteers are welcome all year round to help with the daily treatment of injured sea turtles. No special skills are needed but artistic and technical/maintenance skills can be utilised. Minimum placement is for four weeks. For fieldwork, the busiest times are the beginning and the end of the season.

All volunteers are unpaid, but volunteers can bring tents and stay on designated free campsites with basic sanitary and cooking facilities provided. Applications to Dina Soulantika, at the above address.

Arcturos: 3 Victor Hugo Street, 54625 Thessaloniki, Greece; tel/fax +30 310 555920; e-mail arcturos@arcturos.gr; www.arcturos.gr. *Main targets:* conservation of bear and wolf populations, conservation and management of mountainous ecosystems in Greece and the Balkans. Arcturos is running a bear and a wolf sanctuary for confiscated animals, as well as information centres on these species in rural NW Greece. Volunteers are welcome to assist in the daily chores of the centres and sanctuaries, as well as help with presentations and information kiosks on a number of awareness-raising events. Volunteers usually participate for two weeks minimum from June to September. Arcturos also runs a six-month European Voluntary Service project every year, with various subjects. The EVS volunteers usually assist the scientific teams with the field-work, collection of data, awareness-raising, etc. For more info on volunteer projects, please contact Ms. Sofia Georgeli (georgeli@arcturos.gr).

Conservation Koroni: Post Restante, Koroni 24004, Messinias; fax +30 725 22394. Conservation volunteers are needed for five stints of approximately four weeks each from May to October. Volunteers are welcome to stay for as short or long a time as they wish. The aim is to clean up the local beach and surrounding habitats of the loggerhead turtle near Koroni in the Peloponnese in southern Greece. Duties also include some monitoring of their behaviour, data recording and material preparation. Participants should have a keen interest in conservation, willing to work one to three hours a day, five days a week, and able to subsidise their own stay. There is an accommodation charge of approximately £90 per month. Eight to ten volunteers are required throughout the season and are accepted on a first come basis. Volunteers can enjoy the opportunity of helping to protect these prehistoric animals in their natural environment.

The Greek Animal Welfare Fund (GAWF): 1-2 Castle Lane, London SW1E 6DN; ☎020-7828 9736; fax 020-7630 9816; e-mail admin@gawf.freeserve.co.uk; www.gawf.org.uk. GAWF is a pioneering animal welfare society in Greece; its mission is to bring significant and lasting change to the treatment and status of animals in Greece. GAWF has an ongoing neutering programme for stray animals, particularly the infamous feral cat colonies. It campaigns for the enforcement of EU standards in slaughterhouses, and the improvement of the welfare and status of farm animals. GAWF provides education, veterinary and farriery care for the working animals of Greece (horses, donkeys and mules), subsidising treatment for owners unable to afford it. Volunteer vets from UK work alongside locals helping to improve farriery and veterinary skills. Director, Carol McBeth, co-ordinates humane education programmes in Greek schools, and will be highlighting animal issues during the build up to the 2004 Olympics. GAWF supports the work of 40 local animal welfare groups providing information, veterinary support and grants to encourage and further animal welfare within Greece. This includes causes such as the rescue of exotic animals.

Hellenic Ornithological Society: Vas. Irakleiou 24, 106 82 Athens; tel/fax +30 1 822 8704; e-mail birdlife-gr@ath.forthnet.gr; www.ornithologiki.gr (select English version). Needs volunteers May to October to work in the field constructing and monitoring nests, censusing bird numbers, feeding, habitat monitoring and raising public awarenesss. Accommodation is provided. May be campsite so own camping gear required. Rooms sometimes provided depending on projects. Membership registration fee of about £20 payable. Travel and food at the volunteers' expense. Expenses for the work are borne by HOS. Apply on the HOS website or download form and send by post, fax etc.

Ionian Dolphin Project: Tethys Research Institute, Field Station, 13081 Episcopi-Kalamos, Lefkada; tel/fax: +39 (0)27 2001947; fax +39 (0)27200 1946; e-mail: tethys@tethys.org; www.tethys.org A long-term research programme to protect the common bottlenose dolphin and short-beaked common dolphin in the Mediterranean Sea. Volunteers are needed from June to September for six-day courses: volunteers are involved in all phases of the research programme (observation of dolphins from boat and from land, collection and download of scientific data, maintenance of instruments

They protect loggerhead turtles by tagging nesting females

etc). Cost is from 550-650 euros depending on the season. Volunteers share the base at Episkopi with the research staff and help with cooking and housekeeping.

Katelios Group for the Research/Protection of the Marine Terrestrial Life: Katelios 28082, Kefalonia, Greece; tel/fax +30 26710 81009/81426; e-mail katelios@hol.gr. The Katelios group was started in 1994. Kefalonia is the largest of the seven Ionian islands and its highest point is Mt. Ainos (1628m). Kefalonia has endangered wildlife, notably loggerhead sea turtles and monk seals. Katelios is a small fishing village on Kefalonia. About 40 volunteers a year are accepted. During the turtle nesting season volunteers patrol the beach at night and collect information (size, weight etc) during the nesting procedure. Volunteers also keep the beaches free of litter so as not to impede the progress of hatchlings on their way to the sea. Tasks may vary according to the season and include tagging hatchlings, raising awareness amongst tourists and locals through posters and leaflets. Volunteers are expected to attend Greek lessons as part of the programme. Placements are for a minimum of one month and a minimum of six. Volunteers with knowledge of veterinary nursing and experienced biologists especially welcome. Accommodation is camping in an olive field and volunteers must provide their own food. There is a participation charge and volunteers must pay half of this when their application is accepted. Volunteers are needed all year round and can apply direct to the above address or through the European Voluntary Service. Volunteers who come independently have to contribute to the project; only those who apply through the EVS get pocket money.

Kefalonian Marine Turtle Project: School of Biological Science, University of Wales at Swansea, Singleton Park, Swansea, SA2 8PP; e-mail BDHOUGHT@swansea.ac.uk. The KMTP project was set up to research and conserve the sea turtle population of the island of Kefalonia. Volunteers have the opportunity to participate in a variety of activities connected with this. Depending on the time of year, these include: nocturnal and daytime surveillance of sea turtle nesting activities, radio tracking experiments, data analysis and public awareness talks. Full participation in the day-to-day chore involved in running of the camp on the southern tip of Kefalonia also required.

The volunteer season runs from 1 June to 22 October. Volunteers come for five weeks at a time. However, at the end of the season there is a two and a half week programme for those who can only manage a shorter time. The cost of £550 (five weeks) or £200 (two and a half weeks) covers food, accommodation and a 4-day training course at the beginning of the stay (to ensure maximum participation), project T-shirt, training and science manuals.

Volunteers are normally, but not exclusively, students of biology, marine science or other related subjects. However applications from people from all walks of life are welcomed. A knowledge of Greek, French, German or Italian is useful, but not essential.

Potential participants can download an application form from www.ex.ac/MEDASSET/kmtp/homepage.htm. or send an SAE to the a above address.

Noah's Ark Animal Shelter: P.O.Box 241, Agia Triada, Akrotiri, Chania, Crete, TK 73100; ☎+30 821 66146; www.archenoah-kreta.com The only shelter on the island of Crete, Noah's Ark cares for hundreds of animals including dogs and cats, donkeys, budgerigars, canaries, parrots, owls and hawks. Volunteers are needed year round particularly in winter. Volunteers carry out tasks such as feeding and cleaning out the animals, basic nursing and collecting donated food scraps from hotels, tavernas etc. Volunteers should be prepared for some distressing sights caused by animal abuse, neglect and starvation and to get dirty. Summers are long and hot; winters wet and muddy.

The minimum is one week and the maximum is unlimited. The age range is 16 to 60 years. Languages spoken are Greek, English and German. Volunteers have to pay for accommodation, which can be arranged locally at reasonable rates. Noah's Ark will assist with finding accommodation and transportation, and will provide breakfast. All other expenses including air fares to Crete are at the volunteer's expense.

Long-term volunteers are welcome and if possible will be provided with on-site accommodation. All enquiries to Silke Wrobel at the above address.

Sea Turtle Project, Rhodes Island: Chelon, Marine Turtle Conservation & Research Programme, (Tethys Research Institute), Viale G.B., Gadio 2, 1-20121, Milan Italy; ☎+39 0272001947; fax +39 0272001946; www.tethys.org Aims to protect loggerhead turtle nesting in the southern part of Rhodes. The project focuses on nest censusing and protection, tagging of nesting females and behaviour observation. Also raising conservation awareness amongst locals and holiday-makers. July, August & September. Two weeks. US$600 per two weeks includes meals but own tent needed. All other expenses are borne by the volunteers. Longer stays possible. Volunteers' work involves assisting researchers with the above as well as botanical census and study of birds of prey. Includes night-time work observing turtle nesting. English and Italian spoken and Greek useful.

Greek Embassies

Australia: Corner of Turrana Street & Empire Cct. Yarralumla, ACT 2600; ☎02 6273 3011.

Canada: 76-80 MacLaren Street, Ottawa, Ontario K2P OK6; ☎613 238 6271; fax 613 238 5676.

UK: 1A Holland Park, London W11 3TP; ☎020-7221 6467; fax 020-7243 3202.

USA: 2221 Massachusetts Avenue, NW, Washington DC 20008; ☎202-939 5800; fax 202 939 5824.

Iceland

Iceland's place in Europe is an anomalous one. Although classed as part of Scandinavia, it is nearer to Greenland. It is Europe's second largest island after Britain, yet its population of 260,000 is smaller than Luxembourg's. It lies just below the Arctic Circle and is an active volcanic island, which has earned it the soubriquet 'Land of Ice and Fire'. It does not belong to the EU but is part of the European Economic Area. It also has notoriously expensive living costs so any job volunteering, or as a trainee would almost certainly have to come with an offer of bed and board if there were no pay.

The Viking invaders from Norway brought most of the Icelandic animals' ancestors to Iceland in the ninth century including ponies, sheep, cattle and dogs. Sheep farming is the most common type of animal agriculture. However, there are at least 80,000 horses of the Icelandic pony type on Iceland and several companies run pony trekking holidays there during the summer months. It might be possible, by contacting proprietors to get a groom job in return for keep. The Iceland Chamber of Commerce (Hus verslunarinnar, Kringlan 7, 103 Reykjavik; ☎+354 5886666) could provide addresses of riding stables.

Although not quite a disease-free paradise for animals, there are relatively few viral and bacterial diseases that affect cattle and horses and Iceland's dogs are free from rabies and distemper. There is a total ban on importing or reimporting horses but dogs are allowed in after quarantine.

Vets

Iceland has no veterinary school and Icelandic vets train mainly in Oslo, Copenhagen and Germany. There are 51 public sector veterinarians and 24 private practitioners. Of necessity practitioners do mixed work and outside Reykjavik small animal practices are rare. Veterinarians are allocated a region by the government, which cuts down

competition between vets and is probably necessary for their economic survival.
Icelandic Veterinary Association:
Dyralaeknafelag Islands, Lagmuli 7, 108 Reykjavik; ☎+354 5689545; fax +354 568 9802; e-mail: eggun@rhi.hi.is;
Chief Veterinary Officer's website: www.cvo.is
Animal & Bird Welfare, Protection And Conservation
Icelandic Federation of Animal Protection: P.O. Box 993, 121 Reyjavik.
Icelandic Society for the Protection of Birds: Fuglaverndarfelag Islands, P.O.Box 5069, 125 Keykjavik; ☎ +354 562 04 77; fax +354 562 04 64.

Icelandic Embassies & Consulates:
Australia: Consulate, Kennedy Street, Kingston, ACT 2604; ☎02-6295 7110.
Canada: 485 Broadview Avenue, Ottawa, Ontario KT8 2L2; ☎613 724 5982; fax 613-724 1209.
UK: 2A Hans Street, London SW1X OJE; ☎020-7259 3999; fax 020-7245 9649; e-mail icemb.london.utn.stjr.is; www.iceland.org.uk
USA: Suite 1200 1156 15th Street, NW, Washington DC 20005; ☎202-265 6653/5.

Ireland

The island of Ireland is less than a third the size of Britain and has a small population of 3.5 million. It has benefited hugely from membership of the EU and has successfully modernised into one of the high technology and service providers of Europe while still remaining in touch with its literary and artistic roots. Massive inward investment and a rich culture are an attractive combination and Ireland is a pleasant place to live although high taxes, high unemployment and the very high cost of living are major detractions. Ireland is still largely an agricultural nation, which probably accounts for the proportionately high number of vets there.

Work Scheme for Students from North America, South Africa, Jamaica, Argentina and Ghana
US nationals who can prove Irish ancestry may be eligible for unrestricted access to Ireland. If this is not the case, American and Canadian students are eligible for an 'Exchange Visitor Program Work Permit' valid for up to four months at any time of year for Americans and for Canadians a year. The scheme also applies to the other countries mentioned above. Applicants should be aged 18 to 30 and have a (guideline) sum equivalent of about £400-£600 ($800-$900) in funds to support themselves while they are looking for work. The Union of Students in Ireland Travel Service (19-21 Aston Quay, O'Connell Bridge, Dublin 2; ☎+353 1-677 8117; www.usit.ie). In the USA applicants should contact the CIEE in New York (633 3rd Ave. New York, NY 10017) and SWAP/Travel Cuts (45 Charles St East, Suite 100, Toronto, Ontario M4Y 1S2) in Canada.

A privately run organisation, Dublin Internships (8 Orlagh Lawn, Scholarstown Road, Dublin 16; tel/fax +353 1-494 5277) undertakes to find internships of varying durations (usually one semester starting September or January, or in summmer)in the student applicant's field of interest. The work is non-salaried but can earn North American college credits. There is a fee charged.

Vets
There are over 1,800 practising vets in Ireland and a further 180 working abroad, mostly in the UK. There are veterinarians working in Ireland from other EU countries including

Germany, Italy and the Netherlands. The public sector employs 460 vets and the rest are practitioners. Despite Ireland's reputation as a horse-mad nation only about 40 of these are specialised horse practitioners, some of whom are involved with Ireland's lucrative trade in thoroughbreds, while others are doctors for all types of horses.

Currently, the majority of veterinary practices deal with farm livestock, however this is likely to decrease in the future and small animal practices (currently about 70 in number) will increase. A potential employment opportunity for EU vets is the Headquarters of the Food and Veterinary Office of the European Union which has been based near Dublin since 1998.

Foreign vets should register with the Veterinary Council (53 Lansdowne Road, Ballsbridge, Dublin 4; ☎ +353 1 668 44 02; fax +353 1 660 43 73).

Horses
In popular perception Ireland and horses are inextricably linked.

Irish racing & breeding organisations:
Irish Horseracing Authority: Leopardstown Racecourse, Foxrock, Dublin 18; ☎+353 1 2892888; fax +353 1 2892019.
Association of Irish Racehorse Owners Ltd.: Dumurry House, Co Kildare; ☎+353 45 522944; fax +353 45 522935.
Irish Racehorse Trainers Association: Curragh House, Dublin Road, Co Kildare; ☎ +353 45 522981; fax +353 45 522982.
Irish Thoroughbred Breeders Association: Greenhills, Kill, Co Kildare; ☎+353 45 877543; fax +353 45 877429; e-mail: tba.@indigo.ie
The Irish Master Farriers Association: Ballinamullen Farms, Omagh, County Tyrone; ☎+353 45 521889; fax +353 45 88 550602.

Zoos
Cork: Fota Wildlife Park, Fota Island, Carrigtwohill, County Cork; ☎+353 21 812678; fax +353 21 812 744; e-mail fota@indigo.ie; www.fotawildlife.ie.
Dublin: Royal Zoological Society of Ireland: Dublin Zoo, Phoenix Park, Dublin 8; ☎+353 1 6771425; fax +353 1 6771660; e-mail info@dublinzoo.ie; www.dublinzoo.ie.

Animal & Bird Welfare, Protection And Conservation
Irish Society for the Protection of Animals: 300 Lower Rathmoines Road, Dublin 6; ☎+353 1 4977874; fax +353 1 4977940.

Ornithological organisation
Birdwatch Ireland (Cairde Eanlaith Eireann): Ruttledge House, 8 Longford Place, Monkstown, Co Dublin; ☎+353 1 2804 322; fax +353 128 44407; e-mail: bird@indigo.ie

Farm Work
There is little chance of finding paid work because of high rural unemployment. WWOOF Ireland (Harpoonstown, Drinagh, County Wexford) enables those who pay a subscription fee, to find placements on organic farms in return for board and lodging. There are about 90 farms on their list.

Irish Embassies
Australia: Arkana Street, Yarralumla, ACT 2600; ☎ 02-6273 3022.
Canada: 170 Metcalfe Street, Ottawa, Ontario K2P 1P3; ☎613-233 6281; fax 613-233 5835.
UK: 17 Grosvenor Place, London SW1X 7HR; ☎020-7235 2171; fax 020-7245 6961.

USA: 2234 Massachusetts Avenue NW, Washington, DC 20008; ☎202-462 3939; fax 202 232 5993.

Italy

The long boot-shaped outline of Italy projects into the Mediterranean. Also part of Italy, are the large Mediterranean islands of Sardinia and Sicily and many smaller islands. The population of 57.5 million is most dense in the industrial north around Milan and Turin and sparse in the south, except for the area around Naples. The north is also vastly wealthier than the south. The acrimony caused by the cost to northerners of subsidising the Mezzogiorno (south) has led to the formation of a separatist movement, the Lega Nord which wants the north to form a separate state.

Vets

Veterinarians total 18,000 of whom nearly 6000 are state employees divided amongst 400 local sanitary units. Italy is notorious for its inneficient and financially wasteful state bureaucracy and the veterinary service is no exception. In Italy veterinary services come under the National Health Ministry. Currently the service is undergoing a streamlining and cost efficiency reorganisation which includes enabling state veterinarians to offer services in direct competion with private veterinarians which is bound to make the already difficult lot of veterinarians worse. Italy has no fewer than 13 veterinary faculties which between them turn out 850 new graduates annually and there is no doubt that there will soon be a large number of them unable to find employment with the state or in small or large animal practice as all three areas have reached saturation. Foreign vets have to register with the *Ministero della Sanitá:* Direzione Generale degli Ospedali-Divisione VI, Viale dell'Industria, Rome; ☎+39 6 5994 920; fax +39 6 5994 2665.

Volunteers monitor bear's feeding habits

Horses

Racing authorities & organisations:

AGRI (Amateur Riders Association: Piazza San Alessandro 6, 20123 Milano; ☎+39 2 874 079; fax +39 2 865 673.

Associazione Nazionale Allevatori Cavalli Purosangue (ANAC): Via del Caravaggio 3, 20144 Milan; ☎+39 2 4801 2002; fax +39 2 48194547. Thoroughbred breeders association and sales.

Associazione Nazionale Fantini (Jockeys Association): Via E Montale 9, 20150 Milan; ☎ +39 2 4521 234; fax +39 2 4820 2297.

ANACG: Trainers Association, Via E Montale 9, 20151 Milan; fax +39 2 4820 5006.

Federippodromi (Racecourse Association): Via Nomentana 134, 00161 Rome; ☎+39 6 8632 3490; +39 6 8632 4362.

FENAG: Ippodromo Capannelle, Via Appia Nuova 1255, 00187 Rome; fax +39 6 7180 326. Trainers Association in Rome.

Jockey Club Italiano: via Portuense 96/D, 00153 Rome; ☎+39 65 8330925;fax +39 65 8330921.

Tortoises are monitored by radio tracking

Societa degli Steeple-chases d'Italia: Via Apulia 9, 00183 Rome; ☎+39 6 70493447; fax +39 6 7096 386.

UNPCP: Piazzale dello Sport 12, 20151 Milan; ☎+39 2 4042 416; fax +39 2 700 410.

Zoos & Aquaria

Federation of Italian Zoos and Aquaria: Unione Italiana degli Zoo ed Acquari (UIZA), c/o Giardino Zoologico e Museo di Zoologia Roma, Viale del Giardino Zoologico 20, 00197 Rome; ☎+39 6-321 541 691557; fax +39 6 3218263.

Animal & Bird Welfare, Protection & Conservation

Cetacean Foundation: Fondazione Cetacea, Via Milano 63, 47838 Riccione (RN);

☎+39 541 691557; fax +39 541 606590; e-mail: cetacea@iper.net; website 194.184.164.48/CETACEA/Foundation dedicated to the protection and conservation of whales, porpoises and dolphins etc.

Lega Anti Vivisezione(LAV): Via Sommacampagna 29, 00185 Rome.

Lega Italiana Protezione Uccelli (LIPU): via Trento n.49, 43100 Parma; ☎+39 521273043; fax +39 521 273 043.

Organisations needing Volunteers

Abruzzo National Park: Head Office, Viale Tito Livio 12, 00136, Rome; ☎+39 6 35403331; fax +39 6 35403253. Operates fifteen-day volunteer programmes all year round. About 300 volunteers are taken on annually and they work in groups of two or three equipped with radio telephones and other essentials. Free lodging is provided and a contribution to food expenses is given.

Volunteers are needed to help carry out checks and censuses of the fauna, and also animal protection, maintenance and helping with visitors to the park. Activities take place under the supervision of the park's staff of scientific researchers, technicians, guards etc. Volunteers must be aged 18 minimum. Apply 30 days before proposed departure to the above address. Further details are available from the local Park office in Pescasseroli (0863-1955) or Villetta Barrea (0864-9102/fax 0864-9132. There is a fee for accident insurance. Payment should be made to postal account 11833670 to the favour of: Ente Autonomo Parco Nazionale d'Abruzzo – Direzione, 67032 Pescasseroli.

*Brown Bears, Central Italy: (*see also the above) project carried out by reasearchers from the National Forest Service in the Abruzzo, the sole habitat of a species of brown bear which has been brought back from the edge of extinction to a population of 100 thanks to active conservation. Volunteers help researchers collect data on the bears' behaviour patterns, movements and feeding habits. Minimum age 16. One week July or September. Volunteers must be capable of walking long distances. Cost US$320. Applications through CTS (see address below).

Carapax: European Centre for Conservation of Chelonians, International Rana Foundation, C.P. 34, 58024 Massa Marittima (GR); ☎+39 (0566) 940083; fax +39 (0566) 902 387; e-mail carapax@novars.it; www.novars.it/carapax/index; www.carapax.org. The RANA (Reptiles, Amphibians in NAture) Foundation works on behalf of reptiles and amphibians. The Carapax centre concentrates on the rescue and rehabilitation of tortoises. Once released into the wild tortoises are monitored through radio tracking or other means. Volunteers help with this work and also aid experts with scientific research in this field. The project takes place on the west coast of central Italy 18kms from the sea in Tuscany. Volunteers come for two weeks mid-April to Mid-October. Minimum age 18 years.

CTS: Centro Turistico Studentesco E Giovanile: Via A Vessalio 6, 00161 Rome, Italy; ☎+39 06 44111473; fax +39 06 4411 1401; e-mail: ambiente@cts.it; www.cts.it/ambiente/). Italy's largest youth organisation organises a range of projects involving endangered species, animal behaviour, habitat conservation and management and archaeology. Programmes to date cover bears, dolphins, turtles, wolves, ibex, whales, flamingos and more. Projects can be in the Alps, Mediterranean sea, coast and islands and in the National Parks. Projects outside Italy are in Mexico, Cuba and Costa Rica. The minimum age is 16. Length of service six to 15 days. Costs €250-€700 (approx £170-£450) excluding food and travel. Current projects include Loggerhead Sea Turtles in Linosa an island south of Sicily ten to 12 days June to September. Can also be contacted through Ecovolunteer Network.

Europe Conservation Italia: Via del Macao 9, 00185 Rome; ☎+39 064741241/2; fax +39 06 4744671; e-mail eco.italia@agora.stm.it. ECI supports university research programmes by providing volunteers mostly around the Mediterranean and Central

Italy. Projects involve whales, dolphins and wolves. Periods of service from six days to a month. Minimum age 18 and ability to swim required for marine projects. Costs from US$200-1,200.

Italian League for the Protection of Birds: LIPU_Lega Italiana Protezione Uccelli, Via Trento 49, 43100 Parma; ☎+39 521 273043; fax +39 521 273419; e-mail info@lipu.it; www.lipu.it. LIPU was founded in 1965 and is the Italian representative of BirdLife International. It supports a range of programmes which affect the interests of birds including environmental education programmes, campaigning for public awareness, conservation of endangered species and bird rescue centres. Volunteers taken on from June to October for seven to ten days for activities such as ringing and data collection, bird counts, fire prevention, trail maintenance etc. on the Mediterranean coasts and islands, temperate forests, the Alps and various Italian locations. Some projects require expert ornithologists. Costs US$300-$700.

Mediterranean Fin Whale Programme: Tethys Research Institute, c/o Aquario Civico, Viale Gadio 2, 20121 Milan; ☎+39 02 72001947; fax +39 02 72001 946; e-mail: tethys@tethys.org; www.tethys.org The Institute has been conducting research into fin whales since 1987. The whales can be found in large numbers in the Western Ligurian Sea and around Corsica. The programme studies the ecology, habitat use, dynamics and behaviour of the whales. Other projects involve Striped and Risso's dolphins and sperm and pilot whales. Volunteers must be at least 18 and available for six to 12 days or longer from June to September. Training in research activities is given. Volunteers help with cleaning and cooking. Live on board ship. Costs US$500 for six days or US$1000 for 12 days. Travel, insurance and food are not included.

Monte Adone Wildlife Protection Centre: Via Brento 9, 40037 Sasso Marconi (Bologna); tel/fax +39 (051) 847 600; e-mail info@centrotutelafauna.org; www.centrotutelafau na.org. Rescue and rehabilitation organisation for wild animals including indigenous and exotic species. Offers 24-hours emergency rescue service for animals. The organisation is also open to visitors and offers guided visits to schools and families as part of an educational programme.

   Volunteers are needed to work 8-10 hours a day depending on the season. Duties include feeding, cleaning and care of animals, day and night rescue of wounded animals, building and maintenance and a share of housekeeping chores. English and Italian are spoken. Volunteers have a week's trial period and contribute €80 (about £50) for insurance and food for the first week. Stays after a successful trial period should be for a minimum of 20 days and board and lodging will be provided free. Long-term stays may be negotiable with the Director. No particular animal qualifications requested but would be useful. Must also be able to live and work in a community, be adaptable and responsible.

WWOOF: c/o 109 Via Casavecchia, 57022 Castegneto Carducci (LI); ☎0565-765001; www.wwoofitalia@oliveoil.net Working placements on organic farms in return for board and lodging.

WWF Italia: Servizio Campi, Via Donatello 5/B, 20133 Milan; ☎02 295 13 742). The Italian branch of the WWF claims to be the largest of any of its national branches with responsibility for 70 animal refuges, As well as projects in Italy, WWF Italy has projects in Brazil, France, Greece, Hungary, Ireland, Scotland, Slovenia, Spain, Tunisia and Venezuela. For Italian projects volunteers come for 2 weeks (minimum is 5 days) all year round to help with field studies, restoration and fire prevention. Costs are a minimum of US$35 up to a maximum of US$2,500 which includes insurance, accommodation and food. Also publishes a list of ecological workcamps in Italian only.

Italian Embassies
Australia: Grey Street, Deakin, ACT 2600; ☎02-6273 3333.

Canada: 21st Floor, 275 Slater Street, Ottawa, Ontario KIP 5H9; ☎613-2322401; fax 613-233 1484.
UK: 14 Three Kings Yard, London SW1X 8AN; ☎020-7235 9371; www.ambitalia.org.uk
USA: 1601 Fuller Street, NW Washington, DC 20009; ☎202-328 5500; fax 202-483 2187.

Luxembourg

The Grand Duchy of Luxembourg, one of Europe's smallest countries, comprises just under a 1000 square miles of territory tagged on to eastern Belgium and wedged between Germany and France. The total population is 412,800 of whom 138,000 are non-Luxembourgeois nationals, principally Portuguese and Italians. The national languages are French and German.

Vets
The number of vets in Luxembourg has tripled in twenty years and there are about 89 practitioners, 35 in mixed or large animal practices and the rest are small animal practitioners and several equine only practices. An additional 11 vets hold government posts covering animal welfare, meat inspection and the National Veterinary Laboratory. There is a national 24-hour veterinary service organised by the Veterinary Association of Luxembourg. Luxembourg lacks its own veterinary school so training takes place elsewhere, in Germany, France, Belgium and Austria. However, Luxembourg views the resulting diversity of training as an asset.

Association of Veterinarians of Luxembourg: Association des Médecins-Vétérinaires du Grand-Duché de Luxembourg (AMVL), 27 rue Quatre-Vents, 7562 Mersch; ☎ +352 32 01 26; +352 32 52 25.

Administration des Services Vétérinaires: 93 rue d'Anvers, B.P. 1403, 1014 Luxembourg; ☎+352 478 2540.

Animal & Bird Welfare, Protection & Conservation
Association Luxembourgeoise pour la Protection des Animaux: 35 rue des Etats-Unis, 1477 Luxembourg; ☎+352 48 83 95. Luxembourg animal protection organisation.

Luxembourg League for the Protection of Nature and Birds: Ligue Luxembourgeoise de protection de la Nature et des Oiseaux, Kräizhaff, rue de Luxembourg, 1899 Kockelscheuer; tel/fax +352 29 05 54 04.

Ministére de l'Environment: 18 montée de la Pétrusse, 2918 Luxembourg; ☎+352 4781; fax +352 40 04 10.

Natura: 6 Boulevard Roosevelt, 2450 Luxembourg; ☎+352 47 23 12. Nature conservation.

Luxembourg Embassies
UK: 27 Wilton Crescent, London SW1X 8SD; ☎020-7235 6961; fax 020-7235 9734.
USA: 2200 Massachusetts Avenue NW, Washington DC 20008; ☎202 265 4171/2; fax 202-328 8270.
Canada: deal with the Washington embassy.

The Netherlands

Another of the small nations of Europe, The Netherlands, like Belgium is roughly the size of Maryland or half the size of Scotland. The country is mostly flat apart from the hilly area of Limburg. The Netherlands is the least wooded country in the EU with just 8% woodland; 54% of the land is used for agriculture. The population is about 16 million.

Vets

The veterinary profession in the Netherlands totals just over 4,000 practising vets. There are several hundred Dutch vets employed in other countries, notably the UK. The number of veterinarians working alone is declining because of an increasing tendency to form group practices that usually employ several assistants as part of their veterinary staff. The Netherlands' sole veterinary faculty is in Utrecht and it is the only European veterinary faculty to be accredited by the USA and Canada.

Although considered generally a humane country, the Netherlands is nevertheless one of the largest producers of intensively farmed meat. There are a staggering 106 million poultry birds, not to mention 13.5 million pigs and 4.2 million beef and dairy cattle under production at any one time. Foreign vets should register with the Rijksdienst voor de keuring van Vlees en Vee (RVV): Foreburg, Burgemeester Feithstraat 1, P O Box 3000, 2270 JA Voorburg; ☎+31 70 357 88 11; fax +3170 387 65 91.

Other Veterinary addresses:

Royal Netherlands Veterinary Association: Koninklijke Nederlandse Maatschappij voor Diergeneeskunde (KNMvD/RNVA), P.O.Box 14031, 3508 SB Utrecht; ☎+31 30 251 01 11; fax+31 30 251 17 87; e-mail knmvd@pobox.ruu.nl

Veterinary Services, Ministry of Agriculture, Nature Management and Fisheries: Veterinaire Dienst, Ministerie van Landbouw, Natuurbeheer en Visserj, Bezuidenhoutseweg 73 Postbus 20401, 2500 Den Haag; ☎+31 70 379 3037; fax +31 70 381 5856; www.mininv.nl.

Dogs and Cats

The Dutch are keen on companion animals with 2 million cats and 1.4 million dogs kept. Further information on dogs can be obtained from the following:

Organisation for the Protection of Dogs: Bond tot Bescherming van Honden (BHH), Hondenbescherming, Statenlaan 108, 2582 GV The Hague; ☎+31 70 3556981; fax +31 70 3500202.

Horses

The Dutch horse population numbers nearly 400,000 and the equine industry provides employment for an estimated 12,000 people. Further information on horses and horse establishments from:

Dutch Equestrian Sport Federation: Stichting Nederlandse Hippische Sportbond: Amsterdamsestraatweg 57, 3744 MA Baarn; ☎+31 (0)35-5483600; fax +31 (0)5411563.

Dutch Federation of Horse-riding Establishments: Federatie van Nederlandse Rijscholen (FNRS), Postbus 456, 3740 Al Baarn; ☎+31 35 5483660; fax +31 35 5483625.

Racing Authority:

Dutch Federation of Stallion Owners: Federatie van Bonden van Hengstenhouders: Lindenboomsweg 3, 3417 XC Montfoort; ☎+31 0348-470078.

Stichting Nederlandse Draf en Rensport: Paleisstraat 5, 2514 JA Den Haag, Postal: P.O. Box 454, 2501 The Hague; ☎+31 70 3021675; fax +3170 3021650.

Zoos, Aquaria & Animal Parks
Alphen a/d Rijn: Birdpark Avifauna, Hoorn 65, Postbus 31, 2400 AA Alphen a/d Rijn; ☎+31 1724-87575; fax +31 1724 87506.
Amersfoort: Dierenpark Amersfoort, Barchman Wuytierslaan 224, 3819AC Amersfoort; ☎+31 33-4227120; e-mail MHoedemaker@amersfoort.zoo.nl. Animal Park
Amsterdam Zoo: Artis Zoo, Natura Artis Magistra, Plantage Kerklaan 38-40, 1018 Amsterdam; ☎+31 20 5233400; fax +31 20 5233 419; e-mail info@artis.nl; www.artis.nl.
Apeldoorn: Stichting Apenheul, J.C. Wilslaan 21-31, 7313 HK Apeldoorn; ☎+31 55 3575 700; fax +31 553575 701; e-mail w.jens@apenheul.nl.
Arnhem: Burgers' Zoo, Schelmseweg 85, 6816 SH Arnhem; ☎+31 26 442 4534/445 0373; fax +3126 443 0776; e-mail: info@burgerszoo.nl; www.burgerszoo.nl
Bergen aan Zee: Aquarium Bergen aan Zee, Bergen aan Zee; ☎+31 2208 12928; fax +31 2208 18214.
Emmen: Noorder Dierenpark, Postbus 1010, 7801 BA Emmen; ☎+31 591 850850; fax +31 591 850851; info@zoo-emmen.nl; www.zoo-emmen.nl. Animal park.
Harderwijk: Dolfinarium Harderwijk, Strandboulevard-Oost 1, 3841 AB Harderwijk; ☎+31 3410-467467; fax +31 3414 25888; e-mail: info@dolfinarium.nl;www.dolfi narium.nl
Hilvarenbeek: Safari Beekse Bergen, Beekse Bergen 31, 5081 NJ Hilvarenbeek; ☎+31 13 536 0035; fax +31 13 535 7966. Safari park; e-mail curator@beeksebergen.nl.
Huizen: Endangered Animal Foundation, Driftweg 124, 1272 AC Huizen.
Leuwarden: Aqua Zoo Friesland, de Groene Ster 2, 8926 XE Leeuwarden; ☎+31 511 43 1214; fax +31 511 43 1260; e-mail zodiaczoos@zodiaczoos.nl; www.aqualutra.nl.
Rhenen: Ouwehands Dierenpark, Grebbeweg 111, Postbus 9, 3910 AA Rhenen; ☎+31 317 650 200; fax +31 317 613 727; e-mail info@ouwehand.nl; www.ouwehand.nl. Animal park.
Rotterdam: Rotterdam Zoo, van Aerssenlaan 49, 3039 KE Rotterdam; ☎+31 10 443 1431; fax +31 10 467 7811; e-mail info@rotterdamzoo.nl; www.rotterdamzoo.nl.
Wassenaar: Wassenaar Wildlife Breeding Centre: Raaphorstlaan 28, 2245 BJ Wassenaar; ☎+31 70 5178028; fax +31 70 5119268; wwbc@planet.nl.

Animal & Bird Welfare, Protection & Conservation
It may be worth applying to any of the following to offer your services as a volunteer:
Dutch Society for the Protection of Animals, Utrecht and surrounding areas: P O Box 757, 3500 A T Utrecht.
European Centre for Nature Conservation: Warandelaan 2 – Y Building, P.O. Box 1352, 5004 BJ Tilburg; tel+31 13 466 3240; fax +31 13 466 3250; e-mail: drucker@ecnc.nl
International Bear Foundation: Postbus 9, 3910 Rhenen; ☎+31 317 650 200; fax +31 317 613 727; e-mail: berenbos@worldonline.nl
  The Ecovolunteer Program: Central office, Meijersweg 29, 7553 AX Hengalo, Netherlands; ☎+31 74 2508250; fax +31 20 8645314; e-mail: info@ecovolunteer.org; www.ecovolunteer.org The Ecovolunteer programme runs about 25 projects with hands-on experience in wildlife conservation. The UK agent is Wildwings (www.wild wings.ecovolunter.co.uk
International Bear Foundation: Postbus 9, 3910 AA Rhenen; ☎+31 317 650 200; fax +31 317 613727; e-mail: berenbos@worldwonline.nl Protection society for the European Brown Bear and nature protection in the Arctic.
Nederlandse Vereniging van Deirentuinen-NVD: c/o Artis Zoo, Postbus 20164, 1000 HD Amsterdam; ☎+31 20 5233 402; fax +31 20 5233 481. The Dutch Association of Animal Parks.
Pro-Primates: Morsstraat 53, 2312 BL Leiden; ☎+31 71 514 9894; fax +31 71 512 6031; e-mail: primates@dsl.nl

Stichting Conservation Centre: Jouberstraat 24, 3851 DM Ermelo; ☎ +31 341 558356; fax +31 341 559395. Sanctuary conservation centre.

Stichting Lekker Dier: Lorenseweg 26, 1221 C.M. Hilversum. Animal protection organisation.

De Harpij Sanctuary: P.O.Box 532, 3000AM Rotterdam; ☎+31 10 443 1434; fax +31 10 443 1443. Zoo for endangered animals.

Nederlandse Vereniging tot Bescherming van Dieren: De Dierenbescherming, Floris Grijpstraat 2, Postbus 85980, 2508 The Hague; ☎+31 70 3142700; fax +31 70 3242777. The Dutch equivalent of Britain's Royal Society for the Protection of Animals.

Sophia-Vereeniging tot Bescherming van Dieren: Informatiecentrum voor Gezelschapsdieren, N.Z. Voorburgwal 153, 1012 Amsterdam; ☎+ 31 20 6236167; fax +31 20 6268023. Animal protection organisation.

Stichting Dieren Rampenfonds: Papenvoortse Heide 8, 5674 SL Neunen; ☎+31 40 2834685. Helps animals that have been in accidents/disasters.

Stichting Zeehondencrèche Pieterburen: Hoofdstraat 94-A, 9968 AG Pieterburen; ☎+31 595 526526; fax +31 595 528389. Seal rescue and rehabilitation.

Stiftung Panthera: Grindweg 22, 8422 Nijeberkoop. Big Cats Foundation. Director: Mr A. Van der Valk.

Vogelbescherming Nederland: Driebergseweg 16-C, 3708 J.B. Zeist; ☎+30 6937700; fax +31 30 6918844. Main bird protection organisation.

Werkgroep Roofvogels Nederland (WRN): Aekingaweg 3,8426 GN Appelscha; ☎+31 516 432660; fax+31 516 4326600. Birds of Prey organisation.

Animal Shelters *(Dierenasielen)*

Dierenbejaardentehuis Seniorenclub de: Zijdeweg 56, 2245 BZ Wassenaar; ☎+31 70 511 38 92. Shelter for elderly animals.

Dierenzorg Dierenpension: Kralingseweg 347, 3065 RC Rotterdam; ☎+31 10 202 18 65. Deals with sick and elderly animals.

Dierenpension Dierenzorg: Kralingseweg 347, 3065 RC Rotterdam; ☎+31 10 202 18 65. Deals with sick and elderly animals.

Dierencentrum Zaanstreek Stichting As: Dr H G Scholtenstraat 40, 1509 AR Zandam; ☎+31 75 616 32 04.

Dierenopvangcentrum: Abraham van Stolkweg 33, 3041 JA Rotterdam; ☎+31 10 437 42 11. Animal treatment centre for strays etc.

Hoogendam's International Animal Hotel: Lutkemeerwerg 300, 1067 TH Amsterdam; ☎+31 20 619 41 80.

North Amsterdam Animal Shelter: ☎+31 20 636 84 42.

Vogelbescherming Nederland: Netherlands Society for the Protection of Birds, Dreibergseweg 16c, P.O. Box 925, 3700 AX Zeist; ☎+31 30 69 37700; fax +31 30 69 18844; e-mail birdlife@antenna.n.

Netherlands Embassies

Australia: Empire Cct, Yarralumla, ACT 2600; ☎02-6273 3111.

Canada: Suite 2020, 350 Albert Street, Ottawa, Ontario K1R 1A4, Canada; ☎613-237 5030; fax 613-237 6471.

UK: 38 Hyde Park Gate, London SW7 5DP; ☎020-7590 3200; fax 020-7581 5276; www.netherlands-embassy.org

USA: 4200 Wisconsin Avenue NW, Washington DC 20016; ☎202-244 5300; fax 202-537 5124.

Norway

With one of the smallest populations in Europe at 4.3 million, the Norwegians have a reputation of being a well-ordered nation. The capital, Oslo has a population of less than half a million. Norway is set at the edge of the North Sea and the Arctic Ocean (more than half of the coast lies above the Arctic Circle and the southernmost tip barely descends to the latitude of northern Scotland. It is on the edge of Europe politically as well as geographically: Norway showed its independence by declining to join the EU in a national referendum held in 1994. However, for western Europeans, working in Norway is facilitated by its membership of the European Economic Area.

Vets

For a small country, there are a lot of vets; an estimated nearly 2000 of them of which about 850 are practitioners and 700+ work as public employees for the government, or as academics. About 70% of veterinary students are women. The Norwegian School of Veterinary Science, the country's only veterinary faculty is in Oslo (The Norwegian School of Veterinary Science, Ullevålsveien 72, P.B. 8146 Dep, 0033 Oslo; ☎+47 22 96 45 00; fax +47 56 57 04; e-mail sekretariatet@veths.no; www.veths.no). Before entering vet school, prospective students have to work with animals for at least one year either as veterinary nurses or as farm workers. There is a surplus of large animal vets and small animal practices are increasing. About 120 Norwegian qualified vets are employed outside Norway. There is a shortage of vets in the food hygiene sector. Fur and fish farming are very important industries in Norway and there are hundreds of veterinary jobs in this area. Sheep farming is also developed with 1.04 million sheep and lambs at any one time. Pig farming is also big in Norway. About half of practitioners are single workers and practices total 300. Farming clients in rural areas tend to be rather remote necessitating a lot of travelling and limited social opportunities.

The Norwegian Animal Health Authority: P.O.Box 8147 Dep, N0033 Oslo, Norway; ☎+47 23 21 65 00; fax +47 23 21 65 01; e-mail post@dyrehelsetilsynet.no; www.dyr ehelsetilsynet.no; international co-ordinator Keren Bar-Yaacov; ☎+47 23 21 6503.

The Norwegian Veterinary Association: Den norske Veterinaerforening, General Birchs gate 16, 0454 Oslo; ☎+47 22 59 16 50.

Horses

The main racing bodies' web-links are:

For more information contact Mr Tore Hoff at the Biri Horses Racing; ☎+47 61 18 78 82; e-mail torehoff@rikstoto.no; www.biritrave.no/biri_info.htm

Norsk Jockeyklub: Postboks 53, 1342 Jar, Oslo; ☎+47 22956200; fax +47 2295 62 62; e-mail alopp@online.no.

Norwegian Riding Association: Norske Rytterforbund, Serviceboks, 1 Ullevål Stadion, 0840 Oslo; ☎+47 21 02 96 50; fax +47 21 02 96 51; www.rytter.no.

The Norwegian Horse-owners Association: Norsk Hesteeierforbund (NHF): c/o Mr. Ingve Dubland, Møllevegan 8, 4360 Varhaug; ☎+47 51 43 00 45/511 78 67 52/916 00 637; www.travsport.no/.

Fjellrittet (Recreational Riding Organisation): 2953 Beitostølen; ☎+47 61 34 11 01; fax +47 61 34 15 24; e-mail post@fjelrittet.no; web www.fjellrittet.no.

Gløvik Miljøhestesenter (Recreational riding organisation): c/o Mathias Toppsvei, 2803 Gjøvik; ☎+47 61 17 55 00 57 85; e-mail: post@miljohestesenter.no.

Norsk Hestesenter (Norwegian Horse Centre): Starum, 2850 Lena; ☎+47 61 16 55 00; fax +47 66 16 55 40; e-mail hhest@nhest.no; www.hest.org.

Hasle Ridesenter: 1454 Nestoddtangen; ☎+47 66 91 51 45; fax +47 66 91 70 75; e-mail mheltzen@c2i.net.

Some other relevant recreational riding organisations are listed at www.hest.no.minisite/
?club_id=02010003, but not all of them are in English.

Zoos & Aquarium
The Norwegian Zoological Foundation *(Norsk Zoologisk Forening),* is at P.B. 102
Blindern, 0314 Oslo; e-mail nzf@zoologi.no; www.zoologi.no/linker.htm
Kristiansand Zoo & Amusement Park: 4609 Kardemmommeby; ☎+47 38 04 97 00; fax
+47 38 04 33 67; www.dyreparken.com
Bergen Aquarium: Nordnesbakken 4, P.B. 1870 Nordnes, 5817 Bergen; ☎+47 55 55 71
71; www.akvariet.com/cgu
Oslo Zoo: Norsk Zoologisk Forening, Zoologisk Museum, Sars g 1, 0562 Oslo; ☎+47
22 85 16 00.

Animal & Bird Welfare, Protection & Conservation
Animal Rights Organisation: Norsk Liga for Dyrs Rettigheter, c/o Sonia Løchen,
Sannergt. 1B 0557 Oslo; ☎+47 22 35 11 50.
Animal Welfare Organisation: Dyrebeskyttelsen Norge, Akersg. 67, 0810 Oslo; ☎+47
22 20 23 00; fax +47 22 20 23 25.
Dyrebskyttelsen Norge: Akersgt 67, 0180 Oslo. Norwegian animal protection
organisation.
NOAH: Osterhausgate 12, 0183 Oslo; tel/fax +47 22 11 41 63; e-mail
noah@noahonline.org; www.noahonline.org/english. Animal rescue organisation.
Contacts: Anton Krag & Siri Martinsen. NOAH is for animal rights and is an
organisation based on volunteer work by members.
The Norwegian Federation of Animal Protection: Karl Johansgate 6, 0154 Oslo;
☎+47 23 13 92 50; fax +47 23 13 92 51; e-mail post@dyrebeskyttelsen.no;
www.dyrebeskyttelsen.no
Norsk Ornitologisk Forening (NOF): Norwegian Ornithological Society,
Seminarplassen 5, 7060 Klaebu; ☎+47 72 83 11 66; fax +47 7283 12 55; e-mail:
norornis@online.no
The Norwegian Kennel Club: Norsk Kennel Klubb, Nils Hansens v 2, 0667 Oslo; ☎+47
22 65 60 00; fax +47 22 72 04 74.

Other Useful addresses
Directorate for Nature Management: 7485 Trondheim; ☎+47 73 58 05 00; fax +47 73
58 05 01; e-mail kirstine.stene@dirnat.no; www.english.dirnat.no/
Avifauna: Post Box 674 Sentrum, 0106 Oslo; ☎+47 22 50 21 32; e-mail:
avifauna@hotmail.com

Temporary Farm Work
There are a couple of organisations aimed at young people who want to work on farms.
Not all farms have animals and it is up to the applicant to state their wish to work with
animals at the outset to avoid disappointment.
Atlantis: the Norwegian Foundation for Youth Exchange: Kirkegata 32, 0153 Oslo; fax
+47 22 47 71 79; e-mail post@atlantis-u.no; www.atlantis-u.no/index2_eng.html,
runs a programme which allows people aged 18 to 30, of any nationality to spend
from two to three months on a rural farm. In return for 35 hours work a week, bed,
board and pocket money (minimum £56 weekly) are given. Americans should apply
through WISE (303 S Craig St., Suite 202, Pittsburgh, PA; ☎412 681-8187; e-mail:
wis+@pitt).
APØG (Work on Organic Farms): Elias Hofgaardsgt. 43, 2318 Hamar, Norway; ☎+47
62 53 36 16; fax +47 62 53 36 17; e-mail: biodynfo@frisurf.no; www.oikos.no. The
Norwegian organic farm organisation will supply a list of about 40 farms. Some

farmers want trainees who will stay for a year, others just want temporary summer helpers. Some farms provide board and lodging; others also provide pocket money. Not all farms have animals; it is up to you to request this. Animal related work includes handmilking. The booklet of participating farms costs £10. Further details by post or from their website. Most farmers can reply in English.

Norwegian Embassies

Australia: Hunter Street, Yarralumla, ACT 2600; ☎02-6273 3444.

Canada: Suite 532, Royal Bank Centre, 90 Sparks Street, Ottawa, Ontario K1P 5B4, Canada; ☎613-238-6571; fax 616-238-2765.

UK: 25 Belgrave Square, London SW1X 8QD; ☎020-7591 5500; fax 020-7245 6993; e-mail emb.london@mfa.no; www.norway.org.uk

USA: 2720 34th Street NW, Washington, DC 20008; ☎202-333-6000; fax 202-337 0870.

Portugal

Portugal occupies the southwestern extremity of Europe and accounts for 15% of the landmass of the Iberian Peninsula, shared with Spain. Around the west and south of Portugal stretches 500 miles (804km) of Atlantic coastline. Other Portuguese territories include the Madeira archipelago (the two main islands are Madeira and Porto Santo) off the west coast of Morocco, and the Azores, a group of islands in mid-Atlantic.

Portugal still has many inhabitants, including farmers, living at subsistence level. This is despite huge EU subsidies which have however transformed the infrastructure over the last ten years. The opportunities for work are fewer than in other European countries. The population numbers 9.1 million.

Portugal has a mostly humane attitude towards animals. For instance the Portuguese Association of Veterinarians forbids cosmetic mutilation (e.g. ear cropping) and vocal cord resectioning of dogs to prevent barking.

Vets

There are just under 2,000 practising veterinarians of whom about 70% are employed in government service, which includes inspections of abbatoirs, animal health programmes, teaching and research. There is a tendency for state employees to boost their government salaries by running private clinics after work. This means that the number of practitioners is nearly 1,000. Of private practitioners, 41% work in and around the Lisbon area and 70% in the south. However, small animal clinics are increasing in rural areas offering good employment prospects for new graduates of whom 40% are women. Portugal has four veterinary schools; the two newest in Porto and Evora were opened in 1995 and 1996 respectively.

Veterinary addresses

Direcçaio Geral de Veterinaria: Lg da Academia Nacional de Belas Artes 2, 1200 Lisboa, Portugal; ☎+351 21 323 9500; fax +351 21 346 3518. Main veterinary organisation.

Sindicato Nacional dos Medicos Veterinarios: Rua Victor Cordon No 30, 2nd Floor E, 1200 Lisbon; ☎+351 21 346 59 29. National Union of Veterinary Surgeons.

Ordem dos Medicos Veterinarios: rua Victor Cordon No 30, 2nd Floor, 1200 Lisbon; ☎+ 351 21 346 44 67; fax +351 21 342 54 00. Equivalent of the UK's Royal College of Veterinary Surgeons. Foreign vets should contact this organisation if they wish to become established in Portugal.

Horses
Portugal, is popular for horse riding and trekking holidays. Foreign-run stables are concentrated in the Algarve region in south but they are also found in other regions including the Alentejo (the province above the Algarve). There are an estimated 21,000 horses in Portugal. There are several employers that employ British staff. The following may be worth contacting:

Riding Stables
Campo Hipico de Serzedo: Apartado 89, 4411 Praia da Granja, Godex; ☎+351 2 762 8552.
Pinetrees Riding Centre: Ancao, Almancil, 8135 Portugal; ☎+351 89 394369; fax +351 89 394489. Manège and hacking and distance riding. Also dressage on Lusitano horses. Offers working pupil arrangements.
QPA Riding Centre: Quanta do Pariase, Alto Bensafrim, 8600 Lagos; ☎+351 82 6872 63; fax +351 82 687507. Trekking holidays and hacking. Proprietor: Jinny Harman.

Zoos, Aquaria & Animal Parks
Oceanario de Lisboa: Esplanada D. Carlos 1, 1990-096 Lisboa; ☎+351 2189170; fax +351 2189 55762/17051; e-mail ramoedo@oceanario.pt; www.oceanario.pt). Opened mid-1998. Built around a vast central tank 110 feet across. The aquarium houses a total of 8,000 specimens representing 250 species. As well as fish and other marine life there are sea birds and otters.
Aquario Vasco da Gama: Vasco da Gama Aquarium, Rua Direita-Dafundo, 1495 Lisbon; ☎+351 21 419 6337; fax +351 21 419 3911; e-mail: aquariovgama@mail.telepac.pt; www.aquario.vgama.pt
Jardim Zoologico de Lisboa: Estrada de Benefica 158, 1500 Lisboa; ☎+351-21723 2900; fax +351 21723 2901; e-mail eric@zoolisboa.pt; www.zoolisboa.pt.
Museu e Aquario Municipal do Funchal: Museum and Aquariam of Fundhal on Island of Madeira, rua da Mouraria 31, Funchal, 9000 Madeira; ☎+351 91 229761; fax +351 91 225180.

Animal & Bird Welfare, Protection & Conservation
Animal: Apartado 52.101, 4200 Porto. Animal protection and welfare organisation.
Lagos Animal Protection Society: c/o Mrs Bridget Hicks, Correio Monte Ruivo, Odixere, 8600 Lagos, Algarve.
The Donkey Sanctuary: Estombar, Apartado 117, 8400 Lagoa.
Liga Para a Proteçcao da Natureza (LPN): Estrada do Calhariz de Benfica 187, 1500 Lisbon; ☎+351 21 778 00 97; fax +351 21 778 32 08.

Portuguese Embassies
Australia: Culgoa Cct, O'Malley, ACT 2606; ☎02-6290 1733.
Canada: 645 Island Park Drive, Ottawa, Ontario K1Y OB8, Canada; ☎613-729 0883; fax 613-729 4236.
UK: Silver City House, 62 Brompton Road, London SW3 1BJ; ☎020-7581 8722; www.portembassy.gla.ac.uk *USA:* 2125 Kalorama Road, NW Washington, DC 20008; ☎202-328 8610; fax 202-462 3726.

Spain

Spain the second largest country in the EU after France and occupies 85% of the landmass that forms the Iberian Peninsula at the southwestern extremity of Europe. Territories include the Balearic and Canary Islands, which are in the Mediterranean, and off the north-west African coast respectively. Only ten miles (16km) separates Spain from Africa across the Straight of Gibraltar.

Spain has lagged behind other EU countries in providing a comprehensive legislation for animal protection. Spain has no national system of animal legislation, responsability for which devolves on the 17 autonomous communities which make up the country. Most of the autonomous communities have now formulated their own code of regulations governing the treatment of livestock and domestic animals. A raft of legislation to protect animals has been passed since Spain joined the EU in 1974. However, anomalies remain including bull fighting (fiercely defended as an art form in Spain) and shockingly inhumane customs at some village fiestas.

Vets

Government veterinary services are regulated by the autonomous communities (see above). There has been a 50% increase in the number of active veterinarians in Spain since the early 1990s largely due to the increase in veterinary faculties of which Spain has ten. The proliferation of veterinary graduates has produced a youthful profession with 36 being the average age of 75% of small animal vets. There is some concern in the profession about future employment prospects in Spain and the likely prospect of them having to diversify away from hands on animal work to areas including quality control, environmental work and consultancy.

Livestock practices are most prolific in the northern and central areas. A speciality peculiar to Spain is the Association of Veterinary Specialists in Tauromachy (for bulls) which has 500 members.

The contact authority for foreign vets is:
Subdireccion General de Titulos, Convalidaciones y Homologaciónes, Ministry of Education and Culture, Paseo del Prado 28, 4a, 28014 Madrid; ☎+34 91 506 56 00 or +34 91 42007 67; fax +34 91 420 35 35.

Other organisations for vets are:
Consejo General del Collegio de Veterinarios de España: c/o Villanueva 11, 28001 Madrid; ☎+34 91 435 35 35; fax +34 91 578 34 68.
Colegio Oficial de Veterinarios: Alcala 155, 28028 Madrid; ☎+34 91 575 34 89 /72 80.

Useful publications
Albeitar: Asis Veterinaria S.L.,Plaza Anel Sanz Briz 7, 2nd Floor H. 50013 Zaragoza; ☎+34 976 42 34 11; fax +34 976 42 54 11; e-mail:(asisvet@sendanet.es). Magazine aimed at veterinary surgeons working with farm animals.
Animalia: Elsevier Prensa, S.A. Av.Parallel 180, 08015 Barcelona; ☎+34 93 325 53 50;fax +34 93 423 54 99. Circulation of 7000 copies to small animal vets, trainers, breeders, laboratories and specialised shops.

Dogs & Horses

General information on canine matters can be obtained from the following organisation:
The Royal Dog Society: Real Sociedad Canina de España: Calle de los Madrazo, 26, 3er piso, 28014 Madrid; ☎+34 91 522 24 00/+34 91 521 84 19.
The official estimate for the number of dogs is 3.5 million. For horses there are an

estimated 248,000 and double that for mules and donkeys. Spain, has an ancient, originally military, tradition of equestrianism and there are prized regional breeds like the Andalusian. Riding holidays notably in Andalucia, are popular with foreigners and provide job openings for qualified or trainee stable staff.

Racing authorities and organisations

Agrupacion Espanola de Proprietarios (Thoroughbred Owners Association): c/o Fernaflor 6, 28014 Madrid; ☎+34 91 369 4093.

Asociacion de Criadores de Pura Sangre Ingles de España: Spanish Thoroughbred Breeders' Association, c/o Fernanflor 6, 28014 Madrid; ☎+34 91 369 4093.

Sociedad de Fomento de la Cria Caballar de España: (Jockey Club), c/o Fernanflor 6, 28014 Madrid; ☎+34 91 427 7068.

Other equine addresses

Association for the Purebred Spanish Horse: Associación Nacional de Criadores de Caballos de Pura Raza Espanola (ANCE):, C/Adriano, 19 bajo, 41001 Sevilla; ☎+34 95 421 77 58; fax +34 95 421 70 45.

Can Sort: Bascara 17483, Girona; tel/fax +34 72 560335; Spanish-run stables specialising in trail riding holidays.

Centro de Adiestramiento Victor Alvarez: Centro Kono, Can Bonic, Afores, 17462 Sant Marti Vell, Girona; ☎+34 (9) 72/49 10 46. Offers riding holidays for adults, children and family groups. Also dressage up to Grand Prix level, breaking and schooling Spanish horses, career training exams (British and Spanish).

Club Hipic Montanya: c/o Dels Cavalls, S/N urbanitzacio el Montanya, Seva 08553, Spain; ☎+34 93 884 04 84. Riding Holidays.

Epona Equestrian Centre: Apartado de Correos No 86 Carmona, 41410 Seville; ☎+34 90 8155359/+34 95 593247; fax +34 90 8657740. Riding holidays for children.

Escuela de Capacitacion Agaria Ecuestre (ECAE): c/o Mayor S/n Hospitalet de Llobregat; ☎+34 93 3370157; fax +34 93 3384656. Riding school.

El Noble Bruto: Camino Colinons, s/n Sant Pol de Mar, 08395, Barcelona; ☎+34 93 76 00795; mobile 908 740142. Riding centre.

Mas Gall Riding Centre: Camino Fernells, Campllong, Girona 17457; ☎+34 97 2 463201.

La Gerencia Centro Ecuestre: Miono Cantabria, Biltas; ☎+34 9 42 879138; fax +34 9 42 879069.

Member of the World Farriers Association: Jordi Fortuni Gimenez, Mas Fortuny, 17474 Torroella de Fluvia, Girona.

Member of the World Farriers Association: Marti Sala Bayes, Crue del Mercer 121, Victoria, Catalonia; ☎+34 93 889 4798.

Spanish Arab Horse Association: Associacion Espanola de Criadores de Caballos Arabes (AECCA), c/o Hermosilla 20, 28001 Madrid; ☎+34 91 575 90 65; fax +34 91 416 13 66.

Zoos, Aquaria & Animal Parks

Almeria: Parque de Rescate de la Fauna Sahariana: Estación Experimental de Zonas Aridas, General Segura 1, 04001 Almeria; ☎+34 950 281045; fax +34 950 277100; e-mail mar@eeza.csic.es; www.eeza.csic.es Animals of the Sahara.

Barcelona: Parc Zoologic de Barcelona: Parc de la Ciutadella, 08003 Barcelona; ☎+34 93 225 6780; fax +34 93 221 3853; e-mail zoobarna@mail.cinet.es.

Barcelona: Barcelona Aquarium, Moll d'Espanya del Port Vell s/n, 08039 Barcelona; ☎+34 93 221 74 74; fax +34 93 221 26 61; e-mail jingles@aspro-ocio.es; www.aquariumbcn.com.

Gran Canaria: Palmitos Park, Apartado 107, Maspalomas, 35109 Gran Canaria; ☎+34

928 141158; emphasis on parrots.

Jerez de la Frontera: Jardin Zoologico y Botanico Alberto Duran, Jardines de Tempul, Calle Taxdirt s/n, 11404 Jerez de la Frontera; ☎+34 956 18 2397/4207; fax +34 956 311 586; e-mail direccion.zoo@aytojerez.es; www.webjerez.com/ciudad/zoo/portada.asp.

Safari Madrid: Aldea del Fresno 28620; 28620 Madrid; ☎+34 91 862 23 14; fax +34 91 862 23 76.

Madrid: Zoo-Aquarium de la Casa de Campo de Madrid, Casa de Campo, 28011 Madrid; ☎+34 91 5123770/80; fax +34 91 7118163; e-mail comzoo@zoomadrid.com; www.zoomadrid.com.

Puerto de la Cruz/Tenerife: Loro Parque, Punta Brava, 38400 Puerto de la Cruz/Tenerife; ☎+34 922 374081; fax +34 922 375021; e-mail loroparque@loroparque.com; www.loroparque.com. Focus on parrots, dolphinarium and aquarium.

Santillana del Mar/Cantabria: Santillana del Mar Zoo, Zoológico de Santillana del Mar, Antonio Sandi Ave, 39330 Santillana del Mar; ☎+34 42 81 8125; fax +34 42 81 8365; e-mail: zoostantillana@cantabriainter.net; www.cantabriainter.net/zoosantillana. Focus on insects, waterbirds and butterflies.

Tenerife: La Orotava-Tenerife, Zoo Landia, C/El Ramal 35, La Orotava, Tenerife; ☎+34 922 35 2223/3509.

Valencia: Jardin Zoologico de Valencia: Viveros Municipales, C/Pintor Genaro Lahuerta, 46010 Valencia; ☎+34 963 600822; fax +34 96 3 932868; e-mail valenciazoo@terra.es; www.zoovalencia.drago.net.

Vigo, Pontevedra: Vigo Zoo, Monte de la Madroa-Candean, CP 36.317 Vigo; ☎+34 986 273187; e-mail freitas@vigozoo.com; www.vigo.org.

National Animal & Bird Welfare & Protection Groups

Commission for the Protection of Animals: Comision de Defensa Animal, c/o Palma 34, 28004 Madrid.

Association for Animal Rights: Associacion para la Defensa de los Derechos del Animal (ADDA), Headquarters c/o Valencia 265, 3rd Floor, 08007 Barcelona; ☎+34 91 577 33 76.

National Association for the Protection of Animals: Asociacion Nacional para la Defensa de los Animales: c/ Gran Via 31, 5th Floor, 28013 Madrid.

Sociedad Espanola de Ornitologia (SEO/Birdlife): Spanish Ornithological Society, Carretera de Humera, no 63, 1, 28224 Pozuelo de Alarcon, Madrid; ☎+34 91 351 1045; fax +34 91 351 1386; e-mail: seo@quercus.es

Spanish Federation of Societies for the Protection of Animals and Plants: Federacion Espanola de Sociedades Protectoras de Animales y Plantas, c/D. Ramon de la Cruz, 101 28006 Madrid and Riera de San Miguel 7, ppal. 08006 Barcelona.

Regional animal & bird welfare & protection

Amigos de Animales Abandonados de Marbella 'Triple A': Apartado de Correos 18, 29600 Marbella (Malaga).

Animal Rescue Centre K9: Correos Apartado, Adeje, Tenerife, Canary Islands.

Asoc. Andaluza Para la Defensa de los Animales (ASANDA): Apartado Corres, 4 365, 41080 Seville.

Asociacion Para La Proteccion y Defensa de los Animales de Jose ma Quadrado: 10, Mahon 07703, Menorca.

Centro Canino Internacional: Internation Canine Centre,Calle Jesus 21, Palma 07010 Mallorca.

Benidorm Animal Home: Spap, Partida Fluixa S/N, Apdo. Correos 292, 03500 Benidorm.

Sociedad Protectora de Animales y Plantas: C/Lane Mediana S/N, El Rinconcillo,

Algeciras (Cadiz).

Animal Projects Needing Volunteers
There are a number of volunteer projects in Spain where volunteers pay their own costs and make a weekly contribution towards board and lodging.
Estación Biológica de Donana: Equipo de Seguimiento de Procesos Naturales, Reserva Biologica de Donana, Apdo Correos 4, 21760 Matalascanas, Almonte, Huelva, Spain.; ☎+34 959 440032/36; fax +34 959 440033; e-mail joseluis@ebd.csic.es Volunteers needed for various activities related to the migration of passerines in Donana National Park. Work takes place from sunrise to sunset daily from 1 September to 9th November to help ring birds and enter data in the project data base. Ringers need to have knowledge of moult and biometric measurements, and be able to cope with a lot of birds and data. For assistant ringers no previous experience necessary. Knowledge of Spanish is very helpful. Accommodation is provided free to volunteers. Contact José Luis Arroyo at the above address or e-mail joseluis@ebd.csic.es.
Pilot Whale Conservation Project Tenerife Spain: The Ecovolunteer Program: Central office, Meijersweg 29, 7553 AX Hengalo, Netherlands; ☎+31 74 2508250; fax +31 20 8645314; e-mail: info@ecovolunteer.org; www.ecovolunteer.org The UK agent is Wildwings (www.wildwings.ecovolunter.co.uk). The project is run by Proyecto Ambiental Tenerife and volunteers are required as naturalist guides and to help with research, workshops, education, conference, promotion of educational whale watch trips etc. Weekly fee US$150; cheaper if two or three weeks are booked.
Ringing Programme of Migratory Passerines: Estacion biologica de Donana (Csic), Charo Canas, Apartado de Correos 4, 21760 Matalascanas, Almonte, Huelva; ☎+34 59 440 032/440 036; fax +34 59 440 033; e-mail jilam-1@teleline.es; www.ebd.csic.es/ringing/ Volunteers are needed to help ring migratory birds arriving at Donana National Park in the autumn. Other jobs include assisting schoolchildren arriving at the Centre. On days off, volunteers are encouraged to assist any of the research teams working in the area. Cost details from the organisation.
Whale and Dolphin Project, La Gomera, Canary Islands: M.E.E.R. e.V., Bundesallee 123, 12161, Berlin, Germany; ☎+49 30 2928033; fax +49 30 8507 8755; e-mail meer@infocanarias.com; www.m-e-e-r.de. Scientific study aboard a small whale-watching vessel. Volunteers take part in whale, dolphin, other marine mammals, turtles and shark observation, collecting and entering data. Help with everyday tasks. For the latest details contact M.E.E.R. or apply through the Ecovolunteer Network.

Farmwork
It may be possible to get work on organic farms with animals by contacting Spain's organic farming movement (*Amics de l'Escola Agrària* de Manresa; aeam@agrariamanresa.org) by e-mail and requesting a list of farms that will take working volunteers in return for board and lodging. Note that applicants should have a primary interest in organic farming rather than learning Spanish.

Spanish Embassies
Australia: Arkana Street, Yarralimla, ACT 2600; tel02-6273 3555.
Canada: Suite 802, 350 Sparks Street, Ottawa, Ontario K1R 7S8, Canada; ☎613-237 2193/4; fax 613-236 9246.
UK: 24 Belgrave Square, London SW1X 8SB; ☎020-7235 5555/6/7; fax 020-7235 9905; .
USA: 2375 Pennsylvania Avenue, NW Washington, DC 20037; ☎202-452 0100/728 2340; fax 202-833 5670.

Sweden

Sweden occupies the eastern sector of the Scandinavian peninsular and at twice the size of the United Kingdom (but with one seventh of its population), is the fourth largest EU country. About half the country is forested and 100,000 lakes and rivers criss-cross the landscape. Sweden lies in the same northerly latitudes as Alaska and is 15% above the Arctic Circle.

Vets & Veterinary Nurses

There are about 1,600 practising vets of which about 500 are private practitioners, 300 are government appointed District Veterinary Officers and 800 are involved in veterinary administration dealing with animal health, meat inspection, industry and research. There is no pattern to private practices: some are individuals while others may work in a group practice, others in an animal hospital with over 20 vets on the staff. There is a single veterinary faculty in Sweden, in Uppsala. About 50% of veterinarians are women and their percentage of the profession is likely to increase. There are specialist veterinarians in canines, felines and equines. Specialism requires at least three years' full-time training at an approved animal hospital. Foreign vets should contact *Jordbruksverket* at Valgatan 8, 55182 Jünköping; ☎+46 36 15 50 00; fax +46 3630 8182.

Other veterinary organisations:
The Swedish Association of Veterinary Surgeons: Box 12709, 112 94 Stockholm; ☎+46 8 654 24 80; fax +46 8 65170 82.
Society of Veterinarians Employed at Animal Hospitals: Djursjukhusanställda Veterinärers Fürening, P.O. Box 12709, 112 94 Stockholm; ☎+46 8 654 24 80; fax +46 8 651 70 82.
SCATAN: Swedish Veterinary Nurses Association, Region Djursjukhuset, Oskarshalls 9.6, 55303 Jo[um]nko[um]ping.

Dogs

Dogs, of which Sweden has 600,000, are required to have an indentifying tattoo or microchip. Further information on dogs in Sweden can be obtained from the Kennel Club:
The Swedish Kennel Club: Rinkebysvängen 70, 16385 Spanga; ☎+46 8 795 30 00; +46 8 795 30 40.

Horses

Information about racing in Sweden can be obtained from the racing authorities:
Scandinavian Racing Bureau AB: P.O. Box 14, 18205 Stockholm; ☎+46 8 753 1457; fax +46 8 753 7686.
Svenska Galoppsportens Central Forbund (Swedish Jockey Club): Hastsportens Hus, 16189 Stockholm; ☎+468 627 20 00; fax +46 8 764 50 28; e-mail: info@galoppsport.se; www.galoppsport.se
Details of riding stables can be obtained from:
The Swedish Equestrian Society: Box 27857, 115 93 Stockholm; ☎+46 8 567 56 70; fax +46 8 567 56 70.

Useful Address

The Ministry of Agriculture, Food and Fishery: 10333 Stockholm; ☎+46 8 405 10 00; fax +46 8 20 64 96.

Animal & Bird Welfare, Protection & Conservation
The National Association of Animal Lovers: Davidshallsgatan 12, 21145 Malmö; ☎+46 40 26 99 00; fax +46 4026 99 47.
Sveriges Ornitologiska Förening (SOF): Swedish Ornithological Society, Ekhagsvägen 3, 10405 Stockholm; ☎+46 8 612 25 30; fax +46 8 612 25 36; e-mail: falkdalen@swipnet.se
The Swedish Association for the Protection of Animals: Box 10055 Stockholm; ☎+46 8 659 21 55; fax +46 8 659 0420.
Swedish Society for Nature Conservation:
Asögatan 115, 11691 Stockholm; ☎+46 8 702 65 00; fax +46 8 702 08 55.
Svenska Djurskyddsforeningen: Swedish animal protection organisation, c/o Erik Dahlbergsgatan 28, box 10081, 10055 Stockholm.
Sveriges Djuskyddsforeningars Riksforbunnd: Association of Swedish animal protection organisations, Markvardsgatan 10 41r, 11353, Stockholm.

Farmwork
The WWOOF organisation has a representative for Sweden: c/o Andreas Hedren, Hunna, Palstorp, 340 30 Vislandia (☎+46 470-75 43 75) which has about 20 member farms.

Swedish Embassies
Australia: Turrana Street, Yarralumla, ACT 2600; ☎02-6270 2700.
Canada: Mercury Court, 377 Dalhousie Street, Ottawa, Ontario K1N 9N8; ☎613-241 8553; fax +613-241 2277.
UK: 11 Montagu Place, London W1H 2AL; ☎020-7724 2101; fax 020-7724 4174; www.swednet.org.uk/sweden
USA: 1501 M Street, NW, Washington, DC 20005; ☎202-467 2600; fax 202-467 2699.

Switzerland

Switzerland is the neutral heart of Europe. It belongs neither to the EU nor the European Economic Area, and workers of any nationality have to acquire a combined residence/work permit. For non-EU citizens only this must be obtained through their employer in advance of entering the country. Most stay/residence pursuits are for one year (renewable if the employer can prove he still needs you). Short-trerm, (4-month) permits are also available at cantonal level. Other ways of getting a work permit include schemes enabling those following vocational training to get temporary trainee (*stagiare* positions in Switzerland. These are applicable to young Europeans and North Americans. There is also a farm volunteer scheme for young western Europeans.

Temporary Trainees
Permits for temporary trainee placements should be obtained from the Emigration and Trainees Section of the Swiss Federal Aliens Office (Quellenweg 9, 3003 Berne, Switzerland; ☎+41 31 322 29 96; fax +41 31 322 44 93) The trainee position must be arranged in the vocational field of the applicant. UK applicants should contact the Overseas Labour Service (Department of Employment, W5 Moorfoot, Sheffield S1 4PQ).

Vets & Veterinary Nurses
There are approximately 2,000 practising vets in Switzerland and 1,255 of them are private practitioners spread between 882 practices. Nearly 800 are in mixed/large animal practices, 400 in small animal practices and 60 in horse practices. The Swiss Veterinary

Society (*Gesellschaft Schweizerischer Tierärzte*) to which 86% of vets belong, is also responsible for the highly organised training of veterinary nurses.

Many Swiss practitioners do part-time work for governmental or cantonal authorities which, although it is demanding as it involves providing informatative and educative programmes, it is also lucrative. The Swiss are very keen to ensure that both vets and farmers undergo continuing education on veterinary matters. Small animal clinics in cities are very well equipped technologically and there are many specialists.

The Swiss Veterinary Society: Gesellschaft Schweizerischer Tierärtzte (GST)/Société des Vétérinaires Suisses (SVS), Länggass-Strasse 8, P.O.Box 6324, 3001 Bern, Postfach 6324; ☎+41 31/307 35 35 38; fax +41 31 307 35 39; e-mail gst@lite.mirs.ch; www.gstsvs.ch.

Swiss Veterinary Office: Schwarzenburgstrasse 161, 3097 Liebefeld-Berne; ☎+41 31 323 85 02; fax +41 31 324 82 56; www.bvet.admin.ch.

Horses
Swiss racing authorities:
Schweizer Galopprennsport-Verband: Kanalstr 17, Postfach, 8152 Glattbrugg; ☎+41 1 880 14 40; fax +41 1880 14 60. Swiss racing association.
Schweizer Pferderennsport-Verband: Kanalstr. 17 Postfach, 8152 Glattbrugg; ☎+41 880 15 10.

Zoos
Despite being one of the smaller European countries, Switzerland has more than 75 zoos, wildlife, deer and bird parks, single species parks and other animal collections. Some of them, including large city ones are listed below.

Basel: Tierpark Lange Erlen: Erlen-Verein Basel, Erlenparkweg 110, 4058 Basel; ☎+41 61 6814349; fax +41 79 2059247; www.tierpark-langeerlen.ch.
Basel Zoo: Zoologischer Garten Basel, Binningerstrasse 40, Postfach, 4011 Basel; ☎+41 61 295 3535; fax +41 61 2810-005; e-mail: zoo@basel.zoo.ch; www.zoobasel.ch
Bellevue: Parc d'Accueil Pour Animaux, 33 route de Valavran, 1293 Bellevue; ☎+41 22 774 3808; fax +41 22 774 3070; e-mail info@parc-challandes.ch; www.parc-challandes.ch. Animal reception centre.
Tierpark Daehlhoelzli: Stadt Bern, Tierparkweg 1, 3005 Bern; ☎+41 357 1515; fax +41 31 357 1510; e-mail daehlhoelzli@bern.ch; www.tierpark-bern.ch
Biel: Tierpark Biel-Bözingerberg, Zollhausstrasse 103, 2504 Biel; ☎+41 32 342 5917; e-mail hysek@bluewin.ch; www.tierpark-biel.ch.
Crémines: Zoo jurassien, Siky Ranch, 2746 Crémines; ☎+41 32 939052.
Frauenfeld: Plättli Zoo, Hertenstrasse 41, 8500 Frauenfeld; fax +41 52 721 8845; e-mail info@plaettli-zoo.ch
Geneva: Service des Espaces Verts et de l'Environment Bois de la Bâtie, 120 rue de Lausanne, 1202 Geneva 6; ☎+41 22 418 5000; fax +41 22 418 5001; e-mail: roger.beer@sev.ville-ge.ch. Indigenous animals and rare breeds.
Geneva: Terrarium du Muséum d'Histoire Naturelle: Ville de Géneve, Route de Malagnou 1, case postale 6434, 1211 Geneva 6; ☎+41 22 418 6300; fax +41 22 418 6301; e-mail: volker.manhert@mhn.ville.ge.ch; www.ville-ge.ch/musinfo/mhng/index.htm Rescue centre for exotic reptiles and coordinator of the Swiss bat protection studies.
La Chaux-de-Fonds: Parc Zoologique de la Ville de la Chaux-de-Fonds, c/o Musée d'histoire naturelle, Passage Leopold Robert 63, 2300 La Chaux de Fonds; ☎+41 32 913 3976; fax +41 32 913 3976; e-mail mhnc@ne.ch; www.mhnc.ch.
Langenthal: Tierpark Langenthal, Verschönerungsverein 4900 Langenthal; ☎+41 62 922 0860.
Lausanne: Vivarium de Lausanne, Boissonnet 82, 1000 Lausanne; ☎+41 21 652 7294;

fax +41 21 652 7369.

Le Vaud: Fondation du parc zoologique La Garenne, 1261 Le Vaud; tel/fax +41 22 366 1114; e-mail lagarenne@vtx.ch Specialises in European animals and birds of prey.

Marin-Neuchâtel: Papiliorama-Nocturama Tropical Gardens, Marin Centre, 2074 Marin-Neuchâtel; ☎+41 32753 4350; fax +41 32 7534675; e-mail: cbijleveld@papili orama.ch; www.papiliorama.ch. Specialises in tropical fauna and flora and is involved in nature conservation projects in Belize.

Oberwil: Werner Stamm-Stiftung (Werner Stamm Foundation for Wild Equids), zur Erhaltung seltener Einhufer, Im Müllerhägli 4, 4104 Oberwil; tel/fax +41 61 721 2003; e-mail info@wst-foundation.ch.

Olten: Wildpark Mühletäle Olten, Postfach 2019 4600 Olten; ☎+41 62 2962674; e-mail: wildpark@olten.ch; www.olten.ch.

Rapperswil: Knie's Kinderzoo: Swiss National Circus Children's Zoo, Oberseestrasse, 8640 Rapperswil; ☎+41 55 220 6767;; fax +41 55 220 6769; e-mail: b.sinniger@kni eskinderzoo.ch; www.knieskinderzoo.ch.

Servion: Zoo de Servion, 1077 Servion; ☎+41 21 903 1671; fax +41 21 903 1672. Small primates, mammals and birds.

St. Gallen: Wildparkgesellschaft Peter und Paul, Kachelweg 12, 9000 St Gallen; ☎+41 71 245 113; ☎+41 71 30 7711.

Studen-Biel: Zoo Seeteufel, 2557 Studen-Biel; ☎+41 32 3742555; fax +41 32 3742559; www.seeteufel.ch.

Theille: Kleintierpark Rothaus: 2075 Thielle; tel+41 32 832764. Small animals park.

Unterseen-Interlaken: Manorfarm, 3800 Unterseen-Interlaken; ☎+41 36 222264.

Zofingen: Wildpark und Voliere der Stadt Zofingen,   4800 Zofingen; ☎+41 62 519116.

Zürich: Zoologischer Garten Zürich, Zürichbergstrasse 221, 8044 Zürich; ☎+41 1-254 2500; fax +41 1-254-2510; e-mail: zoo@zoo.ch; www.zoo.ch.

Swiss Farm Work

The Swiss Farm Work Volunteer Programme is organised by the *Landdienst Zentralstelle* and involves spending three to eight weeks helping a German or French-speaking Swiss farmer and his or her family with the daily running of the house and farm. This takes place mostly in spring and summer, but there are a few winter stints available. The age limits are 17-30 and a basic knowledge of French or German (occasionally Italian) is required. Not all the farms have animals so you have to state your preferences at the outset. Additionally, there is a tendency for female volunteers to be given more domestic chores, so again you should state your preference to be employed mostly with animals to the organisers. Volunteers pay an inscription fee and make their own travel arrangements. The farmers provide board and lodging and a daily allowance. Sundays are free. Hours tend to be long up at dawn and finish at 8pm or 9pm. The compensation is to be treated as a member of the family and join them on outings and trips to market to sell produce etc. The farm animals may be cattle, goats, geese, chickens etc.

Further details from the Llanddienst-Zentralstelle/Service Agricole (Central Office for Voluntary Farm Work, Mühlegasse 13 (Postfach 728), 8025 Zürich; ☎+41 1 261 44 88; fax +41 1 261 44 32; e-mail admin@landdienst.ch; www.landdienst.ch).

WWOOF Switzerland (Postfach 59, 8124 Maur, Switzerland) has a list of about 50 Swiss farms that you can contact. To obtain details of the farms, you will have to join WWOOF.

Animal & Bird Welfare, Protection & Conservation

Société Genevoise pour la Protection des Animaux (SGPA): Refuge de Vailly, Case postale 2151, 1233 Bernex; ☎+41 22 757 1323. Situated just outside Bernex, the compound has room for 50 dogs and a dozen cats.

Swiss Association for the Protection of Birds: Schweizer Vogelschutz (SVS) – Birdlife Schweiz Verband für Vogel – and Naturschutz Association Suisse pour la protection des Oiseaux (ASPO) – Birdlife Suisse, 8036 Zürich, Postfach; ☎+41 1/463 7271; fax +41/461 47 78; e-mail: birdlifesvs@access.ch

Swiss Association for the Protection of Animals: Schweizer Tierschutz (STS)/Protection Suisse des Animaux (PSA), Dornacherstr. 101, Postfach, 4008 Basel; ☎+41 61/361 15 16; fax +41 61/361 15 16.

Swiss Youth Society for the Protection of Animals: Schweizer Jugend-Tierschutz/ Jeunesse Suisse pour la Protection des Animaux, Tierparkweg 1, 5622 Waltensschwil; ☎+41 56/622 36 67.

Organisation for animal rights: Verein für Tierrechte, Büschiackerstr. 59, 3098 Schliern; ☎+41 31/971 00 91.

Swiss Foundation for Birds of Prey: Fondation Suisse pour les Rapaces/Schweizerische Stiftung für Raubvögel, Clos Gaspard, 2946 Mié court; ☎+41 66/72 22 02.

Rare species foundation: Stiftung Pro Specie Rara, Engelgasse 12a, 9000 St Gallen; ☎+41 71 222 74 20; fax +41 71/223 74 01.

Swiss Embassies

Australia: Melbourne Ave, Forrest, ACT 2603; ☎02-6273 3977.

Canada: 5 Marlborough Avenue, Ottawa, Ontario K1N 8E6; ☎613 235 1837; fax 613 5631394.

UK: 16-18 Montagu Place, London W1H 2BQ; ☎020-7616 6000; fax 020-7724 7001; www.swissembassy.org.uk

USA: 2900 Cathedral Ave, NW Washington, DC 20008; ☎202 745 7900; fax 202-387 2564.

Central & Eastern Europe & Russia

The fall of Communism in Eastern Europe has brought with it political and economic upheavals. Some countries including Poland, the Baltic States, Slovenia, and the Czech Republic have embraced the free market economies with enthusiasm and are progressing towards full integration with the European Union. Others including Albania and the Russian Federation face an uncertain future as they are in turmoil politically and economically.

Most westerners working in eastern European countries have to contend with low pay and a lack of resources, poor organisation, fluctuating prices, poor quality accommodation and a host of other problems including the language barrier. Generally however, experiences are likely to be positive largely due to the inhabitants of these countries whose resourcefulness and ability to cope in adverse conditions are truly awesome. There is in fact, something to be said for visiting the former eastern bloc countries before they join the EU and become just as commercialised as the rest of Europe.

Entry Regulations & Work Permits
Entry regulations vary from country to country. Anyone going to take up a work will need a work and residence permit obtained in advance from the relevant diplomatic representation in their country.

COUNTRY GUIDE

Bulgaria

Bulgaria in south-eastern Europe has its eastern edge on the Black sea, Romania to the north, Yugoslavia and F.Y.R. Macedonia to the west and Greece and Turkey to the south. Approximately a fifth the size of Spain, it covers 111,000 square kilometres and has a population of eight and a half million people. Like its neighbour Romania, Bulgaria is mountainous to the west with an eastern plain towards the coast. Its mountain ranges include the Rhodope, Stara, Rila and Pirin. The Turks held Bulgaria in the Ottoman empire until the late nineteenth century and are responsible for the term Balkans which is used to designate south-eastern Europe in general and not Bulgaria in particular.

Following the demise of communism, Bulgaria has been slow in adapting to a market economy and suffers high unemployment. One of the major new growth areas is bio-technology.

Vets
The Bulgarian veterinary profession is regulated by the National veterinary service, part of the Ministry of Agriculture, Forests and Agrarian Reform. Reform is necessary in Bulgaria to carry out a transition from state to privatised farming begun a decade ago.

The public sector veterinary service is responsible for nearly 100 veterinary hospitals and over a thousand local veterinary offices in 117 districts located in 28 regions. Livestock is prone to regular outbreaks of infectious diseases like foot and mouth and sheep pox which are rare in western Europe. The prevalence of such maladies makes disease control and prevention a priority. The two veterinary faculties are in Sofia and Stara Zagora. After 3 years at university, veterinary students spend six months in practice before producing a scientific thesis and sitting their final exam. Before being eligible for a private practice licence, they have to notch up five years post graduation experience in a practice. Private practice has only been instituted since 1992 and most of the 300 or so practitioners to date deal with companion animals.

Veterinary Addresses
National Veterinary Service: 15A Pencho Slaveikov Blvd., 1606 Sofia; ☎+359 252 1345; fax +359 254 29 25.
Association of Private Veterinarians: c/o Dr Stoian Stoianov, PSlaveikaov Blvd 15, Sofia; ☎+35 92 54 971.

Zoo & Aquarium
Sofia Zoological Gardens: Srebarna Str. 1, 1407 Sofia; ☎+359 268 2043/31; fax +359 268 3202; e-mail sofzoo@omega.bg
Varna Aquarium: Research Institute of Fishing Resources, Boul. Primorski 4, Varna; ☎+359 5223 1852/5225 7856; fax +359 5225 7876; e-mail ife@abcis.bg

Animal and Bird Protection
Bulgarian Society for the Protection of Animals: Mladost 2, Block 223, ENTR 4, APT 65, 1199 Sofia.
Bulgarsko Druzhestvo za Zashtita na Pticite (BDZP): Bulgarian Society for the Protection of Birds (BSPB), P.O. Box 114, 1172 Sofia, Bulgaria; ☎+359 2 68 94 13; fax +359 2 62 08 15

Volunteer Project
Wildlife Rehabilitation in Stara Zagora: c/o British Trust for Conservation Volunteers, 36 St Mary's Street, Wallingford, Oxfordshire OX10 OEU; ☎01491-839766; fax 01491-824602; e-mail information@btcv.org.uk; www.btcv.org.uk. Work at a centre for the treatment, rehabilitation and release of wildlife including the rare black vulture, buzzards and eagles. Foreign and local volunteers, work together to construct fencing and specialised bird aviaries, and enjoy opportunities to observe and assist the centre's work. Two weeks in August. Minimum age 18 years.

Bulgarian Embassies & Consulate
British passport holders require a visa to stay in Bulgaria for longer than 30 days and US citizens need a visa to enter the country. Longer-term visitors require a residence and work permit. Enquiries about these should be made to the Bulgarian consulate or embassy before departure.
Australia: Consulate, Carlotta Road, Double Bay, NSW 2028; ☎02-9327 7581.
UK: 186-188 Queen's Gate, London SW7 5HL; ☎020-7584 9400/0891 171208; www. bulgarianembassy@yahoo.com; www.bulgaria-embassy.org.uk
USA: 1621 22nd Street NW, Washington DC, 20008; ☎202-387 7969.

Croatia

Croatia occupied a northern position in former Yugoslavia. It is shaped, for want of a better description, like a butterfly and its territory incorporates a touristically important stretch of the Dalmatian Coast including Split and Dubrovnik. Croatia shares borders with Slovenia, Hungary, Bosnia-Herzegovina and Yugoslavia. The country has a population of nearly five million.

Vets

Croatia has nearly two and a half thousand practising vets over 1000 of which are in private practice. Practices vary in size from two to a staggering 100 vets each. Specialities include wildlife, aquaculture and apiculture (bees). The state veterinary service is organised efficiently and covers the country evenly. As in some other European countries, annual rabies vaccination and registering of dogs is compulsory. Croatia suffered heavy livestock losses during the Yugoslavian conflict and restocking was necessary. The current growth area is in small animal private practice. The single veterinary faculty is in the capital, Zagreb.

Veterinary address
Croatian Veterinary Association: Hrvatska Veterinarska Komora: Planinskia 2a, 1000 Zagreb; ☎+385 1 215830; fax +385 1 215 830.

Zoo
Zagreb Zoo: Zooloski vrt grada Zagreb: Zoological Garden Zagreb, Maksi Mirski Perivoi BB, 10000 Zagreb; ☎+385 1 2302 198/9; fax +385 1 2302 198/9; e-mail zoo@zoo.hr.

Animal, Bird & Nature Protection
Croatian Society for Bird & Nature Protection (CSBNP): Ilirski Tr. 9, 10000 Zagreb; tel/fax +385 1 345 445.
Slavonian & Baranian Animal Protection Society: A Waldingera 11, 31000 Osijek.

Conservation Projects
Blue World/Adriatic Dolphin Project: Zad Bone 11, Veli Losinj, 51551, Croatia; ☎+385 51 520276; fax +358 51 520275; e-mail adp@adp.hr; www.adp.hr.
Blue World/ADP carries out research on bottlenose dolphins collecting data in the field and then analysing it. All aspects of the methodology will be taught to volunteers. ADP also raises awareness of the project through lectures and preparation of materials in 5 languages.

30-40 volunteers are accepted annually. Volunteers are involved in all aspects of research dependent on skills and motivation. Of particular interest to the project are students of biology/environmental sciences and geography. EU nationalities and US citizens (visa required). Volunteers must be English-speaking and conservation minded. Volunteers should be in good health and able to spend long hours under the sun up to 35 Celsius. Programmes last 12 days between June and September. Accommodation is provided, but no expenses.

Scientific papers and other information about volunteering free from the website.
Applications should be made direct to the above address.

Griffon Vulture Conservation Project – Island of Cres: Eco-center Caput insulae-Beli, Beli 4, 51559 Beli; tel/fax +385 (51) 840-825; e-mail caput.insulae@ri.tel.hr; www.caput-insulae.com.
The aim of the project is to study griffon vulture biology and ecology with a view to determining the factors most likely to ensure their survival and to use the data to formulate a conservation plan. Numbers in Croatia are down to 120-150 breeding pairs.

Volunteers are needed for a conservation project where they record Griffon sightings and observe and record the cliff colonies in May, June, September and October. Volunteers can stay for a minimum of a week, but two weeks or longer is also possible.

Volunteers can also participate in the volunteering programmes for protecting the natural and cultural-historical heritage on the Island of Cres throughout the year.

Accommodation is in the Eco-Centre house, which has 20 volunteer beds and bathroom and kitchen facilities. Volunteers are expected to help with the housekeeping and cooking. Cost is $149 per week. Volunteers are also offered lectures on a variety of ornithological topics.

Apply direct to the above address or website.

Slavonsko-Baranjsko Drustvo: "Zivot", Gornjodravska Obala 84, 31000 Oswek, Croatia; ☎+385-31-283-445; fax +385-31-284-415; e-mail zivot@zivot.hr; www.zivot.hr
Croatian organisation that operates an animal shelter, manages the protection of wild birds and animals on the edge of a national park, and monitors animal transport. Volunteers are needed to help in the shelter everyday and with other animal activities. No special qualifications are needed but volunteers with previous relevant experience are preferred. Help is needed all year round. Accommodation is provided but not food. The work is unpaid.

Anyone interested in helping should contact Davorko Feil, preferably by e-mail (zivot@zivot.hr).

Croatian Embassies & Consulates
Australia: Embassy, Jindalee Crs, O'Malley, ACT 2606; ☎02-6286 6988.
UK: 21 Conway Street, London W1P 5HL; ☎020-7387 1970; fax 020-7387 0574; www.croatiaemb.org .
USA: 2343 Massachusetts Avenue NW, Washington DC 20008; ☎202-588 5889; fax 202 588 8936.

The Czech Republic

The Czech Republic was until 1993 part of the Republic of Czechoslovakia, a state cobbled together in 1918 from the Austro-Hungarian territories of Bohemia, Moravia and Slovakia. Following the bloodless overthrow of communism ('The Velvet Revolution') in 1989 the Czech and Slovak politicians decided to split into the Czech Republic and Slovakia (see below). Unlike Slovakia the Czech Republic has elected to join the EU, which seems likely to happen soon.

Slightly smaller than Austria, the Czech republic has a population of ten million which includes German, Slovak, Hungarian, Ukrainian and Polish minorities. The climate is colder in winter than Britain and warmer in summer and has been described as similar to that of the north-western United States. Czech is the official language but German and English are widely spoken.

Vets
There are about 3,000 practising veterinarians who until 1991 were all state employees. Privatisation has led to two-thirds of these opting for private, mostly mixed practice, and mostly on an individual basis. There are about 100 large animal practices, 250+ small animal practices and 50 or so horse specialist practices. About 200+ practices involve two partners. 100 or so employ an assistant.

The state veterinary service deals with infectious diseases prevention and control, food inspection, registration of veterinary medicines, animal welfare and environmental protection.

All Czech vets practising in the Czech Republic are obliged to be members of the Chamber of Veterinary Surgeons. Chamber membership is also open to other vets. The single veterinary faculty is in Brno, which also accepts foreign students for whom a parallel course is run in English.

Useful Addresses
The Chamber of Veterinary Surgeons of the Czech Republic: Komora Veterinárních
    Lékaŕu, České republiky (KVL CR), Palackeho 1-3, 61242 Brno; ☎+420 5 756 407;
    fax +420 5 756 407; e-mail vetkom@mbox.vol.cz; internet: www.vetkom.cz.
University Faculty of Veterinary Medicine: Vysokà Škola Veterinární a Farmaceutická,
    Fakulta Veterinarního Lékaŕsvi, Palackého 1/3, 61242 Brno; ☎+420 5 4156 1111; fax
    +420 5 4156 88 41; e-mail HORIN@DIOR.ICS.MUNI.CZ; Erasmus exchanges: c/o
    Emilie Sedlářova; ☎+420 5 4156 2002.

Racing authority
Jockey Club Czech Republic: Lamačova 914, P.O. Box 8, 15200 Prague 5; ☎+420 2
    5816091; fax +420 2 5814785.

Animal & Bird Protection
Česka Společnost Ornitologická (CSO): Czech Society for Ornithology (CSO),
    Hornoměcholupska 34, 10200 Prague 10; tel/fax +420 278 66 700.
League for the Protection of Animals: C R, Hrádek, 67401 Třebíč.
Moravian Society for the Protection of Animals: Interpespension Brno, Kocianka 23,
    61200 Brno.
Nadace Na Ochranu Zvířat: Olbrachtova 3, Prague 4, 14000.

Zoos
Brno-Bystré: Zoologická Zahrada Města Brna, 63500 Brno-Bystré; ☎+420 5 4621
    0143; fax +420 5 4621 0000; e-mail zoo@zoobrno.cz.
Chomutov: Podkrušnohorsky Zoopark Chomutov, 43001 Chomutov; tel/fax +420 396
    624 412;; e-mail zoopark@zoopark.cz.
Decin: Zoologická zahrada Děčin, Stadt Děčin 40502 Decin; ☎+420 412 531164; fax
    +420 412 531626; e-mailinfo@zoodecin.cz; www.zoodecin.cz.
Dvur Králové nad Labem: Zoologická zahrada Dvur Králové nad Labem, Stefanikova
    1029; 54401 Dvur Kralove nad Labem; ☎+420 499 329; fax +420 499 320564; e-
    mail zoo.dk@zoodk.cz; www.zoodk.cz.
Hluboká nad Vltavou: Zoologická zahrada Ohrada, 37341 Hluboká nad Vltavou;
    ☎420 38 700 2211; fax +420 38 796 5445; e-mail info@zoo-ohrada.cz; www.zoo-
    ohrada.cz.
Jihlava: Zoologická zahrada Jihlava, Brezinovy sady 10, 58601 Jihlava; ☎+420
    567573730; fax +420-567302839 e-mail jizoo@zoojihlava.cz
Liberec: Zoologicá Zahrada Liberec, Masarykova 1347/31, 46001 Liberec; ☎+420 482
    710-616; fax +420 482-710-618; e-mail info@zooliberec.cz; www.zooliberec.cz.
Olomouc-Svatý Kopeček: Zoologiká Zahrada Olomouc; ☎+420 585385; fax +420
    585385 260; e-mail info@zoo-olomouc.cz; www.zoo.olomouc.com.
Ostrava: Zoologická zahrada Ostrava, Michalkovicka 197, 71000 Ostrava; ☎+420
    59 624 1269; fax +420 59 624 3316; zuzoostrava@volny.cz; www.mmo.cz/zoo/
    index.htm.
Plzen: Zoologická a Botanika zahrada Města Plzně, Pod Vinicemi 9, 30116 Plzen;
    ☎+420 19753 0916; fax +420 19753 3764; e-mail mail@zoo.plzen-city.cz;
    www.zooplzen.cz.
Prague: Zoologiká Zahrada Praha, Stadt Praha, U.trojskeho zamku 3/120, 171000
    Praha 7; ☎+420-2-688-1118; fax +420 2 688 0624; e-mail zoopraha@zoopraha.cz;
    www.zoo.cz.
Usti nad Labem: Zoologická zahrada Ústí nad Labem, Stad Ústí nad Labem, Drazdanska
    23, 40007 Ústí nad Labem; ☎+420 475503-354/284; fax +420-475503-451; e-mail

zoo@zousti.cz zoousti@mbox.vol.cz
Zlin: Zoologická zahrada a Zamek Zlín-Lesná, 76314 Zlín-Lesná; ☎+420 5779 14180/
1; fax +420-5779-14053; office@zoolesna.cz; www.zoolesna.cz.

Czech Embassies
EU and US citizens do not need a visa to enter the Czech Republic for a short time, and
may remain for up to 30 days before a residence permit is required. Visa information on
090 6910 1060 and www.czechembassy.org.uk
Australia: Culgoa Cct, O'Malley ACT 2606; ☎02-6290 1386.
UK: Visa section, 26-30 Kensington Palace Gardens, London W8 4QY; ☎020-7243
1115; fax 020-7243 7926; e-mail london@embassy.mzv.cz; www.czech.org.uk
USA: 3900 Spring of Freedom Street, NW Washington DC 2008; ☎202 274 9100; fax
202 363 6308; e-mail washington@embassy.mzv.cz; www.czecg,cz/washington

Estonia

One of the three Baltic States, Estonia has a population of one and a half million,
remarkable if compared with the Netherlands, which is only slightly smaller in area, but
whose inhabitants number 15.6 million. The Estonian population was devastated by wars
in the 18th and 20th centuries and was briefly freed from Russian domination in 1918
only to be invaded by Germany in 1941 and returned to Russian ownership in 1945.
Finally after a period of stealthily progressing its independence, Estonia re-emerged as
a republic in 1991.

With its large forests, marshes and lakelands, Estonia has more than a passing
resemblance to Finland. It shares borders with Russia to the east and Latvia to the south.
Its territory includes the two large Baltic islands, Hiumaa and Saaremaa, and two-thirds
of its people live in the mainland capital Tallinn. The Estonian language bears some
similarities to Finnish. However, since independence, English has taken over from
Russian as the most learnt second language.

Vets
Estonia has about 900 practising vets about 450 of whom work in mixed practices and
300 or so are employed by the public sector including universities. The importance of
small animal and companion animal practice in increasing but the sole veterinary faculty
at Tartu is short of teachers in this field. The faculty usually has a small intake of students
from Finland.

Under the Soviets, Estonian agriculture and animal production was carried out on large
state and collective farms which have been gradually broken down into smaller units,
privatised or closed down. Currently 250 vets work as veterinary inspectors responsible
for the control of food hygiene and infectious diseases. This is an important area for
Estonia, which needs to meet EU standards before becoming a member.

Veterinary addresses
Estonian Veterinary Association: Eesti Loomaarstide Ühing (ELÜ/EVA), 62 Kreutzwaldi
St., 2400 Tartu; ☎+3727 42 14 97; fax +372 7 42 25 82.
State Veterinary Department: Riigi Veterinaaramet, Väike-Paala Street 3, 0014 Tallinn;
☎+372 6 38 00 79; fax +3726 38 0210.

Dogs
Estonian Kennel Union: Siili 21-100, EE0034 Tallinn; ☎+372 2 521 063; fax +372 654
2448.

Zoo
Tallinn Zoological Garden: Stadtverwaltung, Paldiski Mnt. 145, 0035 Tallinn; ☎+372
694 3300; fax +372 657 8990; e-mail zoo@tallinnlv.ee; www.tallinzoo.ee.

Nature & Bird Protection
Eesti Ornitoloogiaühing (EOÜ): Estonian Ornithological Society (EOS); P.O. Box 227,
2400 Tartu; +372 7 430198; fax +372 7 427 033; e-mail margus@linnu.tartu.ee
Union of Estonian Protection Areas (EKAL): ☎+352 32 44 675; fax +372 23 44 575.

Voluntary Work
Native Horses of Estonia, Saarema: c/o British Trust for Conservation Volunteers,
36 St Mary's Street, Wallingford, Oxfordshire OX10 OEU; ☎01491-839766; fax
01491-824602; e-mail information@btcv.org.uk; www.btcv.org.uk. Work to preserve
traditional grazing areas for Estonia's native horses, which are unique and pure bred.
You can take riding lessons on the native horses and stroll through their meadows. Two
weeks end of July/beginning of August.
It may be possible to get contacts for other wildlife programmes in Estonia by asking
the following organisation for assistance:
Estonian Ministry of the Environment: Toompuiestee 24, 0100 Tallinn; ☎+372 626
2810; fax +372 626 2801; www.envir.ee.

Estonian Embassies & Consulates
EU nationals and US passport holders do not need a visa for stays of up to 90 days in
any one year.
Australia: Consulate, Louisa Road, Birchgrove NSW 2041; ☎02-9810 7468.
UK: 16 Hyde Park Gate, London SW7 5DG; ☎020-7589 3428; fax 020-7589 3430.
USA: 2131 Massachussets Avenue NW, Washington DC; ☎202 588 0101. *Estonian
Consulate:* Suite 2415, 630 Fifth Avenue, New York, NY; ☎212-247 1450; fax 2121-
262 0893.

Hungary

The relatively flat country of Hungary covers 93,000 square kilometres and its 10.2
million inhabitants share their borders with seven countries; more than any other country
in Europe. These are with the Slovak Republic to the north, the Ukraine and Romania to
the east, the rump of Yugoslavia to the south, Croatia to the southwest and Austria and
Slovenia to the west. The population is 96.6% Hungarian-speaking Magyars, and the
rest are minorities including German-speakers and gypsies. The country is dotted with
lakes of which the largest and best known is the vast Lake Balaton, which is a traditional
tourist area.

Vets
As in other post-communist countries, Hungary's veterinarians are now free to set up in
private practice. There are over 3,000 vets of whom approximately 500 run some type of
private practice outside full-time jobs working for the state and a further 900 or so work
part-time as civil servants while running their private practices. Cattle production has just
about halved since the reform of state and co-operative farming into private enterprise.
Reform has also proved the economic downfall of many farmers. The knock-on effect
on vets' employment has made diversification essential and there has been an increase in
city-based, small animal practices. Simultaneously, there has been a rise in the number of
women applying to study veterinary science (currently 40% of vet students are female).

This will help redress an under-representation of women in the profession; just 15% of vets are female. There is a single veterinary faculty in the country, the University of Veterinary Science in Budapest and the course is difficult to access with six applicants for every place.

Veterinary Organisations
The Hungarian Veterinary Association: Istvan utca 2, P O Box 2, 1400 Budapest; ☎+36 1 343 71 04; fax +36 1 142 65 18.
Chamber of Hungarian Veterinarians: Lehel u. 43, 1135 Budapest; ☎+36 1 350 6116; fax +36 1 350 6116. (Founded 1996).

Racing Authority & Equestrian Associations
National Horse Racing Ltd: 1087 Budapest, Kerepesi, Ut 9; ☎+36 1 334 2958; fax +36 1 210 0785.
Hungarian Equestrian Association: Magyar Lovas Szövetség, 1087 Budapest, Kerepesi út 7; ☎36 1 313 0451.
Hungarian Equestrian Society: Magyar Lovas Egylet, 1087 Budapest, Kerepesi út 9; ☎36 1 313 5817.
Hungarian Horse Breeding and Equestrian Sport Society: Magyar Lótenyésztő és Lovassport Szövetség, 1134 Budapest, Lőportár u. 16; ☎36 1 412 5010.
Hungarian Horseracing Co.: Magyar Lovasfogasdást Szervezö Kft, 1087 Budapest, Kerepesi út 9; ☎36 1 334 2958.

Zoos
Budapest: Budapest Zoo and Botanical Garden: Stadt Budapest, P.O.Box 469, 1371 Budapest 5; ☎+36 1 363 3820; fax +36 1 363 2971; e-mail allakert@zoobudapest.c om; www.alba.hu/zoobudapest.
Debrecen: Nagyerdei Kultúrpark Debrecen, Ady E. u. 1, 4001 Debrecen; ☎+36 52 310 065; fax +36 52 315 864.
Nyíregyhza-Sostofürdo: Sosto-erdei Szabadido Park Nyiregyhaza-Sostofürdo: Sosto-erdei Szabadidö Park Nyieregyhaza. 4431 Nyirgyhaza-Sostofürdo; ☎+36 424 79702; fax +36 424 79702.
Pecs-Dömörkapu: Pécsi Allatkert és Akvárium-Terrárium: Mecseki Kulturpark, Munkácsy Mihály u. 31, 7621 Pecs; ☎+36 72317005; fax +36 72 213 114; zoo@dravanet.hu; www.zoo.hu/Pecs/.
Szeged: Szegedi Vadaspark Zoo Szeged, Cserepes-sor, 6701 Szeged; ☎+36 62 542 50; fax +36 62 445 299; szeged.zoo@tiszanet.hu; www.zoo.szeged.hu.
Veszprem: Kittenberger Zoo Veszprem, Stadverwaltung, Kittenberger u.17, 8200 Veszprem; ☎+3688 421088; fax +3688321 287.

Animal, Bird & Nature Protection
Hungarian Federation of Animal Welfare & Nature Protection: Vadasz U 29, 1054 Budapest; ☎361 302 1686.
Hungarian Ornithological & Nature Conservation Society: Magyar Madártani és Természetve-Delmi Egyesület MME/Birdlife Hungary: Kültöu. 21, Pf. 391, 1536 Budapest; ☎+36 1 393 17 11; fax +36 1 395 8327; e-mail mme@mme.zpok.hu

Farmwork
WWOOF: contact Andrea Bódi of the Biokultúra Egyesület (Kitaibel, P.u. 4, 1024 Budapest; ☎1-316 2138/fax 1-316 2139).
ETO Farm: 2687 Bercel-Jákotpuszst (035-384715) or Department of Applied Ethology, Pater Karoly u. 1, 2103 Gödölló (028-410131; matine@nt.ktg.gau.hu). EU students with an interest in innovative agricultural techniques are welcome to participate in

summer training activities at the ETO farm, where these are researched by academics from the university of Gödölló.

Hungarian Embassies

Australia: Beale Crs., Deakin, ACT 2600; ☎02-6282 3226.

UK: 35 Eaton Place, London SW1X 8BY; ☎020-7235 5218; www.huemblon.org.uk; website for the Government Portal is www.ekormanyzat.hu/english

USA: 3910 Shoemaker Street, NW, Washington DC 20008; ☎202 362-6730; fax 202 362-6730; www.hungaryemb.org

British and EU citizens do not require a visa to enter Hungary and remain for 90 days (six months for British citizens). Work and residence permits should be arranged in advance by the employer in Hungary. Foreigners wishing to stay for a year or longer must apply for a residence permit after six months from the police station in their town of residence.

Latvia

Latvia, similar in size to fellow Baltic state Lithuania, has a population of 2.5 million including 650,000 Russian-speakers. Its other borders are with Estonia to the north and Russia and Belarus to the east and southeast. Latvia's long Baltic coast includes the Gulf of Riga and the important port of that name.

Vets

Latvia has 3,000 registered veterinarians. Vets have to be licensed (since 1992). The majority of the thousand or so practices, are mixed large animal ones. There are fewer than 150 small animal practices and a dozen or so specialist horse practices. The growth area is likely to be in small animal practice.

Veterinary addresses

State Veterinary Department: Ministry of Agriculture, Rupublikas laukams 2, 1981 Riga; ☎+371 7 325 446; fax +371 7 322 727.

Latvian Association of Veterinarians: Skolas iela 3, 1010 Riga; ☎+371 7 28 87 47; e-mail lvb@apollo.lv.

Zoo

Riga Zoo: Rigas Zoologiskais Darzs, Mezha prospekts 1, 1014 Riga; ☎+371 7 518 409; fax +371 7 540 011; e-mail rigaszoo@latnet.lv.

Bird Protection

Latvian Ornithological Society: A.K. 10, 1047 Riga; ☎ +37172 21 580; fax +371 72 21 580; e-mail putni@lanet.lv.

Latvian Embassies & Consulate

EU citizens and US passport holders do not need a visa to visit Latvia for up to 90 days in any one year.

Australia: Consulate, Parnell Street, Strathfield, NSW 2135; ☎02-9745 5981.

UK: 45 Nottingham Place, London 1M 3FE; ☎020-7312 0040; fax 020-7312 0042.

USA: 4325 17th Street NW, 20011 Washington DC; ☎202-726 8213; fax 202 726 6785. Consular office open from 10 to 12 am; www.latvia-usa.org.

Lithuania

The Baltic state of Lithuania has a larger population (3.7 million) than northern neighbour Latvia, despite being of a similar size. The capital Vilnius is home to 600,000 Lithuanians. Other borders are with Poland and the Russian enclave of Kaliningrad to the southwest, and Belarus to the south east. Lithuania became part of Russia for the first time in 1772, re-emerging as an independent state in 1918 only to be illegally occupied by the Soviets in 1940 and 1945. Finally, in 1990 it became independent again.

Vets
Lithuania has 2,264 registered vets, of whom 529 are official veterinarians, 524 authorised to carry out official supervision, and 1,211 are private practitioners. The country's first Small Animal Veterinary Association was founded in 1995.

Veterinary addresses
State Food and Veterinary Service of Lithuania: Siesiku 19, Vilnius 2010; ☎+370-5-2404361; fax +370-5-2404362; e-mail vvt@vet.lt; www.vet.lt. This governmental institution implements state policy veterinary matters and authorises foreign vets to practice in Lithuania.
Lithuanian Veterinary Association: Tilzes 18, Kaunas 3022; tel/fax +370-37-267971; lvga@lva.lt. A body uniting the veterinarians of Lithuania.
Lithuanian Veterinary Academy: Tilzes 18, Kaunas 3022; ☎+370-37-36 23 83; fax +370-37-36 24 17; e-mail reklva@lva.lt; www.lva.lt. The Lithuanian Veterinary Academy is the only higher school in Lithuania qualifying veterinary surgeons.

Cats and Dogs
The main law on animal welfare is the Law on the Care, Keeping and Use of Animals passed in 1997 by the Lithuanian Parliament. The two main animal protection organisations are:
The Lithuanian Society for the Protection of Animals (LiSPA): Radvilų dvaro 33-, Kaunas 3026; tel/fax +370-37-363333; e-mail: LGGD@takas.lt
Vilnius Region Animal Welfare and Protection Society: M.Horodničienes 18, Vilnius; ☎+370-5-2711629, GSM +370-698-00952; e-mail danga.eva@aiva.lt

The national organisation for pedigree dogs is:
The *Lithuanian Kennel Society:* V Maciulevičiaus 53, Vilnius 2050; tel/fax +370-5-2446901; e-mail lkd@centras.lt

The national organisation for pedigree cats is:
Lithuanian Felinology Association: Šv. Gertrudos 46, Kaunas 3000; tel/fax +370-37-324545; e-mail bubaste@animal.lt

Horses
The main racing body is:
Lithuanian Equestrian Association: Kedrų 6, Vilnius; ☎+370-5-2160415; fax +370-5-2163957.

Zoo & Aquarium
Kaunas Zoo: Lithuanian Zoo, Radvilenu pl. 21, 3028 Kaunas; ☎+370-37-332540; fax +370-7-332196; e-mail; Izs@is.lt.
Klaipeda: Lithuanian Sea Museum, Smiltynès 3, 5800 Klaipeda; ☎+370-46-490740; fax +370-46-490750; e-mail: ljm@juru.muziejus.lt; www.juru.muziejus.lt.

Ornithological organisation
Lithuanian Ornithological Society: Naugarduko 47-3, Vilnius 2009; tel/fax +370-5-2130498.

Lithuanian embassies
London: 84 Gloucester Place, London W1H 3HN; ☎020-7486 6404; www.users.globalnet.co.uk/lralon.
USA: 2622 16th Street NW, 20009-4202 Washington DC; ☎202-234 5680; www.ltembassy.org

Poland

Poland is the second largest eastern European nation after the Ukraine. It has an area equivalent to almost 90% of Germany but with 38.6 million inhabitants, has only 50% of that country's population. Poland has a Baltic coast to the north and shares a border with Germany to the west and other borders with Russia, Lithuania, Slovakia and the Czech Republic. 45 years of Russian domination came to an end in 1989 and Poland is aiming to join the European Union in the early years of the next millennium.

Some parts of Poland, notably Gdansk and Silesia, are heavily industrialised, but this is contrasted with vast tracts of mostly unspoiled natural landscapes including Bialowieza, the last remnant of primeval forest in Europe, which is home to 225 species of birds, 65 species of mammals (including wolves and the rare European bison) as well as numerous flowers and plants. You can work in this unique environment as a volunteer (see below).

Vets
As a result of the post-communist shake up veterinarians regained their liberal profession status in 1990 and the Polish Veterinary Chamber was constituted as a self-governing body in 1991. Membership is compulsory for practising veterinarians. There are nine and a half thousand registered practising vets and a further 2691 are employed in the public sector.

A growth area is in laboratories providing private diagnostic services for vets. This is partly linked to rise in the number of small animal practices. The number of rural practices on the other hand is declining along with animal production.

Another relatively new veterinary body, The Polish Society of Veterinary Sciences has 17 regional branches which organise scientific and professional conferences around Poland. The Society also has 12 specialist sections. Veterinary specialists are appointed by the Ministry of Agriculture, and areas covered include, bee diseases, fur animals, laboratory animals and fish.

Veterinary Addresses
Polish National Veterinary Chamber: Al Przyjaciol 1, 00950 Warsaw; ☎+48 22 628 93 35; fax +48 22 622 09 55.
Polish Society of Veterinary Sciences: Ul. Akademica 12, 20033 Lublin; ☎+48 81 53 329 12; fax +48 81 53 329 12.
Veterinary Department: Ministry of Agriculture and Food Economy, ul WSpolna 30, 00930 Warsaw; ☎+48 22 628 85 11; fax +48 2 623 14 08.

Horses
Racing Authority: Sluzewiec Tory Wyscigow Konnych W Warszawie Spolka: Ul Pulawska 266, 00-976 Warsaw; ☎+48 22 43 14 41; fax +48 22 43 66 49.

Zoos

Bydgoszcz: Ogró Fauny Polskiej, Lesny Park Kultury i Wypoczynku, ul. Gdanska 173-175, 85674 Bydgoszcz; ☎+48 52 372 1865/1405/1215; fax +48 52 372 1437; e-mail bcee@bcee.bydgoszcz.pl; www.bcee.bydgoszcz.pl.

Gdansk: Gdansk Zoological Garden, ul Karwienska 3, 80328 Gdansk; ☎+48 58 552 0042; fax +48 58 552 1751; zoo@zoo.gd.pl; www.zoo.gd.pl.

Katowice: Slaski Ogród Zoologiczny, POB 385, 40954 Katowice; ☎+48 32 599472; fax +48 32 599472; e-mail zoo.kat@grot.com.pl.

Kraków: Fundacja – Miejski Park i Ogród Zoologiczny Kraków, Stadt Kraków, ul Kasy, Oszczednosci M Krakówa 14; ☎+48 12 4253551/2; fax +48 124252710; e-mail zoo@kraknet.pl; www.zoo.kraknet.pl.

Lódz: Miejski Ogród Zoologiczny w Lodzi, ul. Konstantynowska 8/10, 94303 Lodz; ☎+48 42 6329290; fax +48 42 632 9290; e-mail zoo@lodz.pdi.net; www.zoo.lodz.pl.

Opole: Ogród Zoologiczny Opole, ul Spacerowa 10, Skr.poczt. 5, 45094 Opole; ☎+48 77 4542858; fax +48 77 456 4264; e-mail zooopole@miramex.com.pl

Plock: Miejski Ogród Zoologiczny, ul. Warszawska 30; 09402 Plock; ☎+48 24 262 4163; +48 24 264 6324; anzooplock@data.pl.

Poznan: Poznan Zoo, Stadt Poznan, ul Browwarna 25, 61063 Poznan; ☎+48 618 768 209; fax +48 618 773 533; e-mail zoo-pozn@man.poznan.pl; www.zoo.poznan.pl.

Warsaw: Miejski Ogród Zoologiczny w Warzawie, Stadt Warszawa, ul Ratuszowa 1/3, 03461 Warsaw; ☎+48 22 619 4041; fax +48 22 619 5898; e-mail zoo@zoowarzawa,pol.pl; www.zoo.warzawa.pl.

Wroclaw: Miejski Ogrod Zoologiczny Wroclaw, Stadt Wroclaw, ul Wroblewskiego 1/5, 51-618 Wroclaw; ☎+48 71 3483024; fax +48 71 3483768; e-mail lutra@zoo.wroc.pl; www.zoo.wroclaw.pl.

Zamosc: Ogród Zoologiczny im Stefana Milera, ul Szczebrzeska 12, 22400 Zamosc; ☎+48 84 3934 70/79; fax +48 84 639 3470; e-mail zoozam1@wp.pl

Animal & Bird Welfare, Protection & Conservation

Ogólnopolskie Towarzystwo Ochrony Ptaków (OTOP): Polish Society for the Protection of Birds, 4/2 Hallera Str. 80-401 Gdansk; ☎+48 58341 26 93; fax +48 58341 26 93; e-mail office@otop.most.org.pl

The Polish Society for the Prevention of Cruelty to Animals: Towarzystwo Opieki nad Zwierzetami, Zarzád Glo[ac]wny, ul. Noakowskiego 4, 00666 Warsaw; ☎+48 22 825 7535; fax +48 22825 6049.

The Polish Society for the Prevention of Cruelty to Animals: Towarzystwo Opieki nad Zwierzetami 'Fauna' W. Rudzie Slaskiej, UlBijoczka, 41700 Ruda Slaska.

Animal Organisations Needing Volunteers

Bieszczady Wolf Project: The Ecovolunteer Program, Meijersweg 29, 7553 AX Hengelo, Netherlands; ☎+31 74 250 8250; fax +31 20 8645314; UK agent is Wildwings (www.wildwings.ecovolunter.co.uk).

This project in the Bieszczady National Park, 300km south of Krakow aims at improving the protection of wolves in Poland. Researchers collect droppings and prey leftovers, observe prey species, attach transmitters to wolves and red deer in order to track them and collect date on wolves territories to ascertain their resting and congregating places. Other animals, which may be seen include brown bears, lynxes and elk. Volunteers come for two weeks any month except December and need to be able to walk 15km a day with ease. Volunteers should also have a commitment to nature and animal protection and a co-operative attitude towards working with Europeans of varying nationalities. Cost is approximately US$730 for 2 weeks and covers accommodation and food, a permit for working in the park, and transfer from

Krakow. In winter the temperature can drop to minus 30 degrees Celsius.

Polish Consulates & Embassies
Australia: Turrana Street, Yarralumla, ACT 2600; ☎02-6273 1208.
Canada: 1500 Pine Ave West, Montréal, H3G 1B4; ☎514-937 9481.
UK: Consulate, 73 New Cavendish Street, London W1M 8LS; ☎020-7580 0476; fax
020-7323 2320; www.poland-embassy.org.uk
UK: 47 Portland Place, London W1N 4JH; ☎020-7580 4324; fax 020-7323 4018.
USA: 2640 16th St NW, Washington DC 20009; ☎202-234-3800; www.polishworld.com/
polemb. Consulates also in New York, Los Angeles and Chicago.
British passport holders may enter Poland and remain for six months without a visa. For
US passport holders the limit is 90 days. Applications for work and residence permits
should be made from outside the country.

Romania

Romania is bordered by Moldova, and Ukraine to the north, Bulgaria to the south and
Hungary and Serbia to the west. Like Bulgaria, eastern Romania reaches the Black
Sea. The country is divided into four parts, mountainous and forested Transylvania
and Moldavia in the north are separated by the Carpathian mountains. A continuation,
(Carpatii Meridionali) of the main range, divides the mountainous north from the flat
Danube plain of Wallachia in the south and east.

The population of Romania is nearly 23 million with two million of them living in the
capital, Bucharest.

Romania was one of the few countries of former Soviet-dominated eastern Europe that
marked the end of communist rule with violence directed at their hated former dictator,
Nicolae Ceausescu, who was executed by shooting and without a trial.

Romania was rejected by the EU to be in the first wave of former eastern European
countries to join on financial grounds.

Vets
There are about 8,500 practising vets in Romania of whom over 6000 work in the public
sector. The state sector is organised into 40 districts, which are responsible for over 400
local food hygiene units and 3000 state practices. State practices usually consist of a
veterinarian and a technician or animal assistant. There is an excess of graduates from
the five veterinary schools with the result that one in three has had to find non-veterinary
employment. The Romanian veterinary profession suffers from a lack of equipment and
pharmaceuticals and an increasing black market in drugs. Younger veterinarians are
tending to go into private practice running small animal clinics in the cities.

Veterinary addresses
Associatia, Medicilor Veterinari din Romania (AMVR/RVA): Romanian Veterinary
Association, Spaiul Independentei 105, P.O. Box 35, 76201 Bucharest; ☎+40 1 638
68 83.
Agentia Nationala Sanitaria Veterinaria: National Veterinary Sanitary Agency, Ministry
of Agriculture and Food Industry, Bd. Carol 1, No 24, Sectorul 3, 70033 Bucharest;
☎+40 1 615 7875.
Veterinary University-Bucharest: www.medvet.go.ro/indexen.html

Dogs
There are more than 40 dog owners' clubs in Romania. The national authority for dogs'

rights, protection and recognition is:
Asociaţia Chinologică Română: 61 Popa Tatu Street, 70771 Sector 1, Bucharest, Romania; www.ach.ro (under contruction). Has 14 regional offices.

Miscellaneous Animal Organisations
Birds and Small Animals Growers Association: Asociatia Crescatorilor de Pasari Si Animale Mici Bucuresti: P-ta Sahia Alexandru 66, Bucharest; ☎+40 21 6154979.
Bee Growers Association: Cal. Dorobantilor 134, Bucharest; ☎+40 21 6154979.
Children Love Animals Foundation: Copiii iubesc animalele, Str. Sebastian nr.211 B, sector 5, Bucharest; tel/fax +40 21 410 34 69; 411.60.54; fax +40 21 410 32 80; e-mail fcia@xnet.ro

Zoos
Gradina Zoologica Bucuresti: Bucharest Zoological Garden, Str. Vadul Moldovei nr. 4, Sector 1, Of Postal 18, 71588 Bucharest; ☎+40 1 230 4510; fax +40 1 231 4135; e-mail zoo@digicom.ro; www.ici.ro/romania/bucharest/bu – zoo.htm.
Oradea Zoo: www.oradea-online.ro/oradea/9/zoo.htm

Other zoos
Gradina Zoologica Birlad in Birlad
Gradina Zoologica Resita in Resita
Gradina Zoologica in Sibiu
Gradina Zoologica Turgu-Mures, Turgu-Mures
Aquarium Galatia (Galatia town)

Animal & Bird Protection
Association for the Protection of Animals: Fidelius Street, Vulcan No. 1-3, Of. Post No 7, 3900 Satu Mare.
Societatea Ornitologica Romana (SOR): Romanian Ornithological Society, Str Gheorghe Dima 49/2, 3400 Cluj Naponica; tel/fax +40 64 43 80 86; e-mail sorcj@codec.ro

Project needing volunteers
Carpathian Large Carnivore Project: organised by the Munich Wildlife Society. A study of wolves and bears in the Brasov area, 180 km from Bucharest. Volunteers spend two to four weeks helping to study the daily habits and movements of wolves and bears using radio tracking, collecting biological samples, following wolf tracks in the snow (winter) and caring for captive wolves. Cost US$630 weekly. Food and accommodation in mountain log house or converted farm are provided. Volunteers have to make their own way to Brasov (there is a train from Bucharest). Applications to Dr. Ioan Senchea Street 162, 2223 Zarnesti, Romania; ☎+40 94 532 798; ☎+40 68 223 081; e-mail info@clcp.ro; also through Ecovolunteer Network (www.ecovolunteer.org).

Romanian Embassies
Australia: Dalman Crs.,O'Malley, ACT 2606; tel02-6286 2343.
Canada: 655 Rideau Street, Ottawa, ON K1N 8L5; ☎613-789 5345.
UK: Arundel House, 4 Palace Green, London W8 4QD; ☎020-7937 8125; www.roemb.co.uk
USA: 1607 23rd Street, NW Washington, DC 20008; ☎202-328 8610; www.roembus.org
British passport holders need a visa to enter Bulgaria but US citizens do not for visits of up to 30 days. Those working or looking for work need to register at the local police station. Residence and work permits should be arranged in advance in your own country.

Russia And The Republics

Russia refers to the Russian Federation or Commonwealth of Independent States (CIS), created in 1991 when the Russian leaders met their newly independent opposite numbers from Ukraine and Belarus, and created a new union for the former Soviet empire, thus making the USSR the CIS.

RUSSIA

Racing authority

Russian Racing Authority: Moscow 125284, Begovaya 22 K, Hippodrome; ☎+7 95 945 0437; fax +7 95 200 3200.

Zoos

Bolsherech'ye: Bolscherech'yenskii Zoopark: Omskaya oblast, ul. Sovetov 67, 646420 Bolsherech'ye; ☎+7 92063/91799.

Ekaterinburg: Ekaterinburgskii Zoopark, ul. Mamina-Sibiryaka 189, 620055 Ekaterinburg; ☎+7 3432 5554 69/37; fax +7 3432 563940; e-mail zoo@uralregion.ru; www.zoo.uralregion.ru.

Kaliningrad: Kaliningradskii Zoopark, Prospekt Mira 26, 236000 Kaliningrad; ☎+7 0112 218924; fax +7 41531 64003; e-mail postmaster@zoo.koenig.su; www.enet.ru/ zoo/.

Lipetsk: Lipetsksi Zoopark, Petrovskii proezd 2, 398002 Lipetsk; ☎+7 0742 77 8570/ 2514; fax +7 742 778662.

Moskva: Moscow Zoo, Bolshaya Gruzinskaya ul. 1, 123242 Moskva; ☎+7 095 2556 034; fax +7 095 973 2056; tanya@zoopark.msk.ru; wwwlzoo.ru/moscow.

Novosibirsk: Novosibirsk Zoo, ul. Gogolya 15, 630005 Novosibirsk; ☎+ 7 3832248766; fax +7 3832 248766.

Penza Zoo: Krasnaya ul 10, 440026 Penza.

Perm: Perm Zoological Gardens, ul Ordzhonikidze 10, 614600 Perm; ☎+7 8412-330-156; fax +7 3422 34 2621.

Rostov na Don: Rostov-on-Don Zoo, ul. Zoologicheskaja 3 Rostov na Donu; ☎ +7 8632322741;fax +7 8632 32 5918; e-mail zoo@rostov.don.sitek.net; www.don.sitek.net/home/zoo/.

Sankt Petersburg: St. Petersburg Zoo, Aleksandrovskii Park 1, 197198 St Petersburg; ☎+7 812 2328260/4828;fax +7 812 232 4828; e-mail lenzoo@mail.convey.ru; www.lenzoo.convey.ru.

Seversk/Tomskaya region: Seversk Zoo, pr. Commun.45-A,a/ya 581, 636070 Seversk/Tomskaya region; ☎+7 8 38242 48242; fax +7 8-382-772470; e-mail zoo@seversk.ru.

Sochi-Adler: Institute of Medical Primatology, Veseloye 1, 354597 Sochi-Adler; ☎+7 8622 919250; fax+7 095 9561711; e-mail iprim@sochi.net; www.iprim.sochi.net.

Tula: Tula Exotazium, Oktyabr'skaya ul. 26, 300002 Tula; ☎+7-872-775392; fax +7-872-779577.

Animal & Bird Protection and Conservation

Ekaterinburg Society for the Protection of Animals' Rights: Generalska St. 6, Ekaterinburg.

Russian Bird Conservation Union (RBCU): Soyuz Ochrany Pits Rossii, office 110, Kibalchicha Str. 6, Building 5, Moscow 129278; ☎ +7 95 283 12 02; fax +795 283 12 02; e-mail rbcu@glas.apc.org.

Society for Saving & Protecting Homeless Animals 'friends': Chiukova Street 23-29,

400131 Volgograd.

Projects Needing Volunteers
Baikal Centre for Ecological and Citizen Initiatives: e-mail irkutsk@glas.apc.org
Volunteer opportunities in the Baikal-Lena Nature Reserve including the ones given below.

Baikal Volunteer Corps: Assistance for the Baikal-Lena Nature Reserve: Baikal Centre for Ecological and Citizen Initiatives, P.O. Box 1360, Irkutsk 664000; tel/fax +73952 381-787; e-mail irkutsk@glas.apc.org. The project involves working in a protected and restricted area. In 1996 system of trails and huts was begun with help from volunteers. Work needed includes a continuing development of the trail system, hut construction, boundary marking, and counting and census work on the animal population of brown bear, deer and moose. Work takes place in Eastern Siberia on the north-western shore of Lake Baikal, near the source of the Lena river. The reserve is not easily reached and so transport from Irkutsk will be provided (bus, boat and on foot with a pack). Volunteers come for three to six weeks and different tasks are done depending on the period: June to August (trail construction), February to March (counting bears and hoofed animals), April to September (bird census). Maximum age of volunteers is 45 to 50. For counting work, knowledge of the species and training is needed. A knowledge of Russian would help greatly. Costs: US$500 includes round trip Irkutsk-Reserve and meals. Visa cost is US$40 per two weeks. Accommodation and breakfast in Irkutsk US$20 per night. For population census cost is around US$30-40 per day (lower for groups). Own tent and sleeping bag needed. Physical fitness essential and tolerance of low temperatures.
From the USA travel arrangements can be made through:
Uniglobe Connoisseur Travel, 353 Sacramento Street, Suite 1020 San Francisco, CA 94117; ☎+1 415-272-0700; fax +1 415272 0729; e-mail uniglobect@aol.com.
If at all possible application forms should be completed in Russian and sent to Baikalo-Lenskiy, c/o Baikal Centre via e-mail or fax. After the participant is accepted a formal invitation will be sent which is necessary to obtain a visa. Allow two weeks for visa processing.

Beluga Research Project – Russia: The Ecovolunteer Program, Meijersweg 29, 7553 AX Hengelo, Netherlands; ☎+31 74 250 8250; fax +31 20 8645314; UK agent is Wildwings (www.wildwings.ecovolunteer.co.uk). Volunteers are needed to help study a large annual grouping of belugas (white, polar dolphins with no dorsal fin) in the Solovetski Islands, Archangelsk District, southern White Sea. This happens in July and August during the 'white nights' when there is 20 hours of daylight in every 24 hours. The study into Beluga socialising behaviour, especially the introduction of young belugas to the adults, mothers and young, and sexual behaviour and communication is conducted by scientists from the Shirshov Oceanological Institute of the Russian Academy of Sciences. Volunteers carry out observations, inform visitors to the project, construct observation posts, maintain the encampment, prepare food, gather timber, cut wood, collect groceries, fish etc.. The cost is (US$725) for two weeks in June, July or August. Camping accommodation, meals and ground transport in Russia included. Not included are visa for Russia plus administration charge), flights to Russia, and insurance. Volunteers provide their own tenting equipment for camping close to the shoreline. Supper is taken around 11pm or midnight (because of the 'white nights'). This takes some getting used to.
Zapovednik Central Forest Reserve Wolf Research: The Ecovolunteer Program, Meijersweg 29, 7553 AX Hengelo, Netherlands; ☎+31 74 250 8250; fax +31 20 8645314; UK agent is Wildwings (www.wildwings.ecovolunter.co.uk). Volunteers needed to help research into wolf migration in the Central Forest Nature Reserve in the southern taiga (coniferous forest) of central Russia. The reserve lies about 350km

north west of Moscow. Cost US$1000 for two weeks, US$1,650 for four weeks. For biology students only, there is a special rate of US$20 per day for six weeks. Simple accommodation is provided at the research station or tents in summer. Sometimes volunteers stay with Russian reserve workers' families. Living conditions are primitive and there is little provision for privacy. Flights to Moscow, visa and personal expenses not included.

Volunteers have to be physically fit, able to walk long distances through the forests in search of wolf trails (faeces and footprints) that lead to wolf resting and feeding places. In winter the tracking is done by snowmobile and skiing. Overnight stays in ranger huts (no facilities) in the forest possible. Other species which inhabiting the reserve include brown bear, lynx, mink, moose and a variety of birds. Little or no English is spoken by the Russian reserve workers.

Researchers analyse wolf calls

Russian Embassies
Australia: Arkana Street, Yarralumla, ACT 2600; ☎02-6281 2716;
Australia: Canberra Avenue, Griffith ACT 2603; ☎02-6295 9033.
Canada: 285 Charlotte Street, Ottawa, ON K1N 8L5; ☎ 613 235 4341.
UK: 13 Kensington Palace Gardens, London W8 4QX; ☎020-7229 8027; fax 020-7727 8624; www.russialink.com
USA: 2650 Wisconsin Avenue NW, Washington, DC 20007; ☎202-298 5735; www.russianembassy.org.

Slovakia

The Republic of Slovakia which became independent from Czechslovakia in 1993, comprises 49,036 square kilometres and has a population of 5.4 million. The capital, Bratislava has under half a million inhabitants. The official language is Slovak but Hungarian is widely spoken.

Vets
Slovakia has about 2,500 active veterinarians about half of whom work in the public

sector. Private practice has been permitted since 1992 and there are about 1,000 practitioners. Livestock production has about halved since the end of the Communist era but the number of companion animals is rising. The sole veterinary faculty is in Kosice.

Veterinary addresses

Slovak Veterinary Chamber: Komora Veterinárnych lekácrov SR, Botanická 17, 84213 Bratislava; ☎+421 7 723 385; fax +421 7 720 883.

Slovak Veterinary Association: Slovenská Spoloçnost Veterinárnych Lekárov, Hlinkova 1/A, 04001 Kosice; ☎+421 95 633 20 11; fax +421 95 633 18 53.

Zoos

Bojnice: Zoologicka zahrada Bojnice, zamok a okolie 6, 97201 Bojnice; ☎ +421 862 540 2975; fax +421 862 540-3241; e-mail zooboj@isternet.sk; www.zoobojnice.sk.

Bratislava: Zoologicka Zahrada Bratislava, Mlynska Dolina 1, 84227 Bratislava; ☎+421 862-540-2974; e-mail zoo@zoobratislava.sk; www.netax.sk/zoobratislava.

Kosice-Kavecany: Zoologicka Zahrada Kosice, Siroka 31, 04006 Kosice-Kavecany; ☎+421 95 633-1517/8103/4; fax +421 95 633 9531.

Animal & Bird Protection

Society for the Protection of Birds in Slovakia (SOVS): Spoloçnost pre Ochranu Vtactva Na Slovensku, P.O. Box 71, 09301 Vranov nad Top'lou; ☎+42 931 61120; fax +42 931 62120; e-mail sovs@changenet.sk

Spolok Na Ochranu Zvierat Na Slovensku: Slovakian Animal Protection Organisation, c/o Dana Herrmanova, Bjorresonova 3, 81105 Bratislava.

Volunteer Projects

The British Trust for Conservation Volunteers(BTCV): 36 St Mary's Street, Wallingford, Oxon OX10 OEU; ☎01491-839766; fax 01491-839646; www.btcv.org. Alpine mammal (marmot, chamois, wolf, lynx) and raptor (golden eagle) monitoring, and also wolf and bear conservation in the Tatra mountains. Contact BTCV for more information.

Slovak Embassies

Australia: Culgoa Cct, O'Malley, ACT 2606; ☎02-6290 1516.

Canada: 50 Rideau Terrace, Ottawa, ON K1M 2A1; ☎613-749 2496.

UK: 25 Kensington Palace Gardens, London W8 4QY; ☎ 020-7243 0803. There is an 0891 number which gives general visa information, or you can write to the Visa Department and ask for the details to be sent to you which would be cheaper.

USA: Suite 250, 2201 Wisconsin Avenue, NW, Washington DC 20007; ☎202 965 5160; www.slovakemb.com

North Americans and EU citizens do not need a visa to enter the Slovak Republic.

UK and USA citizens should check with the Slovak embassy in their countries about residence permits, which can take two months to be processed as the embassies send applications and documents to the Slovak republic. It can be an expensive business currently costing about œ100.

Slovenia

Slovenia is a small country of 20,256 square kilometres and two million inhabitants. It borders Italy to the west, Austria to the north, Croatia to the south and Hungary to the east. The country is almost, but not entirely, landlocked; it has a short section of Adriatic coastline, which is popular with holidaymakers. Small is often beautiful and Slovenia has celebrated Alpine scenery including the Julian Alps.

The war in former Yugoslavia began in Slovenia, which was also the first country to secede from Yugoslavia and claim its indpendence. It is on course to join the EU in the next few years.

Vets

There are about a thousand practising vets in Slovenia divided almost equally between the public and private sectors. The sole veterinary faculty is in Ljubljana. The biggest upheaval in the veterinary profession since independence has been the disappearance of the huge collective farms each with hundreds of animals. Privatised farming has reduced many farmers to smallholding level and many are going out of business.

Veterinary Addresses
Slovenian Veterinary Chamber: Veterinarska Zbornica Slovenije (VZbS), Cesta v Mesti Log 47, 1000 Ljubljana; ☎+386 61 33 2303; fax +386 61 33 23 03.
Slovenian Veterinary Association: Slovenska veterinarska Zveza, Gerbiçva 60, 1000 Ljubljana; ☎ +386 61 177 91 95; fax +386 61 177 91 99.

Dogs

Slovenian Kennel Club: Kinololoska zveza Slovenije, Ilirska ulica 27, 1000 Ljubljana; tel/fax +386 61 315 474 (office hours 9am-12pm).

Horses

Konjeniska zveza Slovenije: Celovska cesta 25, 1000 Ljubljana; tel/fax +386 61 133 3228. Equine organisation.

Zoos

Ljubljana: Zooloski vrt Mesta Ljubjane, Vecna Pot 70, 61000 Ljubljana; ☎+386 1 2563 768; fax +386 1-2573-160; e-mail ljzoo@guest.arnes.si; www.zoo-ljubljana.si.
Maribor: Mestni Akvarij, Heroja Staneta 19, 2000 Maribor; ☎+386 2 25 12 295; fax +386 2 25 12 291; e-mail akvarj-terarj@florina.si; www.florina.si.

Animal & bird protection & conservation

Bird Watching and Bird Study Association of Slovenia, Langusova 10, SLO-61000 Ljubljana; ☎+386 61 133 95 16; +386 60 962 52 10; e-mail dopps@guest.arnes.si
Lovska zveza Slovenije: Zupanciceva ulica 9, 1000 Ljubljana; ☎+386 61 214 950; fax +386 61 217 994. Wildlife protection and conservation organisation.

Animal protection/rescue organisation

Drustvo proti mucenju zivali: Trubarjeva cesta 16, 1000 Ljubljana; ☎+38661 131 5261.

Slovenian embassies

Australia: Marcus Clarke Street, Canberra City, ACT 2601; ☎02-6243 4830.
Canada: Suite 2101, 150 Metcalfe Street, Ottawa, ON K2P 1P1; ☎613-565 5781.
UK: Suite One, Cavendish Court, 11-15 Wigmore Street, London W1H 9LA; ☎020-7495 7775; fax 020-7495 7776; www.slovenia-embassy.org.uk Visa section 10am to midday.
USA: 1525 New Hampshire Avenue NW, Washington DC 20036; ☎202-667 5363; fax 202-667 4563; www.embassy.org/slovenia. Consulate in New York: ☎212-370 3006.

Ukraine

Ukraine became a separate state from Russia in 1991. For most western Europeans Ukraine is considerably poorer and more basic than most of us are used to, especially for a European country. However, any shortcomings in public services and transport are more than compensated for by the hospitality of its people, and the cheapness of the beer. It has a large population (53 million) in an area slightly larger than France.

Monitoring Steppe Wolves and Bird Migration on the Black Sea
Participation in an organised study by local scientists. Volunteers will study, net, handle and ring birds using nets by the beach and in the interior. Volunteers are also involved in the area's first wolf survey, tracking wolves through sand and studying them from night hides. May also include wolf radio collaring and camera trapping work. Based at a comfortable summer house. Rotating bird and wolf research teams work from research camps near the beach for birds and in the centre of the peninsula for wolves. From 31 Aug-14 Sept and 14-28 September 2003. Join for two to four weeks. Expedition contribution is approximately £990 per two weeks. More details and application form from Biosphere Expeditions, Sprat's Water, Near Carlton Colville, The Broads National Park, Suffolk NR33 8BP; ☎01502-583085; UK website www.biosphere-expeditions.org; Germany website deutschland@biosphere-expections.org

Working in Kiev Zoo
Kiev Zoological Park is a large zoo with an international reputation and is a member of EAZA (European Association of Zoos and Aquariums). A placement there is especially good if you are intending to have a veterinary career as you will be able to observe vets dealing with many different species. The work will be varied and can include all or some of the following: admin (proof-reading English documents, some ad hoc English teaching to staff, and schooling school parties around the zoo), research work in the laboratories, general maintenance (keeping paths clear, cleaning and mucking out cages, feeding animals (under supervision), guarding animals from unauthorised feeding by tourists. Any volunteer studying zoological sciences will be allowed to work in the animal clinic, which treats domestic animals as well as zoo ones.

The placements can be for two months or longer and cost £995 for three months; extra months are £195 per month. The cost covers food and accommodation with a local family. Flights cost about £350 depending on the season. It may be possible to get a free travel pass for local travel during the placement.

The placements are arranged by Travellers Worldwide (7 Mulberry Close, Ferring, West Sussex, BN12 5HY; ☎01903-700478; fax 01903-502595; e-mail info@travellers worldwide.com; www.travellersworldwide.com).

Part III

Worldwide

North America

Australia & New Zealand

Africa & The Indian Ocean

Asia

South & Central America

Animal Charities

Working Overseas

Organisations with

Animal-Related Projects

North America

THE UNITED STATES OF AMERICA

ENTRY & WORKING VISAS

TOURIST VISAS

Even entering the USA as a tourist entails being 'vetted' by their Customs and Immigration, and obtaining a tourist visa, which requires producing proof of financial support and documentary evidence that the applicant will be returning home. British nationals do not need to apply for a tourist visa in advance. They can wait until arrival to obtain a visa-waiver (1-96) which is valid for one entry into the USA for a maximum of three months. Tourist visa holders are categorically forbidden to work.

WORK VISAS

It is very difficult for foreigners to get permission to work in the USA and there are strict regulations and a category of worker's visa for every possible type of employment and a procedure attached to obtaining it. Small wonder that most foreigners entering the USA do so on tourist visas and some are then tempted to take casual work (illegally) with potentially dire consequences; huge fines for the employer and deportation for themselves. Illegal workers will almost certainly be banned from entering the USA for a number of years if caught.

The Visa Branch of the US Embassy (5 Upper Grosvenor Street, London W1A 2JB; ☎09061-500590; £1.50 per minute), can send a brief outline of the non-immigrant visas available. If you live in Northern Ireland, you should contact the Visa Branch of the US Embassy, Queen's House, Queen Street, Belfast BT1 6EQ.

There follows a selection of the visas likely to be useful, though eligibility obviously depends on individual circumstances. There may also be other working visas that would be appropriate. The full list obtainable from the US Embassy (see above).

○ **J-1** is available to participants of government authorised programmes known as Exchange Visitor Programmes (for details of EVPs, see below). You cannot apply for the J-1 without form IAP-66 (Certificate of Eligibility for Exchange Visitor Status) and you cannot get form IAP-66 without going through an EVP which has a sponsoring organisation in the USA.
○ **B-1** Volunteer Visa. Applications for this must be sponsored by a charitable or religious organisation, which is permitted to reimburse your expenses, but not to pay you. This might be useful for working with an animal charity.
○ **H-1B** Temporary Visa for 'pre-arranged professional or highly skilled jobs' for which there are no suitably qualified Americans. A university degree is a pre-requisite.
○ **EP-3** Visa is for skilled workers with at least two years' relevant experience or training, but not necessarily possessed of a university degree. Zoo keepers or animal behaviourists might qualify.

EXCHANGE VISITOR PROGRAMMES

EVPs are aimed mainly at younger people and they exist because of their purported educational value. These exchanges and their quotas are reviewed regularly by the US government. Thanks to lobbying and proof from employers of staff shortages, the numbers have been increasing. A full list of EVPs and other programmes can be obtained by writing to the Fulbright Commission, US Educational Advisory Service, 62 Doughty Street, London WC1N 2JZ (www.fulbright.co.uk) and enclosing a stamped addressed envelope.

BUNAC

BUNAC stands for the British Universities North America Club (16 Bowling Green Lane, London EC1R OBD; ☎020-7251 3472; fax 020-7251 0215) which is open to full-time university students. BUNAC administers several programmes in the USA of which Work America, (a summer programme for students), and OPT-USA (three to eighteen months practical training for students and non-students) could be utilised by someone wanting to work in an animal-related job from veterinary surgeon to jockey or as an intern at a zoo or wildlife refuge.

Work America

Once you have applied to BUNAC, and been accepted on the Work America Programme, and obtained your J-1 Visa, you can travel to anywhere you choose in the United States and look for any job. However, the process of documentation is slow so it is advisable to start applying early, for instance in April for the summer period. Costs include a programme administration fee and the cost of the return flights, plus any living expenses you may need while you are looking for a job on arrival. This programme is open to those aged 18+ studying for a university degree, HND or NVQ 4/5. Those taking a gap year between school and university, who have a confirmed university place, are also eligible. You will also need either a definite offer of employment in the USA and proof that you have bought $500 in American dollar travellers cheques or a letter of sponsorship from a responsible American, if possible a relative, who promises in writing to support you financially if needed, plus supporting funds of $700. Also acceptable, would be a vague letter of support from America plus a higher amount of personal funds ($700) and proof of access to a further $700.

To save the cost of supporting yourself in the USA while you look for a job, try to arrange something to go to in advance. For instance with a zoo, animal or marine theme park such as Sea World (70077 Sea Harbor Drive, Orlando, FL 32821; 407 351 3600). Disney's Animal Kingdom (P.O.B. 1000, Lake Buenavista Fl. 32830; 407-939 7322) and San Diego Zoo (PO Box 120-551, San Diego, CA 92112-0051; 619-231 1515) are other well-known possibilities. Every February BUNAC publishes its annual job directory which is free to members, or you can search the internet under animals, zoos, Disney, Sea World etc.

INTERNSHIPS

One useful way of getting a permit for working in the USA could be an internship organised through BUNAC, the Council on International Educational Exchange (CIEE), or the Student Conservation Association. Internship is American for a trainee post, providing you with a chance to get some experience in your potential career, as part of your academic course or as on-going training in your profession or field. The categories eligible for inclusion are very broad and could be utilised for example by stable management trainees or zoo and veterinary staff (but not vets).

Internships can last a few weeks, or over a year, depending on the programme and the internship sponsor. Internships will not make you rich. If you are lucky you will get free housing and a subsistence allowance or modest wage. In many cases internships are unpaid leaving you with substantial personal costs. A few organisations offer paid work.

THROUGH BUNAC.

The BUNAC internship programme known as Overseas Practical Training or OPT USA is sponsored by International Program Services of the American YMCA. The programme is open to non-students as well as students but must be integrated into six, 12 or 18 months of on-the-job training (i.e. not work experience only). Applicants have to be aged at least 19. Programme fees vary from $250 to $550.

At the heart of the scheme is the training plan compiled by the applicant and the host organisation in the USA. The training must have a purpose and should include details of qualifications which make the applicant eligible, the primary learning objectives of the training, details of the activities to be undertaken during the training period and the supervision and assessment which will be given.

OPT USA is open to applications at any time of year.

THROUGH CIEE UK

Council for International Educational Exchanges (52 Poland Street, London W1V 4JQ; ☎020-7478 2020; fax 020-7734 7322; e-mail infouk@councilexchanges.org.uk; www.ciee.org.uk) helps full-time students to arrange sandwich placements in the USA for up to eighteen months. You have to find your own job, which must be related to your field of study. The range of careers covered is very broad and can include animal related work, although hands-on veterinary work is prohibited. There is also a four-month summer Work and Travel programme, which allows you to take almost any job, anywhere in the USA. CIEE provides some practical advice on making speculative applications to potential employers. CIEE provides legal sponsorship for the J-1 visa, as well as travel insurance, 24-hour support and orientation.

Applicants in France and Germany should apply in their own countries:
CIEE France: 112, ter rue Cardinet, 75017 Paris; ☎01 58 57 20 66.
CIEE Germany: Oranienburger Strasse 13-14, 10178 Berlin; ☎030 2848 590.
Other nationalities should apply through partner organisations in their own countries. Please visit www.ciee.org.uk for eligibility requirements and further information.

THROUGH STUDENT CONSERVATION ASSOCIATION (SCA)

The Student Conservation Association, P.O. Box 550, 687 River Road, Charlestown, New Hampshire 03603-0550; ☎603-543-1700; fax 603-543-1828; e-mail internships@ thesca.org; www.theSCA.org.
A not-for-profit organisation that places candidates in internships and provides training, free housing, stipend for uniform and food and travel grant. Internships are available all year round in conservation projects in national parks, forests and wildlife refuges around the USA. Over 1200 placements annually lasting from twelve to sixteen weeks. Applicants should be a minimum of 18 years old and of any academic background. Also open to those re-entering the work force and retirees. At least 3,000 applications are received annually so apply well in advance. Contact the Director of Recruitment at the above address. A fee of $20 is charged for processing.

Internships involving wildlife ecology such as the ones at Haleakala National Park (see below) in Hawaii can be arranged through the SCA.

OTHER ORGANISATIONS OFFERING INTERNSHIPS

The following organisations are either environmental organisations or animal parks offering internships

Aspen Centre for Environmental Studies: 100 Puppy Smith Street, Aspen, Colorado 81611; ☎970 925 5756; fax 970-925 4819; e-mail acesone@rof.net; www.aspen.com/aces. A 25-acre nature preserve and visitor centre.

Offers summer (June to September) internships for students or graduates with an educational background in natural sciences or environmental education and knowledge of Rocky Mountain flora and fauna.

Responsabilities include teaching environmental awareness to children, maintaining trails, rehabilitating injured animals, caring for resident birds of prey and leading hikes. Sites include the Maroon Bells Snowmass, and around Aspen Mountain.

Weekly pay of $125 and free housing and free participation in ACES's field school courses. Educational credits can be arranged. Applications in writing by March 1st or call or e-mail the Internship Co-ordinator, The Summer Naturalist Intern, Aspen Center for Environmental Studies at the above address.

Audubon Center of the North Woods: P O Box 530, Sandstone, Minnesota 55072; ☎320-245 2648; fax 320 245 5272; e-mailmuskopf@audubon; www.audubon-center.com.

Environmental education centre teaching outdoor skills, natural history, ethics for all ages. Has 20 employees.

Internships include two wildlife interns to care for, feed and train educational raptors and herptiles, and care for animals in rehabilitation. Will also be responsible for teaching natural history and adventure classes to children. Also helping with development of educational materials and maintenance. Duration of six to twelve months. Stipend per month plus free lodging and most meals. Other benefits include on the job training, opportunity to attend workshops and the graduate school credits.

Applications with a cover letter and three references to: Amy Muskopf, Wildlife Co-ordinator, at the above address year round.

Audubon Naturalist Society: 8940 Jones Mill Road, Chevy Chase, Maryland 20815; ☎301-652 9188; fax 301-951 7179; e-mail avernor@audubonnaturalist.org.

Offers environmental education internships. Duties include maintaining a classroom and assisting with the upkeep of a forty-acre, wildlife sanctuary. Duration is for three months in spring, summer, or autumn; $1200-$2400 per duration. Applicants should have an interest in a career in elementary education, environmental education, or another related area such as natural history or children. Open to students and graduates. Those changing careers or re-entering the workforce may also be eligible. Contact the Education Program Co-ordinator at the above address.

Brookfield Zoo: 3300 South Golf Road, Brookfield, Illinois 60513; ☎708-485-0263; fax 708-485 3532; e-mail Zookeeper_Internships@brookfield.zoo.org; www.brookfieldzoo.org.

Large zoo with 400 employees. Takes zookeeper interns for 10 to twelve weeks. Work covers all aspects of zookeeping: animal management including exhibit/enclosure maintenance, animal husbandry, record keeping, food preparation and observation. Unpaid and no housing provided. Apply by 1 February for summer or 1 August for autumn or 1 December for winter. Contact Intern Program Co-ordinator at the above address for application form.

Brukner Nature Center: 5995 Horseshoe Bend Road, Troy, Ohio 45373; ☎937-698

6493; fax 937-698 4619; e-mail brukner@juno.com.
Offers internships lasting three to nine months for education/wildlife rehabilitation assistants. Applicants can be students, graduates, career changers or those re-entering the work force. Duties range from providing education programmes for schools using live animals and assisting in the care of native Ohio species. Commitment to learn about and participate in all parts of the operation is essential. Applicants should have a background in natural history. Possibility of longer employment. Free housing and fortnightly stipend of $150 provided. Applications giving dates of availability should be addressed to Debra K Brill, Administrative Director at the above address.

Clinic for the Rehabilitation of Wildlife (CROW): P.O. Box 150, Sanibel, Florida 33957; ☎239-472-3644; fax 239-472 8544; e-mail crowclinic@aol.com; www.crowclinic.org
Crow Clinic is a non-profit wildlife veterinary hospital that rescues and treats and rehabilitates the injured, ill and orphaned native and migratory wildlife of Lee County. Two interns help medical and rehabilitative teams. Four to eight weeks unpaid, but includes housing. Applicants should be veterinary students or have a background in natural sciences and excellent spoken and written English is a prerequisite. Apply at least 12 months in advance of proposed dates to allow time for necessary visas. Applicants should send a résumé, cover letter, school transcript and two letters of recommendation to the above address.

Carolina Raptor Center, Inc: P.O. Box 16443, Charlotte, North Carolina 28297; ☎704 875-6521; extension 102; fax 704-875 6521; e-mail: lorisparkman@birdsofprey.org; www.birdsofprey.org.
Carolina Raptor Center (CRC) is dedicated to environmental education and the conservation of birds of prey, raptors, through public education, the rehabilitation of injured an orphaned raptors, and research. This mission is accomplished with the help of volunteers and interns. Internships are available year-round. The minimum time commitment is 120 hours. All applications must include three references (in English) with contact information and should be submitted to the Volunteer Co-ordinator at the above address.

Three types of internships are offered. One area of concentration is raptor rehabilitation, assisting with the day to day care of injured or orphaned raptors and the release programme. Applicants should have some biology background (scholastic or life experience). Previous experience handling wildlife is not required but recommended.

Interns are also sought in Environmental education to assist with the care of trained birds of prey and presentations of programmes both at the facility and at off-site displays and exhibitions. Applicants should have a background (scholastic or life experience) in biology and/or wildlife management. Experience in education and public speaking is recommended.

Internships in resident (permanently injured) raptor care are also available. The duties of the position include, but are not limited to feeding, cage cleaning, and training of non-releasable birds of prey. Applicants should have a background (scholastic or life experience) in biology, wildlife management, and if possible experience with wildlife.

Foreign applicants welcome, but should be able to communicate well in English. Internships are unpaid and interns are responsible for their own lodging and transportation, though advice and assistance is available from CRC.

Chattanooga Nature Center: 400 Garden Road, Chattanooga, Tennessee 37419; ☎423-821 1160; fax 423-821 1702; e-mail nature@chattanooga.net; cdc.net/nature.
For over 20 years the centre has been providing environmental education to the public as well as operating a wildlife rehabilitation programme. Housing is not provided for interns but apartments can be rented locally for $400-$450 monthly. Lack of public

transport means interns need their own transport to get to the centre, ten minutes ride from downtown Chattanooga.

Internships include a wildlife rehabilitation assistant. Duties include animal care activities, feeding, administering medication, exercising etc. under the supervision of the rehabilitator. A part of the job also involves educating the public and completing a research paper. Applicants should have a background in biological sciences, experience in handling animals, and interest in conservation and people skills.

Internships generally last ten weeks in summer or twelve weeks in autumn. Interns wanting to stay longer have to undergo assessment. International applications welcomed. Applications to the Internship Director. In-person interview preferred.

Chesapeake Wildlife Sanctuary: 17308 Queen Anne Bridge Road, Bowie, Maryland 20716-9053; ☎301-390 7011; fax 301-249 3511; e-mail bowie@cws@yahoo.com; www.chesapeakewildlife.

Interns are taken on by this non-profit rehabilitation centre that rescues and treats injured and orphaned animals and specialises in providing intensive hands-on training for anyone interested in a wildlife or veterinary related career.

Internships are divided into assisting in the following departments:

Small mammals: includes groundhogs, rabbits, opossums, and squirrels. Interns clean, feed, rear and rehabilitate and maintain care records.

Large mammals: Same duties as above but caring for white-tailed deer. Three months in summer.

Avian interns: Variety of birds. Same duties as above plus emergency response programme for oiled wildlife.

Veterinary: record-keeping, treatments. Minimum 3rd year veterinary student.

Housing provided at a cost. Applicants should contact the Internship Co-ordinator at the above address.

The Conservancy of Southwest Florida: 1450 Merrihue Drive, Naples, Florida 34102; ☎941-262 0304; fax 941-262 0672; e-mail humanresources@conservancy.org; www.conservancy.org

Non-profit nature conservation organisation that operates locally and runs its owns research, education and practical conservation projects. It also operates two nature centres and a wildlife rehabilitation clinic and carries out a programme of events for the public.

The internships that involve animal work are:

wildlife rehabilitation assistants for the care, treatment and release of injured, sick and orphaned wildlife and general maintenance of the facilities. Applicants should be students or graduates with animal experience. Six months stay. Six to nine months. $125 per week and housing.

Sea turtle research conservation assistants for the turtle research programme to monitor and tag nesting turtles and maintaining the security of the nest sites. 4 months stay. Applicants should be graduates with an interest in biology and able to work at night. Duration 3-5 months and

Interns are provided with free accommodation and $100+ a week cost of living allowance. Enquiries should be sent by fax, e-mail or telephone to the Human Resources Director, by phone, fax, and accompanied by a stamped addressed envelope for details of the internships.

Dahlem Environmental Education Center: 7117 South Jackson Road, Jackson, Michigan 49201; ☎517-782 3453; fax 517-782-3441; internet: www.jackson.cc.mi.us/Dahlem_ Center.

The Center promotes the understanding of ecological and environmental principles through its public and schools education programmes. It has 3 full-time, 2 permanent part-time and one or two seasonal staff and is a unit of Jackson Community College. There is one `internship' for a wildlife biologist/naturalist whose work includes coordinating a community-based restoration project for the eastern bluebird. This involves monitoring and record keeping 400 nesting boxes and providing on site assistance to volunteers and property owners. Applicants must have organisational and research and field skills and the ability to work well with others. Position lasts from the beginning of March to mid-August and is open to students, graduates, postgraduates and career changers. There is a small salary $206 per week, free housing and travel reimbursement.

Applicants should contact the Program Co-ordinator enclosing a formal application, CV, three references by 1 February. A telephone interview is required.

Dolphin Research Centre: 58901 Overseas Highway, Grassy Key, Florida 33050-6019; ☎305-289-1121 Ext. 230; fax 305-743-7627; e-mail drc.ur@dolphins.org; www.dolphins.org.
Internships include an *Animal care and training intern* to assist trainers working with sea lions and dolphins, helping with public tours, data collection, maintenance etc. Also an a*nimal husbandry intern,* duties to include preparing food and supplements, data collection and observation, food stock taking and ordering, maintaining husbandry and medical files. Also a *dolphin/child therapy intern* to assist the dolphin therapy staff, preparation and maintenance of equipment used, assisting the participants and their families etc. All internships last 3-4 months and are unpaid. Apply by February 1 for summer and October 1 for winter.

Erie National Wildlife Refuge: 11296, Wood Duck Lane, Guys Mills, Pennsylvania 16327; ☎814-789 3585; fax 814-789 2909; e-mail: r5w_ernwr@mail.fws.gov.
Sanctuary for migrating birds. Offers an internship for a biologist for surveys and data collection. Applicants must have a background in biology or a related area. The position is unpaid. Housing discussed at the time of application. No meals provided. Address application to the Volunteer Co-ordinator at the above address.

Exotic Feline Breeding Compound Inc: HCR 1, Box 84, Rosamond, California 93560; ☎661-256-3793; fax 661-256-6867; e-mail info@cathouse-fcc.org; www.cathouse-fcc.org.
Keeper Internships offered for varying lengths of time. Posts are unpaid and there is a charge for housing. Duties include cage cleaning, health chart maintenance and observation, assisting with medical procedures, food preparation, educating the public and office work.

Farm Sanctuary: 3100 Aikens Road, Watkins Glen, New York 14891; ☎607-583-2225; fax 607-583 4349; e-mail education@farm sanctuary.org; www.farmsanctuary.org.
Operates two shelters (in Watkins Glen, NY and Orland, California) that are home to hundreds of farm animals that have been rescued from abuse and neglect. 60-100 volunteers/interns are taken on annually. Interns must be at least sixteen years old and vegetarian. Interns help with barn cleaning and farm chores, staff the visitor centre and conduct educational tours, carry out bulk mailing and assist with administrative projects. Interns/Volunteers should stay minimum of a month and a maximum of three. Positions start at the beginning of the months and end the last day of the month. Free housing is provided. Transportation to the grocery store is provided once a week. Application can be done on line at www.farmsanctuary.org (go to *volunteer/job link*).

Friends of the National Zoo: National Zoological Park, 3001 Connecticut Avenue, NW Washington, D.C. 2008; ☎202-673 4974; fax 202-673 4890; www.fonz.org.

Washington Zoo is a division of the Smithsonian Institution and was founded in 1890. It has about ten internships relevant to animal behaviour, animal husbandry and veterinary medicine students or graduates.

Animal behaviour/ecology intern: responsible for collecting and analysing data on basic behaviour of exhibited animals and at the Conservation and Research Center.

Zoo animal medicine intern: to assist with the ongoing programme of care for exotic animals. Applicants must be veterinary students.

Veterinary pathology intern: applicants should be veterinary students.

All positions are for 12 weeks and a stipend of $2,400-$3000 is provided. Interns find their own accommodation but a list of possible lodgings will be provided.

Very popular internships with over 500 applicants per year. Write in the first instance for application pack to Friends of the National Zoo (Traineeships), National Zoological Park, Washington D.C. 20008. The deadline for applications is 31 December.

Haleakala National Park: P.O. Box 369, Makawao, Hawaii 96768; ☎808-572-4487; fax 808-572 4428; e-mail HALE_VIP_Coordinator@nps.gov.

Internships involving conservation of wildlife for future generations:

Endangered species management: responsibilities include monitoring endangered species and computer data entry, monitoring traplines for predators that prey on endangered species. Driving licence, able to hike, work independently and fit enough to climb steep hills. Must have several years' experience in wildlife, biology, zoology or other appropriate field.

Duration is three months. A paid internship is not guaranteed unless you apply through the Student Conservation Association (see Internships above) as that comes with food and housing. About 80% of volunteers at Haleakala working with animals are appointed through SCA.

For the latest details contact the Volunteer Co-ordinator at the above address. Applications best sent through the Student Conservation Organisation.

Hawk Mountain Sanctuary: 1700 Hawk Mountain Road, Box 191, Kempton, Pennsylvania 19529; ☎610-756 6961; fax 610-756 4468; www.hawkmountain.org.

Wildlife reserve of 2,500 acres in the Appalachian mountains. Founded in 1934 and privately supported. 16 Employees. Runs an international internship programme open to students and new graduates as well as those committed to a career in conservation.

Applicants should have experience of ringing birds from a small boat

Takes on two biological survey and monitoring interns whose work includes assisting with flora and fauna censuses, maintaining databases, preparing and analysing technical and non-technical reports and some interpretive activities for the sanctuary's visitors. Interns can also work on preparing an independent research project. Duration is four months and the pay rate is $500 per month plus free housing. Some interpretive work with visitors.

Apply to Annette Turner, Senior Education Specialist enclosing a self-addressed stamped envelope for application details. Deadlines for applications are: 15 February for the spring and 15 June for autumn.

Howell Living History Farm: 101 Hunter Road, Titusville, New Jersey 08560; ☎609-737 3299; fax 609-737 6524.

Living history farm demonstrates farming life at the turn of the 20th century. Made relevant to the millennium by turning historical technology to uses of farmers in developing countries.

Internships offered to farm workers to care for the animals, work on crop production and use oxen for farm work. Ten-week stay. $100 per week and free housing. Food, in the form of farm produce is provided free (flour, eggs, vegetables and chicken with the feathers on!). Applicants should demonstrate an interest in international agricultural development of small-scale farming. Previous foreign interns have come from the UK, Japan, Kenya, The Gambia and Tanzania.

Free housing is provided. Apply to Intern Program Coordinator at the above address.

International Crane Foundation: P O Box 447, Baraboo, Wisconsin 53913; e-mail mwell@savingcranes.org; www.savingcranes.org.

Aviculture internships in the crane conservation department. Interns receive intensive hands-on training in the care and management of endangered cranes, including general husbandry, handling techniques, behaviour, captive reproduction, incubation, chick rearing, artificial insemination, health care and genetic management. This position provides training that provides the skills to help interns qualify for a permanent job in their field.

Responsibilities vary by season. Breeding activities are concentrated in the warm season, and facilities maintenance, record keeping, project write-up, occur more in winter. Interns help with all aspects of the management and breeding of the captive crane flock, and in maintaining crane-related facilities.

Working conditions: 5 days a week; 40 hours approximately per week (normally 8am-5pm). Interns also conduct 1-2 after hours incubator and chick checks per week (April-September). Most interns work weekends and have two consecutive days off during the week. Half of work time is spent outdoors, in all weathers found in Wisconsin.

Duration and stipend: 6 months; all seasons. Stipend US$350 monthly and on-site housing.

Qualification: two years of college or equivalent practical experience with knowledge of, and interest in bird conservation. Persons with 4-year college degree preferred. Must be able to carry 50lbs feed bag and do hard work outdoors. Those with previous experience breeding birds or with extensive bird knowledge will be given preference.

Applications to Kelly Maquire, International Crane Foundation, P.O. Box 447, Baraboo, WI 53913, USA, should include three letters of recommendation.

Maritime Center at Norwalk: 10 North Water Street, Norwalk, Connecticut 06854; ☎203 852-0700 ext 269 fax: 203-838 5416; e-mail interncoor.aol.com

Aquarium interns: to assist the aquarist with daily care of the exhibits, animals and school programmes. Students will assist in the collection of new specimens, water testing, exhibit interpretation for visitors, husbandry of the animals and teaching the

Aquarium's educational programmes. Forty hours per month minimum, six weeks minimum. Students must be interested and involved in marine biology or other marine science. Aquarium internships are unpaid and no meals or accommodation are provided. There is a possibility of full-time employment. Write to the Intern Co-ordinator, Lauren Sikorski. In-person interview preferred.

Massachusetts Audubon Society: South Great Road, Lincoln, Massachusetts 01773; ☎617 259 9506; www.massaudubon.org.
Founded in 1896. Amongst the many internships available are *wildlife interns* whose responsibilities include animal care, feeding, administering medical preparations, training animals and assisting with the rehabilitation of wild birds of prey. Candidates should have experience of working closely with wild animals and natural history knowledge is preferred. 12 weeks. Unpaid or paid. Contact Mrs. Claudia Veitch, Director of Human Resources at the above address.

Minnesota Zoo: 13000 Zoo Boulevard, Apple Valley, Minnesota 55124; ☎952-431 9200; fax 952-431 9300; e-mail jill.wallin@state.mn.us; www.mnzoo.com.
Conservation facility, entertainment, education facility founded in 1979 and has a workforce of 300. Takes on a variety of interns including those for animal management whose job is to care for exotic and domestic animals, diet preparation, cleaning exhibits and generally learning the techniques of zoo animal management. Communicating with the zoo visitors is also part of the job. Positions are seasonal lasting twelve to fourteen weeks and are unpaid. Open to students and postgraduate students. Applications to the Intern Program Co-ordinator at the above address. Deadline for applications is mid July for autumn and winter and 1 December for spring, mid-March for summer.

National Aquarium in Baltimore: Pier 3, 501 East Pratt Street, Baltimore, Maryland 21202; ☎410-576-3888; fax 410-659-0116; e-mail intern@aqua.org; www.aqua.org.
Described as a 'state-of-the-art' aquatic institution, the Baltimore aquarium is dedicated to the conservation and preservation of the environment and to enlightening the public. It has a staff of 350 and 20 to 40 interns are taken on in a wide range of departments. Internships which involve directly dealing with the sea mammals and other marine and aquatic life include herpetology, marine mammal training, aquarist and aviculture assistants. Applicants should have knowledge of the field in which they wish to work and be planning a career in this field. Foreign applicants must receive a college credit. Help provided in finding housing, but room and board are at the interns' expense. The posts are unpaid.
    Apply to the Education Department Internships and include academic transcripts by 1 April for summer, and 1 November for January. An in-person interview is preferred. Application forms can be printed from the website.

New England Aquarium: Central Wharf, Boston Massachusetts 02110-3399; fax 617-973 5235; e-mail vols@neaq.org; www.neaq.org.
Established in 1969 to protect marine life. Has 230 employees and offers a range of internships including *Animal Observation* to keep a record of a colony of marine animals. Record data for sea turtle project and enter it into database. Assist with set up for turtle project and any other behavioural studies being conducted. Extensive data entry and office work, dealing with student enquiries. Must be over 18.
Aquarist (Fish) to assist staff aquarists with animal husbandry responsibilities including feeding, maintaining aquariums systems and other routine animal care duties in the various fish departments of the aquarium. Marine science, biology etc qualification preferred. Previous experience with animal care desirable. Applicant must be able to lift 50lbs.

Penguin colony assistant to assist staff aquarists with animal husbandry caring for the aquarium's penguin colony. Duties include preparing food for penguins and giant ocean tank. Cleaning include washing the exhibits including the islands which have to be scrubbed free of guano and algae. Feed penguins and record daily intake for individual birds. Maintain observation records. Same requirements are for Fish Aquarist, must be able to lift heavy weights and be over 5 feet, 3 inches so as to stand in the exhibit.

Aquaculture Intern-Lobster Rearing Facility and jelly fish culturing facility. This internship can be a joint appointment with the Research and Fishes Departments. The Lobster rearing facility produces a year round supply of lobster embryos, larvae and juveniles for various research institutions. Assist with daily husbandry and maintenance. General laboratory experience required and good attention to detail.

Whale Watch Interpreter (summer only) to assist Aquarium's professional staff and volunteer efforts to preserve 'the world of water' through teaching whale watch passengers about whales and whale behaviour. Duties include education and whale observation from vessels owned by the Aquarium. Excellent computer and organisational skills required. Ability to work long hours to accommodate whale watch trip schedules.

Giant Ocean Tank Intern No diving required. Care and maintenance of Caribbean Reef exhibit. Feeding barracuda, sea turtles etc. May be assigned special research projects by other staff.

Aquarium Medical Centre Responsibilities Assist the permanent staff with upkeep and animal care. Basic husbandry of patients. Previous animal care and handling essential. A background in basic college-level sciences is desirable.

Applications should be sent to Volunteer Programs and Internships at the above fax or e-mail address. An in-person interview is necessary.

Norlands Living History Center: 290 Norlands Road, Livermore, Maine 04253; ☎207-897 4366; fax 207-897 4963; e-mail norlands@norlands.org; www.norlands.org.
Created in 1974, as a non-profit, educational museum, the Center occupies the historic buildings and 445-acre estate of the Washburns, a nationally prominent 19th century family. Its mission is to preserve the Washburn's family heritage, and to teach the history and culture of rural New England in the Civil War era. The methodology employed is role-playing, demonstrations and hands-on experiences. Visitors can become participants in the daily activities of a farming family. Depending on the season there are 19 employees.

Two internships as agricultural assistants are offered for those willing to participate in 19th century farm activities, work with school groups, and perform chores relating to livestock, as well as general site maintenance. Applicants should be capable of working independently, have good oral communication skills, and a personal interest in the field. Free housing with utilities and a stipend of $50 per week increases to $75 after three months and $100 after 6 months. Meals not provided, except when part of a living history programme in which the intern is participating. Food preparation facilities are provided and interns by their own groceries, or use farm produce, and prepare their own meals. Open to students, graduates, post-graduates, those re-entering the workforce and career changers. Minimum duration is two months. Internships are generally not offered for the months of October to March, except as part of a longer programme. Farming background useful, but not required.

[Please send introductory letter to Judith Bielecki, Executive Director, at the above address. Application materials can be downloaded from internships page on the website. Three references are required, In-person interview is preferred, but telephone interview possible.

Pacific/Remote Islands National Wildlife Refuge: P.O. Box 50167 Honolulu, Hawaii 96850; ☎808-541 1201; fax 808-541 1216; e-mail chuck_monnett@mail.fws.gov.

National wildlife refuge for the preservation, protection and enhancement of fish and wildlife and their habitat in the northern Hawaiian islands.

Ten to twelve seabird monitoring volunteers whose responsibilities include monitoring populations of seabirds and other wildlife duties such as ringing birds and sea turtle counts, assisting with field station maintenance and carrying out specific monitoring tasks. Minimum of three months. Unpaid. Applicants should be experienced in field work and wildlife biology. Housing and meals provided free. Apply to The Wildlife Biologist at the above address.

San Juan/Rio Grande National Forests: 1803 West Highway 160, Monte Vista, Colorado 81144; ☎719-852 5941; fax 719-852 6250; e-mail Is=c.keller/oul=ro2f09a@mhs-fswa.attmail.com.
Offers a range of internships including wilderness rangers, fish, wildlife and range positions. Responsibilities vary depending on the position. Those involving wildlife include biological surveying of fish, birds and other wildlife. Horseback rangers ('Ghost Riders') must have their own mounts. Free housing and limited subsistence (usually $16 per day) is provided in most cases. Duration is three months. Open to students, graduates, postgraduates, career changers and those re-entering the workforce. Contact the Partnership/Volunteer Coordinator, Dale Gomez, at the above address.

National Audubon Society: Sharon Audubon Center: Route 4, 325 Cornwall Bridge Road, Sharon, Connecticut 06069; ☎860-364 0520; fax 860-364 5792; www.audubon.org/local/sanctuary/sharon.
A sanctuary covering 758 acres that carries out wildlife rehabilitation and provides public environmental education. Established in 1961.

Takes on one environmental education intern to teach a wide variety of environmental and natural history topics on and off site, rehabilitating injured, and rearing orphaned birds and range of other tasks related to the day-to-day running of a nature centre. Housing provided free. Duration is three months. Small wage and free housing. Applicants should have a background in natural history and some teaching experience. Contact the Manager, at the above address.

Staten Island Zoo, Education Department: 614 Broadway, Staten Island, New York 10310; ☎718-442 3174; fax 718-981-8711; www.statenislandzoo.org.
Although the internships offered are for educationists one of them involves direct contact with animals: the travelling zoo instructor, who visits New York City's schools in the 'zoomobile' using live animals (turtles, -non-venomous snakes, lizards, rabbits etc.) in education programmes. The intern is also responsible for the feeding and care of live animals used in the outreach teaching programme. The post is for nine months and is paid $250 per week. Interns find their own housing and fund their board and accommodation.

Applicants should be recent college graduates or postgraduate students qualified to teach elementary science to 4-12 year olds. Good driving record and ability to obtain a NY state driver's licence. Applications to the Assistant Director of Education at the above address enclosing a CV and cover letter by 25 February for the summer, May 30 for the autumn.

Theodore Roosevelt National Park: 315 Second Avenue, P.O. Box 7, Medora, North Dakota 58645; ☎701-623-4466; e-mail: bruce_kaye@nps.gov.
National park encompassing the Little Missouri Badlands and 70,000 acres on which is found a diversity of wildlife including bison, elk and mustangs, and birdlife. Established 1947. Employees: 30.

Among the internships offered are two biological science technicians whose responsibilities include resource management (exotic pest control and wildlife surveys). There are no positions that involve full-time work with animals. Some positions do involve working with wildlife during the autumn roundups for bison and wild horses. Applicants must be able to work independently and with others, have good oral communication and research skills. Open to students, graduates and postgraduates, career changers and those re-entering the workforce. Duration is two to three months. Free housing and subsistence (usually $5-$10 daily) are provided. Volunteers have to fund their own food.

Apply to Bruce M Kaye, Chief of Interpretation with a cv, covering letter and two personal references by 15 February for spring/summer.

Three Lakes Nature Centre & Aquarium: 400 Sausiluta Drive, Richmond, Virginia 23227; ☎804-261 8230; fax 804-266-6938; e-mail tt-threelakes@juno.com
Environmental education centre established in 1992. Has four employees. Offers two internships for nature centre assistants to help with all aspects of the day-to-day running including programme planning, setting up exhibits, animal care (includes reptiles, amphibians and a few fish) and general maintenance. Flexible duration. Internships are unpaid and no meals or housing are provided. Applicants should have a background in natural sciences. Applications or résumé should be addressed to Tom Thorp, Nature Center Supervisor at the above address.

Trailside Museums and Wildlife Center: Palisades Interstate Park Commission, Bear Mountain, New York 10911; ☎845-786-2701; fax 845-786-2776; e-mail uncl@icu.com; www.bearmountainzoo.org.
Large park and recreational facility established in 1927. Exists to promote the conservation of natural resources and is home to non-releasable native New York state wildlife. Also operates a wildlife rehabilitation facility.

Takes on four zookeeper assistants whose responsibilities include caring for permanently damaged or orphaned park wildlife in a zoo setting under the supervision of a park ranger/zookeeper. Applicants are expected to have the ability to work independently and with others and plan to have a career in this field. Good oral communication skills also important. Duration from mid-May to mid-August or from the end of August to mid-November. Unpaid. Formal and on-the-job training given and there is a possibility of permanent employment. Applications are considered any time. Applicants must send a CV and an in-person interview is preferred.

Vermont Raptor Center: Church Hill Road, RR 2, Box 532, Woodstock, Vermont 05091-9720; ☎802-457-2779; fax 802-457 1053; e-mail mcox@vinsweb.org; www.vinsweb.org.
Living museum of birds of prey and rehabilitation centre for all type of birds. Part of the Vermont Institute of Natural Science. Offers two to four raptor center internships to help with all aspects of the centre including care and health monitoring of the raptors and environmental education. Applicants should have a background in ornithology, bird handling and veterinary assistance and/or environmental education. The work involves long hours. Must be able to lift 50lbs and have a driving licence. Duration of two to five months. Internships are unpaid but free housing is provided. Applications from students, graduates, those reentering the work force and career changers. Apply to Raptor Center Director at the above address. In-person interview preferred.

Wetlands Institute: 1075 Stone Harbor Boulevard, Stone Harbor, New Jersey 08247-1424; ☎609-368 1211; fax 609-368 3871; e-mail wetlandsinstitute@juno.com; www.wetlandsinstitute.org.
A privately funded non-profit institute for scientific research and environmental education relating to tidal salt marshes and other coastal ecosystems. Occupies 32 acres of a 6,000-

acre area of coastal wetland. Takes on a variety of interns including two aquarists responsible for maintaining aquariums, collecting specimens and interpreting the exhibits to the public. Applicants should be knowledgeable in environmental sciences and have previous aquarium experience. Also needed is an environmental education intern who works with the staff in teaching marsh and ecology through Summer Nature Classes and presentations to visiting public. EE interns also develop a working knowledge of the relevant flora and fauna through working with them in beach and marsh habitats.

Positions last three months and housing is available for summer interns at a cost of $100 monthly. Minimum of 30 hours a week expected. Unpaid. Most interns have part-time jobs. Deadlines for application are 1 March (for summer), 1 August (for autumn) and 15 November (for spring). Applications to: The Intern Co-ordinator at the above address. Interviews can be conducted on the telephone.

Wildlife Care Center: 3200 Southwest 4th Avenue, Fort Lauderdale, Florida 33315; fax 954-524-9415; e-mail silfenr@nova.edu; www.wildcare.org.
Animal hospital established over 30 years. Has 36 employees. Offers 2-8 veterinary internships responsible for assisting the veterinarians. Candidates should have completed courses in the field and be intending to pursue a career in the veterinary field. Duration is flexible. Apply to Dr. Robert Silfen, Executive Director, by fax or e-mail.

Zoo New England: One Franklin Park Road, Boston, Massachusetts 02121; ☎617-989-2000; fax 617-989-2025; e-mail aminterns@zoonewengland.com; www.zoonewengland.com.
Non-profit, private organisation responsible for the Franklin Park Zoo and Stone Zoo. Employees total 150. Takes on one to six animal care interns each season, whose responsibilities include assisting the animal care staff at the Franklin Park and/or Stone Zoo (in Stoneham). Applicants should be able to work independently, oral communication skills, good interpersonal skills and planning a career in a related field. Duration is twelve weeks. All internships are unpaid. Open to students, postgraduates and career changers. On the job training will be given.

Researchers study chimps to find out what makes them happy

Applicants should contact the Internship Co-ordinator, at the above address or fax number. E-mail enquiries can be sent to aminterns@zoonewengland.com Apply by mid-March for the summer, mid-July for the autumn and mid November for the winter.

VOLUNTEER WORK

The concept of the volunteer who not only works for an organisation but pays for the privilege has become very common. Many of the organisations involved are non-profit organisations, which use such means to raise money for their projects. Those dealing with animals are largely research organisations that are also dedicated to conservation and protection of all kinds of creatures, and to raising public awareness.

Some of the following organisations take paying volunteers; others like the ASPCA and the Assisi Animal Foundation take unpaid volunteers.

ASPCA – The American Society for the Prevention of Cruelty to Animals: 424 East 92 Street, New York, NY 10128; ☎212-876-7700; fax 212-348-3031; e-mail volunteer@aspca.org; www.aspca.org.
The ASPCA is the USA's oldest humane society (incorporated in 1866). It works to prevent cruelty to animals throughout the USA, runs New York City programmes, animal shelter assistance, animal hospital, animal behaviour and training centre, humane education, low cost neutering and poison control centre. It has 350-400 active volunteers at any given time. All new volunteers attend orientation and training sessions including working with shelter animals. Minimum volunteer period is usually 6 months but is negotiable depending on circumstances.
Animal placements: include adoptions counsellor, animal socialiser for traumatised animals, dog walker, foster caretaker.
Center for Behavioural Therapy: tester volunteer to see if trained animals pass the Canine Good Citizenship test, and dog training assistant for qualified volunteers to assist permanent ASPCA dog trainers; assistants should make a minimum weekly commitment of 3 hours in a single day per week.

Assisi Animal Foundation: 9221 Lucas Road, Crystal Lake, Ilinois 60039-0143; ☎815-455-9411; fax 815-455-9417; e-mail info@assisi.org; www.assisi.org.
Assisi Animal Foundation operates a non-kill, minimum cage refuge for about 250 average dogs and cats (mostly cats). Provides animal assisted therapy programme to eleven nursing-retirement senior facilities. Also provides education programmes for young people and an adult education programme focusing on African wildlife.

Has 50 regular volunteer staff and six temporary staff. Takes volunteers to help with direct care of animals, office duties, and participation in animal assisted therapy programme. Volunteers are expected to stay for three months minimum and there is the possibility of free accommodation, but no expenses are paid. Contact Isabelle Linklater at the above address or e-mail.

Caretta Research Project: 9841, Savannah, Georgia 31412-9841, USA; ☎912-447-8655; fax 912-447 8656.
A co-operative hands on research and conservation project, involving the threatened loggerhead sea turtles that nest on Wassaw National Wildlife Refuge in Georgia. The work is variable depending on time of season and turtle activity. mid-May through to mid-August is egg-laying season, and participants spend part of each night patrolling 6 miles of beach, looking for nesting female turtles. The turtles are then tagged, all related data is recorded, and the nests are protected either by relocation to a hatchery, or by screening so racoons cannot raid them. Late July through to September is hatching

season and participants monitor nests and escort emerging hatchlings down the beach and into the surf. The work is hard but rewarding.

Approximately 95 volunteers are recruited annually to take part in all aspects of the project's work. The placements last one week, from Saturday to Saturday throughout mid-May to mid-September; some have signed up for three-week placements but one week is the normal duration. Participants must be at least 16 years old (the oldest so far was 78) and in good health, as they may be expected to walk long distances. A positive mental attitude is of particular importance; the project requires upbeat, adaptable, people who can cheerfully endure close quarters, rain storms, insects, and the heat and humidity of a week in the subtropics without air conditioning. Previous volunteers have come from all over the world. The cost of placement is $550 per person per week and covers full training, transportation to and from the island, all food and basic but comfortable housing.

Applications to the above address from 2nd January, and the Centre advises that in 2002, 75% per cent of places were filled in the first 2 days of booking.

Chimpanzee & Human Communication Institute: Central Washington University, Ellensburg, Washington.
Volunteers needed to help study a group of captive chimps at a 930-square meter facility to see what they need to keep them happy and healthy. The project is intended to improve the lot of chimps in captivity generally. Volunteers stay for 12 days during February to October. During the first week, volunteers learn how to care for the chimpanzees and their environment and how to observe them during 15-minute sessions. Each chimp is known by name and observations are critical to determine how chimps use objects and the best mix of features. Described by the organisers as 'an opportunity to have a direct effect on animal welfare.'

Applications through Earthwatch in UK (☎01865-318838; e-mail info@earthwatch.org.uk; www.earthwatch.org/europe). For Earthwatch international agents see Earthwatch entry in Worldwide Organisations section.

Column Muccio: c/o Arcas, Section 717, P.O. Box 52-7270, Miami, FLorida 33152-7270; ☎502-476-6001; www.rds.org.gt/arcas; e-mail arcas@intelnet.net.gt or masako@amigo.net.gt.
Animal rescue and rehabilitation centre in jungle near Lake Peten Itza. Volunteers needed to care for monkeys, parrots, ocelots, jaguars, catimundis and kingajous. Also another centre situated on the Pacific coast involving tracking, patrolling beaches where sea turtles lay their eggs. Accommodation and cooking facilities provided. Volunteers pay $50-$80 weekly towards funding the Centre. Special arrangements made for long-term volunteers.

Headquarters: 3 Clocktower Place, Suite 100, P.O. Box 75, Maynard, MA 07154 USA; ☎978-61-0081 or 800-776 0188; fax 978-461-2332; e-mail info@earthwatch.org.
Provides the opportunity of participating in an established study of bottlenose dolphins in Sarasota Bay, off the central, west coast of Florida.

Volunteers come for one to three weeks from January to September to help with observation of dolphins and documenting their behaviour, collecting environmental data and cataloguing photographs. There are no long-term work opportunities, but volunteers can stay longer by joining successive teams. There is a possibility also of helping to care for stranded dolphins Mote Marine Laboratory's dolphin hospital. Help is also required with day-to-day domestic tasks including shopping, cooking and clearing up.

Cost of $995 (five days) or $1,745 (12 days) includes shared beach condo accommodation and food. Volunteers pay their own travel costs to Sarasota.

For Earthwatch Europe, Japan and Australia offices, see Worldwide Organisations.

Kewalo Basin Marine Mammal Laboratory (KBMML) Hawaii. For more than 20 years KBMML has been researching dolphin sensory perception, cognition and language competence and their findings about these astonishing creatures have helped to raise public awareness of the need to protect them. Volunteers help the lab's scientists, graduate students and interns and staff in their exploration of the dolphin's mind. Volunteers rotate through tasks including monitoring experimental apparatus, recording data from trials, archiving experiments on videotape and entering computer data. Volunteers also help prepare the dolphin's food, help clean their tanks. Importantly for those wanting contact with the dolphins are the tankside socialisation sessions when you interact with the dolphins on a one-to-one basis. Volunteers come for two or four weeks year round or one-week teams from September to May. Volunteer costs are from £850 including shared bedroom condo with all amenities. A weekly food allowance is provided for volunteers to do their own shopping and catering.

Volunteer applications are handled by Earthwatch (UK ☎01865-318838; e-mail info@earthwatch.org.uk) or contact Earthwatch in the USA and other countries.

Loons of Maine: Loons are aquatic diving birds, which have been found to contain high levels of mercury which enters the food chain via pollution from incineration and power plants. Volunteers help catch loon families at night and measure concentrations of mercury in their blood and feathers and also observe the behaviour of marked loon families to see how chick survival correlates with mercury levels. Takes place on Rangely Lakes in Maine, USA. Volunteers stay for ten-day stints during the period mid-June to late August. Volunteers pay £730 for accommodation and shared cooking in a rented house. There is a chance to see abundant wildlife.

Applications through Earthwatch (UK ☎01865-318838; e-mail info@earthwatch.org/ europe) or Earthwatch agents in the USA and other countries.

Marine Mammal Center (TMMC): Marin Headlands, GGNRA, Sausalito, California 94965; ☎+1 415 289 7325; fax +1 415 289 7333; e-mail volunteer@tmmc.org; www. marinemammalcenter.org.
A major rescue centre for the rehabilitation and re-release of marine mammals with hundreds of marine mammals treated annually. The centre is operational 365 days and 24 hours. Volunteers are taken any time but the main period is March to August. Volunteers can stay as long as they want but are unpaid and there is no accommodation. They help prepare food and feed animals, restrain animals for tube feeding, clean enclosures, laundry, medication of animals, weighing animals and maintain chart of observations. Shifts last 6-12 hours. Training is given. The work is physically demanding.

Mission Wolf: P.O. Box 211, Silver Cliff, CO 81252, USA; ☎+1 719 859 2157; fax 719-746 2919; e-mail info@missionwolf.com; www.missionwolf.com.
Mission Wolf runs an isolated sanctuary in Colorado where upwards of 50 captive born wolves and wolf-dog crosses are cared for in their spacious reserves. These animals are so used to people that they cannot be released successfully into the wild. The goal is to provide them with the highest quality of life possible. Daily projects provide hands-on working and learning experiences. Volunteers' tasks are very flexible depending on the individual's skills and interests. Projects range from animal care, fencing, landscaping, construction, office work, educating the public etc. As work is unpaid and voluntary no work permit is needed. Being able to speak and understand English is desirable. There is no restriction on duration of stay but volunteers who stay two weeks or longer will be given food and a place to stay. Accommodation is provided if available on a first come, first-served basis. A small amount of pocket money is given to those who stay two months or longer. volunteers staying less than two weeks should bring a tent and enough food to last. No transport so volunteers have to make their own way to the site.

Oiled Sea Otters: Friends of the Sea Otter (FSO), 125 Ocean View Boulevard, Suite 204, Pacific Grove, CA 93950; ☎831-373-2747; fax 831-373-2749; e-mail seaotter@seaotters.org; www.seaotters.org.

FSO is a non-profit organisation started in 1968 to protect the southern sea otter, as well as other types of sea otter throughout the north Pacific. The organisation works to ensure that current protections for the otters and their habitat are maintained, and to educate the public about the sea otter's uniqueness of behaviour and its dependency for its existence on its habitat.

FSO has occasional need for volunteers. Contact the organisation for details.

Prairie Wind Animal Refuge: 22111 County Road 150, Agate, Co 80101; ☎+1 303-763 6130.

Prairie Wind Animal Refuge is a non-profit organisation that provides a humane home to exotic animals such as lions, tigers, jaguars, mountain lions, bobcats, bears, wolves, etc. Most animals have been rescued from furriers, guaranteed hunts, taxidermists, exotic meat markets, even use as ingredients in folk medicines. Some have been placed at Prairie Wind by the Colorado Wildlife Division. Some are mistreated pets. There are over 60 animals at the refuge at any time.

Volunteers are needed to clean cages, feed and water the animals, mow the lawn, stock the Visitor Center, trim shrubs and trees, clean storage areas, carry out basic maintenance etc. from June to October. No food or accommodation is provided.

Applications to Prairie Wind Animal Refuge, c/o C. Szeibert, 12043 E. Arizona Dr, Aurora, Co 80012.

Reef Environmental Education Foundation (REEF): P.O. Box 246, Key Largo, Florida FL33037; ☎305-852-0030; fax 305-852-0301; www.reef.org.

REEF recruits volunteer recreational divers and snorkellers to conduct REEF fish surveys in regions where REEF has an active Volunteer Fish Survey Project, including coastal North America and the Hawaiian islands, Central America, northern South America and the Caribbean. The number of temporary staff, volunteers and interns annually recruited is in the region of 5,000. Volunteers must supply their own SCUBA equipment and vehicle. Must have some experience of fish identification. Positions are available all year round for varying lengths of time. For the internship program only, there is a stipend and accommodation is provided.

For more details contact Lad Akins at the above address.

Useful Organisation

One World Workforce (OWW) based in California (P.O. Box 3188, La Mesa, CA; tel/fax +619 589 5544; e-mail ebhtour@aol.com) has several projects which vary in location and have taken place in California in the past. For their projects in Mexico and the West Indies see *The Rest of the World, South America*.

CAREER OPPORTUNITIES

VETERINARY

Pet medical care is very big business in the USA and veterinarians employed there are likely to be earning considerably more than British and European counterparts. Sixty per cent of American households keep pets including 52 million dogs and 60 million cats in total. The American Veterinary Association claimed that the total expenditure per annum was a boggling £8 billion plus, nearly double what it was five years ago. This figure is partly explained by the high-technology approach of veterinary medicine which means that open heart surgery for dogs, and organ transplants for cats and dogs are, if not routine, fairly common at a likely cost of around £2,000+ per operation.

Pet insurance has boomed concomitantly with veterinary costs and one of the leaders in this field is Veterinary Pet Insurance. Since an increasing number of Americans think of their pets as 'children' there is little likelihood of them wanting anything other than the best treatment available which is good news for vets and the advance of veterinary techniques.

American Veterinary Association: 1931 N Meacham Road, Suite 100, Schaumburg, IL 60173-4360; ☎847-925 8070; fax 847 925 1329; e-mail awhitsett@avma.org; www.avma.org.

HORSES

American racing is some of the richest in the world with prize money to match. The Breeder's Cup Classic, one of the most important annual races brings $4 million (about £2.35 million) to the winner. Grass courses are almost unheard of and most races are run on dirt tracks.

American Horse Racing Federation: Suite 300, 1700 K Street, NW Washington. D.C. 20006; ☎+1 202-296 4031.

American Association of Equine Practitioners: 410 West Vine Street, Lexington, Kentucky, KY 40507; ☎606-233 0147.

American Jockey Club: 40 East 52nd Street, New York, NY 10022; ☎+1 212 371 5970.

Stable Staff

Stablemate: Belton, Oakham, LE15 9LE; ☎01472-717381; fax 01572-717343; e-mail SRS@stablemate.demon.co uk. Agency that arranges work and training opportunities in the USA for those aged 18-34. For other agencies which might have horsey jobs in the USA see *Agencies* in the *Working with Horses* chapter.

The following equitation establishments are affiliated to the Association of British Riding Schools and may be worth contacting for vacancies:

Cazenovia College Equine Center: Cazenovia, NY 13035; ☎+1 315-655 7186; fax +1 315-655 2190.

Minglewood Farm: P.O. Box 125, Clifford, Pennsylvania 19413; ☎+1 717-222 3028.

Patapasco Horse Center: 2501 Frederick Road, Catonsville, Maryland 21228; ☎+1 410 203 0211.

Winsome Farm: 444 Nealy Road, Newville, Pennsylvania 17241; ☎+1 717 776 5516; fax +1 717 564 3762.

Westmoorland Davis Equestrian Institute: Morvan Park, Route 4 Box 43, Leesburgh, Virginia 22075.

Another possibility is jobs on Dude or Guest Ranches, which are part of the tourist industry in North America. You may however find yourself concentrating your attention as much on the guests as the horses. Instructors and wranglers need stable qualifications and several years' experience. A first aid certificate is also usually obligatory. Pack trail ride leaders need training and a licence. They have to learn a range of skills essential for a wilderness guide including how to load a packhorse, shoeing and mountain riding. One way to do this could be through the International Farm Experience Programme (see below).

Addresses of dude ranches can be obtained from the publication Summer Jobs USA (£14.99) from Vacation Work; ☎01865-241798; www.vacationwork.co.uk), or Peterson's Guides (Princeton Pike Corporate Center, 2000 Lennox Drive, Lawrenceville, NJ 08648; ☎609-896-1800; fax 609-896-4544, or use Dude Ranch brochures from American tourist offices, or find them on the internet.

AGRICULTURE

Agriventure: International Agricultural, Exchange Association (IAEA), Long Clawson, Melton Mowbray, Leicestershire LE14 4NR. Tel 01664-822335; fax 01664-823820; e-mail post@agriventure.com; www.agriventure.com.
Organises international agricultural exchanges. Age group 18-30 with good practical farming experience. Placement destinations include the USA and Canada. Placements begin in Feb/Mar/Apr and last seven to nine months. Candidates have to attend pre-departure meeting. Costs are from £1,725, which includes airfares, visa, insurance, orientation seminar and board and lodging throughout with a host family. Trainees are then paid a realistic wage.

US-based agricultural programmes:

The Land Institute: 2440 E Water Well Road, Salina, Kansas 67401, USA; Offers year-long internships in sustainable and ecological agriculture, for graduates. Apply to the above address for details.

Ohio International Agricultural Intern Program: 113 Agricultural Administration Building, Ohio State University, 2120 Fyffe Road, Columbus, OH 43210-1757; ☎614-292-7720.

Minnesota Agricultural Student Trainee Program: Room R395 Vo Tech Building, 1954 Buford Avenue, St Paul, MN 55108. Tel 612-624-3740; e-mail sjones@umn.edu; www.mast.coates.umn.edu

Tillers International: 5239 South 24th Street, Kalamazoo, MI 49002 USA; ☎616-344-3233. Offers summer schools, which include working with animal traction, visiting Amish farms and western and third world farmers working together.

ZOOS

Zoo keepers wishing to extend and broaden their professional experience by working in a zoo in the USA, could try the American Association of Animal Keepers (635 Gage Boulevard, Topeka, Kansas 66606; ☎+1 800 242 4519; fax +1 785 273 1980). Some larger American zoos and other institutions that might be worth trying are listed below:

Baltimore Zoo: Druid Hill Park, Baltimore, Maryland 21217; ☎+1 410-396 7623; fax +1 410 396 6464. Founded in 1876, the zoo has 150 employees.

Bronx Zoo: 2300 Southern Boulevard, Bronx, New York 10460-1099; fax +1 718 733 4460. Established in 1895. 200 employees.

Brookfield Zoo: 3300 South Golf Road, Brookfield, Illinois 60513; fax +1 708 485 3532. Established in 1934. The zoo has a stated aim to foster appreciation of the earth's biological heritage. 400 employees.

Central Park Wildlife Center: 830 5th Avenue, New York 10021.

Indianapolis Zoo: 1200 West Washington Street, Indianapolis, Indiana 46222; ☎+1 317-630 2041; fax +1 317 630 2041; fax +1 317-630 5114. Established in 1944. 225 employees.

Gladys Porter Zoo: 500 Ringgold St./Brownsville, Texas 78520; www.gpz.org. The GPZ is a non-profit organisation that is active in involving the support of the local community. The zoo has a Foreign Zoological Veterinarian Host programme for visiting veterinarians to learn about veterinary techniques in the USA.

International Center for Gibbon Studies (ICGS): P.O. Box 800249, Santa Clarita, CA 91380; ☎805-943 4915; fax 805 296 1237; e-mail gibboncntr@aol.com. Volunteer primate keeper position for one month minimum. Duties include keeping, collecting and entering behavioural data (on Mackintosh) on approximately 35 captive gibbons, assist with routine annual examination, occasional grounds maintenance.

Volunteers must love animals, be hardworking, knowledgeable or willing to learn, have cage building and gardening skills. No stipend, but housing, transportation to from airport is provided at arrival and departure.

Contact for more information is Patti Dahle, Volunteer Co-ordinator, International Center for Gibbon Studies at the above address.

The Minnesota Zoo: 13000 Zoo Boulevard, Apple Valley, Minnesota 55124; ☎+1612 431 9212; fax +1 612-431 9211. Established 1997. Primarily a conservation facility. Has 300 employees.

National Zoological Park: 3001 Connecticut Avenue, NW Washington, DC 20008; ☎+1 202-673 4974; fax +1 202-673 4890. The National Zoo of America established in 1890. Exhibits include giant panda, a micro Amazonian rainforest, Komodo dragon hatchlings and a cheetah conservation programme.

Staten Island Zoo: 614 Broadway, Staten Island, New York 10310; ☎+1 718-442 3101; fax +1 718-981 8711; www.statenislandzoo.org Established 1936. Applications to the General Curator, Staten Island Zoo at the above address.

Texas Snow Monkey Sanctuary: P.O. Box 702, Dilley, Texas 78017; ☎830 378-5775; fax 830 378 5881; e-mail chango@vsta.com

Volunteer primate keeper. Positions are for a minimum of two months. Cleaning cages, feeding, monitoring health, grounds work, animal censuses and occasional computer work. Must be hardworking, dedicated and willing to learn. Respect for the animals is also important. Knowledge of computer applications (Word, Excel, TSMS) would be useful.

Volunteers should be prepared to cope with the weather conditions: extremely hot summers and very cold winters. No stipend, but free housing and ground transportation provided.

Contact Tanya Bell, Site Manager, Texas Snow Monkey Sanctuary at the above address.

Zoo New England: One Franklin Park Road, Boston, Massachusetts 02121; ☎+1 617-989 2017; fax +1 617 989 2025. Responsible for the Franklin Park Zoo in Boston and the Stone Zoo in Stoneham. Employs 150 staff.

CANADA

ENTRY & WORKING VISAS

TOURIST VISA

British citizens need only produce their passports to enter Canada. The maximum duration of stay is six months. New arrivals may be asked by customs and immigration to show proof of adequate funds to support them during their stay and a return ticket. A list of Canadian contacts may also be necessary.

US citizens do not need a passport to enter Canada but they may have to provide proof of citizenship if requested.

No-one is allowed to take up paid or unpaid work in Canada on a tourist visa.

WORKING VISAS

Canada has high unemployment of about 10% and this is one reason why entering to take up long term work is strictly regulated. Working legally in Canada involves obtaining an Employment Authorisation from a Canadian High Commission or Embassy before leaving your own country.

If you are a full-time student there are several work exchange schemes you can apply to, similar to the schemes for the USA, allowing you to work in Canada for up to a year.

These are based on reciprocal agreements with several countries to take a similar quota of Canadian students.

Nationalities eligible to work in Canada on such schemes include Australians, British, Dutch and Swedes.

US citizens also have to have a job arranged in advance, but they can apply for Employment Authorisation on arrival at the point of entry, rather than in advance from the Canadian High Commission.

Useful Addresses

Canadian High Commission: Immigration Visa Information, 38, Grosvenor Street, London W1X OAA; 020-7258 6600; www.canada.org.uk/visa-info, or use the fax-you-back service (020-7258-6350), or send a large s.a.e. with £1 stamp marked 'SGWHP' in the top right-hand corner to obtain the information document *Student Temporary Employment in Canada.* The processing fee for Employment Authorisation is about £70 ($120).

Canadian Consulate General: Immigration Office, Level 5, Quay West, 111 Harrington Street, Sydney, NSW 2000; (☎ 02-9364 3050). Australians should request an application form for a working holiday visa.

EXCHANGE VISITOR PROGRAMMES

THROUGH THE CANADIAN HIGH COMMISSION

Students who already have a job offer from Canada may be eligible for 'Programme A'. They can apply directly to the Canadian High Commission in London (see above) for an employment authorisation (reference 1102) which is valid for a maximum of 12 months and is not transferable between different jobs.

THROUGH BUNAC

For more flexibility, you should apply through BUNAC's Work Canada programme. This is intended for gap year, full-time undergraduate, or postgraduate students, wishing to spend a maximum of twelve months in Canada. To be eligible you also have to be a British or Irish passport holder, and aged between 18 and 29 at the time of application and entry to Canada.

Work Canada participants can go to Canada to look for a job of their choice virtually anywhere in Canada or they can arrange a job in advance. You need to have personal funds of C$600 if you have a prearranged job and C$1000 if you are going job hunting on arrival.

Those wanting to work with animals should spend some time before departure researching job openings using personal, academic and public sources of help. BUNAC can offer some job listings, the Canadian yellow pages can be consulted in major public libraries and the internet can be used to track down major zoos and animal parks and other animal organisations which tend to have their own websites.

There is a Work Canada registration fee, flights cost approximately £460 to £550 and insurance £120 for four months.

VOLUNTEER WORK

Voluntary work comes into a special category. If you have found a placement with a charitable institution the permit needed takes about a month to process.

PAYING VOLUNTEERS

The following organisations take paying volunteers:

Coastal Ecosystems Research Foundation (CERF): Whale Research Expedition, Tours of Exploration, 1111 Melville Street, Suite 820, Vancouver, British Columbia V6E 3V6; www.toursexplore.com & www.cerf.bc.ca e-mail info@toursexplore.com & info@cerf.bc.ca. CERF operates from shore-based stations and a 40-foot research boat focusing on the distribution, number and movements of summertime visitor grey whales, and also humpback and killer whales and Pacific white-sided dolphins. Actual projects vary from year to year. Research takes place on the central coast of British Columbia between Port Hardy on Vancouver Island and Bella Coola on the mainland in an area of temperate rainforest.

Volunteers stay for six nights/7 days during the period from the end of June to the first week in September. The cost is Can$ 1400 for adults, and Can$ 125 less for students. This covers all meals, camping accommodation, safety equipment and return transportation between Port Hardy BC and base camp. The meals are primarily vegetarian. Participants should be prepared for wilderness and rustic camp conditions. Volunteers who stay longer get a reduction of 10%. Useful skills include photography boat handling. Volunteers are integrated into all aspects of the research operations from boat handling to observation and data collection.

Initial applications should be be by letter or e-mail and addressed to William Megill, Coastal Ecosystems Research Foundation.

Long Point Bird Observatory: British Trust for Conservation Volunteers (BTCV), 36 St Mary's Street, Wallingford, Oxfordshire OX10 OEU; ☎01491-839766; fax 01491-839646; e-mail information@btcv.org.uk; www.btcv.org.uk.

The project is organised with the Federation of Ontario Naturalists. Long Point is an 18-mile sandspit jutting into Lake Erie in the province of Ontario. It supports a range of habitat including forest, dense swamp and an extensive beach. Research is timed to coincide with the renowned spring migrations of waterfowl and songbirds.

Volunteers are needed for two weeks in April to plant indigenous trees and shrubs to provide habitat for breeding and migratory birds at the Long Point Observatory. Volunteers will also explore the Point, observatory and monitor the daily nettings.

Cost of £275 excludes flights to Toronto but includes bunkhouse accommodation.

The following organisations may also take paying volunteers:

ACS Whale Adventures: American Cetacean Society, P.O. Box 1391, San Pedro, California 90733-1391; ☎+1 310 548 6279; fax +1 310 548-6950; e-mail acs@pobox.com; www.acsonline.org

Sea Quest Expeditions/Zoetic Research: P.O. Box 2424, Friday Harbor, WA 98250; ☎+1 360 378 8767.

WWOOF

Willing Workers on Organic Farms (Canada): 4429 Carlson Road, Nelson, British Columbia VIL 6X3; tel/fax 250-354 4417; e-mail wwoofcan@shaw.can; www.wwoof.ca.

WWOOF Canada attracts over 1,000 volunteers annually who wish to experience the country anywhere from coast to coast. There are 400 WWOOF farms in Canada ranging from small homesteads to large commercial farms. You will have to indicate at the outset that you wish to work with livestock, which may include horses, goats, etc.

Volunteers work for a week or much longer (you are free) between early spring and late autumn. The only cost is $30 membership and 5 international reply coupons for postage. Food and accommodation are provided, and volunteers live as family.

OTHER OPPORTUNITIES

HORSES

Racing Authorities

The Jockey Club of Canada: P.O. Box 156, Rexdale, Ontario M9W 5L2; ☎+1 416 675 7756; fax +1 416 675 6378.

Canadian Thoroughbred Horse Society: National Office, P.O. Box 172, Rexdale, Ontario, M9W 5LI; ☎416 675 3602; fax +1 416 675 9405. Useful for obtaining address list of stud farms in Canada.

GUEST RANCHES

Guest ranches are a popular form of adventure holiday. Ranches offer a range of activities including horse back riding, pack horse adventures, wildlife viewing and others.

Guiding by horses in the wilderness is a unique profession, and requires knowledge of the wilderness and horses, as well as resourcefulness and other special skills. Chilcotin Holidays Guest Ranch in British Columbia offers a variety of wilderness guide training programmmes that focus on guiding by horseback in the wilderness. The programmes are intense training modules that can be taken separately or in various combinations to provide a graduated approach. They are based on the theory that the fastest way to learn is by doing. The Seven and fourteen day modules focus on horse riding and handling, horse shoeing and packing, wilderness guiding and backcountry living. Other modules include outfitter training, adventure tourism management, horse logging and angling guide training. The courses range from beginner to advanced, and are registered as a private post secondary education programme in British Columbia. Successful participants receive a certificate and are given an apprenticeship Log Book.

Chilcotin Holidays recruits its staff directly from the training programmes, and has an extensive referral programme. The cost of the modules ranges from CAN $1,397 (one week), to CAN $2,450 (two weeks). Prices do not include Canadian GST (VAT). Further information can be onbrtained from Chilcotin Holidays (Gun Creek Road, Gold Bridge, British Columbia, Canada V0K 1PO; tel/fax 250-238-2274; e-mail adventures@chilcot inholidays.com; www.chilcotinholidays.com).

QUÉBEC

Note that anyone with a job arranged in Québec has to comply with separate and additional immigration procedures.

PAYING VOLUNTEERS

The following animal protection organisations may be able to take volunteers or help provide contacts:

Action pour les Animaux Urbains: ☎514-366 9965. Refuge, education, wildlife awareness programmes

CLAN (wolf protection and conservation): a/s Benoît Ayotte, 1232 Chute Panet, St.-Raymond, Québec GOA 4GO; ☎418-337 6546; fax 418-337-4875

Réseau Secours Animal: C.O. 65131, CSP Place Longueuil, Longueuil, Québec, JK4 5J7; ☎514-745 5743. Animal Rescue Network.

Societé Québecoise pour la Défense des Animaux (SQDA): 847 rue Cherrier, bureau 102, Montréal, Québec, H2L 1H6; ☎514-524 1970; fax 514-524 3740; Carrefour des Animaux, www.intwork.com/sqda

SPCA: 5215 Jean-Talon ouest, Montréal, Québec, H4P 1X4; ☎514-735 2711; fax 514-735 7488

Union Québecoise pour la Conservation de la Nature (UQCN): 690 Grande-Allée, 4e étage, Québec, G1R 2K5; ☎418-648 2104; fax 418-648 0991

ORGANISATIONS NEEDING PAYING VOLUNTEERS

Mingan Island Cetacean Research Expeditions: Mingan Island Cetacean Study Inc., 378 rue Bord de la Mer, Longue-Pointe-de-Mingan, Québec, GOG 2VO; tel/fax +1 418 949 2845; e-mail mics@globetrotter.net; www.rorqual.com.

Marine biology research institute concentrating on Blue, fin, humpback and minke whales. Research activities include biopsies, photo-identification and matching and entering data on the computer. Much of volunteers' time is spent on the water in the Gaspé region of Québec (summer). In winter operations concentrate on blue whale in Loreto, Baja California (February to March) and Silver Bank (February) on humpback whales.

Volunteers stay for seven to fourteen days (up to a month is possible) and must be prepared to spend long periods on water (up to 12 hours) collecting field data (observation notes, photography, biopsies), and assisting with daily logistics and boat preparation.

Costs are from US$1,295 for seven days including accommodation and meals but not air travel or transport from the airport.

Applications direct to the organisation or in UK through Animal Watch (see entry in Worldwide Organisations section or telephone 01732-741612).

ORES – Center for Coastal Field Studies: PO Box 303, 196 Wilson Avenue, Toronto, Ontario M5M 4N7; e-mail lynas@aol.com; www.access.ch/ores.

The ORES Centre specialises in the study of the coastal ecosystem in the St. Lawrence River, and in particular the several species of whale found there. Research takes place in Grandes Bereronnes (Québec), confluence of the St Lawrence and Sanguenay Rivers.

Volunteers are needed from mid-July to mid-October and should be prepared to spend four to six hours per day in a boat. Volunteers have to take a two-week 'introductory course' to broaden their familiarity with the ocean and whales. Anyone who has completed this course is eligible for an 'internship'. These are suitable for those doing independent studies or undergraduate thesis projects. The period of stay is up to 14 weeks. Useful skills include photography, computer, carpentry and boating.

The work involves observation and data gathering from small, inflatable craft (weather permitting) and from the research boat. Also, tracking and plotting whales using GPS (Global Positioning System), profiling analysis of subject mammals, documenting human/whale interactions and much more.

Free food is provided for internship participants. Others pay US$35 per week for food.

Costs of approximately US$950 include accommodation (own sleeping bag required). Volunteers also pay for food and transportation to the centre. Suitable gear is provided for work at sea.

European volunteers can apply to ORES Stiftung zur Erforschung der Marinen Umwelt, Postfach 756, 4502 Solothurn, Switzerland; tel/fax +41 32 623 63 54; e-mail utscherter@gmx.ch; www.ores.org

Apply any time before May to either address.

Australia & New Zealand

AUSTRALIA

Australia's wildlife needs little introduction here. Suffice it to say that existence as an isolated continent has given it some of the world's uniquely wonderful species like the koala, the kangaroo and the duck-billed platypus. There is a strong conservation movement manifested by conservation organisations offering opportunities to work with various native species inland and offshore. There are needless to say, all the usual opportunities for working with animals that you would expect in a highly developed country from veterinary, equine and animal welfare to farming.

ENTRY AND WORKING VISAS

VISITOR'S VISA

Tourists require a Visitor's Visa, for which they will need Form 48 obtainable from the Australian High Commission and many travel agents. This form can also now be downloaded from the Internet at www.immi.gov.au/forms/48.gif. Visitors' visas are classed as either 'short-stay' (3 months) or 'long-stay' (more than 3 months). Short-stay visas are valid for three months from the date of entry into Australia and must be used within 12 months from the date of issue, whilst the long-stay visa is valid either for entry within four years or for the life of the passport (whichever occurs first). There is no application fee for a short-stay visitor's visa, however, a non-refundable fee of $35 is charged for the longer visa.

The three-month Visitor Visa can be applied for by post – allow approximately three weeks for processing. Enclose a large, S.A.E. for the return of your documents. Applications can be made in person at the Australian High Commission in London (☎020-7379 4334), the Australian Consulate in Manchester (0161-228 1344) and the Australian Embassy in Dublin (01 676 1517). The AHC in London can be very busy, especially from September to February, and you should expect a long wait; Monday to Wednesday are generally the busiest days.

It is possible to extend a three-month visitor's visa to one of six months duration whilst in Australia. There is currently a $200 fee for this. If you wish to stay longer in Australia, it is most important to extend the visa before it expires. The Department of Immigration will deport any applicant whose visa has expired. You must leave the country on a valid visa and renew it overseas before returning. Note that some travellers have been refused re-entry into Australia despite leaving Australia on a valid visa and renewing their visas in New Zealand or Singapore.

The Visitor's Visa is now being superseded by Australia's state-of-the-art 'Electronic Travel Authority' (ETA) system, which is currently available to UK and US citizens, and in most EU countries. The ETA is an 'invisible', electronically-stored authority for short-term travel to Australia which can be issued in less than ten seconds at the time of making travel bookings. It is claimed that the ETA is currently the most advanced and streamlined travel authorisation system in the world, permitting visitors to be processed in seconds on arrival at their destination. At this end, the advantages include an end to form-filling, queues and embassy visits: the whole process is completed on the spot. ETAs can be obtained from any participating travel agent or from the nearest Australian diplomatic mission. There are three different types of ETA and travellers should make sure that they obtain the one appropriate to their needs: tourists and those visiting family or friends for a period of 3 months or less need a free Tourist ETA (Type V).

It has recently been reported that some British travel agents are charging up to £15 to issue a free ETA to their clients. The amount of work involved in supplying this visa can in no way justify this charge, and travellers should be alert to this potential rip-off.

TEMPORARY RESIDENCE VISA

Visitors intending to enter Australia temporarily for the purpose of work need to obtain a Temporary Residence visa. There are currently 15 different visa sub-classes, which are issued according to the type of employment the applicant will undertake in Australia. The temporary residence programme is designed to allow people from overseas to come to Australia for specific purposes, which are expected to provide some benefit to Australia. The focus is on the areas of skilled employment, social, cultural and international relations. Those likely to be relevant to those working in various capacities with animals are:

O *Exchange (Category 411)* Allows visitors to come to Australia to broaden their work experience and skills under reciprocal arrangements by which Australian residents are granted similar opportunities abroad. A letter of invitation is required from the organisation offering the position.

O *Special Program (416)* Intended for people visiting under approved programmes for the purpose of broadening their experience and skills. It is generally used for youth exchanges and programmes such as the Churchill Fellowship. A letter of support is required from the organisation.

O *Working Holiday (417)* The Working Holiday Maker Visa aims to promote international understanding by giving young people the opportunity to holiday in Australia, whilst working to supplement their funds. The WHM visa has numerous conditions attached which are explained in the section *Working Holiday* below.

O *Educational (418)* Allows entry of staff to fill academic, teaching and research positions in Australian educational institutions, which cannot be filled from within the Australian labour market. A letter of appointment is required.

O *Visiting Academic (419)* Allows entry of people as Visiting Academics at Australian educational and research institutions, with the intention that their presence will contribute to the sharing of research knowledge. A letter of invitation is required and you may not receive a salary from the host institution.

O *Occupational Trainees (442)* Allows entry of persons for occupational training appropriate to their background and/or employment history, for the acquisition or up-grading of skills useful to their home country. A nomination must be provided unless the training is being given by the Commonwealth of Australia.

People who wish to enter Australia on the temporary residence visas listed above must meet the normal health and character requirements for entry. Some applicants may be asked to have a medical examination before a visa will be granted. In most cases, if you have your application for temporary residence approved, you will then be granted a multiple entry visa for the period of the approved stay. If you need a further re-entry visa, you will need to apply to an office of the Department of Immigration and Multicultural Affairs (DIMA).

STUDENTS

Australia's student visa programme provides for the entry of overseas students who wish to undertake full-time study in registered courses in Australia. Students have the right to work up to 20 hours per week while their course is in session, however, the intention is that income derived from working in Australia should be a supplement to the main source of funding, and applicants will need to produce evidence of their financial resources when apply for a visa. Students may work without restriction during vacation periods. Recent press reports have suggested that some students entering Australia on this type of visa are deliberately enrolling in a minimal course load and maximising their working hours illegally. It is likely that holders of student visas will be more closely monitored in future.

WORKING HOLIDAY

The Working Holiday Maker scheme allows working holiday makers to enjoy an extended holiday by supplementing their travel funds through incidental employment, thus experiencing closer contact with local communities. Australia has reciprocal working holiday arrangements with Canada, Ireland, Japan, Korea, Malta, the Netherlands, and the United Kingdom. Although there are specific arrangements with these countries, the Australian working holiday scheme is applied globally, and applicants from other countries are considered where there might be a benefit both to the applicant and to Australia.

The Working Holiday Maker Visa (WHM) is available to applicants between the ages of 18 and 25 (and in special circumstances, for applicants from arrangement countries, up to age 30). Applicants may be either single or married, but must not have children (even if any children are not in their custody). The visa is valid for 13 months from the day of issue, of which a maximum of 12 months may be spent in Australia. It is best to apply for the WHM visa no more than four weeks before the date of travel, however, if you do not arrive in Australia until some time after your visa is issued, the visa can be 'topped up' to the maximum 12 months at the local immigration office. This must be done approximately two months before the expiry of your visa and currently costs $200.

When you apply for a working holiday visa, you must demonstrate that your main purpose in visiting Australia is to holiday, and that any work you expect to undertake will be solely to assist in supporting you whilst on vacation. You must have a good chance of finding temporary work, and may not enrol in formal studies of any kind. You must also have a return ticket or sufficient funds for a return airfare, in addition to being able to demonstrate £2,000 in funds for your travels (or a parental guarantee for the same amount). If you are over 25 and applying in the UK under the 'special circumstances' clause, you will need to demonstrate that the opportunity to visit and work in Australia will benefit you, and that you are able to offer benefits to Australia in return. A Working Holiday Maker visa usually allows for multiple entry, which means that you may leave and re-enter the country as many times as you like (within the time restriction of your visa). When the visa is granted, ensure that it has been stamped 'multiple entry'. You cannot get an extension on a Working Holiday Visa under any circumstances, and must leave the country on or before the expiry date of your visa.

In 1997-98, 55,000 visas were issued; in 2000 (the year of the Sydney Olympics) this figure rose to 78,000, and it has been rising since. A large part of them were granted to UK nationals. As the system is based on a first come, first served basis, travel specialists in Australian travel suggest you plan to commence the working holiday shortly after the beginning of July, which is the beginning of the annual visa allocation period. Applications made at this time have a good chance of succeeding.

SPECIAL SCHEMES

Australia Work and Travel (AUSWAT)

Run by the Council on International Educational Exchange (CIEE), 52 Poland Street, London W1V 4JQ; ☎020-7478 2020; fax 020-7734 7322; e-mail auswat@ciee.org). Working traveller scheme. Organises 12-month visa and helps find work and accommodation in Australia. Open to British, Canadian, Dutch and Irish passport holders *resident in the UK* and aged 18-30.

BUNAC

BUNAC (16 Bowling Green Lane, London EC1R OBD; ☎020-7251 3472; e-mail downunder@bunac.org.uk) best known for schemes in the USA, also operates a Work Australia programme. It is open to anyone aged 18-25 at the time of application who is also a British, Irish, Canadian or Dutch passport-holder currently resident in the UK or Ireland. It utilises the Working Holiday Visa (see above), and provides additional benefits including back up and support from International Exchange Programs (IEP) in Australia. Under this scheme, you can take any job anywhere in Australia. If you are planning to work with animals it would be advisable to do your research in advance and contact likely organisations before you arrive and if possible arrange something in advance. You are not restricted to one job on this type of visa so you could arrange several jobs lasting a few weeks or a few months each. The total cost of this programme including, flights, orientation and back up services is about £1,500.

If you are looking for a particular telephone number or category of organisation, Australian telephone books, including Yellow Pages, can be accessed through the internet on www.telstra.com.au.

Useful Addresses

BUNAC USA: P.O. Box 430, Southbury, CT 06488, USA; ☎203-264-0901; fax 203-264 0251.

International Exchange Programs PTY Ltd (IEP): 196 Albert Road, South Melbourne, Victoria 3205, Australia; ☎03-9690-5890; fax 03-9645-7496.

Other Programmes

Travel Active Programmes (TAP): P.O.Box 107, 5800 AC Venray, Netherlands; ☎+31 478 55 19 00; fax +31 55 19 11; e-mail info@travelactive.nl; www.travelactive.nl) offer a similar scheme to BUNAC's based on the working holiday visa for Dutch and Belgian people aged 18-30.

World Travellers Network (WTN) Programs: 14 Wentworth Avenue, Sydney, New South Wales 2010; ☎02-9246 1201) offers those with a working holiday visa support and guidance on job-finding after arrival in addition to other services. A fee is charged.

OTHER OPPORTUNITIES

VETS

The Australian Veterinary Association Ltd (National Office): 134-136 Hampden Road, Artarmon 2064, New South Wales, Australia; ☎02 94112733; fax 02 9411 5089; e-mail avahq@ava.com.au

Australian Association of Cattle Veterinarians: P.O. Box 30, Indooroopilly, Qld 4068; ☎073378 7944; fax 07 3878 3559; e-mail avahq@ava.com.au. Re-directs queries to other Australian states.

Australian Equine Veterinary Association: (same address as above.

The Australian Small Animal Veterinary Association: P.O.Box 674, Surry Hills, NSW

2010; ☎02 9211 8899.

HORSES & AGRICULTURE

Racing Authority: *Australian Jockey Club:* Randwick Racecourse, Alison Road, Randwick, NSW 2031; ☎02 663 8400; fax 02 662 6292; e-mail ajc1@interconnect .com.au.

Changing Worlds: 11, Doctors Lane, Chaldon, Surrey CR3 5AE; ☎01883-340960; ww w.changingworlds.co.uk Offers paid placements on Australian farms around Broken Hill, NSW for which an ability to ride is useful.

National Racehorse Owners Association & Asia-Pacific Racehorse Owners Association: P.O. Box 585 Flemington, Victoria 3031; ☎03 9376 6999; fax 03 9372 1699.

South Australian Jockey Club Inc.: Morphettville Racecourse, Morphettville, South Australia 5043 or GPO Box 1695, Adelaide, South Australia 5001; ☎08 8294 2577; fax 08 8376 0401.

Stablemate Staff Agency: 1 Bullridge Road, East Kurrajong, NSW 2758; 02 4576 4444/ STABLEMATE@bigpond.com; UK address: The Old Rectory, Belton in Rutland, Oakham, Rutland LE15 9LE (ep@stablemate.demon.co.uk). This agency deals exclusively with equestrian and thoroughbred staff. However, they may also be able to help place those with limited experience with horses if they want to work as a general farm assistant.

Victoria Racing Club: 400 Epsom Road, Flemington, Victoria 3031; ☎03 9258 4666; fax 03 9258 4743; e-mail rsb@ozacing.net.au.

The Western Australian Turf Club: Ascot and Belmont Park Racecourses, P.O. Box 222, Belmont, Western Australia 6904; ☎09 277 0777; fax 09 277 7722; e-mail cryder@acslink.aone.au; www.waturf.org.au.

Thoroughbred Breeders Australia: 283 Anzac Parade, Kingsford NSW 2032; ☎02 9663 5053; fax 02 9662 8793.

ZOOS

Below are the addresses of some important zoos around Australia:

Taronga Zoo: Bradleys Head Road, Mosman, Sydney, New South Wales 2088; ☎02 9969 2777.

Zoological Gardens: Elliott Avenue, Parkville, Melbourne, Victoria 3052; ☎03-9285 9300; fax 03 9285 9330.

Alma Park Zoo: Alma Road, Kallangur, Brisbane, Queensland 4503; ☎07-3204 6566.

Zoological Gardens: Frome Road, North Adelaide, South Australia 5000; ☎08-8267 3255; fax 08-8239 3921.

Perth Zoo: 20 Labouchere Road, South Perth, Western Australia 6151; ☎08 9367 7988; fax 08 9367 3921.

Bonorong Park Wildlife Centre: Briggs Road, Brighton, Tasmania 7403; ☎03-6268 1184.

Mugga Lane Zoo: Mugga Lane, Red Hill, Australian Capital Territory 2603; ☎02 6295 3610.

About 24 zoos belong to Friends of the Zoos Ltd. (c/- Royal Melbourne Zoo, Elliot Avenue Parkville, Victoria 3052; ☎03 9285 9300; fax 03 9285 9390). The FOZ promotes the role of zoos in understanding and conserving wildlife and its habitats. This organisation has information about individual zoos and their projects.

SEA WORLD

Part of the International Sea World Enterprises. The Sea World complex on the Gold Coast of Queensland, incorporates a marine mammal park and is in the business of entertainment. Many of the jobs with the organisation are related to the business and catering field and are people, rather than animal, orientated. However, there are also posts for marine scientists and keepers and trainers for the marine mammals such as dolphins. You can ask for an application form at any time and if there is no vacancy your application will be held on file for three months. Contact: Human Resources, Sea World (Sea World Drive, Main Beach, Gold Coast, Queensland, Australia, P.O. Box 190 Surfers Paradise, Queensland 4217, Australia; ☎07-5588 2222; fax 07-5591 1056).

VOLUNTEER WORK

Australian Koala Foundation: Level 1, 40 Charlotte Street, Brisbane, QLD 4000, Australia; ☎+61-7 3229 7233; fax +61-7 3221 0337; e-mail research@savethekoala.co m; www.savethekoala.com; akfkoala@gil.com.au; www.akfkoala.gil.com.au.
The Australian Koala Foundation (AKF) is a non-profit, non-government funded, international conservation organisation dedicated to saving the koala and its habitat. Funds research and conservation biology projects, co-ordinates Save the Koala Month and annual conference and arranges field trips and tours. Publishes quarterly newsletter. AKF has offices in Washington DC in the USA and Tokyo, Japan. From simple beginnings the AKF is now a major conservation voice for the future of wild koalas in both domestic and international forums.
   The major scientific research project, the Koala Habitat Atlas, spearheads the thrust of AKF – conservation of the koala and its habitat. Using GIS and satellite imaging technology to identify, map and rank koala habitat, the Atlas provides land-use planners with this vital information in a practical format. Volunteers can assist in fieldwork expeditions that contribute to the Koala Habitat Atlas. Field trips are usually two weeks in duration and occur four times a year. Costs start at AU$1,000 per week, depending on location. Applicants should advise the AKF of any specialist areas of expertise or interest they may have. Check out the website for upcoming field trips.

Batreach: Jungle Walk – Kuranda, P.O. Box 300, Kuranda, 4872 North Queensland, Australia; ☎07-40938858; e-mail tullcourt@bigpond.com; www.batreach.cairns.tc.
Batreach is a rescue and rehabilitation centre for native animals, and specialises in mega bats and micro bats, as well as other marsupials. The centre has a dozen staff, all volunteers. Work involves cleaning, feeding, caring for orphaned and adult native animals. Volunteers are welcome all year round for a minimum stay of three weeks. Must be able to speak English. No special skills required as training is given. Accommodation is provided free of charge. Apply to Pam Tully at the above address.

Conservation Volunteers Australia(CVA): Head Office, P.O. Box 423, Ballarat, Victoria 3353; ☎03-5333 1483; fax 03-5333 2290; e-mail info@conservationvolunteers.com.a u; www.conservationvolunteers.com.au.
A non-profit, non-political organisation which organises practical conservation projects all over Australia. A few projects are animal connected: for instance carrying out surveys and monitoring of endangered species. CVA offers overseas volunteers a six-week Conservation Experience package, which includes food and accommodation and project-related transport in Australia for AUD$ 966 (23 Australian dollars per day). Volunteers supply own sleeping bag and work boots and must also ensure they have comprehensive medical/accident insurance. Write, fax or e-mail for an application form.

Heirisson Prong Biosphere Reserve, Western Australia: Project to reintroduce animals which have become extinct on mainland Australia back to the mainland from the offshore islands where they have survived in small numbers. This is achieved by fencing out predators, which caused their extinction. The reserve needs constant monitoring, and management, to ensure that the experimental populations do not outgrow the space allotted to them. Volunteers from the Earthwatch organisation are divided into rotating day and night crews where they spend afternoons baiting traps for bettongs and bandicoots, and evenings with spotlights to note any predator incursions. At first light trapped animals are given medical checks, and released animals are radio tracked to find their daytime refuges. The predator proof fencing also has to be maintained. Volunteers' hard work is interspersed with breaks to view the Zuydorp Cliffs, blowholes, meet dolphins and explore beaches.

Volunteers pay £1,295 for two weeks in February, June, August or October. Accommodation in shared rooms at a comfortable field station with beds and baths. Breakfast and lunch are casual affairs prepared by the volunteers. Dinner is a three-course served meal.

Applications are managed by Earthwatch (UK ☎01865-318852; e-mail info@earthwatch.org.uk). For US and international Earthwatch agents see Earthwatch entry under Worldwide Organisations.

Involvement Volunteers Association Inc: P.O. Box 218, Port Melbourne, VIC 3207; ☎+61 (0)3-9646 9392; fax +61 (0) 3 9646 5504; e-mail ivworldwide@volunteering.or g.au; www.volunteering org.au.
IVI may be of particular assistance to those wanting to work with animals. For a fee of A$600, a networked programme of volunteer placements around Australia and the world can be arranged. There are conservation and farm-related placements in each state in Australia, with certain placements aimed at those with a background in biology. Current placements include: assisting bat research in Queensland, working at a zoo in South Australia, 'Dolphin Therapy' with disabled children and wild dolphins in Western Australia, and horse riding centres in the outback.

IVI also co-ordinates animal-related placements in Africa, Europe, the Americas and the Pacific Islands. A 'Multiple Placement Program' can be devised for up to one year, allowing the volunteer to gain a variety of experience with different types of projects in different countries during their journey. In the UK Involvement Volunteers can be contacted at IVUK, 7 Bushmead Avenue, Kingskerswell, Newton Abbot, Devon TQ12 5EN; ☎01803-872594; fax 01803-403154; e-mail: ivengland@volunteering.org.au.

Jirrahlinga Koala and Wildlife Sanctuary: P.O. Box 880 Geelong 3220, Australia; e-mail tehree@jirrahlinga.com.au; www.jirrahlinga.com.au.
Jirrahlinga is renowned for its work with sick and orphaned wildlife, which it restores to health and then releases back into the wild. Approximately ten volunteers annually. Volunteers should be aged 14+ and the usual stay is two weeks to a month, but longer stays are possible. Volunteers assist keepers with feeding, cleaning cages and compounds and general maintenance. Volunteers can arrange a placement direct with the organisation but must pay their own travel and accommodation and food costs. Apply to Tehree Gordon, Director, Jirrahlinga Koala and Wildlife Sanctuary, at the above address.

Koala Ecology
Investigating the ecology of a healthy koala population on the quiet volcanic island of St. Bees, Queensland. After proper training volunteers will be be assigned to rotate through koala capture, tracking and field ecology. Caught koalas have to be weighed, measured, tagged and some of them radio collared. Collared animals have to be tracked sometimes at night. Other work includes recording forest composition and collecting plant samples. Volunteers share rooms in mostly solar-powered cottage with mod cons. 12 days. £1,095.
Apply through Earthwatch (UK ☎01865-318838; www. earthwatch.org).

Oceania Research Project: The Oceania Project, P.O.Box 646 Byron Bay, NSW 2481;

☎+61 (0)2 6687 5677; fax +61 (0)2 6685 8998; e-mail trish.wally@oceania.org.au; www.oceania.org.au.
The Oceania Project is a non-profit research organisation that also aims to raise awareness and inform the public about whales and dolphins and the ocean environment generally. For more than eight years the Oceania Project has been carrying out a study, in conjunction with the Queensland Department of the Environment, of the abundance, distribution and behaviour of humpback whales at the Hervey Bay Marine Park, off the northeast coast of Queensland and in the Great Barrier Reef Marine Park. The Hervey Bay study takes place from a research vessel during the ten weeks of annual humpback migration from August to October.

Paying volunteers who join the programme for weekly periods (maximum is ten weeks) to, help to fund research. As well as helping with the on-board research, participants receive detailed education on cetaceans. There are very limited opportunities on the Great Barrier Reef programme.

Applicants need no particular skills but field experience in marine mammal research is useful. A committed interest in whales and dolphins, common sense and a willingness to work long hours with a dedicated research team are essential.

Volunteer fees are A\$650 per week (ages 14 to 18). Graduate or post-graduate students or teaching staff pay \$850 per week; otherwise \$950. Costs include on-board bunk accommodation, all meals, participation in the research, and educational programmes. Volunteers have to pay their own travel and insurance costs. Marine science students may be eligible for credits.

OneWorld Volunteer: Explorations in Travel Inc., 2458 River Road, Guilford, Vermont 05301 USA; ☎802-257-0152; fax 802-257-2784; e-mail info@oneworldvolunteer.org; www.oneworldvolunteer.org.
OneWorld Volunteer is a non-profit organisation which arranges individual volunteer placements in Australia (and also in Central America). Their placement in Australia involves working with fruit bats at a small rescue/rehab project in the rainforests of Queensland. Room and board is provided for US\$15 per day. Placements are available during the dry season (April to November). Applications to OneWorldVolunteer at the above address.

Tolga Bat Hospital: P.O. Box 685 Atherton 4883 Australia; tel/fax +61 7 4091 2683; e-mail jenny.maclean@iig.com.au; www.athertontablelands.com/bats.
Works with flying foxes or fruitbats and occasionally insect-eating microbats. Many of the adult bats have tick paralysis and many of the females have young. October to December usually sees 3-4000 adults and 1-2000 young. Other bats come in injured. The bat hospital is 6km from Atherton (small town) and 90km from Cairns. Volunteer jobs vary depending on the time of year. Minimum stay is a month. Longer preferred. 2-3 volunteers at a time. Accommodation provided for AUS\$15-30 per day including meals and laundry and limited internet access. Happy to help people find other bat volunteer work in other countries. Contact Jenny Maclean at the above address.

WWOOF Australia: Wwoof Pty Ltd, Buchan, Victoria 3885 Australia; ☎(03)5155-0218; fax (03) 5155 0342; wwoof@net-tech.com.au; www.wwoof.com.au.
Willing Workers on Organic Farms in Australia publishes four lists including a directory of over 1,300 host farms and properties all over Australia. Many of the hosts are involved in Landcare and Land for Wildlife organisations. Note not all hosts have animals.

ANIMAL, BIRD & WILDLIFE PROTECTION & WELFARE

The following organisations while mostly unable to offer vacancies themselves may be able to help with contacts.

Animals Australia: P.O. Box 1023, Collingwood, Victoria 3066; e-mail enquiries@a nimalsaustralia.org; www.animalsaustralia.org. Umbrella organisation that represents about 40 animal welfare, rights and conservation organisations. Promotes the causes of animal welfare and rights in Australia and New Zealand. Affiliated to the RSPCA in the UK. Publishes *Animals Today* magazine.

Animal Rescue (Inc): Ms Jenny Solhorst, P.O. Box 364, Deloraine, Tasmania, Australia 7304; ☎0368 1310; e-mail rataak@tassie.net.au.

Animal Societies Federation (NSW): P.O.Box 211, Gladesville, New South Wales, 2111 Australia. ☎02 9817 4892/fax 02 9817 4509.

Animal Welfare League of South Australia Inc. 1-19 Cormack Road, Wingfield, SA 5013; ☎08 8268 4188;fax 08 8268 9545; e-mail wecare@animalwelfare.com.au; www.an imalwelfare.com.au. Dedicated to providing the highest quality care to abandoned, injured, maltreated etc. domestic animals.

Australian Animal Protection Society (AAPS): Corner Chapel & Homeleigh Road, Keysborough, Victoria 3173; ☎03 9798 8044; fax 03 9769 0317. Promotes animal welfare and runs an animal shelter at Keysborough.

Australian Bird Study Association (ABSA): P.O. Box A313, Sydney South, NSW 1235; ☎02-9231 8166; fax 02 9251 7231. Founded in 1962 to support, study and conserve Australian birds. Annual meetings are held in capital cities on a rotating basis. Study expeditions are organised annually at different locations in Australia.

Australian Wildlife Protection Council (AWPC): Victoria Environmental Centre, 247 Flinders Lane, Melbourne, Victoria 3000; ☎03 9650 8326; fax 03 9650 3689. Organisation founded 1969 to prevent cruelty to, and/or extermination of the remaining species of wildlife. Involvement in wildlife rescue and other projects relevant to its aims.

Australians for Animals: Lot 14, Bilin Road, Myocum Byron Bay, NSW 2480; ☎02-6684 3769; e-mail sarnolds@byronit.com. Wildlife group formed in 1981 and specialising in the koala and cetaceans. Publishes bi-monthly newsletter.

Blue Cross Animals Society of Victoria: 26 Homestead Road, Wonga Park, Victoria 3136; ☎03 9722 1265. Concerned with the welfare of unwanted pets. Runs an animal shelter at Wonga Park and investigates allegations of cruelty.

Fund for Animals Ltd. Australia: 113 Mona Vale Road, Terrey Hills, NSW 2084; ☎02 9450 2122; fax 029450 2483. Aiming to save endangered species and halt the exploitation of animals in general. Develops, implements and contributes to conservation, preservation and protection programmes and animal welfare.

Queensland Wildlife Hospital Inc.: Lot 124 Cemetery Road, Cawarral, Qld 4702; ☎07 49279396. Founded in 1995 to provide care and sanctuary for injured wildlife, and wildlife welfare education in schools and elsewhere.

Royal Society for the Prevention of Cruelty to Animals (Victoria) Inc.: P.O. Box E369, Kingston, Australia, ACT 2604; ☎02 6282 8300; fax 02 6282 8311; e-mail rspca@rspca.org.au. Similar to the UK's RSPCA.

Victorian Animal Aid Trust: 62-80 Colchester Road, Kilsyth, Victoria 3137; ☎03-9725 5608; fax 03 9725 4485. To care for and house stray, abandoned and unwanted animals.

Worldwide Fund for Nature Australia: Michael Kennedy, GPO Box 528, Sydney, New South Wales, Australia 2001. ☎02 9299 6266; fax 02 9299 6656; www.faust@ozemail.com.au Part of the WWF international organisation. Highlights conservation problems in Australia and the South Pacific. Works to raise awareness, influence governments and fund projects conserve endangered species and habitats.

New Zealand

New Zealand is a predominantly rural country where sheep outnumber humans and work with animals is most likely to be agricultural or equine. There are also some conservation opportunities for volunteers.

ENTRY AND WORK REGULATIONS

Nationals of the UK can enter New Zealand without a visa for stays of up to six months. North Americans and Europeans can stay for up to three visa free months. These are the visitor regulations and are not for those intending to work there, although some visitors take casual jobs illegally.

WORK SCHEMES

The UK Citizens' Working Holiday Scheme allows up to 2,000 Britons aged 18 to 30 to take temporary jobs in New Zealand annually on a first come basis. To apply you need the relevant Application for Work Visa form, your UK passport, £60 fee, evidence of a return ticket and evidence of supporting funds of about £1,800. Sponsorship from a New Zealand citizen is not considered a substitute for adequate personal funds. A similar scheme is open to a much smaller quota of Irish nationals.

BUNAC's Work New Zealand programme provides those aged 18 to 30 the chance to find their own job and work in New Zealand for up to a year. There is a partner organisation in New Zealand (International Exchange Programs (IEP) to provide back-up and assistance. However, it is advisable to do some research and if possible make contact with an employer before you go as IEP will not necessarily have all the contacts for jobs with animals. Prices were not finalised at the time of press but were likely to be in the region of £1,700 for the whole package including return flights.

CIEE (☎ 020-7478 2020) operate an Internship New Zealand programme and a Work and Travel New Zealand programme. British students can undertake work experience internships lasting six months, which may be extended to 12 months, or they can take part in the working holiday visa scheme for up to 12 months. Participants must be enrolled in full-time further or higher education. Interns must find their own work placements in their field of study.

GETTING A WORK VISA

A cheaper option than BUNAC if you have relatives or contacts who can employ you, and/or you have special skills and a definite job offer from an employer in New Zealand. The employer must be prepared to prove to the Immigration Service that it is necessary to employ a foreigner (rather than a New Zealander). The High Commission's leaflet *Getting a Work Visa* gives further details. This option does not constitute a work permit in itself, but it facilitates obtaining one after arrival.

You can also make no advance preparation and apply for a work permit after arrival, at one of the seven Immigration Service offices in New Zealand. To do this you must obtain a definite job offer from an employer confirming the position offered, duration, evidence that you are suitably qualified and evidence that the employer has made efforts to fill the vacancy with a New Zealander. This is a hit and miss method as a work permit may or may not be granted and may be affected by a number of factors unknown to the outsider.

CONSERVATION

The New Zealand Department of Conservation (DOC) has a branch in each province of the country and may be worth contacting. Most of their projects involve habitat management and/or wildlife monitoring. One such, organised by the Picton branch (in the north of The North Island) is concerned with kiwi preservation. Paul Bagshaw and his girlfriend were working their way around the world volunteering on projects whenever they could. In New Zealand they contacted the Department of Conservation and found out about a conservation project for Kiwis, and in particular the Little Spotted Kiwi. Kiwis are endangered on the mainland because they are flightless and suffer from predators. There is an ongoing programme to remove them to small islands where they can propagate in safety.

Paul describes his experiences monitoring the Little Spotted Kiwi

We spent a week on an island (called Long Island) in the outer reaches of Queen Charlotte Sound. Although we got soaked on the boat trip there, we admired the stunning scenery of the Sound. There were six of us in the team including local people, which made it more interesting, and we had to bring our own tents and camping gear. We also prepared our meals from supplies brought over from the mainland. Our one luxury was a portaloo; there were no showers or any other facilities.

The object of the work is to regularly estimate the number of kiwis on the island to ascertain whether the population is flourishing. As the kiwi is nocturnal, we had to work in the small hours. Since it's dark, it's impossible to count them so we had to spread out and walk up a long slope listening for their call (a high pitched whistling noise). In the daytime they hide in burrows and foliage so it is very rare to see one. One night we heard one rustling around our camp, and my girlfriend went outside with a torch and actually managed to see it. She was so excited that she couldn't speak and resorted to wild gesticulation to describe its big feet and long beak.

We did see many other native birds including the New Zealand robin, silvereye, bellbird, fantail, weka and penguins – many at close quarters.

USEFUL ADDRESSES

The New Zealand Trust for Conservation Volunteers Inc: Three Streams, 343 SH 17, RD3 Albany, Auckland; tel/fax +64 9 415 9336; e-mail conservol@clear.net.nz; www .conservationvolunteers.org.nz. Registers and selects volunteers for projects organised by the New Zealand Department of Conservation, National Parks and Forest and Bird community groups, many of which involve protection and care of wildlife, especially endangered species. Applicants for working with animals are required to have some training and experience. A basic knowledge of English is necessary.

Conservation Volunteers: Department of Conservation at Nelson/Marlborough, Private Bag, Nelson (☎03-546-9355); or Private Bag, Christchurch (☎03-379 9758); or Otago and Southland P.O. Box 743, Invercargill (☎03-214-4589);or Private Bag, Hokitika. Address enquiries to The Co-ordinator.

Earthwatch
The dusky dolphins around Kaikoura Peninsula are a popular attraction for tourists. Earthwatch has a project studying their needs and how to balance them with the demands of tourism and fisheries management. Dusky Dolphins are a critical indicator of the state

of the ocean there. Teams take photos of individual dolphins, carries out behavioural observations, track them, take sloughed skin samples for DNA analysis of population structure. Involves alternating between hours on the water and land-based depending on the weather. Volunteers needed for 12-day stints from January to the first week of May inclusive. After that, please call for details of later teams. The costs are £1,170 including modern house accommodation with laundry and cooking facilities.

Applications through Earthwatch (see Worldwide Organisations or ☎01865-318838 in the UK.

Earthwise Living Foundation: P.O. Box 108, Thames 2815; ☎025-994204; www.elfnz.com. Places international visitors in a variety of ecological and conservation programmes which last 4-14 weeks. Alternatively you can have a work experience/ internship programme tailored to your wishes; useful if you wish to work in contact with animals. There is an arrangement fee of about US$500 plus additional living expenses. Many placements offer accommodation with a local family.

OTHER OPPORTUNITIES

VETS

It tends to be more usual for NZ vets to want to work outside New Zealand than for foreigners to want to go to NZ to practise. As you would expect, work is mainly agricultural. The professional authority is the Veterinary Council of New Zealand, P.O. Box 10-563, Wellington; ☎+64-4-473 9600; fax +64 4 473 8869.

FARM WORK

There are some affordable options such as the Farm Helpers in New Zealand (FHiNZ, 50 Bright Street, Eketahuna 5480, New Zealand; tel/fax 06-375 8955; www.fhinz.co.uk; www.fhinz@xtra.co.nz) which charges NZ$25 for membership including a list of addresses of about 175 farms throughout the country. The list is updated monthly, no experience is necessary, and about 4 hours a day of work is expected on participating farms in return for board and lodging. Visits can last days or months by agreement.

Willing Workers on Organic Farms (WWOOF, P.O. Box 1172 Nelson (tel/fax 03 544 9890; e-mail: wwoof@wwoof.co.nz; www.wwoof.co.nz) is expanding in New Zealand and there are currently about 500 farms on the list (send £13/US$20/NZ$40)which take farm helpers in return for board and lodging. Member farms are often smallholdings off the beaten track run by 'characters'.

HORSES

Racing: New Zealand offers the usual range of possibilities for those with equine experience and qualifications. Vacancies in NZ racing stables are sometimes advertised in the *Racing Post* (☎020-7293 3092). One wellknown racing stable which has advertised for staff is Wexford Stables at Matamata (fax +64 7 888 8780).

New Zealand Racing Industry Board: 106-110 Jackson Street, P.O. Box 38-899 Wellington Mail Centre; ☎+64 04 568 8866; fax +64 04 568 9817; e-mail nzrib@netlink.co.nz; www.racing-new-zealand.co.nz.

Useful Addresses Wellington area
Ashford Park Stud: Te Roto Road, Otaki (☎+64 6 364 7739). Trainer.
Waimanu Stud: Rahui Road, Otaki (☎+64 6 3645067).
Eddie Dickinson: 50 Tasman Road, Otaki Beach, Otaki (☎+6 364 6400. Trainer.
Ken Thomson: 64 Aotaki St, Otaki (☎+64 6 364 7189).

The following agency has a small number of requests for general stable staff in NZ:
A World of Experience, Equestrian Employment Agency: 52 Kingston Deverill, Warminster, Wiltshire; ☎01985-844102/844022 (Mon-Fri 9am-5pm; www.equijobshop.com).

Horse Charity & Trust

The International League for the Protection of Horses (New Zealand): affiliated to the British ILPH, the NZ league investigates equine welfare complaints and approves riding and trekking centres. Work opportunities may be found at ILPH centres listed in *Where to Ride in New Zealand* booklet and on the website www.horsetalk.co.nz.ilph rescues and rehabilitates equines discovered to be at risk. Works to educate, i.e. reduce cruelty caused by ignorance. Can be contacted through The Administrator, ILPH, P.O. Box 10-368, Hamiton; ☎ +64 7 849 0678; fax +64 7 849 9034.

The Wild Horse Trust: c/o The Secretary, P.O. Box 385, Wellington; ☎+64 4 472 8691; fax +64 4 472 8639; e-mail sigmawgtn@extra.co.nz website www.nzsail.co.nz/wildhorses/ The WH Trust incorporates members of lobby and interest groups wanting to safeguard the future of the Kaimanawa Wild Horse herd, including the Maori landowners of the area. The aim is to agree a permanent structure for the management of stock in cooperation with the Department of Conservation.

ANIMAL WELFARE & CONSERVATION ORGANISATIONS

The following organisations may not have vacancies themselves but might be able to help with contacts.

Humane Society of New Zealand (INC): c/o The Secretary, 462 Manukau Road, Epsom, P.O. Box 29060, Greenwoods Corner, Epsom; ☎+64 9 630 0510. Provides sanctuary for mistreated animals and offers a referral system for owners looking to re-home their pets. Also provides financial assistance for owners unable to afford neutering for their pets.

The Rare Breeds Conservation Society of New Zealand: A charity that strives to maintain genetic diversity in livestock by promoting the conservation of breeds, which have reached low numbers. Can be contacted through the Secretary (P.O. Box 20116, Bishopdale, Christchurch) or the Chairman, (Willowbank Wildlife Reserve, 60 Hussey Road, Christchurch 8005; ☎+64 3 359 6226; fax +64 3 359 6212).

The Royal New Zealand Society for the Prevention of Cruelty to Animals: c/o 1 Rankin Avenue, New Lynn, P.O. Box 15-349, Auckland 1232; ☎+64 9 827 6094;fax +64 9 827 0784.

Worldwide Fund for Nature New Zealand (WWF-NZ): Botanic Garden, Glenmore Street (P.O. Box 6237) Wellington; ☎499 2930.

Royal Forest & Bird Protection Society of NZ Inc: 172 Taranaki Street, P.O. Box 631; Wellington; ☎(04)385 7374; fax (04)385 7373; e-mail office@wn.forest-bird.org.nz; www.forestandbird.org.nz.

Elsewhere

Africa & The Indian Ocean

Mention working with animals in Africa, and people tend to think in terms of game wardens and rangers. However, there are also opportunities for zoologists and vets. Veterinary, farriery, and husbandry consultants are also needed to help with farming projects in developing countries. The Middle East, despite its oil wealthy elite, still has many people existing at subsistence level who depend on overworked animals for transport, farm work and income from tourists. Some organisations involved with these types of work are given below.

BOTSWANA

Lion Research Programme
'Hands on' programme in association with researchers working in the Okavango delta. Participants are involved with research such as tracking a pride of lions through the night while they are hunting. 11 days costing from £2,625. Apply through Discovery initiatives (The Travel House, 51 Castle Street, Cirencester, Gloucestershire GL7 1QD; ☎01285-643333; www.discoveryinitiatives.com).

EGYPT

Sinai Wildlife Clinic (SWC)
SWC is concerned with wildlife and environmental conservation and operates wildlife rehabilitation centres in the Sinai peninsula, and human health programmes amongst the nomadic bedouin tribes. Volunteers are needed year round. Specifically, doctors of medicine, veterinarians, conservationists, nurses, environmental teachers and students and post graduates in appropriate disciplines. Volunteers must be able to function in hot weather as much of the work takes place in desert conditions. Knowledge of Arabic is useful. English essential. Medical doctors and veterinarians pay no participation fee. All others pay US$300 a month for which board and lodging is provided.
   Applications to: Sinai Wildlife Clinic,
c/o Domina Club and Hotel, Coral Bay, South Sinai, Sharm El Sheikh, Egypt; ☎+20 62 601 610; e-mail wildlifeclinic@sinainet.com.eg

GHANA

Raleigh International
Raleigh's ten-week expeditions in Ghana include:
Volunteers work with the Wildlife Division in Mole National Park, home to over 90 mammal species, including elephants, baboons and hyena. Volunteers collect base data on elephants and analyse rates of elephant dung decay as part of a study to assess the elephant population.
   Volunteers also work on the western coast of Ghana to help protect the endangered marine turtle population by recording turtle numbers and building hatcheries to protect the eggs.
   Contact the organisation direct: (Raleigh House, 27 Parsons Green Lane, London SW6

4HZ; ☎ 020-7371 8585; fax 020-7371 5116; e-mail info@raleigh.org.uk; www.raleigh international.org).

Short-term Veterinary Placements
Placements are located in Accra. Volunteers work alongside local vets, treating farm and domestic animals. Volunteers could soon become involved in vaccinations, operations, laboratory work, post-mortems, meat inspections and routine treatments. Note that veterinary medicine in Ghana is very basic: equipment is sterilised in hot water (when available) and minor operations such as castration are carried out under local anaesthetic while the owner holds down the animal. Not for the squeamish. £1,795 includes food, accommodation, insurance back-up staff services and travel arrangements. Further details from Teaching and Projects Abroad (Gerrard House, Rustington, West Sussex BN16 1AW; ☎ 01903-859911; fax 01903-785779; e-mail info@teaching-abroad.co.uk; www.teaching-abroad.co.uk

KENYA
Europe-Africa Songbird Migration
Assist a Danish research team at one of three banding stations for migratory songbirds that have arrived from Europe at the Mwea Natural Reserve in Kenya. Volunteers set up and patrol mist nets to trap the birds, which volunteers help to extract from the nets and weigh, measure and blood test them. The data will be used to establish the habitat needs of the songbirds i.e. to ensure that enough habitat remains en route to feed them for their incredible migratory journey. Cost is £1,395 for two weeks. Accommodation is in luxury, safari-style tent camp with toilets and showers and catered meals.

Apply through Earthwatch (UK ☎ 01865-318838; info@earchwatch.org).

MADAGASCAR
Earthwatch
Nearly 80 per cent of Madagascar's plants and animals are found nowhere else. One of Earthwatch's projects for 2003 is to study two of Madagascar's most endangered lemurs. Volunteers need to be fit to collect data on the behaviour of two groups of the largest lemurs in the Ranomafana National Park. Working deep in primary rainforest, volunteers will follow one lemur group for five days of the two week duration. The price is £1,495. Accommodation is at a field research station camping on pre-built platforms with facilities (running water and showers) on site. Meals based on local staples (rice and beans, steamed vegetables, eggs and fruit) are prepared by a local cook.

Applications to Earthwatch (see entry in Worldwide Organisations or telephone 01865-318838 in the UK).

MOROCCO
Society for the Protection of Animals Abroad (SPANA)
SPANA estimates it treats over 300,000 working animals annually in North Africa (Algeria, Tunisia and Morocco) and the Middle East (Jordan and Syria). It also runs an education programme aimed at teaching animal owners and children, the principles of care and respect for their animals. In total throughout these areas it has 18 animal refuges and some mobile veterinary clinics. It has openings for a few qualified veterinary nurses (qualified or in training) in Morocco for July and August. Accommodation provided but all other costs (travel, food, living expenses borne by the volunteers).

Contact SPANA, 14 John Street, London WC1N 2EB; ☎ 020-7831 3999; fax 020-7831 5999; www.spana.org.

NAMIBIA
Population Ecology and Long-term Monitoring of Namibian Cheetah

Expedition work organised through Biosphere. Emphasis is on capture activities (capture, radio-collaring and release), radio-tracking, looking for cheetah tracks and hide-based observation at waterholes and play trees. Location is Central Namibia, near Omitara, about 120km East of Windhoek. Dates for 2003 are 25th Oct-7 Nov, 9-21 Nov and 23 Nov-5 Dec. Volunteer team members can join for two, four or six weeks within the above dates. Cost is £1,250 per two weeks. No experience or scientific knowledge necessary. Observation skills will be taught. Land Rover drivers must have full, clean licence and be prepared to undergo offroad and safety training (as part of the expedition).

Further details from Biosphere Expeditions, Sprat's Water, near Carlton Colville, The Broads National Park, Suffolk, NR33 8BP; ☎01502-583085; e-mail info@biosphere-expeditions.org or www.biosphere-expeditions.org; e-mail in Germany: deutschland@biosphere-expeditions.org

Raleigh International

Project organisers Raleigh International are involved in three projects in Namibia which take self-funding volunteers:

Working in the Waterberg Plateau Park in North Central Namibia on fundamental conservation work, volunteers conduct full-moon game counts and rhino treks with rangers on patrols to assist with research to protect the endangered black and white rhino.

Working with the Rare and Endangered Species Trust (REST) volunteers construct bird viewing hides and aviaries as part of a conservation programme to preserve the endangered Cape Griffon vultures (Gyps Coprotheres).

Working in Khaudom National Park in North East Namibia, home to elephants, lions, leopards, cheetahs and giraffe, along with the endangered species of roan antelope and wild dogs, volunteers help to construct game-viewing hides and basic facilities for the anti-poaching unit.

Contact the organisation direct: (Raleigh House, 27 Parsons Green Lane, London SW6 4HZ; ☎020-7371 8585; fax 020-7371 5116; e-mail info@raleigh.org.uk; www.raleigh international.org).

NIGERIA & CAMEROON

Wisconsin Regional Primate Research Center

The WRPRC has volunteer primate sanctuary supervisor positions at the Drill Rehabilitation & Breeding Center in S.E. Nigeria, and in the Limbe Wildlife Centre in S.W. Cameroon. The Nigerian project has 70 drills and 16 chimpanzees. Emphasis is on conservation and captive breeding with the aim of protected release into the wild. The project is also working the creation of a wildlife sanctuary in 150 square km populated by drill, gorilla, chimps and other species.

The Cameroon project involves the conversion of the former Limbe Zoo to a sanctuary and education centre. It houses gorillas, chimps, drills, several other primate species and other animals.

Volunteers can be in any or all of the following fields depending on staffing at the time: supervision and training of local staff, veterinary, lab work, general animal husbandry, enclosure construction/maintenance, book keeping, quarterly reports, education projects, equipment maintenance, liaison with governmental officers, fundraising and research. Applicants are expected to have an interest in primate and wildlife conservation and preferably experienced in primate/wildlife care. Preference will be given to those with previous African or developing world experience. French fluency is useful for Cameroon. Minimum of one year. In Nigeria all in-country expenses are met. In Cameroon housing is provided and other expenses covered as funding allows. Volunteers pay their own air fares and insurance. More information on the website http://members.xoom.com/Limbe.

Contact for applications is Patricia Gleason, 3000 Lee Highway, B201, Arlington, VA, USA 22201; ☎ 703-243-3003; e-mail p_gleason@hotmail.com

SOUTH AFRICA

African Experience
Offers wildlife volunteer work on the biggest game farms. Work with wild animals, hand rearing baby lions, translocation of wild cheetahs, helping preserve endangered species, bottle-feeding baby baboons, cleaning and maintaining animal enclosures, learning about conservation and working closely with African rural communities. Also volunteer work with poor, sick and terminally ill African children. Average 75-80 volunteers per year. Volunteer period is from 2 weeks up to 12 weeks plus. Average length is 4 weeks. All year. Accommodation is provided and prices start from US$200 per week.

For further details contact African Experience directly at 21a Ashley Drive, Gillitts 3620 Kwa-Zulu Natal, South Africa; ☎ +27 82 433 2319; fax +27 31 705 3635; e-mail louise@african-experience.co.za; www.african-experience.co.za

Bio-Experience
Bio-Experience was formed in 2001 and aims at aiding Nature Reserves and Wildlife Rehabilitation Centres to become self-sufficient through funding, job creation and hands-on volunteers to assist with various projects including five wildlife rehabilitation centres. Volunteers can get involved with cage cleaning and wildlife feeds as well as other tasks. International volunteers are recruited from around the world and pay for their experience and so help fund the various projects. Volunteers can stay from a month to a year and can participate in more than one project. Unlike many organisations, Bio-experience recruits volunteers locally as well. Many locals cannot afford the $600 all told per month that volunteers pay and so are sponsored by the various institutions.

Potential participants should contact Ms. Dreyer on +27 11 964 1900 or e-mail her on natanya@cybertrade.co.za

Centre for Dolphin Studies
In 2002 the Centre for Dolphin Studies in Plettenberg Bay, started a volunteer programme to help generate funds to support their research programmes. Volunteers pay a weekly fee, which includes board and lodging. Research students under Prof. Peter Cockcroft, South Africa's leading dolphin and whale specialist, manage up to four volunteers at time. Volunteers should have a background in zoological, biological or marine sciences and have a keen interest in cetaceans. Volunteers are involved in a number of activities, the most popular of which is recording sightings of whales and dolphins from the research boat. There is also administration work involving filing and categorising of gathered data. Volunteers with an interest can attend post mortems of beached and stranded whales and dolphins. Accommodation is provided in a cottage on Professor Cockcroft's farm. Breakfast and vegetarian suppers are provided and ingredients to make sandwiches for lunch each day. Volunteers are expected to work five days per week and there are plenty of things to see and do on days off.

South Africans only should contact The Centre for Dolphin studies, Postal address: P.O. Box 1856, Plettenberg Bay 6600; Street address: Centre for Dolphin Studies, 17 Laridae, Challenge Drive, Plettenburg Bay, 6600, South Africa; tel/fax +27 (044) 533 6185; e-mail cdswhale@worldonline.co.za; www.dolphinstudies.co.za. Overseas applicants should go through Travellers Worldwide (see entry below).

Dolphin Research
Programme of research on dolphins and whales based in Pletternberg Bay on the southern coast about 500km east of Cape Town. One of the major priorities is to educate the local people. Another of the Centre's activities is the rescue and rehabilitation of sea

mammals after oil spills great and small. Field studies, administration and tour escorting are other likely duties. Paying volunteers can arrange to participate through Travellers Worldwide. The cost for 2 months is £1,595 for up to 2 months or £1,095 for a month. Flights from £650.

For further details contact Travellers Worldwide, 7 Mulberry Close, Ferring, West Sussex, BN12 5HY; ☎01903-700478; e-mail info@travellersworldwide.com.

Micofe Equestrian Centre
Situated in the African Bushveld. Surrounded by wildlife, students are offered the opportunity to work with and train horses, learn different skills such as artificial insemination, and touring South Africa at the end of each course. Places to visit include the Drakensburg Mountains, Kruger National Park, Cape Town and Durban.

The Equestrian Centre has a variety of breeds including American saddlebred, Arabian, Friesian, Appaloosa and thoroughbred. Students are assigned their own horse. Enrolment can be for three, six or twelve months and the all inclusive cost is £685 per month (includes self catering accommodation, all provisions and necessities, course materials, certificates and end of course tours).

For more details contact Annemie Coetzee (e-mail fc@pharmarama.co.za).

Phinda Big Cat Project
Volunteer field assistants needed to help with long-term research on big cats in the Phinda Private Game Reserve in northern KwaZulu-Natal Province. In 2003 volunteers will be helping to track radio-collared leopards and fit collars to new leopards. There is no guarantee you will handle a sedated leopard as capture numbers vary on each trip.

Accommodation is provided in rooms with two sharing as are meals. The work is not physically demanding but entails long hours which can be exhausting and there is a lot of waiting quietly in the open research vehicle. Work begins at 5am and finishes at 11am then from 5pm until well into the night or early morning. Chance to see many other kinds of typical game reserve animals and birds.

For more details contact Dr. Luke Hunter, Carnivore Chairman, IUCN Reintroduction Specialist Group, Dept. of Biological Sciences, Monash University, P.O. Box 18, Victoria, 3800 Australia; ☎+61 3 9905-5602; fax +61 3 9905-5613; e-mail luke.hunter @sci.monash.edu.au.

Pongola Poort Game Park
Pongola Game Reserve was founded in 1894 and is home to a vast array wildlife including over 40 white rhino. Travellers Worldwide can arrange for paying volunteers can get involved in fascinating and varied work sometimes done on foot, sometimes from a vehicle. Tasks include trapping, photographing and releasing small mammals, observing and recording species of birds, plants, elephants etc. and entering data on a spreadsheet. Those experienced with handling snakes and reptiles can collect, photograph and release snakes and reptiles. The cost includes accommodation and meals; the latter sometimes self catered.

Cost £1,795 for up to 2 months. Flights from £700. Extra months £550 each. Apply to Travellers Worldwide, 7 Mulberry Close, Ferring, W. Sussex BN12 5HY; info@travelle rsworldwide.com

Ranger Training Courses
Ranger training courses can be arranged through the British company Discovery Initiatives, which arranges adventure holidays and supports conservation. In addition to treks and tours in remote places it organises a twelve-day introduction to game rangering and safari course in Timbavati, a wilderness reserve, adjacent to Kruger National Park in South Africa. The hands on course is taught by a leading ranger, and focuses on

conservation, ecology, tracking, anatomy, diseases, animal rehabilitation, handling and human impact. No previous experience is necessary. Courses are run once a month from March to November and cost £1,625 (US$1675) per person.

Further information from Discovery Initiatives (The Travel House, 51 Castle Street, Cirencester, Glos. GL7 1QD; ☎01285-643333; e-mail enquiry@discoveryinitiatives.com; www.discoveryinitiatives.com).

Ranger courses can also be arranged direct: if you have a lot of patience, telephone the South Africa Tourist Board head office in Pretoria (+27 12 347 0600) for details.

Rhino and Elephant Foundation

The Foundation was started by Clive Walker, a respected conservationist who is also chair of the African Rhino Owners' Association. As many as half the rhinos in Africa are in privately-owned game reserves. Although most of the reserves employ locals for whom employment is a lifeline, it may be possible to work on one temporarily, particularly if you have skills you can pass on or want to do some useful research.

Try contacting the Rhino and Elephant Foundation, P.O.Box 381, Bedfordview 2008, South Africa. Also worth trying might be the the rhino rehabilitation expert Karen Trendler, (Wildcare Centre for the Rehabilitation of Wild Animals, P.O.Box 15121, Lynn East, Pretoria 0039).

Southern African National Foundation for the Conservation of Coastal Birds (SANCCOB)

Works to rehabilitate coastal birds particularly the African Penguin, which has declined drastically from a combination of factors including pollution from major oil spills. Volunteers are needed to rescue and clean these large, strong birds that do not like being handled, at the organisation's centre, 20 km north of Cape Town. Minimum volunteer stay is two weeks and the maximum is three months. Volunteers join a team and learn skills in which ever area they are interested. Estimated cost per day is $40-$50 and volunteers must pay their own board and lodging costs.

Contact SANCCOB, PO Box 11116 Bloubergrant, 7443 Cape Town; ☎+27 21 557 61 55/6; fax +27 21 557 88 04; e-mail sanccob@netactive.co.za.

White Shark Research Studies

Offers the opportunity to get actively involved in a White Shark study for 12 days based at Bansbaai. Involves looking for the sharks by boats equipped with dive cages. Participate in data and observation collecting with the research teams. Departures monthly; cost £2020. Apply through Discovery Initiatives (☎01285-643333; e-mail enquiry@discoveryinitiatives.com

Wild at Heart

Wildlife clinic that rescues and rehabilitates African mammals and birds. Is also involved in about 15 projects in southern Africa. Currently recruits over 1000 volunteers a year. Needs volunteers with a commitment to helping injured and neglected wildlife. Ideal for those pursuing a veterinary career. Work with wildlife rehabilitation specialists and the South African Parks staff. Duties include vet work, hand rearing baby animals, research, capture and release. No day is the same. No experience needed. English language essential. Transport, transfers, training, certificates all provided. Minimum stay is three weeks, year round. Long-term positions up to a year can be arranged. Volunteers stay at a house near the Clinic at a cost of US$300 (about £200) with board and lodging included.

Contact is Claude Fourie, Wild at Heart, 15 Plantation Road, Hillcrest, 3610 Kwazulu/Natal, South Africa; tel/fax +27 31 765 1818; e-mail claude@wah.co.za; www.wah.co.za/volunteer.asp

Other Useful Addresses

Animal Aid Network of South Africa: Jacqlyn Edge, 1301 Lancaster Marlborough Park, Bath Road, Claremont 7700, South Africa; ☎+27 21 641 562; e-mail info@animals.co.za Regularly updated comprehensive website of all South Africa's animal organisations. Contact Jacqlyn Edge.

Kalahari Raptor Center: Chris or Bev, P.O.Box 1386, Kathu, Northern Cape, South Africa; ☎ +53 712 3536; info@raptor.co.za Cares for injured and orphaned birds of prey and small mammals. Runs educational outreach programme. Contacts: Chris and Bev. May be worth asking if they need volunteers. Expect to pay your way.

SWAZILAND

Project Rhino Rescue

Volunteers are needed all year round for this project in the Mkhaya Game Reserve. Work includes daily monitoring of endangered species (black and white rhinos, elephant, giraffe, leopards etc), nightly support in detecting poaching activity from watchtowers, animal surveys and generally supporting the activities of rangers in the reserve, helping in the research into the wildlife of the area. When there are rescued rhinos in temporary captivity, volunteers may help with food preparation.Volunteers can stay from two to five weeks (the fifth week is free). Costs from £570 for two weeks to £780 for four weeks. Included in the price are basic accommodation including mosquito nets and local food (which is monotonous for westerners but can supplemented at own expense). There is shared preparation of meals.

Applications to Europe Conservation Italia in Rome, Italy (☎+39 6 474 1241; +39 6 4744671; e-mail eco.italia@agora.stm.it. You can also apply through The Ecovolunteer Network in the Netherlands (see Worldwide Organisations for internet and postal address etc.)

UGANDA & CONGO

HELP Congo

HELP is a primate sanctuary which welcomes volunteers to work in the chimpanzee sanctuary and release site. Volunteers' work includes feeding and monitoring the behaviour/health of the chimps which are living free on islands, helping maintain the sanctuary food garden (crops for chimpanzee food), educating and raising awareness of chimpanzee and other wildlife protection, collecting data on the local flora and fauna.

Volunteers should stay a minimum of three months and a contribution of £200 per month is charged which includes food, local travel, gas and cleaning products. Accommodation is provided free. By special arrangement, shorter stays are possible. If however, the stay is less than one month, a contribution of £400 per month is required. Volunteers need to bring pocket money of about £30 per month and pay their own airfare. Volunteers muck in generally at camp helping to keep it clean and participating in communal tasks necessary to keep the project going. The sanctuary is isolated and without radio or telephone.

Further details from and application to Sophie Descamps, Relais Help Congo France, Les Sophoras, Bat B, 10 Allée des Sophoras, 34700 Montpellier, France; tel/fax 04 67 47 08 04; e-mail descamps@mnet.fr; www.cybsnack.mnet.fr/gorilla.htm Address in Congo is:

Habitat Ecologique et Liberté des Primates(HELP), Congo Chimp Sanctuary, Habitat Ecologique et Liberté des Primates, B.P. 335 Pointe Noire, Congo; fax 01 5301 69 95; e-mail help.congo@cg.celtelplus.com; www.help-primates.org

Jane Goodall Institute (UK)

The internationally renowned Insitute was founded in 1989 to support and expand research into the behaviour of chimpanzees whose range in Africa is becoming increasingly limited. Its work involves both conservation of rainforest habitats including tree planting, education and building sanctuaries where rescued chimpanzees, which have been illegally caught, can be kept in semi-wild conditions. There are projects in Congo, Uganda, Tanzania and Kenya.

At the time of press the Institute did not wish to broadcast a need for volunteers for chimp sanctuaries. However the Institute remains a world authority on chimpanzees and anyone interested in working with chimps may need their advice at some time. The UK headquarters are at Orchard House, 61-67 Commercial Road, Southampton, Hants S015 1GG; ☎012380-335660; fax 012380-335661; e-mail info@janegoodall.org.uk; www.janegoodall.org.uk

In Uganda: (P.O. Box 4187, Kampala; ☎+256 41 241574; fax +256 41 236852).

ZAMBIA

Chimfunshi Wildlife Orphanage Trust-Chimp Rehabilitation Programme

Chingola, Zambia; fax +260 2 311293. Chimp rehabilitation programme. May be worth contacting to see if they need volunteers after that. Write or fax Mrs Sheila Siddel.

Munda Wanga Wildlife Park and Sanctuary

Munda Wanga is a charitable trust incorporating botanic gardens, wildlife park and animal sanctuary. Its main aims are environmental education and captive breeding and release programmes for endangered species including the African wild dog. It is situated about 15km from Lusaka. The wild animal sanctuary is the only one in Zambia that accepts pretty much any species. Volunteers (about 10 per year) are needed to for daily running of Munda Wanga. Duties include monitoring animals, providing visitor tours, working with school groups, fundraising, hand-rearing orphaned animals, cleaning enclosures, handing out flyers, building and maintenance etc. Usual volunteer period is 3 weeks but two is possible. Extensions may be possible depending on factors at the time. Basic accommodation is provided with bathroom and cooking facilities. Cost to volunteer is US£600 (GB£400) for food and accommodation, trips to wildlife lodges and airport transfers. Volunteers' contributions are poured back into the projects.

Further details from Emma Stone, Munda Wanga, P.O. Box 38267, Kafue Road, Lusaka, Zambia; ☎+260 1 278 456; fax +260 1 278 529; e-mail environment@zamnet.zm or emzstone@hotmail.com.

Asia

As with other developing parts of the world, opportunities for well paid work in countries such as Malaysia, Indonesia, Sri Lanka, Thailand, Vietnam and Mongolia are rare. The exception until recently was Japan, which at the time of press was experiencing its highest unemployment for 50 years. However, there are possibilities to work with animals as volunteers in a range of Asian and southeast Asian countries.

BORNEO & INDONESIA

Earthwatch

Counting and observing Orangutans, proboscis monkeys, macaques and gibbons in the Tanjung Puting National Park, Kalimantan (Borneo), Indonesia. Mornings and evenings volunteers observe and count endangered species by foot or canoe. Cost of £975 for 11 days includes accommodation in a rustic dormitory at the field camp. Electricity is solar generated and there is no running water. Meals are prepared by a cook.

Applications to Earthwatch (see entry in Worldwide Organisations or ☎01865-318838 in the UK.

Orangutan Foundation's Volunteer Programme

The volunteer programme does not involve direct contact with orangutans, but as volunteers participate in hands-on conservation fieldwork in a national park, they will see orangutans in their natural habitat. The programme consists of four teams of up to 12 people per team. Each team runs for a set period of six weeks from April through to November. The main target area of the programme is Camp Leakey, the historical research site of Dr. Biruté Galdikas, situated within Tanjung Puting National Park. Here work will involve the continuation of a Renovation and Expansion project started in 2000. Proposed activities include repairing existing structures, increasing boundaries of the study area, trail cutting, installing walkways and signs, and developing facilities for conservation education and wildlife appreciation. Taking part in the volunteer programme is an opportunity for adventurous individuals to support a dedicated conservation organisation and to experience the magic of the rainforests.

The Orangutan Foundation organises and runs the volunteer programme in an environmentally and socially responsible way. Volunteers are there to support the work of the Orangutan Foundation whose main aim is to protect the orangutan and its habitat. As such volunteers will not have direct contact with the orangutans. Local people are employed to work on the projects and with the volunteers, and the services of the nearby town are used as much as posssible. There is a charge of £470 made by the Orangutan foundation for participation and you must pay your own travel costs to and from Borneo.

Further details from the Orangutan Foundation, 7 Kent Terrace, London NW1 4RP; ☎020-7724 2912; e-mail info@orangutan.org.uk; www.orangutan.org.uk

Pulau Banyak Foundation – Environmental Programme

At the time of press we heard that that the following project in Indonesia may need volunteers for their conservation and development programme for the Pulau Banyak archipelago, coast of Aceh Selatan, Sumatra, in northern Indonesia. The programme includes measuring, guarding and some tagging of turtles on Bangkaru Island, bird surveys and tropical bee-keeping. Applications at any time of year for one month minimum stay. Cost is $1000 per month including accommodation and food (own bedding required) and local transportation. Transport from Medan, bus to Singkil and boat to islands for arrival date is not included.

Applications to Pulau Banyak Volunteering, FAO A Steeman MSc, Pulau Banyak Foundation, P.O. Box 1021, Medan, Sumatera Utara; tel/fax +62 61 814 644; e-mail pbanyak@ibm.net.

JAPAN

The following animal welfare organisations may be able to help with contacts for volunteering:

Japan Society for the Prevention of Cruelty to Animals (JSPCA): 3rd Floor, Odakyu Minami Aoyama Building, 7-8-1 Minami Aoyama 7-Chome, Minatoku, Tokyo 106; ☎03-3409-1821; fax 03-3409 1868.

Japanese Society for the Humane Care of Animals (JSHCA): Shin Aoyama Building, West 23F, 1-1-1 Minami Aoyama, Minato-ku, Tokyo 107; ☎03-3475-1601; fax 03-3475-1604.

Japan Animal Welfare Society (JAWS): 7th Floor Daigo Tanizawa Building, 3-1-38 Moto Azabu, Minatu-Ku, Tokyo 106-8663; ☎03-3405 5681; fax 03-3478 1945.

MALAYSIA

Earthwatch

Tagging green turtles at Chendor, Pahang (north of Kuala Lumpur) as part of a conservation project. Egg harvesting by Malaysians, who prize the rich source of protein they provide, has reduced the turtle population by 60 per cent in 50 years. Volunteers are needed to patrol the nesting beaches, to record turtle sizes, markings and nesting sites and mark individuals with titanium tags. Egg teams then relocate the nest to the safety of the hatchery and carry out incubation experiments to determine optimum hatching conditions.

Another team of volunteers works at the more rustic site of Pulau Redang where hatching conditions are observed without moving the nests. Volunteers can choose which site they wish to work at.

The stay is two weeks during the period from the beginning of August to the end of September. Costs are £1,150. The Chedor site accommodation in the Turtle Centre has all conventional facilities. Pulau Redang is reachable only by boat and has a solar shower, outdoor cooking and no mains electricity. Dinner at either site is planned and prepared communally using local produce.

Apply through Earthwatch (see entry under Worldwide Organisations).

Pinnewala elephant orphanage

Raleigh International

Raleigh International are involved in projects in conjunction with the Worldwide Fund for Nature and Sabah Parks.

A typical project may involve constructing bird-viewing hides at Likas bird sanctuary, an important breeding site for many coastal birds including the purple heron.

Contact the organisation direct: (Raleigh House, 27 Parsons Green Lane, London SW6 4HZ; ☎020-7371 8585; fax 020-7371 5116; e-mail info@raleigh.org.uk; www.raleigh international.org).

MONGOLIA

Przewalski Horse Reintroduction

At the Hustain Nuruu Reserve in Mongolia, an experiment is underway to reintroduce the Przwalski horse (a.k.a. Takhi) a sturdy looking beast with a thick neck, stripe down its back and zebra stripes on its legs, to semi-wild conditions. The last truly wild takhi died in 1969, after being hunted to extinction in its native habitat. There were however some in private collections from which the present stock is derived.

Volunteers are needed to help monitor and observe the herds on the steppes. This may involve several trips a day on horseback with a Mongolian ranger.

Accommodation is in traditional Mongolian tents with basic, but adequate facilities and Mongolian meals are cooked on a communal basis.

Volunteers are expected to stay for a minimum of three weeks for which the cost, which includes meals and accommodation but not travel, is £695. Extra weeks are £230 each. Tourist visa is extra. Transfers from Ulaanbatar included. Volunteers should be able to ride.

Applications to Eco Volunteers in the Netherlands (see Worldwide Organisations).

SRI LANKA

Home and Abroad Animal Welfare

Home and Abroad works with stray dogs and cats in Negombo, Sri Lanka. They have a veterinary clinic where numerous dogs are bought to be spayed and neutered, vaccinated against rabies and TVD (venereal disease), and mange. The charity also carries out educational work in schools. Volunteers are needed for 2-3 weeks at a time to work in Sri Lanka usually in December, April and July. Volunteers have to pay their own flights and expenses. However, if they help fundraise, half the amount raised will go towards their flight. Accommodation is included in the amount charged for the flight. It is not essential to have qualifications/experience but volunteers should be confident with animals.

For further details of volunteering in Sri Lanka and in the UK contact: Miss Janice Down (Home and Abroad Animal Welfare), 39 Albert Street, Fleet, Hampshire GU13 9RL; ☎01252-629044; e-mail home-and-abroad@yahoo.com. Volunteers can also help without going abroad by assisting with activities from public relations to administration and fundraising.

Kudimbigala Bird Sanctuary

Situated 25 km south of Arugam Bay via Panama and further south Yala East National Park, home to many wild elephants. Run by the Department of Wildlife Conservation (DWLC), 18 Gregory's Road, Colombo 07, Sri Lanka (www.dwlc.lk). The DWLC's assistant director of of Wildlife Health and Management is Tharaka Prasad (tharaka@dwlc.lk). It may be worth asking if they need volunteers; almost certainly you would have to pay your own costs including food and accommodation.

Pinnewala Elephant Orphanage

The Sri Lankan elephant is a sub-species of the Asian elephant and is used in Sri Lanka for moving timber in forests inaccessible to vehicles. Many elephants were badly frightened and killed, deliberately or otherwise as result of the country's civil war. The Pinnewala Orphanage was set up by the government for 50 or more injured and orphaned elephants. It might be worth enquiring if volunteers are needed. You can stay nearby at Elephant View Hotel (Elephant Bath Road, Pinnewala; ☎+94 (0)35 65292/3; fax +94-35 65283).

Sea Turtles Project

There are various turtle nesting sites along the coast near Bentota, south of the capital Colombo in south-west Sri Lanka and conservationists are trying to protect them from development, pollution and disturbance. The ruse is to buy the eggs from local fisherman to discourage them from selling them in the food market (which though illegal is rife). The eggs are then reburied in a protected site until they hatch. Then the hatchlings are released at night to reduce the danger to them from predators. You can take part in this operation in return for a contribution to the project's funds (☎+94 (0)34 75850).

Useful Addresses

Someone who may be able to help with advice and information on animal related contacts in Sri Lanka is Janice Down (Home & Abroad Animal Welfare, 39 Albert Street, Fleet, Hampshire, GU13 9RL; ☎01252-629044; e-mail R.E.Lee@reading.ac.uk). She was urgently looking for volunteers to help with rescuing street dogs in Negombe, Sri Lanka.

Animals' Welfare and Protection Association: 59, Gregory's Road, Colombo 07, Sri Lanka; ☎+94 1 575 325 325; fax +94 1 575 696 71.

THAILAND

Ayutthaya Elephant Camp

Volunteers are needed year round for a minimum of three weeks and a maximum of 3 months to work with elephants. Must take initial training with elephants and an examination before working with them. Those with veterinary or animal science skills are especially welcome, but those with no particular skills are also considered. Two volunteers per year are accepted. Board and lodging provided in a communal bunkhouse. Cost of US$750 per month includes accommodation. Health insurance is compulsory. Two other affiliated elephant projects in Kanchanaburi and Trad provinces.

Further details from: Ayutthaya Elephant Palace & Royal Kraal and Elephant Care Assembly, Pathon Road, Ayutthaya Historical Park, Phranakornsri Ayutthaya province, 13000 Thailand; ☎+66 35 211 001; fax +66 35 211 001; e-mail elephant@ksc.th.com; www.saveelephant.com

Earthwatch

Conservationists fighting to save the rainforest in southern Thailand need volunteers to help assess the stability of the remaining fragments situated in Khlong Saeng Wildlife Sanctuary on small islands. Volunteers will boat to one of three island or mainland sites to carry out sampling procedures: collecting moths from traps, releasing amphibians from pitfall traps and small mammals from live traps, trap birds in mist nets and record their songs, trap butterflies, flying beetles, and collect ants and termites. Conditions are hot and humid with rain, mosquitoes and leeches as irritations.

Volunteers stay for ten days in the period from mid-June to mid-August for which the contribution to costs is £975 which includes own tent or loan hammock at the Thai Royal Forest Department Ranger Station. The station has pit latrines and no electricity except solar power for laptops. Shower in rainwater or bath in the reservoir. Prepared meals and packed lunches provided.

Applications through Earthwatch (see entry under Worldwide Organisations for branch addresses, or ☎01865-318838 in the UK).

Gibbon Rehabilitation Project – Phuket

Volunteers needed all year round to help a rehabilitation and study project rescuing gibbons being kept illegally in conditions of exploitation and abuse. The majority of the gibbons rescued are incapable of being rehabilitated to the wild. The few that are suitable for re-release undergo the process of rehabilitation that can take up to two years. The gibbons are returned to semi-wild conditions on deserted islands where their progress is monitored by staff and volunteers. The project is based near Bang Pae waterfall in the Khao Phra Thaew National Park in the northern, non-tourist, part of Phuket Island. Work at the Centre involves a six-day week, usually for eight hours a day and includes feeding and caring for the gibbons, building cages and informing visitors of the project's aims. Volunteers are not allowed to handle the gibbons and physical contact is allowed only in the presence and under the supervision of the Thai stafff. Volunteers stay a minimum of three weeks and choose their own dates at any time of year. The cost is US$1,169 for the first three weeks and US$130 for each additional week. Volunteers who stay longer than two months and or are studying for a biological or anthropological degree have the opportunity to become assistant researchers or carry on their own research. They pay US$974 for the first eight weeks and US$65 for each week thereafter. Collection from Phuket airport is arranged and meals and accommodation are provided.

Applications through The Wild Animal Foundation of Thailand (WAR), 235 Sukhumvit 31, Bangkok 10110, Thailand; tel/fax (662) 662-0898; e-mail war@warthai.org. Application forms can be downloaded from the website www.warthai.org.

Krabak Koo Gibbon Macaque & Bear Rescue Centre

The Rescue Centre is located 150km east of Bangkok. The nearest town, Sanam Chai Ket, is 30km away from Krabak Koo.

The main purpose of the Rescue Centre is to provide a place for the authorities to send confiscated pets and victims of illegal trade. It is hoped that once they have been cared for and rehabilitated, it will be possible to re-release some of the animals back to the wild. The Centre is home to four types of gibbon, three type of macaque, slow loris, langurs and Asiatic and Malaysian black bears.

Volunteers are needed all year round for periods of three to eight weeks. Those who stay longer than two months can combine their stay with a stint in the Gibbon Rehabilitation Project in Phuket. At Krabak Koo the work is helping to clean the cages and feed the animals. Sick and blind animals need special care and only volunteers who stay for eight weeks or more can help them because it is essential to build up a trusting one-to-one relationship. Long-term volunteers and/or Biology/anthropology students can apply to assist with the Centre's ongoing research, or carry out their own. Visas are required by UK citizens for stays of more than 30 days. Those staying longer than three months have to renew their visa in Thailand.

Costs are £560 for the first three weeks and £70 for each week after. Long-term costs are £430 for the first eight weeks and £35 per week after. Provided for the volunteers is on site: basic bungalow accommodation and all meals.

At the time of press there was no UK organisation handling applications for this project. You can try contacting WAR (Wild Animal Rescue of Thailand) whose address is given below.

Turtle Monitoring, Phra Thong Island

The project is organised in collaboration with the Marine Biological Centre in Phuket and focuses on marine turtles and observation of their nesting for censusing and protection purposes. Several species of turtle nest on the 15km of sandy beaches on Phra Thong island, Phang-Nga province in southern Thailand. The presence of volunteers to help with the programme acts as a deterrent to poachers and helps to raise awareness of the turtles' vulnerability amongst the local community and tourists.

Volunteers are needed for a minimum of a week from December to February to patrol beaches daily in order to estimate the number of nests and protect them. Volunteers also have to visit local villages to involve them in the project and collect information on the local turtle eggs trade which is illegal, but difficult to stamp out. Giving arranged talks to tourists at the Golden Buddha Beach Resort to raise awareness of the needs of the turtles is also important.

The volunteer cost is $600 for two weeks and $250 for additional weeks and covers prepared meals and accommodation. Longer stays may be possible at the organiser's discretion. Training courses for biological and natural science students are organised.

Apply through BTCV, 36 St. Mary's Street, Wallingford, Oxfordshire OX10 OEU; ☎01491-839766; www.btcv.org

Wild Animal Rescue & Education Centre Baan Talae Nork

Created by The Wild Animal Rescue Organisation in 2001, the Centre is based in 600 rais of virgin rainforest near the village of Baan Talae Nork, 80km from the city of Ranong. A further 20 rai was purchased in the village for the creation of an education and visitors' centre. This ambitious project will be accomplished in stages subject to funding coming available. The animal sanctuary accommodates all Thai wild life including reptiles, but the main concentration is on mammals.

Volunteers work a six-day week, usually 8 hours a day. Work includes food preparation, cleaning of cages, assisting in general animal welfare. As the development of the site is ongoing, volunteers are required to become in involved in whatever stage of the project is being processed. Additionally, suitable volunteers will be included in the education programme. Placement costs are the same as for the Gibbon Rehabilitation Project (see above).

No special qualifications are required, but applicants with experience or qualifications in animal-related subjects and those able to give a long-term commitment will be given special consideration.

You can get further information and application forms from The Wild Animal Rescue Foundation of Thailand (WAR), 235 Sukhumvit 31 Bangkok 10110 Thailand; tel/fax (662) 261-9670; e-mail war@warthai.org or, if you are in Thailand you can contact them direct. The Wild Animal Rescue Foundation of Thailand should be able to assist volunteers with visa extensions by providing a special letter of support.

VIETNAM
ZSCSP/Allwetterzoo, Münster
Several possible positions for volunteer project assistants for two projects in north Vietnam dealing with conservation of endangered primates. One project is at the Endangered Primate Rescue Center (ERPC) which houses about 60 primates (langurs, gibbons and loris) which have been orphaned by hunters. The other is the conservation of the extremely rare Tonkin Snub-Nosed Monkey (TSNMP).

Volunteers are needed to conduct field surveys of primate and other animals (reptiles, insects and birds) population/distribution, ecological data, also to help with developing conservation and educational programmes and caring for the animals at the ERPC. Useful but not essential are experience of primate conservation and rehabilitation, wildlife/ecological surveys, Third World living and working, biology or conservation-related degree, animal enclosure enrichment/building/maintenance and veterinary care. Bonus skills include computer knowledge, auto/motorcycle maintenance, teaching English, knowledge of Vietnamese and fund raising.

Volunteers have to be prepared to tolerate basic, rough living conditions in a mostly uncomfortable climate and have an awareness of and concern for the conservation of primates and their habitats. Volunteers have to be self-funding and pay a daily or monthly fee towards board and lodging, transportation and other costs as well as airfares and insurance.

Apply to each project individually with full CV and relevant details such as your dates of availability.

Endangered Primate Rescue Center, Volunteer Program, Cuc Phuong National Park, Nho Quan District, Ninh Binh Province, Vietnam.

Tonkin Snub-Nosed Monkey Project, Volunteer Program, c/o Anh Binh,Ban Quan Ly Du An Bao Ton Thein Nhien, Na Hang, Tuyen Quang, Vietnam. Fortunately, this one has an e-mail address too: snubnose@netnam.org.vn.

South & Central America

ARGENTINA
Refugio del Caraya – Black Howler Monkey Refuge
The refuge is run by Professor Maria Alejandra Juarez and is located 100km from Cordoba in the province of that name. The region is remote (11km to nearest village)

and is 1,250 meters above sea level. Centre accessed on foot, horse or by taxi. No public transport. The centre works to protect the howler monkey for which there is an illegal pet trade. The monkeys at the centre come from seizures, zoos and private hand-ins. The programme consists of teaching the monkeys to be wild again. Other work of the centre includes feeding and care, observations, study and data input, study of individual monkeys, cleaning, maintenance, construction of refuges etc. patrolling the area, care of other animals and vegetable garden. Volunteers contribute US$300. Patience and dedication essential. Spanish very useful. No urban comforts or luxuries. The centre also provides bibliography and study materials, the opportunity to work weekends in the zoo in the capital. Applications by e-mail to refugiodelcaraya@yahoo.com.ar.

BELIZE
Lifeline
Lifeline works to conserve wild cats (jaguar, puma, ocelot etc.). The charity takes in confiscated cats (i.e. former illegal pets) and problem animals (i.e. attackers of livestock). Where possible, cats are rehabilitated and released into the wild. Lifeline also does field research on cats and runs a small wildlife hospital.

Takes up to 48 volunteers annually on 10-day courses, six times a year usually February to August. Duties include helping to care for the Centre's resident cats, observing an monitoring cats' behaviour both at the centre and in the wild, helping to build, maintain and enrich cat enclosures, learning first-hand about human/wildlife conflict as well as basic jungle ecology. Accommodation is provided at a local ranch and the cost is included in the price of the course as are airport transfers and daily transport to and from the site.

For qualified veterinarians there are volunteer positions for 3-12 months with accommodation provided.

Applications to Pat Mansard, Diector, P.O. Box 86, San Ignacio, Cayo, Belize; ☎+501 608 0247; www.li-feline.com; e-mail catsbze@direcway.com.

OneWorld Volunteer
OneWorld Volunteer is a non-profit organisation, that arranges individual volunteer placements in Belize (also Costa Rica, Puerto Rico and Australia). In Belize volunteer work is available at a monkey rehabilitation cnetre. There is a minimum of interaction with the animals at this site. Room and board is provided at US$15 per day. Another placement is available at a howler monkey sanctuary run by the local community. Daily contact with the animals is possible. Room and board is provided for US$15 per day.

Applications to OneWorld Volunteer (2458 River Road, Guilford VT 05301, USA; ☎802-257-0152; fax 802-257-2784; e-mail info@oneworldvolunteee.org; www.onew orldvolunteer.org.

BOLIVIA
Comunidad Inti Warawara Yassi
Operates a wild animal refuge in Machia Park, Bolivia for wild animals which have been rescued from cages and chains in cities all over Bolivia. The animals are then rehabilitated with a view to re-releasing them into the wild where possible. Annual volunteers number about 400. There are also half a dozen intern and trainee posts, and one or two temporary staff. Volunteer work can include construction, maintenance, cleaning and support care of a designated animal. Volunteers stay a minimum of two weeks any time of year. Previous experience is helpful and appreciated, but not essential. Knowledge of Spanish would be extremely useful. The work is unpaid and there is a charge for accommodation.

Applications to Juan Carlos Antezana, Communidad Inti Warawara Yassi, Parque Machia, Villa Tunari-Chapare-Cochabamba, Bolivia; ☎+591-4413-4261; e-mail Ciwy21@yahoo.com; www.intiwarayassi.org.

Jakana/Volunteer Bolivia
Volunteer Bolivia is a new organisation based in Cochabamba and run by expat Americans. Its website (www.volunteerboliva.org/volunteer) includes veterinary jobs at a wildlife rescue centre. The centre needs cat, reptile, tropical bird, monkey and animal nutrition specialists. Minimum stay is three months and preferably a year. You can apply online (info@volunteerbolivia.org) or fax (+1-413 828 8144).

BRAZIL

Humpback Research Project
This project takes place in the Abrolhos Marine National Park where humpbacks come from July to November to reproduce. Volunteers look for jumping and blowing whales observing and recording behaviour and also help with cooking, cleaning and other domestic duties. Volunteers may also be asked to help with other projects run by the Park including censusing and sea turtle protection. Stays are minimum two weeks, maximum three weeks. Accommodation provided in shared rooms or on board research vessel. Cost to volunteers is US$1,300 for two weeks, US$325 for third week.
   Applications through Ecovolunteer Network (www.ecovolunteer.org).

Project Tamar – Sea Turtles
Fundacao Pro-Tamar, Caixa postal 2219, Rio Vermelho-Salvador BA, 40210-970, Brazil; ☎+55 71 6761045; fax +55 71 6761067; e-mail protamar@e-net.com.br; www.tamar.com.br
Sea turtle rescue project in the state of Espirito Santo (the coastal area north of the state of Rio de Janiero) needs volunteers from October to February. Minimum stay is two weeks. The work involves collecting and reburying the eggs, and catching, measuring and marking turtles in shifts which means that some night time work is involved. There is a fee of US$650 for participating in and supporting the research. Volunteers are not taken every year. Apply direct.

CHILE

Raleigh International
Raleigh's ten-week expeditions in Chile include bio-diversity research and radio tracking projects. Typical projects:
Working with an experienced wildlife biologist, volunteers radio track the endangered Huemul deer across rugged terrain in very remote areas. This provides vital data for Chile's National Parks management body, CONAF, helping it to plan how to best protect this species.
   Based in the remote and wild Chonos Archipelago, a group of islands first explored by Darwin, volunteers carry out marine research to assess the diverse flora and fauna and classify and map the dominant communities (biotopes). Volunteers collect lake sediment cores and survey fresh water insects, amphibians and search for traces of freshwater otters.
   Contact the organisation direct: (Raleigh House, 27 Parsons Green Lane, London SW6 4HZ; ☎020-7371 8585; fax 020-7371 5116; e-mail info@raleigh.org.uk; www.raleigh international.org).

COSTA RICA AND PUERTO RICO

It is illegal for foreigners to do paid work in Costa Rica but the organisations listed here offer volunteer work.

Agropecuaria Balve S.A./WorkCamp Bella Vista
The Bella Vista Workcamp is a farm of 15 hectares on the Gulf of Nicoya, on the Pacific Coast of Costa Rica. Volunteers can choose the farming area they wish to work in.

Those with animals are cattle, horses, breeding birds and ornamental fish production. Volunteers should expect to work five to eight hours a day with one day off a week and to make a contribution of approximately £60 a week for board and accommodation. Help is needed all year round and there is no maximum stay. Preferably, applicants should have an interest in biological farming and ecology. Would also suit those who wish to learn Spanish and travel in Costa Rica.

Applications should be addressed to Rudolph Mickass, President, Centro de Diversification, Raizal, Colorado de Abangares, Guanacaste, Costa Rica; tel/fax +506 6780467 or +506 6780464; e-mail balvesa@racsa.co.cr; or to Am Holen Stein 54, 58802 Balve, Germany; tel/fax +49 23 75 21 70.

Associacion de Voluntarios para el Servicio en las Areas Protegidas (ASVO)
ASVO is the main Costa Rican organisation responsible for national parks and reserves. Volunteers are needed for a variety of programmes which can include sea turtle conservation on the Atlantic and Pacific coasts. Students of Biology/Ecology can participate in special projects such as the reintroduction of an animal species into a particular area. The minimum period of stay is a month (two months for special projects). Applications are accepted year round. Knowledge of Spanish is useful. Volunteers pay a daily charge of around US$14 for food and lodging, and pay their own travel costs.

Applications to Volunteer Programme, Servicio de Parques Nacionales, P.O. Box 11384-1000/10104 San José, Costa Rica; ☎+506 257 0922; fax +506 233 4989; e-mail info@asvocr.com; www.asvocr.com.

Caribbean Conservation Corporation
The CCC is an organisation, which has been dedicated to sea turtle and tropical bird conservation in Costa Rica for over 40 years.

Turtle internships revolve around two species the giant leatherbacks (March to May) and the green turtle (June to October). Assistants are needed for two months or longer and are unpaid. Duties include protecting the beaches where they come ashore to lay their eggs, tagging turtles and recording data to reveal the life cycle and migratory patterns of the turtles. Assistants should be biology students, career changers or graduates able physically fit and able to walk six miles in a humid climate.

Bird interns assist researchers on project to study migrant and neo-tropical birds which involves gathering information on the relative abundance of the different species and the physical condition of captured and released specimens. Interns stay for eight weeks or longer. Applicants should be aged at least 20 with a strong interest in wildlife and conservation. A background in biological sciences, wildlife management, environmental education or a field related to these is necessary. Internships are unpaid, but formal training, free board and lodging, letters of recommendation and educational credits all provided as necessary.

Applications by April 1 (Green Turtles) or December 31 (Leatherbacks) by letter, fax or e-mail to Dan Evans, Field Program Co-ordinator; to the Caribbean Conservation Corporation, 4424 NW 13th Street, Suite #A1, Gainesville, FL 32609, USA; fax +1 352-375-2449; e-mail resprog@cccturtle.org; www.cccturtle.org.

Earthwatch
Volunteers are needed for a project to help save Costa Rica's river wildlife around Tortuguero. Censusing manatees, caymans and crocodiles in local waterways, collecting information from local people about the animals, and training local young people to be guides and rangers for the national park are parts of this volunteer programme. One week stays in March and June. The cost is £1,060 for comfortable shared accommodation and meals.

Applications to Earthwatch (see entry under Worldwide Organisations, or ☎01865-

3118838 in the UK).

OneWorld Volunteer

OneWorld Volunteer is a non-profit organisation that arranges individual volunteer placements in Puerto Rico and Costa Rica (also Belize and Australia).

Puerto Rico: placements in Puerto Rico are with an animal/shelter clinic working with dogs, cats and horses and involve hands-on animal care. A one-month minimum stay is requested. Housing is provided. Also in Puerto Rico, placements are available with a private rescue organisation which cares for dogs. Room and board is provided for US$15 per day.

Costa Rica: placements are available at a wildlife rehabilitation centre which works with a variety of rainforest monkeys, other mammals and birds. Room and board is provided at US$12 per day. Also in Costa Rica are placements at a marine centre, which works with dolphins. Room and board provided for US$12 per day. Placements also at a rescue, rehab and release centre for tropical birds, including macaws, parrots, etc. Room and board at US$12 per day.

Applications for all the above to OneWorld Volunteer, 2458 River Road, Guilford VT 05301 USA; ☎ 802-257-0152; fax 802-257-2784; e-mail info@oneworldvolunteer.org or explore@volunteertravel.com or explore@sover.net; www.oneworldvolunteer.org and www.volunteertravel.com.

Punta Banco Sea Turtle Project

This Sea Turtle restoration project concerns Olive Ridley turtles nesting on the beach at Punta Banco. Volunteers (experience in biology, education or phototography useful) are needed to mount night time beach patrols for nesting turtles, moving eggs into the hatchery, tagging and measuring adult turtles, recording data on hatchings and working with the local community and biologists on.

Volunteers pay from US$500 for two weeks up to US$1,200 for two months including full board and lodging.

Further details from STRP, P.O. Box 400/40 Montezuma Avenue, Forest Knolls, California 94933 USA; ☎ +1 415 488 0370; fax +1 415 488 0372; e-mail info@tortugamarine.org; www.seaturtles.org.

Programa Regional en Manejo de Vida Silvestre

The Programa Regional en Manejo de Vida Silvestre puts interested volunteers in contact with rescue centres for injured animals, unwanted pets and wild animals that have been confiscated by the Costa Rican authorities. Volunteers with veterinary knowledge and experience of handling captive wildlife are highly desirable. Work may involve cleaning enclosures, feeding animals, rehabilitation, research, educational programmes and administration. Room and board are provided. It is requested that prospective volunteers contact Dr. Carlos Drews, Programa Regional en Manejo de Vida Silvestre, Universidad Nacional, Apartado 1350, 3000 Heredia, Costa Rica; ☎ +506 277 3600/237 7039; fax +506 237 7036; e-mail cdrews@una.ac.cr.

Raleigh International

Famous for its variety of tropical habitats protected by an impressive system of national parks, Raleigh's projects in Costa Rica offer the opportunity to experience the country's unique flora and fauna first hand.

In a typical project volunteers carry out marine research concentrating on the coastal, estuarine and marine areas around Curu. Curu has a great variety of habitats including forest, mangrove swamp and palm-tree fringed sandy beaches and is home to deer, monkeys, wildcats and iguanas. Volunteers collect comparative research data on the existing artificial reef ecology against that of the new reefs that they will help create.

Their findings will later be presented to the Government as part of a coastal management plan to justify the reasons for protection of this area.

Contact the organisation direct: (Raleigh House, 27 Parsons Green Lane, London SW6 4HZ; ☎020-7371 8585; fax 020-7371 5116; e-mail info@raleigh.org.uk; www.raleigh international.org).

ECUADOR

Black Sheep Inn

A family-run ecological lodge in the Ecuadorian Sierra takes volunteers wishing to learn about low impact sustainable tourism. Lodge managers are also involved in conservation work in the Lliniza Ecological Reserve with over 179 species of birds and the endangered Spectacled Bear. Long-term volunteers welcome after an initial trial period of a week for which the cost is US$8 per day for room and board. After trial period board and room are normally free of charge. Volunteers should be in good health and physically fit with no allergies to animals such as llamas, sheep, dogs, chickens and ducks. Volunteers help in the lodge taking care of guests, general maintenance, domestic chores, animal care and participating in all the hikes, horseback riding and excursions.

Applications to: Andres Hammerman and Michelle Kirby, P.O. Box 05 01 240 Latacunga, Cotopaxi; ☎+593 3 814 587; fax 593 3 814 588; info@blacksheepinn.com; www.blacksheepinn.com.

Earthwatch

A project is underway to study butterfly defence mechanisms in the 2000 hectare Bilsa rainforest reserve in northern Ecuador. The forest is inhabited by all manner of animals and insects. Volunteers hike several kilometres daily in search of butterflies and help to net, number, photograph and release them.

Volunteers stay 16 days during the period from mid-June to early August or late December to mid-January. The cost is £950 which includes accommodation at Bilsa research station's bunkhouse with bathing in nearby stream or under solar shower and meals prepared by a cook.

Applications through Earthwatch (see entry under Worldwide Organisations or ☎01865-318838 in the UK).

GUATEMALA

Arcas

Arcas is a conservation organisation with two conservation project sites in Guatemala. It also runs a sea turtle conservation programme in Hawaii, which also takes volunteers.

The main Guatemalan project is the Wild Animal Rescue and Rehabilitation Centre located in 45 hectares on Lake Petzen Itza near Flores. Volunteers help with feeding and caring for the animals at the Centre including parrots, macaws, spider and howler monkeys, ocelots, coatimundis and kinkajous. Most of these animals have been confiscated from smugglers, and are very young needing constant attention. There are also opportunities to participate in veterinary medical treatment, animal releases and wildlife surveys although the scheduling of these activities is unpredictable. The minimum stay for volunteers is a week. It is possible just to show up on spec at the sites but an e-mail sent a week or two in advance is preferred.

The projects are sustained by volunteers' contributions. Volunteers pay a weekly cost of $100 per week for board and accommodation for the Peten Centre, ($50 a week for the Hawaiian Turtle Project covers accommodation only). Discounts are usually allowed to volunteers who commit for longer than one month.

If you are interested in an internship based on your university studies ask Arcas for a list of possible subjects connected with the environment. Also you will need to stay for longer and speak Spanish fairly well.

Further details on application are on the website (www.arcasguatemala.com) and you can register online. Alternatively, write to Arcas, Section 717, P.O. Box 52-7270 Miami, FL 33152-7270, United States of America; e-mail arcasguatemala@terra.com.gt Please note that Guatemalan post is unreliable so send all mail via the US address. For information only Arcas's street address is 21c 9-44A, Zona 11 Mariscal, Guatemala; tel/fax +502 476-6001, 420-2774.

MEXICO
Earthwatch
Baja Island Predators: Counting spider webs, lizards and plants for the detailing of a preservation plan. Chance to see seabird colonies, whales, dolphins and sea lions. Volunteers stay a week in March, May and July. Costs from £600 includes prepared food (volunteers clear up) and shared field station accommodation. Project takes place in Bahia de Los Angeles, Mexico.

Mexican Forest Wildlife: Volunteers help study the wildlife, particularly the small carnivores, of Mexico's threatened dry rainforest. This involves trapping and sedating ocelots, jaguarundis, coatimundis, coyotes, foxes and pygmy spotted skunks. The animals are then weighed, given an ear tattoo and fitted with a radio collar for distance tracking. Takes place in Chamela, Jalisco, Mexico. Volunteers pay £960 for ten days in January and May, the driest periods of the driest rainforest in Mexico. Accommodation is in the field station at Chamela in shared rooms with hot showers/baths. Mexican food is prepared by a cook.

Applications through Earthwatch (see entry under Worldwide Organisations or ☎01865-318852 in the UK).

One World Workforce
The California-based One World Workforce (OWW) has several sea turtle conservation projects in Mexico.

> **Daniel Bennett, an assistant biologist with the Environment Agency, joined an OWW sea turtle project for three weeks in Cabo San Lucas**
> *I found the project by looking up 'sea turtles' on the internet which produced a list of addresses which I wrote to and chose the one which sounded the best. The good thing about One World Workforce is that they take very good care of you – collect you from the airport, provide tents and campbeds, and prepare all the meals for the team. The downside, is probably that it's expensive, $675 dollars a week plus travel costs. I found my flight on Teletext and it was the cheapest on offer to San José from Gatwick with Continental with a night's stopover in Houston.*
>
> *The work was looking after sea turtles which come ashore just to lay their eggs and then return to the sea immediately afterwards. We had to dig with our hands in the sand to find the eggs and remove them to a safe hatchery. At night we patrolled the beaches and measured any turtles which had come ashore. The hours were pretty flexible and to be honest, this being a brand new project, the work programme was a bit disorganised. I am sure that now the project has been up and running a while things are much better. I did another One World Workforce project with sea turtles at Baja California which involved rehabilitation of confiscated turtles and looking at their feeding biology by attaching tiny cameras to their backs.*
>
> *The best thing about these projects is that there is something for everyone whether you are a trained biologist or not. It's such a magical experience that you fall in love with the sea turtles. It is also very rewarding to know that you are contributing something to the local environment instead of just going there as a typical tourist. I would recommend it to anyone, as long as you don't mind roughing it a bit.*

The fees cover administration, camping fees, ground transportation, food and a field manager/driver/cook. Discounts for students and groups of six or more.
OWW schemes include:
Howler Monkey Project: Pithekos, Via Savona 26, 20144 Milan, Italy; ☎+39 02 8940 5267; fax +39 02 7005 94457; e-mail asspithekos@tiscalinet.it; www.pithekos.it
A project run in part by the Parque de la Flora y Fauna Syvestre Tropical (PFFST), in the Los Tuxtlas region, Veracruz, to conserve the endangered Howler Monkey and its habitat in the tropical rainforest. Volunteers are needed to assist with fieldwork and to raise awareness among the local population. Duration of two weeks minimum up to one month. Longer possible with project leader approval. Should be capable of working independently and walk medium distances in tropical heat. Photographers are especially welcome. Accommodation is provided but own sleeping bag required. There is a fee payable by volunteers.
Sea Turtle Station, Bahia de los Angeles, Baja California, Mexico: volunteers needed to care for confiscated, black loggerheads and hawksbills and to net and re-release wild turtles and assist the camp's regular researchers. One week stints during the second half of May and the first half of October. Cost $675 which includes the ground transportation across 400 miles of amazing desert from the United States.
Cabo Olive Ridley Nesting: Punta San Cristobal, Baja California Sur, Mexico: Volunteers needed for night beach patrols to remove eggs to a protected area for hatching and release of hatchlings to the sea. Data collection and care to be maintained throughout the process. Additionally, to carry out surveys of nearby nesting beaches. Last night treat is a hotel in Cabo. One week in late August and early September. Cost $650. Rendezvous point at Cabo.
Mismaloya Beach Olive Ridley Nesting, La Gloria, Jalisco, Mexico: Work is similar to the above, assisting the University of Guadalajara with some of its field station nesting sites. Second half of September. Cost $575. Rendez-vous at Puerto Vallarta.
Applications to the Field Manager, One World Workforce, P.O. Box 3188, La Mesa, California; tel/fax +619 589 5544; e-mail ebhtour@aol.com.

PERU
Earthwatch
Andean Hummingbirds: study of the different species of the Manu Biosphere Reserve and environs, Department of Cusco, Peru. Volunteers help to set up, move and tend mist nets to catch hummingbirds and other birdlife. Manual dexterity is critical to disentangling these. A miniture instrument is then attached to the birds to measure flight performance in the region's harsh conditions. Expect to wear and use binoculars the whole time to note the foraging and competitive behaviour of different species at nectar sites. Volunteers pay £995 for a two-week stint working at high altitudes requiring optimum fitness. Various accommodation from hotel to camping depending where the team is working. A local cook will prepare good sustaining local food.
Applications to Earthwatch (see entry in Worldwide Organisations below, or telephone 01865-318838 in the UK).

SURINAM
Foundation for Nature Conservation in Surinam (STINASU)
Every year from February to September four species of sea turtle nest in Surinam. The organisation STINASU invites volunteers to help with sea turtle monitoring during the nesting season. The purpose is to identify the species (Green, Olive Ridley, Leatherback or Hawksbill) and count the number of sea turtle nests. Minimum stay is one month. The STINASU provides lodging at the beach and transportation to and from the beach.
For details of the volunteer programme and work contact Ms. Marijem Djosetro, STINASU Research Department; e-mail research@stinasu.sr; www.stinasu.sr/volunteers.

VENEZUELA

ARFA-Associacion de Rescate de Fauna

Volunteers needed for organisation that works for the conservation of wildlife through its educational programmes and a rescue and rehabilitation centre for all kinds of central plains wildlife (including iguana, raptors, alligators, ant-eating bear, turtles, parrots and macaws). Volunteers who are students of biology or veterinary sciences especially welcome, but animal qualifications not essential. Must be physically fit. Work includes feeding the animals, facility maintenance, assistance with educational ecological programmes, wildlife censusing and observations, assistance with wildlife rehabilitation. Some English spoken but knowledge of Spanish helpful. Accommodation and simple meals provided.

Calle La Vista, Edificio La Vista, Apto. 11B, Colinas de Los Caobus, Caracas 1050; ☎+58 212 782 4182; fax +58 212 793 4421; www.geocities.com/arfavenezuela/ index.html.

Appendix

Other Important Organisations to Contact

ANIMAL CHARITIES WORKING WITH ANIMALS OVER-SEAS

Most of the following organisations do not recruit staff or volunteers themselves, but they may be useful sources of contacts for projects, which may need skilled or unskilled helpers abroad.

Anglo-Italian Society for the Protection of Animals: 136 Baker Street, London W1U 6DU; ☎01743-232559; e-mail aispa@clara.co.uk; www.aispa.co.uk.

Anglo-Spanish Animal Welfare Society: Nile House, Nile Street, Brighton, Sussex BN1 1PH; ☎01273-550902.

Animals in Almeria (Spain): Flat 1, 122 Fleet Road, London NW3 2QX; tel/fax 020-7267-4175. Provides funding for domestic stray cats and dogs, donkeys or any animal in need. Funds are used for feeding, neutering, veterinary fees, advertising for rehoming. Recently supplied funds have provided three large kennels in a new sanctuary being built by PAWS group in Mojacan, Almeria; these will house 12 strays. Also funds cat neutering and feeding in Mojacan pueblo. Charity is run by Pamela Baily; e-mail pam@animals-in-almeria.fsn.co.uk; www.animals-in-almeria.co.uk.

BirdLife International: Wellbrook Court, Girton Road, Cambridge CB3 ONA; ☎01223-277318; fax 01223-277200; e-mail: birdlife@gn.apc.org. Acts as a coordinator for bird conservation organisations worldwide. Can provide information on working abroad with BirdLife's partner organisations (specialist knowledge required).

Born Free Foundation: 3 Grove House, Foundry Lane, Horsham, West Sussex RH13 5PL; ☎01403-240170; fax 01403-327838; e-mail wildlife@bornfree.org.uk; www.bornfree.org.uk Animal welfare and conservation charity that campaigns against captivity of wild animals, particularly in zoos and circuses. Through the Zoo Check programme, it investigates and exposes suffering in zoos and campaigns for the phasing out of traditional zoos with cramped conditions, and ultimately all zoos. As an alternative it promotes and supports the protection of wildlife in its natural habitat i.e. keeping wildlife wild.

Born Free's other campaigns include Elefriends, to protect the elephant in its natural habitat and against poachers; Big Cats, Wolf and Bear (wolf sanctuary in Portugal), Primates, Marine and Education.

BP Conservation Programme, Birdlife International/Fauna and Flora International: Wellbrook Court, Girton Road, Cambridge CB3 ONA; ☎01223-277318; fax 01223-277200; e-mail bp-conservation-programme@birdlife.org.uk.www.conservation.bp.com. A tripartite collaboration to assist and guide teams of students wanting to organise conservation research projects. BP Conservation Programme has also developed a series of workshops in biological fieldwork techniques in biological fieldwork techniques for

all kinds of animal surveys and studies, which can be applied worldwide.
Brooke Hospital for Animals UK Office: British Columbia House, 1-3 Regent Street, London SW1Y 4PA; ☎020-7930 0210; fax 020-7930 2386. Provides free treatment for donkeys and horses in Egypt, Jordan, Pakistan and India. Supports five clinics in Egypt, one in Jordan, five mobile clinic teams and a static clinic in Peshawar, NW Pakistan and five mobile clinic teams in Lahore. In addition, there are two mobile teams caring for equines working underground and on tonga stands in Delhi. All vets working for the organisation are nationals of the countries concerned.
Care for the Wild (CFTW): 1 Ashfolds, Horsham Road, Rusper, West Sussex RH12 4QX; ☎01293-871596; fax 01293-871022; e-mail info@careforthewild.com; www.careforethewild.com. An international animal charity that provides practical aid to alleviate animal suffering. Supports projects for all kinds of animals including elephants, black and white rhino, tigers, badgers, foxes, otters and cetaceans.
Cat Survival Trust: The Centre, Codicote Road, Welwyn, Hertfordshire AL6 9TU; ☎01438-716873; www.catsurvivaltrust.org. Concerned with the conservation of endangered species of big cats through captive breeding programmes and habitat protection.
Cheetalert: Grassendale, Woodcombe, Minehead, Somerset TA24 8SB; ☎01643-706736. Project to combat the cheetah's threatened extinction.
David Shepherd Conservation Foundation: c/o Michael Zilka, 61 Smithbrook Kilns, Cranley, Surrey GU6 8JJ; ☎01483-272323; fax 01483-272427. Different focuses but mostly works for endangered mammals.
Dian Fossey Gorilla Fund: 110 Gloucester Avenue, London NW1 8JA; ☎020-7483 2681; 020-7722-0928; e-mail info@gorilla.demon.co.uk; www.dfgfeurope@aol.com Dian Fossey made a lifetime study of the mountain gorillas in Rwanda, of which only a few hundred remain. The organisation campaigns against poaching and provides veterinary and community support, to try and save the rest.
Environmental Investigation Agency: 15 Bowling Green Road, London EC1. Carries out investigations into the illegal trade in rare and endangered species.
Fauna & Flora International: Great Eastern House, Tenison Road, Cambridge CB1 2DT; ☎01223-461471; fax 01223-461481; e-mail info@ffint.org. Works to prevent illegal trading in wildlife worldwide. Also collaborates with the BP Conservation Programme (see above) in assisting teams of students organise conservation research projects.
Fauna & Flora Preservation Society (FFPS): Great Eastern House, Tenison Road, Cambridge CB1 2DT; ☎ 01223-461471; fax 01223-461481. Founded in 1903 as the Fauna Preservation Society, the FFPS works on behalf of endangered animals and plants worldwide. It has members in 100 countries. It was instrumental in campaigning for controls on trade in endangered species and in the creation of the World Wide Fund for Nature. It focuses on a limited number of issues and all its research is backed up by thorough scientific work which is much respected. The society's journal, *Oryx* is published quarterly. There are branches also in Bristol, Chester, Edinburgh and Oxford. See also Flora and Fauna International above.
Greek Animal Welfare Fund: 1-2 Castle Lane, London SW1E 6DN; 020-7828 9736; fax 020-7630 9816; e-mail admin@gawf.freeserve.co.uk; www.gawf.org.uk. Cares for stray dogs and cats in Greece, Provides mobile clinic, neutering service and advice. Campaigns for the enforcement of EU standards for livestock and slaughterhouses. Volunteers needed in the UK rather than Greece.
Greek Cat Welfare Society: 9 Woodfield Crescent, London W5 1PD; ☎020-8998 6867. Education and neutering service provided throughout Greece.
Herpetological Conservation Trust (HCT): 655A Christchurch Road, Boscombe, Bournemouth BH1 4AP; ☎01202-391319; fax 01202-392785; e-mail enquiries@h erpconstrust.org.uk; www.herpconstrust.org.uk. The Trust is committed to improving the conservation status of Europe's threatened amphibians and reptiles by acquiring

sites, managing habitats, field surveying and political lobbying. Works closely with the British Herpetological Society.

International Donkey Protection Trust: Sidmouth, Devon EX10 ONU; ☎01395-578222; fax 01395 579266; the donkeysanctuary@compuserve.com; www.thedonkeysanctuar y.org.uk. Prevents suffering of donkeys worldwide with mobile clinics, sanctuaries and education of the public. Employs full-time and voluntary Welfare Officers. In the UK and Ireland gives permanent sanctuary to any donkey in need of refuge.

International Fund for Animal Welfare: 87-90 Albert Embankment, London SE1 7UD; 0207-7587 6700; info-uk@ifaw.org; www.ifaw.org. Campaigns worldwide for animal welfare and the environment with emphasis on elephants, campaigning for the abolition of fox-hunting and cetacean conservation.

International Gorilla Conservation: Tenison Road, Cambridge CB1 2DT; ☎01223-571000. Works for the welfare of the mountain gorilla in Zaire and its habitat.

International League for the Protection of Horses: Snetterton, Norfolk; ☎0870 870 1927; www.ilph.org. Works for the protection and rehabilitation of equines; rescues and rehabilitates equines at risk, cares for some in final rest homes, raises awareness, educates on equine care and management, sponsors scholarships in equine research at veterinary establishments. In the UK it has four rest and rehabilitation centres. In Europe it works through a Paris office and agencies in several countries. Campaigns against the export of horses for slaughter. Has branches in Israel, Mexico and New Zealand. In developing countries it provides farriery, saddlery and harness and veterinary care training through volunteers. Anyone interested should contact the ILPH for further details.

International Otter Survival Fund: Broadford, Isle of Skye IV49 9AQ; ☎01471-822487; e-mail iosf@otter.org; www.otter.org. Works with scientists around the world (including Chile, India, Turkey, Lithuania, USA, Spain & Russia), for the conservation of otters. Also runs a wildlife hospital specialising in otters. Also runs wildlife holidays in Scotland otter watching. Also, runs one week otter field training courses costing £240 all inclusive per week on Skye and £495 on other islands in the Outer Hebrides.

International Owl Society: 202 Noak Hill Road, Billericay, Essex CN12 9UX.

International Primate Protection League (IPPL): Gilmore House, 166 Gilmore Road, London SE13 5AE; ☎020-8297 2129; fax 020-8297 2099; e-mail enquiries@ippl-uk-org; www.ippl-uk.org. Deals with primate conservation and welfare for apes in the wild and in captivity. Also provides ape sanctuaries and campaigns for export bans from countries of origin and the eradication of illicit trade.

Jane Goodall Institute: Orchard House, 61-67 Commercial Road, Southampton, Hants. S015 1GG; ☎012380-335660; fax 0123880-335661; e-mail info@janegoodall.org.uk; www.janegoodall.org.uk. Works worldwide on behalf of chimpanzees. Volunteers needed in the UK and hopes to have a volunteer programme for Africa in the future.

Japan Animal Welfare Society: Lyell House, 51 Greencoat Place, London SW1P 1DS; ☎020-7630 5563; e-mail jawsuk@freenet.co.uk. Raises funds to support the relief of animal suffering in Japan.

Monkey World, Ape Rescue: Longthornes, Wareham, Dorset BH20; 01929-462537; e-mail apes@monkeyworld.org; www.monkeyworld.org. Rescues apes from around the world. Runs a sanctuary in Dorset for about 100 primates. Takes trainee keepers for a minimum 6-9 months. See entry in *Other Opportunities*

National Canine Defence League: 17 Wakely Street, London EC1V 7RQ; ☎020-7837 0006; fax 020-7833 2701; e-mail info@ncdl.org.uk; www.ncdl.org.uk. The NCDL is working towards the time when all dogs can expect a normal life free from the threat of unecessary destruction. Although most of its work is limited to the UK, it co-hosts a regular international conference in Eastern Europe to discuss important animal welfare issues and to promote good practice at animal shelters abroad. The International Companion Animal Welfare Conference (ICAWC) provides organisations with information on shelter management, animal legislation, animal behaviour and humane education It is designed to offer hope and lots of practical advice for smaller animal shelters.

Orangutan Foundation: 7 Kent Terrace, London NW1 4RP; 020-7724 2912. Registered charity (no. 1042194). The Orangutan Foundation, supports the conservation and research of the orangutan and its rainforest habitat, while caring for and repatriating injured and/or orphaned orangutans back into the wild. The Orangutan Foundation seeks to actively lobby governments and educate the public about the orangutan and its habitat so that it will be saved from extinction. The OF runs several trips to Indonesia, including Red Ape Challenge and the Volunteer Programme.

People for the Ethical Treatment of Animals (PETA): P.O. Box 36668, London SE1 1WA; ☎0207-357-9229; info@petauk.org; www.petauk.org. The British arm of the American non-profit animal rights organisation, which claims three-quarters of a million members worldwide. Founded in 1980 it is dedicated to establishing the rights and improving the lives of all animals through education, lifestyle changing and exposing all forms of cruelty. Broadly, its campaigns are ranged under animals in experiments, food protection, animal based clothing and animals as entertainment. Has offices in Germany and the Netherlands and the USA.

People's Trust for Endangered Species (PTES): Unit 15 Cloisters House, 8 Battersea Park Road, London SW8 4BG; ☎020-7498 4533; fax 020-7498 4459; e-mail enquiries@ptes.org; www.ptes.org. The Trust aims to protect creatures in the wild which are threatened with extinction. It acts by funding scientific research and field work to protect populations in immediate danger, raising public awareness of species in danger, and purchase of land to pursue these aims when possible. Works both in Britain and other countries. It does not recruit volunteers directly, but may be able to provide details of a handful of projects which do. In 2003 these included a black rhino project in Namibia. Office volunteers always needed.

Phoenix Conservation: 3 St John's Street, Goole, East Yorkshire DN14 5QL; ☎01405-769375. Dedicated to conservation particularly through utilising aviation facilities. For instance PTES has an anti-poaching campaign in East and West African game parks to preserve the remaining elephants and rhino there. The project involves park ranger pilot training and a research programme.

Primate Society of Great Britain (PSGB): Dr John Lycett, Centre for Economic Learning and Social Evolution, School of Biological Sciences, Nicholson Building, University of Liverpool, Liverpool, L69 3BX; fax 0151-794 5094; e-mail j.e.lycett@liverpool.ac.uk Promotes research into all aspects of primate biology, conservation and management. PSGB newsletter *Primate Eye* is useful for people enquiring about jobs and field work possibilities as is www.primate.wisc.edu/pin/jobs/index.html.

Royal Geographical Society (with IBG), Expedition Advisory Centre: 1 Kensington Gore, London SW7 2AR; ☎020-7591 3030; fax 020-7591 3031; e-mail eac@rgs.org; www.rgs.org/eac. Issues a regular *Bulletin of Expedition Vacancies* that lists opportunities to join one-off and private expeditions and overseas fieldwork projects. Focuses on expeditions with a scientific basis, including fauna studies. The above website has information about joining an expedition and links to other organisations and websites. The EAC organises workshops on biological fieldwork techniques and assists teams of students with research expedition planning. Holds a reference store of previous fieldwork techniques for fish, small mammals, bats, birds, insects, primates, reptiles and amphibians. The RGS (with IBG) awards funding for overseas field research including the *Expedition Research Grants*. Preference is given to those teams involving host country institutions and nationals. Further details www.rgs.org/grants.

Society for Animal Welfare in Israel: 8 Hamilton Close, Potters Bar, Herts. EN6 3QD. Works to protect the welfare of domestic animals in Israel.

St Petersburg Society for Protection of Stray Animals: 93a Hazel Road, Bognor Regis,

Sussex. Probably Russia's only charity which provides shelters for sick and stray animals.

Tusk Charity for Conservation of African Wildlife: Tim Jackson, 19 Amner Road, London SW11 6AA; ☎020-7978 7100; fax 020-7223 2517; e-mail sales@tusk.org. Conservation organisation that works for all wildlife in Africa.

Wildfowl & Wetlands Trust, Slimbridge: Slimbridge, Gloucestershire GL2 7BT; ☎01453-891900; fax 01453-890827; e-mail enquiries@wwt.org.uk; www.wwwt.org.uk Co-ordinates research and conservation of waterfowl and wetland habitats worldwide.

Wildlife Information Network: Royal Veterinary College, Royal College Street, London NW1 OTU; ☎020-7388 7003; fax 020-7388 7110; e-mail win@wildlifeinformatio n.org; www.wildlifeinformation.org. The Wildlife Information Network (WIN), is a veterinary science based organisation, founded in 1992, and aims to make information on the health and management of captive and free ranging animals and their habitats readily available to wildlife professionals and decision makers worldwide. WIN works towards this goal by developing WILDPro, an electronic encyclopedia on the health and management of captive and free ranging wild animals. Modules can be purchased on CD-ROM and through the website. WIN also provides veterinary experts for specific problems i.e. wasting disease in deer, or emergencies such as big oil spills.

The World Owl Trust: Muncaster Castle, Ravenglass, Cumbria CA18 1RQ; ☎01229-717393; fax 01229-717107; e-mail admin@owls.org; e-mail admin@owls.org; www.owls.org. The world's leading global owl conservation organisation. One of the finest owl collections on view to the general public at its World Owl Centre in Cumbria. Field projects always on going, both in the UK and abroad.

World Parrot Trust: Glanmor House, Hayle, Cornwall TR27 4HY. Dedicated to the preservation, protection and improvement of parrots. Has projects in 11 countries.

World Pheasant Association: 7-9 Shaftesbury Street, Fordingbridge, Hants, SP6 1JF; ☎01425-657129.

World Society for the Protection of Animals (WSPA): 89 Albert Embankment, London SE1 7TP; ☎020-7587 5000; fax 020-7793 0208; e-mail wspa@wspa.org.uk. WSPA promotes co-operation between animal protection and conservation organisations around the world and to undertake conservation and protection projects. Also campaigns for animal welfare worldwide against whaling, sealing, fur trading, illegal trafficking in wildlife, animal experiments and bull-fighting. Also works for improving humane slaughter, conditions for livestock transportation, stray animal control and in disaster relief.

WSPA maintains a database of relevant professionals including zoologists and veterinary consultants. Posts with the organisation itself involve being based at the UK office with trips to projects abroad. Recruitment occurs through adverts in The Guardian or from the database. WSPA cannot help people find jobs abroad but supplies some addresses e.g. primate refuges in Kenya and organisations that organise projects overseas.

World Wide Fund for Nature: Panda House, Godalming GU7 1XR; ☎01483-426444; www.wwf.org.uk. WWF – a global environment network – is the world's largest conservation organisation, working in the UK and around the world to conserve endangered species and protect endangered spaces, and address global threats to people and nature by seeking long-term solutions to the world's environmental problems. Has headquarters in Switzerland (World Wide Fund for Nature – International, Avenue du Montblanc, 1196 Gland, Switzerland; ☎+41 22 364 9111; fax +41 22 364 3238).

The British branch of WWF spends approximately one third of the money it raises on projects in this country and the rest on international projects. WWF national organisations in individual countries usually employ their own nationals for work on projects. The WWF does not recruit volunteers but may be worth contacting for information about national projects for nature conservation. Some of these may involve work with animals.

Zebra Foundation: The Penthouse, Braxfield Court, St Anne's Road West, St Anne's on Sea, Lancs. FY8 1LQ; tel/fax 01253-392289; e-mail faecasimiae@aol.com; www.zebra@bvzs.org. A foundation for Veterinary Zoological Education, affiliated to the BVA and BVZS that helps veterinary surgeons from any country to expand their experience or qualifications in the field of wild and zoo animal medicine.

WORLDWIDE ORGANISATIONS WITH ANIMAL-RELATED PROJECTS

The following organisations take volunteers for a variety of conservation, agricultural and veterinary projects.

Biosphere Expeditions
Sprats Water, Near Carlton Colville, The Broads National Park, Suffolk, NR33 8BP; ☎01502-583085; www.biosphere-expeditions.com.
Biosphere Expeditions aims to send out paying volunteers who contribute their labours and cash to animal conservation projects around the world. Volunteers work alongside experts and scientists and their contribution of £1,495 upwards includes board and lodging but not flights. Current survey/monitoring expeditions include Namibian cheetahs, Peruvian monkeys, macaws, and other wildlife, snow leopards and other animals in the mountains of the Altai republic, Central Asia, steppe wolf and bird migration on the Black Sea Kinburn peninsula, Crimea.
For more information visit the website above, or ask for a brochure.

Cedam International
One Fox Road, Croton-on-Hudson, NY 10520, USA; ☎ +1 914 271-5365; fax +1 914 271-4723; e-mail cedamint@aol.com; www.cedam.org.
CI is a non-profit organisation which works for conservation, marine research, archaeology, raising awareness of environmental issues and raising funds. Its main objective is to promote research in the field of marine sciences carried out in tropical seas e.g. Mexico, Seychelles, Galapagos, Kenya, Australia, Belize and many others worldwide. Programmes are conducted by expert divers, photographers and marine biologists. Volunteer helpers are needed all year round for periods of seven to ten days. Scuba qualifications are an asset but not essential. Other appropriate skills include underwater photography/video and cartography. Cost minimum US$1,500 up to US$4,000. Minimum age is 18.

Coral Cay Conservation
13th Floor, 125 High Street, Colliers Wood, London SW19 2JG, United Kingdom; ☎0870-750 0668; fax 0870 750 0667; e-mail info@coralcay.org; www.coralcay.org.
CCC grew out of a joint universities expedition to examine the impact of fishing on Belize's coral reef. By 1990 the area had been declared a World Heritage Site. Since 1986 thousands of international volunteers have joined CCC projects worldwide to help protect threatened coral reefs and tropical forests. CCC is non-profit and based in the UK, from where it sends teams of volunteers to survey some of the world's endangered coral reefs and tropical forests. There are Coray Cay projects in Honduras (coral reef survey), Malaysia (reef and rainforest survey), the Philippines (reef and rainforest conservation), Fiji (reef and forest conservation), The Caribbean (reef and island surveys). In the UK, CCC has run a series of expeditions to survey the marine life around the Isles of Scilly off Cornwall in southwest England.

Volunteers do not need to be biologists or even have a scuba diving qualification. Volunteers can be gap year students or any kind of professional taking time out. CCC's field scientists and other expedition staff provide training courses which include health and safety briefings and training, diving instruction to PADI Advanced Open Water Driver and Medic First Aid Diver (if not already qualified) during the first week of the expedition. Further qualifications are also possible. Also provided are one or two-week Skills Development courses conducted by the expedition science staff including training in tropical ecology and survey techniques.

After training, volunteers begin the serious work of surveying, gathering information on the diversity, distribution and abundance of plants and animals (rainforest) or, physical features and fish (reefs).

Reef Projects: consist of a two-week training course (£700) plus an unlimited number of Conservation Weeks (£100-£300 per week). Non-divers have to arrive a week earlier to complete a £400 scuba diving course.

Forest Projects: consist of a one-week training programme (£350), plus conservation weeks costing £100-£200 per week.

Prices do not include flights, insurance, transfers and personal gear.

Discovery Initiatives
The Travel House, 51 Castle Street, Cirencester, Gloucestershire GL7 1QD; ☎01285-643333; fax 01285-885888; e-mail enquiry@discoveryinitiatives.com; www.discoveryi nitiatives.com.
Discovery Initiatives is part holiday company organising holidays, treks and journeys to the world's most remote places, and part hands-on wildlife and conservation supporter for small groups who want to participate in wildlife programmes. In 2002/3 the range of projects included helping a researcher in the Gobi desert and Altai mountains track snow leopards, counting game in Chobe National Park in Botswana and Orang-u-tan study and support touring in Borneo.

Game Ranger Course: DI also organise introductory 10-day game ranger courses in Kruger National Park in South Africa (see *Rest of the World, Africa*).

Qualified medical staff receive discounts on tours for which medical cover is required.

Earthwatch Institute International
3 Clocktower Place, Suite 100, P.O. Box 75, Maynard, MA 01754 USA; ☎+1 978-461-0081; or toll-free in the USA 800-776-0188; fax 978-461-2332; e-mail info@earthwatch.org; www.earthwatch.org
The Earthwatch Institute was founded in 1971 and was the first green organisation to recruit paying volunteers for conservation projects. It is truly worldwide in that it has 140 projects related to species (including rhinos, mountain lions, dolphins, snakes, birds, crocodiles, echidnas, chimpanzees, wolves and more) and habitats covering every continent. About 40 projects involve hands on work with animals. It also boasts 60,000 member supporters worldwide of whom approximately 7% participate in expeditions as volunteers.

Volunteers come for one to three weeks year round to help with research and their contributions of US$650 to US$3,695 help fund the research. Food and accommodation is included in the costs. Volunteers have to pay their own travel costs. There is separate scheme for teachers which offers reduced costs.

Earthwatch Agents
Australia: Earthwatch Institute,126 Bank Street, South Melbourne, Victoria 3205; ☎+61 3 9682-6828; e-mail earth@earthwatch.org
Japan: Earthwatch Institute Japan, Sanbancho Ty Plaza 5F, Sanbacho 24-25, Chiyoda-

Ku, Tokyo, 101-0075 Japan; ☎+81 (0)3-3511-3360; fax +81 (0)3-3511-4663; info@earthwatch-japan.gr.jp
Europe: Earthwatch Institute Europe, 267 Banbury Road, Oxford OX2 7HT, United Kingdom; ☎01865-318838; fax 01865-311383; e-mail info@earthwatch.org.uk; www.earthwatch.org.

Some Current Earthwatch Projects
Cheetah Conservation in Namibia: assessing the status of the cheetah's ecosystem by counting game, tracking animals and analysing vegetation. This will help to plan the cheetah's long-term conservation. Feeding and caring for captive cheetahs on site, radio-tracking collared cheetahs, and data entry are primary tasks.
Madagascar's Lemurs: following lemur groups on foot through jungle to study their social behaviour in order to make appropriate decisions concerning the protection of their habitat.
Costa Rican Sea Turtles: monitoring nesting leatherbacks, measuring and tagging them, recording nest position, and counting eggs to determine which factors influence nesting success.
Crocodiles of the Okavango: helping with a research and monitoring project in the Okavango to see how sensitive the crocodile population is to hunters and crocodile farmers in order to supply a plan for managing crocodiles. Task includes catching smaller crocodiles by noose or by hand. Also questioning villagers about crocodile impacts on their communities.
Malaysian Bat Conservation: Assisting a specialist from Boston University in assessing the impact of logging on 40 species of bat that exist in the rainforest. Includes monitoring bat population sizes and recording bat foraging behaviour and roosting sites and patterns. Assist with with harp-trapping, examining and banding bats and describing them.
Caring for Chimpanzees: this project involves evaluating captive chimpanzee environments to improve primate care. Based at a specially built captive chimp facility at Central Washington University, volunteers help prepare the chimps enclosures with various objects and observe how the chimps use them. There is no direct contact with the chimps, but you will be able to use sign language to try to communicate with them. The object of the study is to improve the lot of chimpanzees in captivity by providing them with stimulation that is sufficient for their needs.
Ecuadorian Forest Birds: the rare birds include 20 species of humming bird and 12 other species which are using the rain forest of Loma Alta Ecological Reserve. volunteers work in the field and in the local community. A scientist from Kansas University needs help in surveying these remote tropical forests to track seasonal shifts in bird populations. Includes setting up and checking mist nets, checking captured birds physical condition, conducting bird surveys, and documenting forest structure and food surveys.
Elephant Seals of the Falkland Islands: elephant seals, especially the male of the species are colossal animals weighing up to 3,000kg. Volunteers assist with census taking and classing seals by size/age. Also mapping individuals using GPS and observe harems to record behavioural events. May also help weigh and tag weanlings.
Tanzanian Forest Birds: Netting birds in the Usambara Mountains of Tanzania to examine how rainforest fragmentation affects bird populations.

Further details of all the above and other Earthwatch projects under individual countries in the *Worldwide Section,* or contact Earthwatch direct.

Eco Volunteer Program
Central Office: Meijersweg 29, 7553 AX Hengalo, Netherlands; ☎+31 74 250 8250; fax

+31 20 864 5314; e-mail info@ecovolunteer.org; www.ecovolunteer.org.
The EVN runs a programme of about 25 projects in countries including Colombia, Russia, Spain, Mongolia, Peru and Croatia. Projects include the reintroduction of Przewalski's Horse in Mongolia, caretaking in Thai animal rescue centres and a chimpanzee rehabilitation programme in Sierra Leone. The projects offer hands-on experience in wildlife conservation, wildlife research, assisting with fieldwork, monitoring research and in wildlife rescue and rehabilitation centres. There may be additional housekeeping and visitor management duties. Volunteers are expected to work with local conservationists, researchers and rangers and to adapt to the local culture. Volunteers pay a participation fee which varies according to the project: US$260 for a two week monk seal project in Turkey, US$ 625 for eight-week gibbon project in Thailand and US$1,000 for three weeks on the Przewalski horse project in Poland. Volunteer stays vary from one week upwards depending on the project. There are also long term possibilities for students wishing to apply their research in zoology, biology, veterinary science, wildlife management etc.

EVN Agencies
Belgium: www.ecovolunteer.be
Brasil: www.br.ecovoluntarios.org
International: www.ecovolunteer.org
Netherlands: www.ecovolunteer.nl
UK-Atlantida: www.ecovolunteer.org.uk
UK-Wildwings: www.wildwings.ecovolunteer.co.uk

Europe Conservation Italia
A not for profit organisation, that works for the conservation of natural resources, and supports projects in different developing countries. Currently these include:
Project Pro Tamar (turtles on the Brazilian coast)
Project Rhino Rescue (Swaziland)
   Volunteers are needed for all the above projects (see Rest of the World section for further details). Applications to Europe Conservation Italia (via del Macaoa, 00185 Rome; ☎06 4741241; fax 06-4744671; e-mail eco.italia@agora.stm.it; www.agora.stm.it.

Frontier
50-52 Rivington Street, London EC2A 3QP; ☎0207-613 1911; fax 0207-613 2992; e-mail harriet@frontier.ac.uk; www.frontier.ac.uk.
The conservation organisation Frontier conducts vital research into some of the world's most threatened wildlife and habitats. Current projects are focused on bio-diversity conservation and management issues in Madagascar, Vietnam, and Tanzania (rainforest, savanna, coral reef and mangrove areas). Projects are organised in association with the host countries' relevant institutions, usually a university of a resource management authority. Projects typically involve biological surveys and socio-economic research, rather than direct care or contact with animals. However, volunteers may be involved in trapping, tagging and re-releasing animals depending on the project. The projects are of most value to those interested in a career in overseas development and conservation.
   Volunteers are expected to raise their own participation funds, starting from £2,100, covering visas, local travel, food, accommodation, science equipment and vehicle maintenance on a 10-week expedition (excluding flights and insurance). Each expedition runs four times a year. No scientific experience is required ass full training is given in the field, leading to an optional BTEC qualification in Tropical Habitat Conservation.

Raleigh International
Raleigh House, 27 Parsons Green Lane, London SW6 4HZ; ☎020-7371 8585; fax 020-

7371 5116; e-mail info@raleigh.org.uk; www.raleighinternational.org.
Raleigh International organises ten-week expeditions in Malaysian Borneo, Ghana, Namibia, Chile and Costa Rica/Nicaragua, for volunteers aged 17 and over. Projects change from year to year, but currently include biodiversity monitoring projects, marine research, mammal tracking and the construction of viewing hides.

Each participant completes one community, one environment and one adventure project in remote areas. To take part in the expedition each volunteer is asked to fundraise towards the charity.

Note that participants' living conditions are rugged and that fundraising entails raising over £3,000. The organisation gives advice on getting sponsorship to raise this.

Teaching & Projects Abroad
Gerrard House, Rustington, West Sussex, BN16 1AW; ☎01903-859911; fax 01903-785779; e-mail info@teaching-abroad.co.uk; www.teaching-abroad.co.uk Organises volunteer work projects worldwide. Animal-related projects include veterinary medicine in Ghana and India, and animal care in China, Mexico, Russia and Ukraine. Placements last three months and volunteers pay from £1,395 all inclusive.

United Nations Volunteers (UNV)
PO Box 26011, D53153 Bonn, Germany; ☎+49 228 815 200; fax +49 228 815 2001; e-mail information@unvolunteers.org; www.unvolunteers.org.

The United Nations Volunteer Programme is open to specialists in a range of fields. Thousands of volunteers have participated in programmes in many developing countries, co-operating with local organisations and communities offering teaching or their professional skills. About 10% of the UNVs projects are to do with a wide range of environmental or conservation issues. Animal projects include working in a panda reserve in China. The minimum age for volunteers is 25 but volunteers tend to be older – many are in their thirties owing to the requirement for professional working experience – two years is the minimum. Assignments are usually for two years, but shorter terms may be authorised.

University Research Expeditions Program (UREP)
University of California, One Shields Avenue, Davis, California 95616, USA; ☎+1 530 752-0692; www.urep.ucdavis.edu

UREP offers paying volunteers the opportunity to take part in a range of opportunities to participate in field research around the world, including wildlife projects. Species studied include monkeys, foxes, manatees, birds and frogs. Projects take place in various locations in North, Central and South America, Africa, Europe and Polynesia from March through to August. Volunteers spend two to four weeks with a project. Previous field experience is not essential but curiousity, flexibility and cooperativeness are. Skills such as photography, diving, drawing, observation techniques and wilderness experience are useful. Minimum cost to volunteer is US$800 up to a maximum of US1,900 including food and lodging.

Vetaid
Pentlands Science Park, Bush Loan, Penicuik, Midlothian, EH26 OPZ, Scotland; ☎+44 (0)131 445 6241; fax +44 (0)131 445 6242; e-mail vetaiduk@gn.apc.org; www.gn.apc.org/vetaid.

Vetaid is a specialist non-governmental development organisation started in 1989 to help people in developing countries the majority of whose inhabitants depend on livestock for their food and income. The organisation generally arrives in areas where wars or famine have just ended and things are at a low ebb because livestock has been reduced to a few wretched specimens in very poor condition. The charity also works in countries where livestock is suffering from endemic but treatable diseases which can be devastating if they are not bought under control. Vetaid works with local organisations to prevent suffering and hunger by active promotion of improved animal welfare and husbandry using its own field staff recruited from a number of countries. By enhancing the animals' lives the charity aims to improve the lives of the people who depend on them for survival.

Vetaid is supported by a range of donors from major ones like the European Union and the Department for International Development to public donations of any size.

Projects have included animal health and husbandry and upgrading livestock markets among the Maasai in Tanzania, a post civil war cattle restocking project in Mozambique, reinstating agricultural veterinary support services in Somalia and a post civil war cattle vaccination programme in southern Sudan.

Vetaid employs a number of expatriates for its overseas projects. All employees are professionals with considerable experience of the tropics and a relevant MSc qualification. As well as veterinarians, the charity employs those working in the disciplines of animal production, social anthropology and social science.

Voluntary Service Overseas
317 Putney Bridge Road, London SW15 2PN; ☎020-8780 2266; fax 020-8780 1326. VSO recruits and posts overseas, people with relevant skills and qualifications and normally five years' experience, to work for a minimum of two years, in various fields a few of which (livestock agriculture and veterinary) are animal related. The work mainly involves training people in developing countries and passing on skills. For the first time ever, VSO received a request for a blacksmith to work at an equine hospital in Pakistan in 1999. At the time of press this vacancy was unfilled. Other vacancies on offer at the time of press included included an ostrich farmer and a piggery project advisor for Zimbabwe, a vet to act as a provincial livestock advisor in Cambodia, and a research officer in animal husbandry for The Gambia. VSO pays various grants and allowances to make a long-term commitment in a poor country feasible, and the employer pays a salary at local rates and provides accommodation.

Whale and Dolphin Conservation Society (WDCS) Brookfield House, 38 St. Paul's Street, Chippenham SN15 1LY; e-mail info@wdcs.org; www.wdcs.org. The Society aims to raise awareness of the threats to dolphins and whales worldwide.

Wildwings
1st floor, 577-579 Fishponds Road, Fishponds, Bristol BS16 3AF; ☎0117-965 8333; fax 0117-937681; www.wildwings.co.uk and www.ecovolunteer.org.uk
Wildwings is the UK agent for the Dutch-based ecological organisation, EcoVolunteer (see entry above). Paying volunteers can join over 20 animal projects in Africa, eastern Europe and Thailand. These include:
Thai Wildlife Sanctuary: minimum three weeks (£550)
India bats and monkeys: minimum two weeks (£470)
Mongolia Horses: minimum three weeks (£765-860)
Poland Wolves: minimum a week (£402, extra weeks £267)
Bulgaria horses, dogs and sheep: minimum two weeks (£589)
Turkey seals: minimum two weeks (£289)
La Gomera cetaceans: minimum two weeks (£599)
Scotland dolphins: £522 per week.
Swaziland rhino: two weeks £729.
Brazil humpbacks: two weeks £909.
New Zealand kiwi and kokako: minimum three weeks (£729).
Further details of the above projects and others on the Wildwings and EcoVolunteer websites.

World Association of Zoos and Aquariums(WAZA)
WAZA Executive Office, P.O. Box 23, 3097 Liebfeld-Berne, Switzerland; Visitors' address: Lindenrain 3, 3012 Berne, Switzerland; ☎+41 31 300 20 30; fax +41 31 300 20 31; e-mail secretariat@waza.org; the website www.waza.org has a list of member zoos and aquariums worldwide divided by region.

World Wildlife Fund (WWF) International
The WWF International has its headquarters in Switzerland (1192 Gland, Switzerland) and national branches in many countries. Volunteers should contact their national WWF office for details of projects in their own countries rather than for projects abroad. This is because WWF branches in individual countries recruit experienced, qualified professionals from amongst their own nationals.

USEFUL WEBSITE

www.worldanimalnet.com – global information on animal protection, welfare etc organisations. Contacts for animal-connected campaigns worldwide.

Vacation Work Publications

	Paperback	Hardback
Summer Jobs Abroad	£9.99	£15.95
Summer Jobs in Britain	£9.99	£15.95
Supplement to Summer Jobs Britain and Abroad *published in May*	£6.00	-
Work Your Way Around the World	£12.95	-
Taking a Gap Year	£11.95	-
Taking a Career Break	£11.95	-
Working in Tourism – The UK, Europe & Beyond	£11.95	-
Kibbutz Volunteer	£10.99	-
Working on Yachts and Superyachts	£10.99	-
Working on Cruise Ships	£10.99	-
Teaching English Abroad	£12.95	-
The Au Pair & Nanny's Guide to Working Abroad	£12.95	-
The Good Cook's Guide to Working Worldwide	£11.95	-
Working in Ski Resorts – Europe & North America	£11.95	-
Working with Animals – The UK, Europe & Worldwide	£11.95	-
Live & Work Abroad – A Guide for Modern Nomads	£11.95	-
Working with the Environment	£11.95	-
The Directory of Jobs & Careers Abroad	£12.95	-
The International Directory of Voluntary Work	£11.95	-
Buying a House in France	£11.95	-
Buying a House in Spain	£11.95	-
Buying a House in Italy	£11.95	-
Live & Work in Australia & New Zealand	£10.99	-
Live & Work in Belgium, The Netherlands & Luxembourg	£10.99	-
Live & Work in France	£10.99	-
Live & Work in Germany	£10.99	-
Live & Work in Italy	£10.99	-
Live & Work in Japan	£10.99	-
Live & Work in Russia & Eastern Europe	£10.99	-
Live & Work in Saudi & the Gulf	£10.99	-
Live & Work in Scandinavia	£10.99	-
Live & Work in Scotland	£10.99	-
Live &Work in Spain & Portugal	£10.99	-
Live & Work in the USA & Canada	£10.99	-
Drive USA	£10.99	-
Hand Made in Britain – The Visitors Guide	£10.99	-
Scottish Islands – The Western Isles	£12.95	-
Scottish Islands – Orkney & Shetland	£11.95	-
The Panamericana: On the Road through Mexico and Central America	£12.95	-
Travellers Survival Kit Australia & New Zealand	£11.95	-
Travellers Survival Kit Cuba	£10.99	-
Travellers Survival Kit Lebanon	£10.99	-
Travellers Survival Kit Madagascar, Mayotte & Comoros	£10.99	-
Travellers Survival Kit Mauritius, Seychelles & Réunion	£10.99	-
Travellers Survival Kit Mozambique	£10.99	-
Travellers Survival Kit Oman & The Arabian Gulf	£11.95	-
Travellers Survival Kit South America	£15.95	-
Travellers Survival Kit Sri Lanka	£10.99	-

Distributors of:

	Paperback	Hardback
Summer Jobs in the USA	£10.99	-
Internships	£19.99	-
World Volunteers	£10.99	-
Green Volunteers	£10.99	-
Archaeo-Volunteers	£10.99	-

**Vacation Work Publications, 9 Park End Street, Oxford OX1 1HJ
Tel 01865-241978   Fax 01865-790885**

**Visit us online for more information on our unrivalled range of titles for work,
travel and gap years, readers' feedback and regular updates:**

www.vacationwork.co.uk